S0-BND-725

8086/8088
16-Bit MICROPROCESSOR PRIMER

By
Christopher L. Morgan
and
Mitchell Waite

BYTE/McGraw-Hill   70 Main St.   Peterborough, N.H. 03458

Copyright © 1982 by Christopher L. Morgan and Mitchell Waite.
All rights reserved. No part of this book may be translated or
reproduced in any form without the prior written consent of the
authors and McGraw-Hill, Inc.

The authors of the programs provided with this book have carefully
reviewed them to insure their performance in accordance with the
specifications described in the book. However, neither the authors
nor BYTE/McGraw-Hill makes any warranties whatever concerning
the programs. They assume no responsibility or liability of any kind
for errors in the program or for the consequences of any such
errors.

Library of Congress Cataloging in Publication Data
Morgan, Christopher L.
    8086/8088 16-bit microprocessor primer.
    Includes index.
    1. INTEL 8086 (Computer) 2. INTEL 8088 (Computer)
I. Waite, Mitchell. II. Title.
QA76.8.I292M66   1982   001.64   82-12913
ISBN 0-07-043109-4

10 9 8 7 6

Edited by Bruce Roberts.
Design and production by Ellen Klempner.
Production editing by Tom McMillan.
Typesetting by LeWay Composing Service, Fort Worth, Texas.
Printed and bound by Halliday Lithograph Corp., Arcata Company,
Massachusetts.

Acknowledgements

Any book worthy of reading requires contributions beyond those of the authors writing it. This becomes most obvious when the authors have completed their first draft. Because they have nursed, loved, and nurtured the subject for so long, they frequently find it impossible to evaluate what they have finally created! Knowing we would reach this stage given the immensity of this subject, the authors used friends, wives, students, consultants, and computer professionals to evaluate, criticize, suggest, and correct. We are forever indebted to these individuals and would like to thank them here.

First, and most important, we would like to thank each other. Our mutual respect and admiration for each other's skills and contributions was a major ingredient in making this book not just a great one to read, but also an inspiring one to work on.

For her extreme patience and encouragement through many revisions of the manuscript, and for putting up with the numerous calls, questions, and messages between the authors, we would like to pay our kindest respects to Carol Morgan. We are particularly indebted to her for the tremendous amount of proofreading and valuable suggestions she gave on how to make this book more readable, all the while raising one child and giving birth to another!

Alan Orcutt is owed our heartfelt thanks for all his contributions. As a student under Dr. Morgan, he wrote the comments for the example programs for the 8251 and 8255 Programmable Interface Controller Chips. After graduating and becoming a Marketing Engineer at Intel Corporation, he provided a liaison with Intel and a chance for us to run some crucial software. Alan spent many hours helping us get the example programs for the 8087 Numeric Data Processor working on an Intel Development System and getting the 8089 I/O Processor programs assembled.

For their valuable reviews and comments of the first manuscript, we would like to thank Marvin Winzenread, Alan Orcutt, Philip Lieberman, and David Fox. These experts all helped turn an interesting if slightly confusing manuscript into a great manuscript with balance and clarity. We would also like to pay our kindest respects to David Fox for the extra time he put in to run all the 8088 examples in Chapter 7 on his Compupro computer. His comments have helped us immensely in making these programs better teaching tools.

We would like to thank Bruce Roberts and Tom McMillan at Byte Publications for the careful and quick job they did in editing the manuscript.

Many thanks are due Intel Corporation for their encouragement and cooperation in writing this book. Their chips are certainly among the most powerful, popular, and best supported 16-bit processors on the market. This made our book exciting to write, and their great documentation made it easy for us to dig as deeply as we wanted while researching for it. Their technical writing stands above all others as an example of ''how it's done.'' We wish them tremendous success with their fantastic chips!

Christopher L. Morgan and Mitchell Waite

Contents

Chapter 1   Perspectives   1
Chapter 2   BASIC Concepts of 16-bit Microprocessors   15
Chapter 3   The 8086 and 8088 General-Purpose Processors
Chapter 4   The 8087 Numeric Data Processor   155
Chapter 5   The 8089 Input/Output Processor   189
Chapter 6   The 8086/8088 Support Chips   217
Chapter 7   Eleven Sample Pograms for the 8086/8088   249
Chapter 8   The Current Scene: 8086/8088 Products and
            Programs   305

Appendices

Appendix A   The iAPX 186 and the iAPX 286   319
Appendix B   The Intel iAPX 432 32-bit Microprocessor   323
Appendix C   8086/8088 Instruction Set   339

Index   349

Preface

The new, powerful 16-bit microprocessor units from Intel — the 8086 and the 8088 — represent the latest magic in solid-state integrated circuits. These new microprocessors are expected to eclipse the popular 8-bit microprocessor units of the past as the best choice for a microcomputer-based product. This is because the processing throughput of the 8086 16-bit chip may be from 2 to 4000 times more than that of its 8-bit predecessors. The lower figure would occur when the 8086 is performing ordinary 16-bit integer arithmetic computations and the higher figure could easily happen when the 8086 CPU is teamed up with the 8087 number-crunching coprocessor on double-precision, floating-point calculations. Furthermore, the amount of code needed for equivalent programs is up to 50 percent less. In fact, these new 16-bit microprocessors have built-in integer multiply and divide routines, string instructions, and so many other features that the instruction set is almost like a high-level language.

In addition, the 8086 and 8088 general-purpose processors use such advanced architectural concepts as memory management, multi-level vectored interrupts, and coprocessing — concepts explained in this book. These features give the new 16-bit chips a great lead over the early 8-bit microprocessors, allowing them to be used in synergistic combinations in which the final processor complex is greater in power than the sum of the individual parts would imply.

Besides covering the basic concepts of 16-bit microprocessors, this book details how special coprocessors can work with the 8086 and 8088 to enhance performance manyfold. In particular, it covers the incredible 8087 Numeric Data Processor and the highly flexible 8089 Input/Output Processor. The 8087 and 8089 coprocessing chips enhance the 8086 by performing certain time-consuming tasks for it. The 8087 number cruncher can execute powerful math instructions in hardware much faster than the same functions performed in software by the 8086 alone. The 8087 NDP actually extends the instruction set of the 8086 CPU, giving the programmer the equivalent of a built-in scientific calculator with trigonometric, logarithmic, and other transcendental functions. The 8087 can represent numbers as large as 10 to the 4000th power! The 8089, for example, can perform intelligent dual-channel interleaved I/O operations while the 8086 hums along with the main program. With the addition of these coprocessor chips an 8086 or 8088 may have up to 100 times the throughput of an 8086 alone!

Using a down-to-earth primer approach, this book is the first to explain how the incredible 8086 and 8088 16-bit microprocessors and their coprocessors work. The book also is the first to explain the Intel 186 (an enhanced and updated 8086), the Intel 286 (an 8086 with built-in memory management), and the upcoming Intel 432 (an ultimate super-powerful, 32-bit microprocessor).

The first chapter begins with an explanation of what 16-bit microprocessors are all about and then gives an overview of the book. It then details what makes the 16-bit microprocessors so special, explores the kinds of products possible with 16-bits and gives a sneak preview of the 8086 and 8088. A software overview and a description of the book's organization are also included.

The book then covers basic 16-bit concepts and mechanisms such as the makeup of a typical 16-bit microcomputer with graphics peripherals, data types and numbers, physical memory organization, memory management, multi-processing and coprocessing, and how the 8086 and 8088 differ. The different levels of programming, from high-level **languages to assembly language to microcode and finally to nanocode are** described as is the development of assembly language programs on 16-bit microprocessors.

Next, in Chapter 3, the book introduces the 8086 and 8088 general-purpose processors, covering them in depth, describing their electrical nature, structure, instruction sets, and so forth. Chapters then follow on the 8087 Numeric Data Processor and the 8089 Input/Output Processor. There is also a chapter on the complete 8086 family of support chips so you can maximize the use of chips from a single source. Chapter 7 goes on to demonstrate 8086 programming by presenting 11 short sample programs you can type in and try. These have been optimized for simplicity and cover putting the letters ''HI'' on the computer screen, counting on the screen, a quick memory test, dumping EU registers, typing in a line, and single stepping the 8086. Finally, there is a chapter on the current hardware and software available for these processors and a look at the new IBM Personal Computer. Appendices cover the larger and more sophisticated 32-bit 432 from Intel, as well as the new 186 and the 286.

Throughout the book are numerous diagrams and sample programs that help to illustrate the operations. The three-dimensional drawings also make them more interesting. We have avoided complex timing diagrams and reference information of the type found in manufacturers' manuals and some of the more advanced books. We have taken a more visual approach and presented the subject of 16-bit microprocessors in an interesting, readable, and learnable text. All programs used in this book (except the last) are short and to the point. An entire sequence was developed on an 8085/8088 Dual Processor board for the S-100 bus using the CP/M operating system and the Microsoft cross-assembler. The programs for the 8087 coprocessor were debugged at Intel.

The 8086 and the 8088 are the first of a remarkable breed of third-generation, high-power 16-bit microprocessor chips. Comparatively speaking, they make the first microprocessors look like Model T Fords. You can be certain that the products born from these new chips will cause a giant leap in the capability of low-cost computers. The authors hope that this book will help you to understand and harness the awesome power of these 16-bit devices and the products they spawn.

Christopher L. Morgan, Ph.D.
Mitchell Waite

8086/8088
16-Bit MICROPROCESSOR PRIMER

Chapter 1

Perspectives

WHAT IS A 16-BIT MICROPROCESSOR?

The 16-bit microprocessors are a new generation of computer chips from the wizards of silicon, the integrated-circuit chip makers. The 16-bit microprocessors are larger, more powerful devices designed to replace or supplement the 8-bit microprocessors of the seventies that started the microcomputer revolution. These new 16-bit microprocessors are important because in certain configurations and on certain calculations they are up to 4000 times more powerful than the older 8-bit chips and yet will cost about the same. This awesome power is about to be unleashed in the form of intelligent products that will make an incredible impact on society. This is because 16-bit microprocessors allow products to have significant intelligence. Thus, they make it extremely likely that we will see a revolution in end products, such as machines that talk and listen, three-dimensional color displays, advanced communication networks allowing you to access giant data bases via your telephone, intelligent, computerized automobiles, and smart houses that follow the inhabitants' movements in the house and adjust for maximum energy utilization.

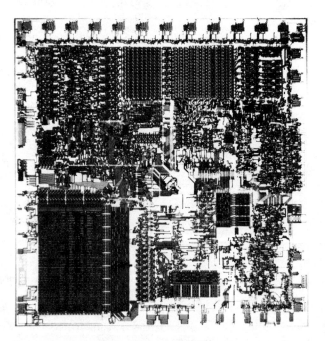

Figure 1.1a: Magnified photo of the 8086 chip.

Figure 1.1b: The 8086 in an IC package.

**WHAT IS THIS
BOOK ABOUT?**

This book is about one of the first, most powerful, and most popular of the 16-bit microprocessors — the Intel 8086. (The book is also about the 8086's cousin, the 8088. When we say 8086, we normally mean both.) This book will show you how the 8086 works, how it fits together, and how to take advantage of its power. The powerful 8086 16-bit chip was the first on the market and has, therefore, established the largest following of users and manufacturers of support products. It is also the least expensive of the major 16-bit chips on the market.

This book is designed to teach you in a simple down-to-earth fashion about the 8086, along with its entire family of support chips, and its sister chips (the 186, 286, and 432). If you are familiar with the older and extremely popular 8080 chip from Intel, then you will certainly want to know all about the more powerful 8086. Since the 8086 is a logical extension of the 8080, it is easy for 8080-oriented people to assimilate. This introductory book uses a visual primer approach to cover the basics of the 8086 and family. It is not a reference manual, but rather a basic book for the beginner who has already been exposed to the 8-bit world and wants to know about the new 16-bit technology.

**WHAT IS SPECIAL
ABOUT 16-BIT
MICROPROCESSORS?**

What makes the new 16-bit microprocessors stand out is the fact that they can deal with information in multiples of 16 bits instead of 8 bits. Actually, these newer processors can deal with data in various basic sizes including both 8 bits and 16 bits, but the underlying mechanisms of the 16-bit processor are twice as large as those in their 8-bit counterparts. Also, because each piece of data can be twice as large, the processor can be many times more accurate. The largest number that can be represented with 8 bits is 255; with 16 bits you can represent a number as large as 65535, which is about 256 times larger! Thus, the range and/or the accuracy can be greatly increased in the various number representation formats. It is interesting to note that the 8086/8088 still uses a byte-oriented instruction set. That is, a machine language instruction for the 8086/8088 takes up from 1 to 6 bytes of memory. On the older 8080-type processors a machine language instruction takes from 1 to 3 bytes, and so a newer processor will have a much richer and more versatile instruction set. At the same time, by dealing with 16-bit data chunks, the processor grabs its instructions at the faster rate of 2 bytes at a time. The 16-bit capability also leads to a much faster microprocessor in other ways. For example, the 16-bit device can send and receive a 16-bit data value in one transfer, whereas the 8-bit device often requires two separate operations to do this. Furthermore, software can be more efficient because it is easy to represent and operate upon larger 16-bit values in the registers of the CPU. In an 8-bit microprocessor you must often do 16-bit operations in two steps, often taking as many as four times the number of instructions to do the job of one 16-bit instruction.

But the 16-bit basis of the microprocessor is only a small part of the whole story. The manufacturers of these devices decided to let out all the stops and increase the computing power beyond what a doubling of the data word would imply. To do this, they used more complex circuitry on the chip. Keep in mind that microprocessors are nothing more than computers made of thousands of tiny transistors (transistors are tiny amplifiers that allow the flow of electronics to be precisely controlled) housed in a tiny chip. The transistors are *etched* onto thin crystal slabs, using photographic techniques of miniaturization. The crystal slabs are *cooked* in an electrical chemical environment and then cut and packaged into lots of computer chips.

The degree of miniaturization that can be achieved controls how many transistors can be packed into the computer. And the more transistors, the more sophisticated things can be done. At the time the 8086 was developed, a better manufacturing technique was needed to allow smaller dimensions for the transistors. A new silicon manufacturing process called HMOS (pronounced h-moss) was implemented for the 8086 family. HMOS allowed putting up to 70,000 (or more) transistors on a single micro chip. With this many transistors manufacturers could include extensive hardware circuits. For example, they could now include on-chip multiply and divide instructions. Since multiply and divide are now built into the chip and not simulated in software, math operations can be performed much faster. With so many transistors there can be sophisticated interrupt structures (some with built-in priority circuitry) right on the chip. This allows the controlling of many I/O devices in efficient ways with little additional hardware.

There are other things about 16-bit chips that extend them far beyond their 8-bit little brothers. For example, the size of memory that the 16-bit chips can use is huge compared to that of the 8-bitters. The 8086 and 8088, for example, can access over a million bytes of read/write memory. Contrast this to the maximum of about 64,000 bytes for most 8-bit microprocessors. With such large memory, programmers can design much more powerful and sophisticated computer programs. It is possible with memory sizes of about 256,000 bytes to run advanced operating systems which can support the very best of computer products. Having lots of memory also means it's easy to have several users sharing the same computer. It is reasonable to imagine a word processor with 1 megabyte of memory serving 16 users. Each user would have a terminal with its own built-in 8088 that communicates with a central 8086.

But perhaps the most relevant, mysterious and trend-setting aspect of the new 16-bit microprocessors is the way in which their designers have distributed their intelligent features. The new 16-bit chips have mechanisms that support much more powerful computing structures than a single processor doing a single task. Whereas older microprocessors usually did all the computing in a system, the new 16-bit micros have divided up the computing into subfunctions available in optional special-purpose chips. That is, you don't need these chips for simple operations, but they are available for you when you want to add them. Today there are special chips for doing floating-point mathematics including computation of trigonometric functions. There are also chips for doing specialized I/O automatically, without the use of the main processor.

These supplemental processors, or coprocessors, are not just simple support chips. They are really complete microprocessors dedicated to special purposes that previously would have required many large circuit boards to contain. In fact, sometimes they are called special-purpose processors. An example is the Intel 8087 Math Chip. It is a very powerful microprocessor itself, with its own programming language. It can perform high-precision computations in an incredibly short time. Whereas a computation of a double-precision square root (53 bits of accuracy) executed on the 16-bit processor in software might take almost 20 milliseconds, with a math chip it takes about 36 microseconds, more than 500 times faster! (Of course, you should not expect to sustain such a performance ratio over the long range during typical operations.) Such a high-speed math chip eliminates the need for lengthy, memory-intensive emulation routines. Using such a chip with a language like BASIC or Pascal means that the language will not only run very fast but use up much less memory space and be cheaper and more reliable.

These math chips,, or coprocessors, are not limited to use in scientific processing or in extending high-level language instruction sets. It is possible, for example, to build a low-cost very high-performance industrial controller using the math chip and the 8088. This allows complex equations to be performed in real time. Digital recording, spectrum analysis, music synthesis, speech recognition, communications, and so on are all untapped applications for this new speed.

In addition to giving the 16-bit microprocessor creative connections, the designers have performed several neat tricks with it. With the dropping cost of computer hardware, it is the programming of computers, a complex and time-consuming chore, that is the most expensive development aspect of any microprocessor-based product, be it for a process controller, business machine, or personal computer. Designers have incorporated features in the new 16-bit chips that allow programs to be easily moved around memory without a lot of difficulty. Moving programs around easily in memory is important if you want powerful software. This ability, for example, allows a program to reconfigure itself on the fly, creating a custom version for the amount of memory available in each unique application. It is likely that because numerous programs for the new 16-bit microprocessors can easily relocate programs, they will also be quite able to work in harmony with programs from different manufacturers.

Another area of enhancement in the 16-bit microprocessors is in error checking. Error checking is a subject largely overlooked by the microcomputer industry, and a program that doesn't handle errors properly can create major operation problems. For example, if the error checking is poor on your computer, the error may not be detected and the results of the program may become suspect. Or if the error recovery is poor, you may find your computer program "dead in the water" and unable to be restarted without destroying lots of your work. On the other hand if the recovery process is good and an error occurs, the program may be able to fix itself and continue automatically. All the new 16-bit units have strengthened error checking. This is especially true for the new math processor. For example, if there is an error in the divide instruction, such as an overflow or divide by zero, the microprocessor notices this and causes an interruption of the processing. Your program can deal with this interruption in a smooth and logical fashion, sending a message to the console, returning control to the program, inserting more realistic values, or whatever you desire. With such sound error-recovery mechanisms, it is possible to design programs that just can't be hung up or crash the system.

With such sophistication you can be sure you will see many high-level languages and operating systems such as C, UNIX, Pascal, Forth, and Ada becoming available on low-cost computers that use these fantastic 16-bit chips.

The 8086 provides the potential for a host of consumer products which use its ability to quickly and efficiently execute complicated programs. Any particular product that currently uses a computer chip is subject to the enhancing effects of the 16-bit microprocessor. Consumer products that are most likely to use the first 8086-type chips are high-performance personal computers (such as small business machines with graphics), video arcade games, automobiles, kitchen machines, typewriters, answering machines, and radios.

Because of the power of the 16-bit chips, it is certain that voice communications will become the bottom line for the computerized products of the 1980s. For example, personal computers will soon feature programs that ask you questions and listen to your answers. Vending machines will have no buttons, just a coin entrance and a heavily grilled speaker and microphone. The sight of people talking with these intelligent boxes will become as commonplace as the sight of someone using a drinking fountain.

Because the 8086 doesn't cost much more than the 8080, and will eventually cost even less, it is possible to use it in places where weight, cost, and superior intelligence are critical, such as in aircraft, and, unfortunately, weapons. With the various subsystems of an airplane controlled independently by 8086's in a *slave* mode, the entire aircraft could operate more precisely, quickly, and reliably than ever before. The math processor would allow navigation control so the 8086 could tie into the auto-pilot system. It is easy to imagine that with enough of these processors the jet fighter itself could be given so much intelligence that a pilot could be on the ground in a simulation cockpit, dogfighting via the computers.

But the first appearance of the 8086 will no doubt be in the personal and home computer market, an increasingly competitive market. In August of 1981, IBM announced their first Personal Computer. Besides shocking the world by going out and making a computer that could run much of the existing 8-bit software on the market, the IBM designers also used the powerful 8088 chip. The 8088 is exactly like the 8086 internally, but externally it uses an 8-bit data bus. This allows it to easily use current, inexpensive, 8-bit I/O and memory chips. With IBM using the 8088, it is clear that its computer will be among the most powerful on the market. By using an 8088 in the computer, the IBM people will be able to develop and use extremely powerful software. Moreover, the IBM Personal Computer has a socket for an 8087 number-cruncher chip, and in typical IBM fashion this socket will be filled and utilized to the hilt to make the IBM Personal Computer a mathematical wizard.

It is not too likely that the 8086 will show up in low-cost TV games, but it may appear in top-of-the-line telephone-answering machines. With the 8086, a number-cruncher chip, and an I/O processor, you could store your messages in random-access memory (RAM) inside the machine rather than on tape. With the 8086's powerful language structure, it is easy to imagine that the answering machine would incorporate more than just the message-taking computer system, and will probably include an appointment reminder program, as well as electronic mail capability.

Another place where the 8086 will probably be used in conjunction with the telephone is the digital private branch exchange (PBX). A PBX is a device that allows the many telephones of a business to be connected to the outside and monitored by one or more attendants. Some PBX's turn each telephone in the system into an intelligent station. Most PBX's have one or more attendants who handle the incoming calls and some long-distance outgoing calls. With the 8086 the attendants may be replaced with a voice-synthesized, intelligent computer, capable of answering a call to the company with "Good afternoon, this is XYZ Company. May I help you?", and capable of reacting successfully to spoken phrases such as: "Harvey Mudd, please." Furthermore the computer will *always* say the greeting message in a positive, up way that the calling person can understand (as opposed to some human operators who get bored and start to mumble on the 3000th call). An automatic PBX could even immediately connect any incoming calls it couldn't handle to a human operator or receptionist and explain why it got stuck!

Without a doubt, 16-bit microprocessors such as the 8086 will have an amazing major impact on the way machines of our world operate, the performance that they are capable of, and the way in which human beings relate to them. One only hopes that these devices will make the world better rather than more difficult.

SNEAK PREVIEW OF THE 8086/8088

Since this is an introductory chapter, we will now give a brief overview of the most basic features of the 8086 and 8088. This will prepare you for the upcoming chapters which cover the entire chip family in more depth.

The 8086 and 8088 are 16-bit microprocessors that are a logical extension of the extremely popular 8080. The 8088 is like the 8086 internally, but it is designed to work with an 8-bit bus and, in fact, is compatible with many existing 8-bit buses. The 8086, on the other hand, interfaces to a 16-bit data bus. The 6 in 86 means 16 bits, the 8 in 88 means 8 bits. Both refer to the hardware data-bus width. Internally, they have identical data sizes and instruction sets.

Both the 8086 and 8088 use the concept of *instruction queuing* to improve the speed of the computer. An area inside the chip called the *instruction queue* holds several bytes of an instruction. When the computer is ready for the next instruction, it doesn't need to fetch many bytes from memory since the entire instruction may already be in the queue. Thus, the address and data bus are not subject to periods of intense overuse, as is common in the buses of 8-bit devices which are constantly accessing memory. Computer buses are sort of like freeways — they have quiet times and rush hours. The secret of the 8086 is that its queue tends to cut down on rush-hour traffic by spreading the traffic into the slack periods and thus controlling the traffic flow more efficiently. By using the bus more efficiently, the *bandwidth* of the bus and the number of possible operations per second are increased, as more time is available for other devices to use the bus. The 8086 queue is 6 bytes long while the 8088 queue is only 4 bytes long. This is related to the fact that the 8086 is more efficient than the 8088.

The 8086 can access 1 megabyte of read-write memory (2^{20} bytes). However, it uses a memory-addressing scheme called *segmentation* in

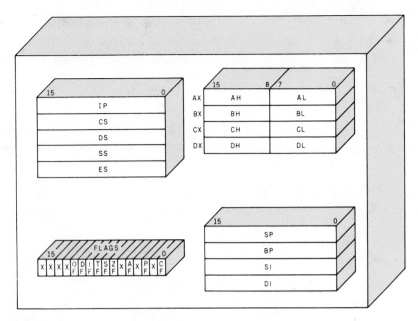

Figure 1.2: 8086 16-bit microprocessor structure.

which certain *segment registers* supply a base address which is automatically added to every 16-bit user address in the machine. Although there are four segment registers in the 8086, the possible base addresses (given by the segment registers) can be evenly placed at intervals of 16 bytes throughout the entire megabyte addressing space. Just how and why this is done will be explained in Chapters 2 and 3.

Part of the address and all of the data bus are multiplexed onto 16 pins.The remaining 4 bits of address are implemented by four additional address pins which are also used for status. An off-the-chip clock is required and an off-the-chip bus controller is used for demultiplexing the address data bus. The figure below illustrates the internal register set structure of the 8086/8088. The shaded registers are the 8080 subset.

The 8086 has a powerful interrupt structure. Almost all 8-bit microprocessors require additional external chips to allow good interrupt operations. In the 8086, about a thousand bytes are set aside for holding up to 256 vector pointers. The 8086 does I/O operations in a separate space from memory called the *I/O space.* It is up to 64 K bytes long. For use of the coprocessors, a special TEST input pin is provided for allowing the 8086 to know when the coprocessor has completed its task. When a WAIT instruction is issued, the 8086 will stop and wait for the external coprocessor, or any other hardware, to give the go-ahead by changing the TEST pin.

The 8086 contains structures for position-independent code and stack processing. (Don't worry, we will explain these terms soon.) It has 16-bit signed arithmetic instructions, including multiply and divide, superior bit manipulation, and interruptible string operations which automatically scan a text string and stop when the text matches or fails to match. This is great for word processing, allowing you to have very fast operations.

The 8086 contains some new kinds of registers in addition to the ones found in the 8080. First, the 8080's three register pairs (HL, BC, and DE) are now called the BX, CX, and DX. They can be treated as pairs of 8-bit registers but also like 16-bit registers with respect to almost all 16-bit operations. The 8080 accumulator register, A, is now 16 bits long and is called AX, but its "lower" half can still be used as an 8-bit accumulator. There are four new 16-bit registers in the 8086 that you will hear more and more about as the chip competition heats up. They are the segment registers, shown as CS, DS, SS, and ES in figure 1.2. These are used with the 8086's *segmentation* addressing scheme. With these registers you can separately and dynamically tell the computer where in the 1-megabyte address space to locate a program, data, and the stack.

There are four other 16-bit registers: the stack pointer (just like the 8080's), the base pointer, and two index registers — the source index and the destination index register.

The 8086 is very fast. If a 5-MHz clock is used, an absolute load of the accumulator from anywhere in the 1-megabyte space takes 2 microseconds. At 8 MHz this instruction takes only 1.25 microseconds. Even faster versions will be available — perhaps soon it will be practical to do this operation in under a microsecond! The 8086 has 29,000 transistors on a 225-mil chip. It is only 27 percent larger than an 8080 so its price will be low.

In addition to the 8086 there are two coprocessor chips available. The 8087 Numeric Data Processor provides very quick floating-point operations for the 8086. It is designed to overlay the 8086 local-address data bus so it can be added with few jumper changes and little extra hardware. The 8087 monitors the 8086 instruction stream looking for its own instructions. It executes them without the help of the 8086. The second coprocessor is the 8089 Input/Output Processor. The 8089 is a chip designed for the efficient movement of blocks of data. It has two channels and can easily interleave both input and output at the same time. It too overlays on the local bus and has its own instruction set. With these two chips the 8086 forms the basis of a very powerful computer.

8086 SOFTWARE

This is a very important subject. Everyone has heard the statement "without software a microprocessor is nothing." What this refers to is that to fully use the microprocessor you must have plenty of available computer programs that will work on your computer. Today the 8-bit microprocessor-based computers have a huge number of *application programs* available. For the popular 8080, there are literally thousands of vendors with programs. But the new 16-bit microprocessors have their own unique (and more powerful) instructions. You can't just take an 8-bit program and put it on a 16-bit computer. You must hire a programmer to create a new version of the program that runs on the 16-bit microprocessor. The new computer is better BUT it will take a long time for programs to appear for it. Therefore you will be stuck with a computer with little software for it for some time. Fortunately, this is not going to be a large problem for the 8086 because there is a very close correspondence between the old 8080 registers and instructions and a subset of the new 8086 registers and instructions. Of course, the names have been changed to protect the innocent. Clearly, the 8086 designers had this problem in mind when they designed the 8086. There are actually only a small number of large-sized, low-level programs which need to be translated over or else developed directly. Once these are done, then a vast number (literally ''tons'') of high-level application programs which were developed for the 8080 will work on the new machine.

To make this conversion process even easier there are special translation programs that convert 8080 code to 8086 code. The designers of the 8086 and others including ourselves have developed such a program. Perhaps you will want to write one when you have finished this book. Translation is almost, but not totally, an automatic process. The programmer must still go inside and *tweak* the code to initialize the segment registers, to deal with incompatibilities between assemblers, and to fix any really sneaky 8080 machine-level programming (stuff that's poor programming practice to begin with). Translation also does not produce optimal code, but in spite of these drawbacks, it certainly speeds the conversion process. What this means is that companies that supply good 8080 software packages today will very soon be selling versions for the 8086.

At the core of the software crunch is the problem of dealing with operating systems. This is a rather strange yet extremely important issue. Almost any useful program you might wish to run on an 8086 requires that a certain program called an *operating system* be already in place. The operating system is like the mother program — it oversees the demands of the application program you are running. It helps your program to operate by providing standard ways for it to access the various devices in your computer system such as the keyboard, floppy disk, and printer. It helps make your program independent of your particular system and thus provides a larger marketplace from which to obtain programs. The problem is that there are several operating systems available for your 16-bit computer. Which one you get may determine the range of software you can acquire. To further complicate things there are low-end and high-end operating systems. For example, control program for microprocessors (CP/M) is a typical, low-end operating system. It is one of the most popular operating systems. (For more details on CP/M see *CP/M Primer,* by Steve Murtha and Mitchell Waite; Howard W. Sams &

Co., Inc., Indianapolis, Indiana.) CP/M is inexpensive and fairly simple to use but it has certain drawbacks too. More sophisticated high-end operating systems such as OASIS or UNIX are more expensive but offer incredible flexibility. Even Intel has its own operating system, ISIS-II. The bottom line, however, is that whichever operating system you choose sets the range of vendors' programs that you can run on your machine.

Operating systems designed especially for the 8086 and 8088 are becoming available on the market at an increasingly rapid pace. One of the first operating systems for the 8086 is CP/M-86 from Digital Research, Inc., the maker of CP/M-80, the most popular operating system in the world. CP/M-86 is much like CP/M-80 but has some special features allowed by the 16-bit chip. There are a few problems with it, however. It has poor error-recovery procedures and must be modified rather extensively for each computer it is used on.

Another 8086 operating system has been created and is available from Microsoft called MS-DOS. MS-DOS is written in the C programming language and can be recompiled to work on the Z8000 and the 68000 and, for that matter, on almost any 16-bit microprocessor that comes out. It is downward compatible with a UNIX-like operating system called XENIX from the same company. It is partially modeled after CP/M-80 and actually emulates all its system calls. Thus, 8-bit programs that worked under CP/M can be translated to 8086 code, and the calls to CP/M will naturally become correct calls in MS-DOS! It uses device-independent I/O. This means each device is like a file — it is opened and closed, read or written to. Thus, all MS-DOS programs can say "send this to the screen" and, regardless of the hardware kinks of your particular screen, the message will get to the screen properly. MS-DOS is relocatable, allowing all programs to take advantage of the 8086's segmentation scheme.

Perhaps the hottest feature of MS-DOS is its device-independent graphics, long awaited in the microcomputer industry. MS-DOS uses the ATT standard for Teletex transmission, an enhanced Telidon format, called Presentation Level Protocol (PLP). Since ATT owns the bulk of the nation's telephone network, an operating system containing commands that interpret the PLPs has tremendous potential. It allows programmers to write the graphics without any particular computer in mind. Remember that, although the Apple has incredible graphics capability, it took programmers years before they could adapt their code to it because of its rather bizarre hardware design. With PLP the programmer doesn't care about the hardware. The hardware designer makes a display that can interpret the commands of the PLP. The commands are character sets, instructions for geometric shapes, etc.

The new IBM Personal Computer runs a version of MS-DOS called IBM Personal Computer DOS. Most experts are predicting that the MS-DOS will outdistance CP/M-86 as the most popular operating system for 16-bit computers. A list in the last chapter describes some of the software available at the time of the writing of this book. The list is growing very fast, so you'll have to check out the market yourself. Included are operating systems; high-level languages like BASIC, FORTRAN IV, and Pascal; tools such as macro assemblers, cross assemblers, linking loaders, editors; and even an adventure game! Without a doubt, you will see a flurry of activity in new software products for the 8086. And the performance will be so much superior to the versions of these products that run on the 8-bit machines as to render them obsolete.

HOW THIS BOOK IS ORGANIZED AND HOW TO USE IT

This book is organized into eight chapters. It is designed to be read sequentially, from Chapter 1 to Chapter 8, but skipping around will work if you keep the following things in mind:

This first chapter, "Perspectives," is an introduction to 16-bit microprocessors, particularly the 8086.

Chapter 2, "Basic 16-Bit Concepts," presents the first-time reader with a complete introduction to the world of 8- and 16-bit microprocessing and to the various new concepts associated with the new, 16-bit processors. In this chapter you will be introduced to the architecture and nomenclature of a typical microprocessor-based microcomputer, and then to the 8086/8088 family and the even larger 8000 family. Next, the chapter gets into some basic concepts you need to know to appreciate the 16-bit machine. It covers data types and numbers, from bits and nibbles to strings and pointers. Also covered here are physical memory organization, memory management, coprocessing, and instruction queues. The chapter ends with a description of the software used to create the programs for this book.

Chapter 3, "The 8086 and 8088 General-Purpose Processors," covers the ins and outs of these specific chips, including the similarity to the 8080 and 8085, the major features, power requirements, pipelining architecture, signals and pinouts, and so on. The instruction set is introduced in groups by function, such as data transfer, binary arithmetic, string manipulation, etc. Finally, we offer a few very simple, very short sample programs for the reader to examine. You should definitely read this chapter.

Chapter 4, "The 8087 Numeric Data Processor," is a very exciting chapter that shows how this number cruncher does its crunching. It covers the concepts of floating-point notation, then explains how the NDP works as a coprocessor, and details how it extends the software, architecture, hardware, and marketing of the 8086/8088. You'll learn about the 8087 data types (the kinds of numbers the 8087 can play with — big), its stack, its powerful instruction set, and its "exception" handling. Sample programs that run on the NDP conclude the chapter.

Chapter 5, "The 8089 I/O Processor," explains this amazing, intelligent, high-speed DMA-like device and how to best use it. This chapter is a mini-book in itself. Sample programs showing how to use an

8089 IOP end the chapter. If you don't care about this device you can skip this chapter.

Chapter 6, ''The 8086/8088 Support Chips,'' surveys the entire family of 8200 chips. A family of support chips is a group of chips that can all operate together to help the main processor. A good understanding of the family will help you appreciate the possible configurations of the 8086/8088-based computer system.

Chapter 7, ''Making the 8086/8088 Run,'' presents a series of instructional CP/M application programs that are designed to teach you about programming the 8086. The programs are short and sweet and easy to learn. Each program introduces a new set of instructions. For example, we start with the data transfer group of instructions and show how to use them to put the word ''HI'' on the screen. Next, we cover looping instructions and show how to perform multidigit counting on the screen (a combination of two processes), and so forth. For serious potential programmers of the 8086 this is an important chapter. Those just wishing to get to know the chip on a less intimate basis can skip it.

Chapter 8, ''The Current Scene,'' covers the evolution of hardware and software for the 8086, the development of the chip, the IBM Personal Computer, and then goes on to give a partial list of the equipment and software available for this chip today, and a list of the manufacturers of the vendors of 8086-based products.

Throughout the book we have used many three-dimensional drawings and figures to aid your understanding. As you read this book, keep in mind that by understanding the 8086 you will be in a good position to write programs for computers like the IBM Personal Computer. The authors believe good programmers for such machines will soon be in extreme demand and command outrageous salaries. In simple terms, the 16-bit market is a wide open, totally virgin, super-big-bucks game, and the rush is on to be a winner in it. Why not start today by reading the next chapter!

Chapter 2

Basic Concepts of 16-Bit Microprocessors

In this chapter we will cover some basic concepts as they relate to modern 16-bit microprocessors. These topics include: the organization of a typical modern microcomputer; an overview of Intel's extensive family of microprocessor and microprocessor support chips; some concepts particular to the new 16-bit processors, such as segmentation, memory management, and multiprocessing; various common data types; and a quick introduction to assembly-language programming (and even lower levels).

We will discuss many of the basic concepts introduced here in other places throughout the book as they relate to the particular chips under discussion. In subsequent chapters we will introduce other basic concepts not covered here as we need them.

MICROCOMPUTERS FROM OUTSIDE TO INSIDE

Most people are familiar with the outside trappings of the modern microcomputer. There is usually a keyboard, a video screen, a couple of floppy disk drives, and a printer. There also might be other devices such as digital plotters, joysticks, and digitizing tablets (see figure 2.1). All of these devices are connected by cables to a box in which the actual computer is located. Sometimes this box also houses the keyboard, video screen, or perhaps the disk drives, but, even so, we can think of the *computer system* as a *computer* with peripheral devices attached.

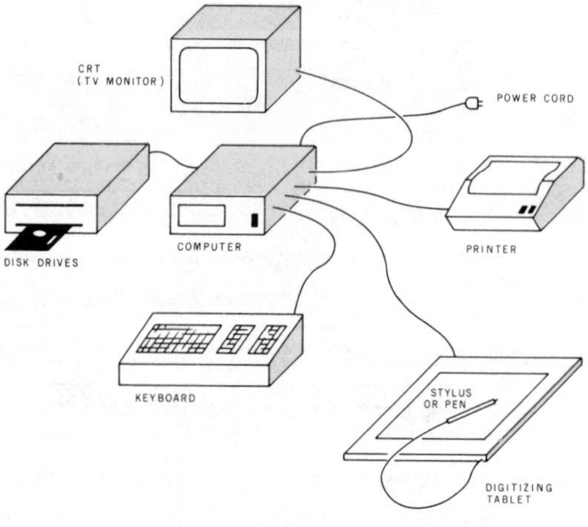

CRT (TV MONITOR)

POWER CORD

DISK DRIVES

COMPUTER

PRINTER

KEYBOARD

STYLUS OR PEN

DIGITIZING TABLET

Figure 2.1: A typical computer system.

Bus-Based Architecture

Now let's look inside the computer. Usually there is a main bus with various devices attached to it. This bus looks like a bunch of electrical conductors running in parallel through the computer. In the famous S-100 bus computers, there is a big board, called the motherboard, usually lying along the bottom of the computer, which houses this bus. In the S-100 bus, all 100 signal lines run in parallel from one end of this board to the other. Physically, these signals are carried within deposits of metal, called traces, on the board's surface. There are anywhere from 5 to over 20 connectors, each of which runs across and is attached to all of the S-100 bus signal lines (traces). S-100 bus boards plug into these connectors. The boards house important functions such as memory, the central processing unit (CPU), and input/output interface logic. As you can see from the figure below, the connectors are all parallel to each other, but perpendicular to the S-100 bus signal traces. This is a very simple example of the principle of *orthogonality* (perpendicularity) in which two different qualities or quantities interact in an absolutely uniform way. Here each connector gets access to exactly the same arrangement of signal lines from the bus as every other connector. Thus, you can place your S-100 boards into these connectors in any order you please, although you might find that certain arrangements tend to reduce noise levels in your system.

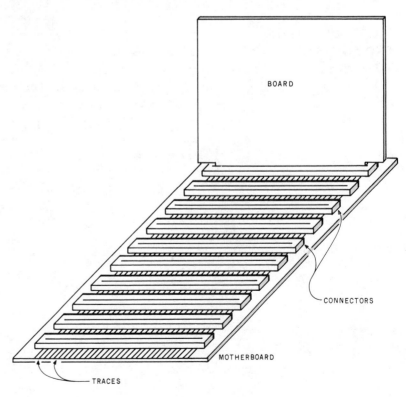

Figure 2.2: A typical bus—the S-100 bus motherboard.

The S-100 bus with its various electrical conductors has essentially no *active* electronic components. That is, it doesn't usually have transistors or integrated circuits, although some manufacturers have included a few components to form what is called *termination circuitry* to keep the electrical noise along the bus to a minimum. Sometimes part of the power supply is on the motherboard. However, with the exception of termination circuitry and, of course, the main power supply, all the active electronics are housed on boards which plug into the connectors on the S-100 bus (see the figure below for a block diagram of a typical S-100 system). On non-S-100 bus computers, there is often a main circuit board, containing all basic components of the computer, and often the motherboard which houses the bus is plugged into this main circuit board. Sometimes the functions of the main circuit board and the motherboard are combined on one board. In spite of these different arrangements, it is still very useful to always retain a *logical* model of the *computer* as a *bus* with devices attached to it.

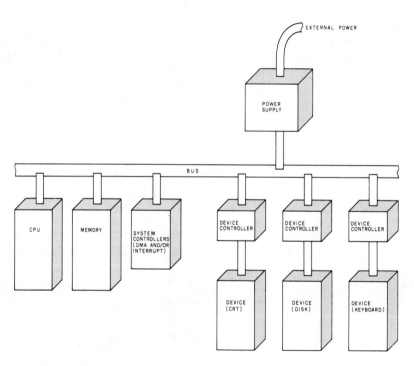

Figure 2.3: Block diagram of a bus-based system.

The main bus of a computer is divided into various *subbuses*. These are: 1) power, 2) control, 3) address, and 4) data.

Power

The *power* subbus carries electrical power from the power supply to the various components in the computer. The older 8080-based S-100 bus had to have several lines in the power bus because the 8080 CPU chip requires three different voltage supplies in addition to a return line (commonly called the ground). Since the newer chips (both microprocessor and support chips) require only one voltage (+ 5 volts, direct current), this subbus now need only consist of two wires: the 5-volt supply and the ground. Thus the older + – 18-volt lines are no longer needed for today's chips.

It is often convenient to send a higher voltage with a slight 60 or 120 hertz (Hz) *ripple* (not to be confused with the wine by that name), and then each board can smooth and lower the voltage to obtain a direct current of + 5 volts *locally* on the board. This greatly reduces the problems of noise, *voltage drops* along the power bus, and *crosstalk* between boards over the power supply lines. It also reduces the price of the equipment.

Control

The *control* subbus carries information back and forth regarding such things as timing (the system clock signal), commands (memory or I/O access), direction of data (read versus write), busy signals (the READY line), and interrupts.

Address

The *address* subbus carries special control signals which carry *selection* information throughout the computer. This information is used to distinguish both the various I/O devices and the many thousands of memory cells in the computer. For example, if you wish to move some information from one memory cell to another, you might go through the following sequence of events: the address of the first cell is put on the address bus, next the data is moved from the currently addressed memory cell (the first memory cell) onto the data bus (which is described in the next section), then the address of the second memory cell is placed on the address bus, and finally the data is moved from the data bus to the currently addressed memory cell (this time, the second memory cell).

The addresses are transmitted along the address bus in a binary code with each conductor carrying a signal corresponding to a different *binary digit* (bit). A high voltage (above a certain limit) might indicate a binary 1, and a low voltage (below a certain value) might indicate a binary 0. Due to losses and other kinds of inaccuracies in the system, the two-state yes/no or 1/0 logical or binary values are represented by certain *ranges* of voltages.

According to the rules of binary arithmetic, if you have *n* binary digits, then you can represent 2 to the *n*th power different binary numbers. The earlier 8-bit processors such as the 8080, 8085, or Z80 had 16 signal lines and thus could produce 2^{16} = 65,536 different addresses. It was once thought that this was more than enough for most microcomputer applications. Now, however, with the cost of memory ever dropping, a medium-size microcomputer could profitably use over 100,000 memory cells, requiring a different address for each. At the same time modern high-level languages such as Pascal and now Ada are requiring ever larger amounts of memory — much more than 64 K. The proposed IEEE standards for the S-100 bus specify 24 address signal lines, thus giving an addressing range of

$$2^{24} = 16,777,216$$

or over 16 million possible addresses! This is enough to store about 16 copies of the Bible!

Data

The *data* subbus carries the actual information throughout the computer. On the 8080-, 8085-, and Z80-based machines as well as the newer 8088-based machines, the data bus has eight connectors carrying eight signals in parallel. This means that the data bus can be used to carry units of data, each of which consists of eight binary digits. Only one such unit of data can be carried at a time on this bus. With 8 bits, each data unit can range in value from 0 to $2^8 - 1$ = 255 as a binary number. However, in the newer 16-bit machines (perhaps using the 8086 CPU chip), the 16 data signal lines running in parallel can be used to represent numbers which range from 0 to $2^{16} - 1$ = 65,535. Giant computers have data subbuses of up to 64 conductors, yielding binary numbers as large as about 1.8 times 10^{19} in one shot! We will see later in this chapter how numbers larger and smaller than this, as well as other types of data such as characters and fractional numbers, can be represented on the smaller machines as groups of several smaller 8-bit and 16-bit pieces. The smaller machines have the capability of representing the same-size numbers as the larger machines, but require many more machine cycles to do so, thus operating at significantly slower speeds than the larger machines. However, a smaller machine with few users will often outperform a larger machine with everybody under the sun using it!

In Figure 2.3, you can see a variety of ''devices'' attached to the main bus. Among them are: the power supply, the central processing unit, some memory, and various device controllers. Starting with the power supply, we shall now look at each of these in turn.

Power Supply

The job of the power supply is to convert the outside electric power (usually 120-V, 60-Hz alternating current) into the kinds of power required by the power bus. This might be about 8 V with a small ripple or waviness if the final power regulation is done on the boards. On the other hand, for the older 8080-based S-100 bus, there are, in addition, supplies with plus and minus approximately 20 V, again with a small ripple.

The Central Processing Unit

The central processing unit forms the brains or control center of a computer. Looking at any modern computer as a whole, the CPU usually consists of a board or set of boards which is plugged into the main bus. However, on many machines, the CPU occupies just a portion of the main circuit board. In any case, we can envision the CPU as a distinct device which "hangs" on the main bus, feeding on power from the power subbus, sending and receiving control signals over the control subbus, sending addresses over the address subbus, and transferring data back and forth to the data subbus. In minicomputers and maxicomputers, the CPU circuitry may consist of an array of low-density (in the logical sense) electronic components, usually mounted on separate chips. However, in a microcomputer the CPU usually consists of just a few (one, two, or possibly three) high-density (LSI and/or VLSI[1]) chips, forming what is called a *microprocessor* together with perhaps as many as 40 less dense MSI and SSI support chips. Thus, although we often call the microprocessor chips CPU chips, they are normally not quite the entire CPU of the computer.

Sometimes the CPU will consist of several microprocessors forming a cluster, and sometimes there are several such clusters in a computer. We will explore these situations as we study the concepts of *coprocessing* and *multiprocessing* later in this chapter and in Chapters 4 and 5.

The Memory

The memory of a computer is really just another device which is connected to the main bus. It is usually housed on one or more boards in the system. Its job is to store data and programs, usually on a temporary basis. The memory can be thought of as a collection of individual cells, each with a number assigned to it called its address. A given cell doesn't store this address; instead the CPU and the control circuitry in the memory use this address to *select* a particular memory cell. All transfers

---

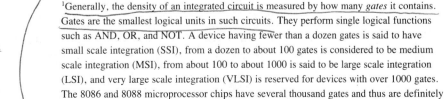

[1]Generally, the density of an integrated circuit is measured by how many *gates* it contains. Gates are the smallest logical units in such circuits. They perform single logical functions such as AND, OR, and NOT. A device having fewer than a dozen gates is said to have small scale integration (SSI), from a dozen to about 100 gates is considered to be medium scale integration (MSI), from about 100 to about 1000 is said to be large scale integration (LSI), and very large scale integration (VLSI) is reserved for devices with over 1000 gates. The 8086 and 8088 microprocessor chips have several thousand gates and thus are definitely VLSI devices.

of data from cell to cell or between cells and the CPU are made via the data bus, using the address bus for selection purposes and the control bus to initiate and monitor the process.

Most microprocessors allow transfers from one memory cell to another (memory-to-memory transfers as opposed to CPU-to-memory or memory-to-CPU transfers) only under a special mode called direct memory access (DMA). In this mode, the CPU turns control of the main bus over to a special device called a DMA controller. We will study a single-chip version of such a device in Chapter 6.

Most main memory is built out of chips (semiconductor integrated circuits). There is an older way of building memory, using little magnetic *cores,* but this is no longer used because it is so much more expensive (each little core had to be individually wound with little wires). When computers' memories were made entirely of this older core type of construction, then the *main* memory was called *core* memory.

There are two logically different types of memory commonly used in microprocessors today: RAM and ROM. RAM stands for random-access memory. This does not mean that you will get completely random results when you access this type of memory. Instead, it means that you can directly access any memory call you might want to specify (at random). Both RAM and ROM (read-only memory) are memory with random access. The difference is that RAM can be both *written to* (store information) and *read from* (retrieve information) successfully, where ROM can only be successfully read from. ROM can be written to during a very special process called *programming* or *burning*. During normal operations, trying to write to ROM will not "blow up" the computer; it will just not cause any change to the contents of the intended destination memory cell.

Perhaps a more accurate scheme for naming memory would be this: RAM would include all of what is now called RAM and what is now called ROM, since these are both technically random-access memory. Thus, the entire main memory would be called RAM. RWM (read and write memory) would be the new name for what is now called RAM, and ROM would retain its old name and definition. The name "SAM" (sequential access memory) would be used for external memory such as magnetic tape in which a whole sequence of cells has to be accessed to get to the desired one (see the table below). Having said this, let's not use this new system because RAM and ROM are so easy to say and almost everybody has a fixed idea of what they mean.

	RWM	ROM
RAM	Random Access Read and Write 1	Random Access Read Only 2
SAM	Sequential Access Read and Write 3	Sequential Access Read Only 4

Examples:
1. Main memory you can directly modify.
2. Main memory you cannot directly modify.
3. Magnetic tape.
4. Paper tape (once it's punched).

Table 2.1: Types of memory.

Even on the larger 16-bit machines, memory is usually organized in 8-bit (1-byte) memory cells. This is because even 16-bit machines are required to work with 8-bit data. Indeed, modern 16-bit and even 32-bit processors now have instructions to work with a variety of data sizes which includes the 8-bit byte. For example, processing byte-sized types of data such as characters from a keyboard is essential for entering and editing programs. On a 16-bit machine the bytes can then be grouped together in pairs to form 16-bit *words*. In such a pair, the bytes have consecutive addresses, and the *address of the pair* is where the pair begins, that is, the address of the first byte of the pair. If you start at address 0, then the entire memory can, and indeed is, divided into a series of such pairs. The first byte of each pair is at an *even* address and the second byte of the pair is at an *odd* address (see figure 2.4). In this scheme each word has an even address. On some machines such as the Motorola MC68000 or the Digital Equipment Corporation LSI-11 and PDP-11, this is the only way you can access a 16-bit quantity. In particular, on a PDP-11 an attempt to access a 16-bit word with an odd address will cause the operating system to scold you with an error message.

In contrast to the Motorola and Zilog processors, the 16-bit Intel 8086 microprocessor puts no such restriction on the programmer, although there is a price to pay in performance, in that an access to a word with an odd address will take longer on an 8086 than an access to a

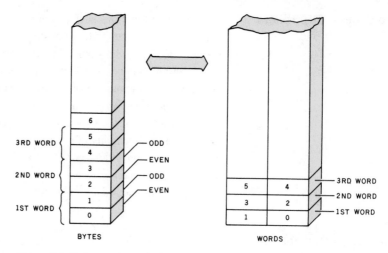

Figure 2.4: Bytes and words in memory—two views.

word with an even address. This is because accessing a word with an odd address requires two different fetches by the 8086: one for the word containing the odd byte (and the unneeded byte below), and one for the word containing the even byte (and the unneeded byte above). The processor then puts together the appropriate bytes to form the word and throws out the inappropriate ones (see the figure below).

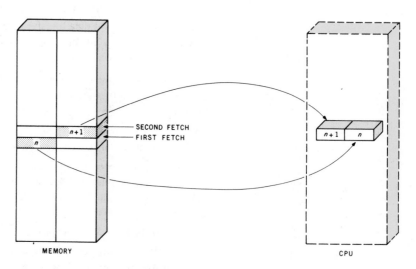

Figure 2.5: Accessing odd words.

The System Controllers

Certain functions such as transferring of blocks of information from one place to another (DMA transfers) or control of the I/O interrupts are better done by devices other than the main CPU. Thus, it is desirable to have certain *system controllers* to perform these tasks. Having such devices not only makes certain functions possible, but also relieves the CPU of the time-consuming "overhead" of certain tasks by *distributing* the intelligence of the system to places outside the CPU. Our bodies also do this for us, for many of our reflex reactions occur without any processing by our brain (our CPU) until after the reflex has happened!

Later in Chapter 6 we shall explore two system-controller chips, the 8237 Programmable DMA Controller and the 8259 Programmable Interrupt Controller.

The Device Controllers

When we looked at the whole computer system, we saw that there were a number of devices such as keyboards, video monitors, floppy disks, and printers connected to the computer. These may generally be called input/output (I/O) devices. I/O devices never connect directly to the main bus of the computer. Instead, each such device has some sort of cable which connects to its own (or a shared) *device controller* which in turn connects to the main bus. Thus, device controllers *interface* the devices to the computer whereas *system controllers* perform internal functions.

The various system and device controllers can be assigned addresses just as each memory cell is assigned an address. On the Intel and Zilog microprocessor chips, the addresses assigned to I/O devices are kept in a separate *space* from the memory space. Control signals on the control bus help distinguish the difference between memory and I/O accesses, and, in the processor, different data transfer instructions are used for each (IN and OUT for I/O and MOVe, LoaD, STore for memory). On the Motorola and Digital Equipment Corporation PDP-11 machines, the I/O devices and the memory cells are all in the same area or space and are only distinguished by their addresses. Hence there are two philosophically different places to locate the I/O addresses: in a separate space or in part of the memory space.

Often each set of device controllers is housed on a separate board. A few years ago you would, in fact, have had to buy a separate I/O controller board to plug into your bus for each additional I/O device. Each such board would have been filled with an assortment of less dense SSI and MSI chips. This *assortment of chips* would thus have formed the device controller. Intel and other manufacturers such as Motorola and Texas Instruments have been incorporating this board-level logic into chips. For example, you can now buy a *single chip* which contains all the logic of a floppy disk controller. A number of other device controllers chips have been developed, some of which are *special purpose* such as a floppy disk controller or a CRT controller, and some of which are *general purpose* such as a parallel interface controller or a serial interface controller. These last two can, in fact, be used to hook up a wide variety of different devices to a computer. System controllers such as DMA controllers and interrupt controllers have also been placed on single chips. There are now even chips such as the Intel 8256 Multifunction Universal Asynchronous Receiver/Transmitter that perform many functions including system control.

This miniaturization process has had a profound effect on board manufacturing, greatly simplifying board design and making it possible to design boards which perform a large variety of functions, including system functions as well as I/O functions. Recent board designs will now include connections for several parallel and serial interfaces as well as timers and interrupt controllers.

With miniaturization has come increased flexibility and sophistication. System and device controllers are now *programmable*. That is, they can be put into various modes and can perform various functions under software control. In Chapter 6, we will study several examples of different types of programmable system and device controllers. These include the 8259 Programmable Interrupt Controller and the 8237 Programmable DMA Controller, which are both system controllers; the 8251 Programmable Serial Interface Controller and the 8255 Programmable Parallel Interface Controller, which are general-purpose device controllers; and the 8275 Programmable CRT Controller and the 8272 Programmable Floppy Disk Controller, which are specialized device controllers. We shall also use these chips as support chips in our model computers later in this chapter.

Integrated Design and the Use of "Glue"

Intel's line of chips is so complete that it is theoretically possible to build a complete computer using just chips manufactured by this one company, as we shall do in our example computers. Usually, however, a designer selects a small number of LSI and VLSI microprocessor chips and special-function chips to achieve the major goals of the particular design and then "glues" the system together with a multitude of smaller less complex chips. Here "glue" means logical circuitry needed to connect major components together. In contrast to the major components which are LSI and VLSI chips, typically constructed using some variation of the metal oxide semiconductor (MOS) technology, the "glue" chips are very often constructed using some type of bipolar technology formed into what is called transistor-transistor logic (TTL), with densities which are small-scale integration (SSI) and medium-scale integration (MSI). (For an explanation of the differences between the MOS and bipolar technologies see Meindl, James D., "Microelectronic Circuit Element." *Scientific American*. September, 1977.) Texas Instruments is a leading manufacturer of the popular TTL devices and has one of the most complete catalogues of these SSI and MSI chips. Though there are many other manufacturers of such TTL circuits, the numbering scheme as described in the Texas Instruments catalogue has become the industry standard.

Using this "glue" from Texas as well as a little Intel "glue," an engineer can encode and decode the control signals as well as separate and combine address and data signals from the processor and controller chips. In present systems, signals have to be combined because there are more signals needed than there are lines to carry them. For example, the 8086 microprocessor chip has only 40 pins, but produces many more logically different signals. This seemingly impossible problem can be overcome in two fundamental ways: *time multiplexing* and *encoding* (see the figure below).

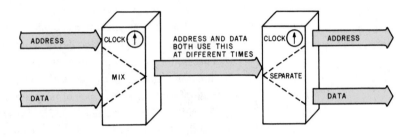

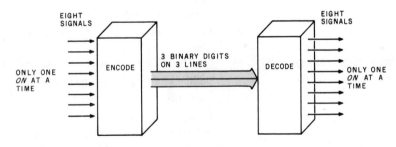

Figure 2.6: Time multiplexing and encoding.

Time multiplexing

Time multiplexing depends upon the fact that not all signals need be sent at once. With this method the same set of signal lines (coming through the pins on the chips) is used to send different sets of signals during different time periods. For example the 8085, 8086, 8087, 8088, and 8089 processors use the same pins for both address and data (on the 8-bit data machines only the lower 8 bits of address share pins with the data). During any memory access, the address is always sent during the first clock cycle and then the data is sent during later clock cycles. To help the external circuitry ("glue") separate these two types of signals, there is a signal called address latch enable (ALE). The ALE signal indicates when these lines contain address information. This allows certain circuitry outside the CPU to "latch" or hold onto the address information and ignore the data information, while other circuitry ignores the address information and "latches" the data.

Encoding

Encoding depends upon the fact that only certain combinations of signals will ever occur. With this method groups of signals are *encoded* into numbers before they are set and *decoded* before they can be used. For example, there are eight different ways that an 8086 can use the system bus. Each different way corresponds to a different "state" that the processor and, indeed, the system can be in. These eight states can be encoded using the numbers 0 through 7, and thus can be represented by three-digit binary numbers. Thus with 3 pins we can send out 8 signals.

For control purposes one would like to have separate signals for each such state. Each such control line would turn on during a certain time period only when the processor is in the appropriate state. In actual practice some states require no control lines, some require one, and some even have two. For example, during the *memory-read* state, at just the right microsecond, there must be a signal line from the processor to the memory to tell the memory when to send the data. In one of its two operating modes, an 8086 actually has two such memory-read signals, one to give advance warning to slower memories to help them prepare for a read and one to indicate when to actually release the data.

All in all (that is, for all possible states), the 8086 requires about seven such state control signals. In one of its operating modes (the minimum mode) it produces a minimal set of these signals itself, and in the other mode (the maximum mode), it instead sends a three-digit binary number, which encodes its state, to the 8288 Bus Controller. The 8288 Bus Controller combines these with the clock signal to produce the actual full set of control signals. By sending only the three-digit binary code (on three lines), Intel saves 4 pins on the 8086 processor, but forces you to use another device, the 8288 Bus Controller, to do the decoding. Because of its role in sorting out these signals, we can think of the 8288 Bus Controller as an example of Intel "glue" or perhaps "rivets" because they drop into place rather neatly.

Intel has developed its own bus, the Multibus, with a complete set of boards to populate it, thus "integrating" logic at a higher level than just the chip level. In particular, it has a line of single board computers (iSBC), using the 8080, 8085, 8086, and 8088 CPU chips; a large assortment of memory boards; various general purpose I/O boards; and several floppy-disk controller boards. It offers several chassis, including a heavy duty industrial chassis and the Intellect Development Systems. Most of the single board computers can either stand alone or work in conjunction with the Multibus. For the single board computers which use the 8086 and 8088 CPUs, (the iSBC 86/12A and the iSBC88/40) there is a special module (iSBC 337) which replaces the CPU by a PCU *cluster* consisting of an 8086/8088 CPU coupled with an 8087 NDP.

The Multibus is popular with the industrial, rather than the personal, hobby, or professional market. Many industrial control and monitoring devices use these boards. These devices are built by other companies called Original Equipment Manufacturers (OEMs) and incorporate these Intel boards, often as stand-alone computing devices. Other companies such as AMD and NEC are now also manufacturing boards for the Multibus.

Intel processor and controller chips are also often used to produce digital systems which conform with designs and standards other than Intel's. For example, Intel chips are often used to provide key functions for computers which use the popular S-100 bus. The S-100 bus has different control, timing, and multiplexing (as well as power) requirements than the newer 8086, 8088, 8089, and 8087 processors because it was based upon the older 8080 CPU chip. A lot of SSI chips are typically used to ''glue'' such systems together.

In a complete system today, there are typically more SSI and MSI chips than there are LSI and VLSI chips (although this is changing — see for example the Commodore VIC and the Atari 800). Thus, though the bulk of the logic is on the latter type of chip, much of the space and power is consumed by the former. The trend for tomorrow is to have just a few powerful chips hooked together in a simple, elegant manner. Intel is right on track in providing this larger type of chip.

8086/8088-BASED SYSTEMS

The figure below shows a block diagram of a system in which a number of Intel chips are interconnected to form a computer. Almost all the chips used will be discussed somewhere in the next four chapters of this book.

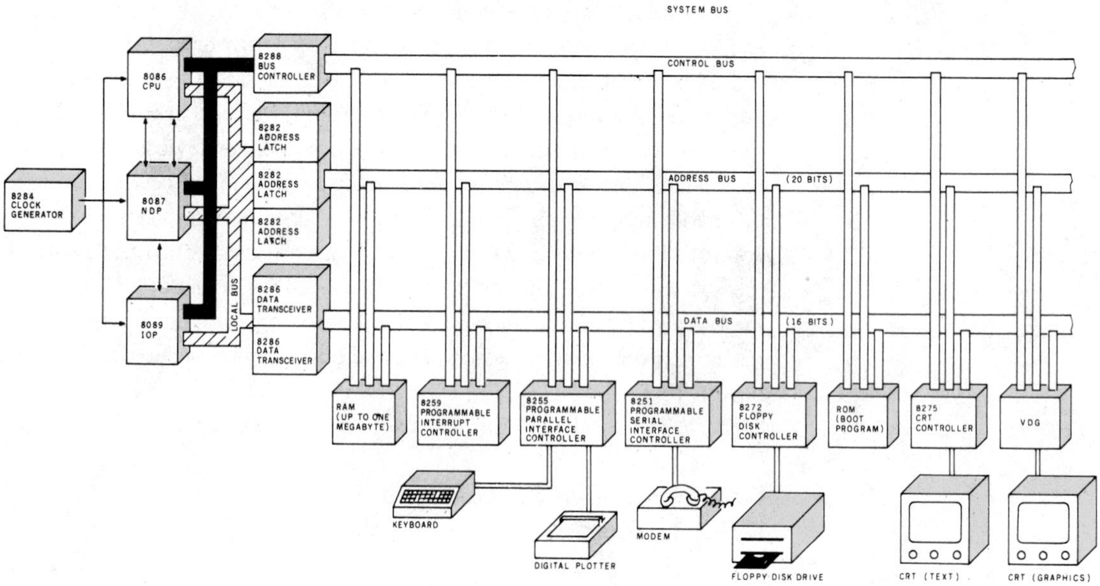

Figure 2.7: Block diagram of a 16-bit computer based on the 8086 CPU.

In particular, this block diagram shows how to connect together the three Intel processors:

the 8086 Central Processing Unit
the 8087 Numeric Data Processor
the 8089 Input/Output Processor

These three processors form a high-power, number-crunching complex which is located on the left side of the figure. The 8086 central processing unit (CPU) is the general manager of the whole system, delegating tasks to the other two processors. High precision arithmetic computations get delegated to the 8087 Numeric Data Processor (NDP) and the 8089 Input/Output Processor (IOP) is in charge of moving blocks of data within the video display memory and between the main memory and the video display system.

This cluster has its own *local* bus structures. Control lines running directly from the 8086 CPU to the 8087 NDP and then to the 8089 IOP help decide who has control of this local address/data bus at any given moment (only one may use this bus at a time).

There are three bus interface chips:

the 8288 Bus Controller
the 8082 Octal Address Latch
the 8286 Octal Data Transceiver

A single 8288 Bus Controller, three 8282 Octal Address Latches, and two 8286 Octal Data Transceivers are used to connect the local bus shared by the three processors to the system (non-local) bus. These chips are needed for two reasons: 1) to rearrange the various signals and 2) to supply the power necessary to drive the numerous devices attached to the system bus. A different type of chip is used to interface with each different subbus: the 8288 Bus Controller is used to interface with the control subbus, the 8282 Octal Address Latch is used to interface with the address subbus, and the 8286 Octal Data Transceiver is used to interface with the data subbus. A fourth bus, power, is not shown, but it has the power supply attached to it, and every device in the system draws power from it.

There are two programmable system controller chips:

the 8259 Programmable Interrupt Controller
the 8237 Programmable DMA Controller

These two system controllers perform the internal functions of DMA transfer and interrupt controller as we discussed previously.

There are four programmable device controller chips:

the 8251 Programmable Serial Interface Controller
the 8255 Programmable Parallel Interface Controller
the 8275 Programmable CRT Controller
the 8272 Programmable Floppy-Disk Controller.

Each external device is connected to one of these four device controllers which is in turn connected to the main system bus. Notice that two devices (a digital plotter and a keyboard) share the 24-bit 8255 Programmable Parallel Interface Controller.

In addition there is one other device controller not covered: a video graphics controller. The video graphics is not yet available from Intel (hint . . . hint). However, there are several such chips available on the market right now; for example, the Motorola 6847 Video Display Generator (VDG), and the new NEC 7220 Graphics Display Controller chip (which is perhaps not quite ready). The Motorola has a medium resolution up to about 192 vertical by 256 horizontal, while the NEC is a high-performance device with more resolution available than an ordinary display could possibly use as well as other features such as built-in line-drawing commands. There have been several fully functional video graphics controller systems on the market for some time whose logic is distributed among a whole set of SSI and MSI chips on integrated circuit boards. Manufacturers such as Digital Graphic Systems, Cromemco, Cambridge Development Laboratory, and Scion produce such one-, two-, or three-board systems.

Notice that memory is just another "device" to the processors! Our system can hold up to 1 megabyte of RAM and ROM. The ROM is used to store a short *bootstrap* program to get the floppy-disk controller started. The program causes the first sector of the disk to be loaded into memory. This contains a program which loads the rest of the operating system into memory. The operating system then initializes the various controllers and signs on, ready for your commands.

With very little modification to our block diagram (actually several simplifications) we could replace the 8086 CPU chip by an 8088 CPU. The 8088 CPU chip has an 8-bit-wide external data bus, and, thus, the data bus for our computer will now be only 8 bits wide. This actually simplifies matters in terms of connecting the various I/O device controllers because they mostly use 8-bit data buses. The 8087 NDP and 8089 IOP are designed to work with *either* the 16-bit data bus of the 8086 CPU *or* the 8-bit data bus of the 8088 CPU. Although the 8-bit system is easier and less expensive to build, the 16-bit system will perform better. This is because a 16-bit data bus can move data up to two times faster among the 16-bit components which include the CPU, memory, and video graphics display system (which we can operate in either an 8-bit or 16-bit mode). In particular, instructions can be fetched faster and pictures displayed faster with the 16-bit system.

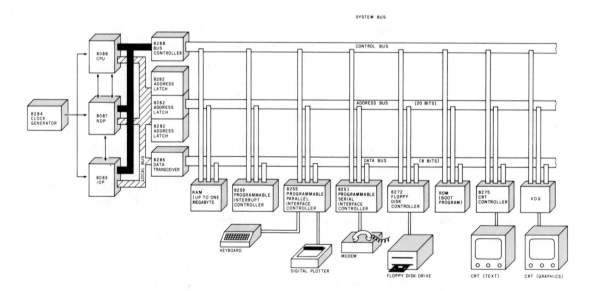

Figure 2.8: An 8-bit computer based on the 8088 CPU.

Either computer design would be useful as a graphics development system. The video graphics controller would display pictures of simple or complex mathematical shapes, artistic renderings, or animated pictures of complex scenes. Both the 8087 Numeric Data Processor, and the 8089 Input/Output Processor will be valuable tools to help rapidly manipulate these types of pictures. The digital plotter would then draw high-resolution line drawings of these shapes. The keyboard would be used to enter and modify programs. The floppy disk would be used to store programs (and pictures), and the modem would hook the computer to a large computer network to gain access to large data bases and some public programs. The CRT controller would be used to display the text of programs and other nongraphics information.

The display of video graphics will put the most demand on the system. Because of this we will discuss its requirements in some depth. We will suppose that we have a fictitious video graphics display system set up as follows: Each picture will require 96 K bytes. This is because there are three different primary colors with a resolution of 480 vertical dots by 512 horizontal dots. This is one of the standard high resolutions for ordinary broadcast signal. There are $480 \times 512 = 245,760$ dots (pixels) altogether. Each pixel requires 3 bits (1 for each color), and thus 737,280 in all. This is 92,160 bytes (737,280/8), more than the 64 K bytes that can be directly addressed by an 8080 or 8085 CPU. In fact, even the 8086/8088 CPU, with its 20-bit addressing, can only hold about 11 such pictures in its main memory (without paging[2]) at once! To produce animated effects we will need to hold four or five different pictures in memory at a time. This is necessary so that we can build more complex pictures out of simpler ones, perhaps assembling a picture of an animal from separate head, arm, and leg pieces. It is also necessary so that we can flash back and forth between two or more pictures (or parts of pictures) to simulate motion. There are other ways to produce animated effects, but because our system is a development system we wish to use all sorts of methods including those which use a lot of memory.

Our video system produces a standard broadcast video signal which can be displayed on an ordinary television monitor. This means that the complete picture is redrawn or *refreshed* 30 times a second by the video

---

[2]Paging is the use of several *planes* or *pages* of memory, all with the same addresses. Only one such page is visible to the processor at any one time, even though the other pages still retain whatever information was stored there. Selection of which page is visible is done under software control, usually through an I/O port. Usually the memory has at least one section which is not paged. The paging control software is usually located in nonpaged memory so that page changes can be completed successfully, although it is possible to get around this problem by having duplicate copies of the crucial portions of the software on all pages.

display circuitry. Actually a full *frame* (complete picture) is broken up into two *interlacing fields,* each of which is displayed in 1/60 of a second. Interlacing means that each field shows every other line with the two together giving the entire picture. This scheme was developed as a compromise which is synchronized with the 60 cycles used by ordinary house current and at the same time reduces *flicker* on the video screen. An interlaced rate of about 30 frames per second is quite adequate to eliminate flicker for most ordinary television pictures. The kind of high-contrast pictures produced by computer graphics, however, requires a higher refresh rate of about 40 frames per second. This is what the broadcast standard should be. Unfortunately, U.S. broadcast standards were developed long before video computer graphics was feasible.

To achieve animation we will need to change scenes at the rate of about 10 frames per second. This animation speed is not to be confused with the faster refresh rate necessary to eliminate flicker. Thus, the video hardware usually displays each new picture several times before the computer causes it to be changed. This is quite fortunate, because most computers find it very difficult to recompute a new picture at 30 to 40 times a second (the refresh rate), but can easily do it at 10 times a second (to get smooth animation). The entire process is done as follows: As one scene is being shown, a second hidden scene is being drawn. When the second scene is finished, it is shown and the first one is hidden, ready to be used to draw the third scene. Each time a new scene is shown, it must appear "instantly". That is, it must appear entirely in place on the next frame. This effect is very difficult (expensive) to achieve if the picture is being computed as it is being displayed or if it is "shoved" into place by moving it from one location in memory to the display area. Even the 8089 IOP cannot move 92 K bytes that fast. With a 16-bit data bus running at 5 MHz, the IOP will take about .075 seconds to make such a transfer. To achieve an "instantaneous" change, the transfer should really be done in between two refreshes, that is, during what is called the *vertical retrace*. For the U.S. broadcast standard, this lasts about .000833 seconds, much too short a time for such a transfer. It is better to have a hardware switch which allows you to quickly change which part of the memory is currently being displayed.

We will often want to move just part of the scene, perhaps just a small rectangle or just one of the colors. If we restrict our calculations to move just a *patch,* which is say 20 $\times$ 20 pixels, then we would have 20 $\times$ 20 $\times$ 3 bits to move. This is

$$20 \times 20 \times 3/8 = 150 \text{ bytes}$$

Now 150 bytes can be moved in about half a millisecond, even by the 8-bit-at-a-time 8088 CPU. In fact, if we use the 8089 IOP in a 16-bit system (8086-based), we could move a 52 $\times$ 52 square on the screen within one vertical retrace, thus "instantaneously."

At times we will wish to move whole pictures. But this will be done as we develop pictures "behind scenes." In this case, .075 seconds to move a picture is not bad.

We have seen how the 8089 IOP will help us move parts of as well as whole pictures around. Now let's look at how the 8087 NDP will help.

The 8087 NDP will be a valuable asset in crunching numbers to produce our mathematical models for graphics pictures. One of the key steps in building such models is matrix multiplication. In Chapter 5, the chapter on the 8087 NDP, we show such a matrix multiply program and discuss why it is so essential.

Very briefly, suppose we wish to display a three-dimensional wire-frame drawing (our model) in many different possible viewing positions, perhaps achieving the effects of animation and perspective. To move such three-dimensional line drawings around, we usually use 4×4 matrices. These 4×4 matrices will allow us to conveniently represent the entire range of rotations, translations, magnifications, and perspective transformations using what are known as homogeneous coordinates. The 4×4 matrix multiply routine given in Chapter 5 will multiply one point of our display by a 4×4 matrix in less than 1 millisecond (ms). Thus, about 100 points can be processed in 1/10 second. This is just the frame rate we need for animation. With an older 8085-based system we would be lucky to achieve one tenth of this throughput.

DATA TYPES AND NUMBERS

A *data type* is a format or encoding scheme for representing data for storage within the computer. Modern 16-bit microprocessors use a variety of different standard formats for representing both numbers and other types of data such as text. We won't in this book give a detailed description of each type of data; we will, however, give an overview. When we get to the 8087 NDP in Chapter 5, we will discuss floating-point notation in considerably more detail.

In our discussion of the S-100 bus we saw an example of *orthogonal* design. That is, the conductors of the bus run perpendicular to the boards and connectors. With data storage and representation we have a similar situation, only on a more abstract level. This time the two different quantities run perpendicular to each other on an allocation chart (see the figure below). These orthogonal quantities are *units of memory* (bits, bytes, words, etc.) and *data types* (logicals, ordinals, integers, floating-point numbers, etc.). Very figuratively speaking, the *units of memory* are our conductors (they actually carry the information) and the *data* types are our connectors (they need access to the different units of storage). Just as not all boards need all conductors of the S-100 bus, not all data types will use all possible units of storage (as you can see from the chart).

For those of you who like to think in mathematical terms, the relationship between data types and data storage is not in itself a "mapping" because a given data type will "correspond to" (use) several possible sizes of data storage, and a given storage unit will "correspond to" (be used by) several different data types.

The figure below shows the common storage requirements for the various data types. Brief descriptions of each unit and type follow after the figure.

	UNITS OF STORAGE							
DATA TYPES	BIT	NIBBLE	BYTE	WORD	DOUBLE WORD	QUADRUPLE WORD	80-BIT WORD	BLOCK
LOGICAL	*		*					
ORDINAL			*	*	*	*		
INTEGER			*	*	*	*		
FLOATING-POINT					*	*	*	
BCD DIGIT		*						
BCD NUMBER		*	*	*	*	*	*	*
CHARACTER			*					
STRING								*
POINTER					*			

Figure 2.9: Data types and how they are stored.

Units of Memory

We begin with units of memory starting with the smallest, the bit, and going to larger units such as the block. See the figure below for a picture of the various units of storage.

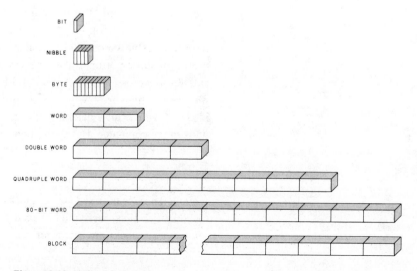

Figure 2.10: Units of storage.

Bit

A *bit* is the smallest unit of data in a computer. The term "bit" stands for "binary digit." A bit is stored and transmitted as a two-state signal, either on or off. It can be used to store individual logical variables (sometimes called flags) or numbers belonging to a very simple clock arithmetic (modulo 2 arithmetic in which the "clock" has just two hours "0" and "1"). Bits can also be combined with other bits to store more complicated types of data. The name "bit" is a misnomer, because we are actually dealing with a unit of memory, and not a type of data as the expanded name "binary digit" implies. Now that we've mentioned this, try not to let it bother you.

Nibble

A *nibble* consists of 4 bits and thus is half a byte (discussed next). A nibble is useful for storing one binary-coded digit (BCD) (equals decimal 0 through 9) or one hexadecimal-coded digit (equals decimal 0 through 15).

Byte

A *byte* consists of 8 bits and thus 2 nibbles. A byte is useful for storing a single character (usually encoded in ASCII), a number from 0 to 255, two BCD numbers (0 through 99), or eight 1-bit flags.

Word

Contrary to popular belief, a *word* can consist of a fixed but arbitrary number of bits. The present generations of microcomputers commonly have 16-bit words, 32-bit words, 64-bit words, and 80-bit words. In this book on 16-bit microprocessors, the term "word" by itself as a unit of memory almost always means a 16-bit word, the term "double word" means a 32-bit word, and the term "quadruple word" means a 64-bit word. These require 2, 4, and 8 bytes of memory storage, respectively. In a book on 32-bit processors, the term "word" might refer to a 32-bit word. Words, double words, and quadruple words are useful for storing ordinals and integers. Double words, quadruple words, and 80-bit words (10 bytes) are useful for storage of floating-point numbers. The word "word" is a poor word because it conjures up the idea of "words" of a natural language such as English instead of storage units in the computer. But again, don't let this bother you.

Block

A *block* is a longer group of contiguous memory cells (bytes or words). There is no fixed size to blocks, although within certain contexts (such as disk files) there might be a definite size such as 256, 512, or 1024 bytes. Blocks are useful for storing strings, sections of text, or sections of programs.

Data types

Now let's look at *what* is being stored in these various storage units, namely the data. Each *type* of data has a certain format, or encoding, which takes up a number of bits of memory. Without a description of the particular format or code used, data becomes completely meaningless and unreadable. This is especially true for complicated data types such as floating-point number representations. See the figure below for an overview of how the various data types are encoded (according to a proposed IEEE standard used by Intel and others). Almost all of these data types are constructed out of pieces which use the base two, or binary, numbering system. We assume that the reader can "speak" in binary, and understands why computers work so well in this number base. At various times throughout the book, we will use base 16 or hexadecimal numbering. We assume the reader is also familiar with this system. Hexadecimal numbers within the text will be distinguished by placing an uppercase *H* after them. If you need a refresher, see the Waite, Mitchell; Pardee, Michael *Microcomputer Primer*. Indianapolis, Indiana: Howard W. Sams & Co., Inc.

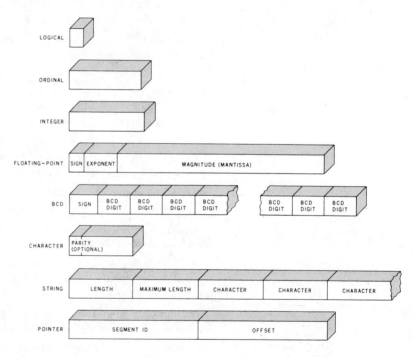

Figure 2.11: Data type encodings.

Let's begin with a data type which we call a *logical,* requiring one bit of storage, and work our way to data types such as *strings* which require many bytes. We will not describe floating-point number representation in much detail here because it is covered quite thoroughly in Chapter 5 in conjunction with the 8087 NDP.

Logical

A *logical* is a two-state quantity and can be stored in a single bit. Two-state means that there are only two possible values. These possible values can be thought of as: true versus false, on versus off, yes versus no, or 1 versus 0. Logicals are useful for such purposes as status flags to let you know when devices are ready for input and output or for conditional flags to help with branching during program flow.

Ordinals

Ordinals are unsigned whole numbers or counting numbers where the count starts with 0. They are sometimes referred to as unsigned integers. Ordinals are stored in the computer in different-sized binary representations (of which we show eight). With 8 bits, ordinals can be represented ranging in value from 0 to 255; with 16 bits, ordinal values from 0 to 65,535 can be represented; and with 32 bits and 64 bits, values can range from 0 to 4,294,967,296 and over 1.84E19, respectively.

Integers

Integers are signed whole numbers (i.e., $+-$). On all of today's well-known microprocessors, integers are represented by two's complement binary representation. There are other systems such as one's complement and sign-magnitude, but we won't need to discuss them here. In the two's complement scheme, the extreme leftmost bit does double duty as part of the number and as a sign bit for the number. An easy way to understand two's complement is to think of the numbers wrapped around a "number wheel" in a couple of different ways. For a given number n of bits for storage, you can represent *ordinals* (unsigned numbers) from 0 to $2^n - 1$. If we wrap this number strip around a wheel, so that the last number is just before the first, then we have a gigantic clock and can use the rules of clock arithmetic. If we now break this wheel halfway around and start assigning negative integers to positions on the broken wheel, counting backwards from 0, we will get the two's complement number representation scheme (see the figure below). The wheel is broken precisely at the point where the leftmost bit changes sign so that all nonnegative numbers have their leftmost bit equal to 0, and all negative numbers have their leftmost bit equal to 1. The leftmost bit is appropriately called the sign bit.

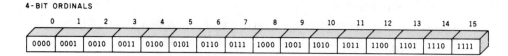

4-BIT ORDINALS

0	1	2	3	4	5	6	7	8	9	10	11	12	13	14	15
0000	0001	0010	0011	0100	0101	0110	0111	1000	1001	1010	1011	1100	1101	1110	1111

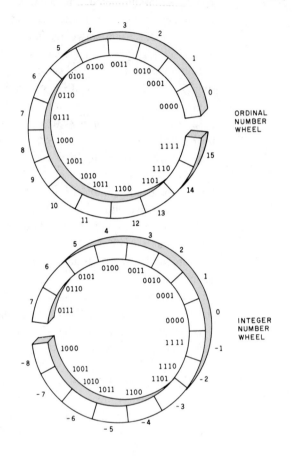

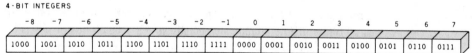

4-BIT INTEGERS

-8	-7	-6	-5	-4	-3	-2	-1	0	1	2	3	4	5	6	7
1000	1001	1010	1011	1100	1101	1110	1111	0000	0001	0010	0011	0100	0101	0110	0111

Figure 2.12: Two's complement numbering.

In the two's complement numbering system with 8 bits (1 byte), you can represent integers ranging in value from –128 to +127; with 16 bits (1 word), you can represent integers ranging in value from –32,768 to +32,767; and with 32 bits (a double word), you can represent integers from –2,147,483,648 to +2,147,483,647. There is even a 64-bit (quadruple word) size integer which can be used to represent numbers between approximately plus and minus 9E18! (That's 9 with 18 zeroes behind it.)

Floating-Point

Floating-point representations of numbers are designed to provide good *approximations* of real numbers. The floating-point representation system is closely related to the familiar scientific notation for numbers in which there is a sign, exponent, and magnitude. Floating-point representations commonly come in the following sizes: 32 bits (double word), 64 bits (quadruple word), and 80 bits. The first two formats (32-bit and 64-bit) are called short and long reals, respectively, and are specified by the proposed IEEE standard for floating-point numbers (see A Proposed Standard for Binary Floating-Point Arithmetic. Draft 8.0 of IEEE Task P754. *Computer Magazine*. IEEE. March, 1981). The third format (80-bit) is used internally by the 8087 NDP and is called the temporary real format by Intel.

The short real format uses its 32 bits as follows: 1 bit for the sign, 8 bits for the exponent, and 23 bits for the magnitude. The smallest possible positive number is 2^{-126} which is approximately 1.175×10^{-38} and the largest possible positive number is about 2^{128} which is approximately 3.40×10^{38}. There are actually 24 binary digits in the magnitude; the first bit is always understood to be a 1 and is never actually stored.

The long real format requires 64 bits: 1 bit for the sign, 11 bits for the exponent, and 52 bits for the magnitude. The smallest possible positive number is 2^{-1022} which is approximately 2.23×10^{-308} and the largest possible positive number is about 2^{1024} which is approximately 1.80×10^{308}. Again, there is actually one more bit in the magnitude which is understood but not stored (making 53 bits altogether).

The temporary real format requires 80 bits: 1 bit for the sign, 15 bits for the exponent, and 64 bits for the magnitude. The smallest possible positive number is 2^{-16382} which is approximately 3.36×10^{-4932}, and the largest possible positive number is about 2^{16384} which is approximately 1.19×10^{4932}. This format is different from the others in that all bits of the magnitude are actually stored. The 64 bits of precision yield more than 18 decimal digits of accuracy.

For a more detailed discussion, including the concepts of precision and range, see the chapter on the 8087 NDP.

Binary-Coded Decimals

With the *binary-coded decimal* (BCD) representation of numbers, each digit of a number in decimal notation is stored in a separate nibble (1 nibble = 4 bits = half a byte). The 8087 NDP can work with an 18^n digit binary-coded decimal format (18 nibbles = 9 bytes plus an extra byte for the sign). (That's right, 1 whole byte for the sign bit. But where else are you going to put the sign bit?) As a result, the entire number takes up 10 bytes or 80 bits when it is stored in the memory of the computer or within an NDP register.

This BCD notation is a favorite with business applications in which every cent in a dollars-and-cents number is important in calculations involving millions or even billions of dollars. The 8086/8088 CPU has special instructions (DAA, Decimal Adjust for Addition, and DAS, Decimal Adjust for Subtraction) to help process this type of number representation.

Characters

Characters are used to represent the letters of the alphabet and other symbols such as number digits (0-9) and punctuation marks. The standard method of representing these symbols is to use the ASCII code which, incidentally, is now an 8-bit code. In this ASCII code, each symbol is assigned a unique number. For example, *A* is represented by decimal 65, *B* is represented by decimal 66, and so on, and *0* is represented by decimal 48, *1* is represented by decimal 49, and so on. Most assembly language manuals and programming cards have a chart of the ASCII code. Most of today's computers employ a 7-bit subset of the 8-bit code, and there is even a 6-bit subset. With the 6-bit subset, you cannot represent lowercase letters, but with the 7-bit code, you can. These various versions of the ASCII code are usually stored in 8-bit bytes. Sometimes the extra bit or bits are used for error detection (see Chapter 5 for more on error detection and correction codes), or for indicating reverse video blinking, and other attributes.

Strings

Strings are formed from sequences of characters and can be used to carry textual messages. For example, sign-on messages and error messages are strings, and some text-editing programs consider the whole document which is being edited to be one long string, perhaps consisting of thousands of characters. Since strings have dynamically variable lengths, extra information is often included which specifies the maximum and the current length of a string. For example, string variables in some implementations of BASIC have a hidden internal 3-byte *prelude* with the first byte containing a number which signifies that the data is a string, the second byte containing the maximum length for that string, and the third byte containing the current length of the string. In other situations, the length of the string is not stored at all. Instead, there is a special character (perhaps a carriage return indicator) which tells where the end of the string is located. The current crop of 16-bit processors do not have special formats for strings, but often do have special string instructions with very general and powerful ways of dealing with various formats. In particular, the 8089 IOP has ways to end string transfers and transformations either on a *count* or a *terminator character* (or both).

Pointers

Pointers are used by the Intel 16-bit CPUs to "point" to physical addresses in memory. They are used in conjunction with segmentation which we will discuss next. With the 8086/8088 microprocessors, a physical address in memory is stored as *two* 16-bit quantities. These quantities are combined in a special way, which we will describe next, to form the actual 20-bit address. A pointer is a double word which stores these two 16-bit quantities, the *segment number* and the *offset*.

In general, Intel has a different manner of assigning storage to longer data types than Zilog or Motorola. Intel specifies that the lower (least significant) parts of a number be stored in lower-addressed bytes of memory, while the other two manufacturers specify that lower parts of the numbers be stored in higher-addressed bytes (see the figure below).

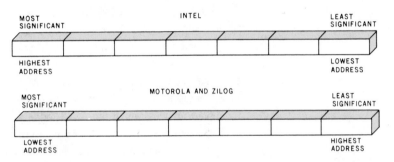

Figure 2.13: Addressing the data—Intel versus Motorola and Zilog.

These differences really come out with BCD number representations. In contrast to Intel's method of storing binary digits in increasing order from right to left, the Motorola MC68000 and the Zilog Z8000 store BCD digits in just the opposite order, increasing from left to right.

Another difference in general is that Motorola and Zilog require that data needing multiple bytes must start on *even* addressed bytes, while Intel allows these data types to be stored starting on any byte address. However, because the 8086 CPU has to access two different words to get the one it needs, it has a speed penalty for longer data types which begin at odd addresses.

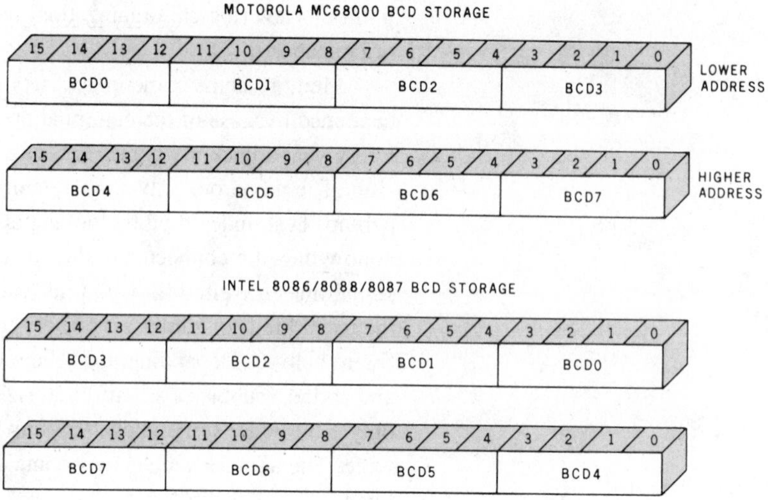

MOTOROLA MC68000 BCD STORAGE

INTEL 8086/8088/8087 BCD STORAGE

Figure 2.14: Motorola and Intel BCD storage.

SOME 16-BIT CONCEPTS

In this section we shall explore several concepts found in 16-bit microcomputers which are either not found in the older 8-bit machines or else are significantly different in the newer 16-bit processors. We shall first turn our attention to memory: the way it is organized and the way it is managed. We shall describe both the physical and the logical organization of memory. "Physical" refers to the way the memory is organized as it appears on the computer's main bus, and "logical" refers to the way it appears to an assembly-language programmer. In today's more sophisticated systems such distinctions begin to appear and become important in multiuser applications.

We shall study two methods for *physical* organization of memory: *straight linear* and *physical paging;* and two methods for *logical* organization of memory: *segmentation* and *logical paging.* We will then see how to use memory management to connect the logical and physical organization together. Next (and last) we shall look at the concept of having several processors in one system and, in particular, within one computer. We shall see that processors can either be organized as equals or in a master/slave relationship. Within the master/slave arrangements we shall describe two common arrangements: *coprocessing* and *multiprocessing.* We shall see how these can greatly increase the power of a microcomputer system.

Physical Memory Organization

The organization of memory in a digital computer depends not only upon the particular computer, but also upon your vantage point within the computer (see figure 2.15). Let's start at the memory chip and work our way toward the system level (physical organization of memory). Later we will explore the organization of memory from the programmer's point of view (logical organization) toward the system level (physical organization).

Memory chips come in a variety of different sizes. This has happened because of the continual breakthroughs in memory technology. Every year somebody comes out with a way of packing more bits on a chip. The numerous ways that memory is arranged on chips can be perhaps best understood by looking at the pinouts of these chips, that is, at how they are connected to the outside world. For a memory chip, the signal lines traveling through pins leading off the chip form a bus with the usual kinds of subbuses: power, control, address, and data (see the figure below). Depending upon the model number of the chip, the data and address subbuses are different sizes. Sometimes the data subbus is only 1 bit wide, sometimes it's 4 bits wide, and sometimes it's 8 bits wide. The address subbus may contain anywhere from 10 to 16 signal lines.

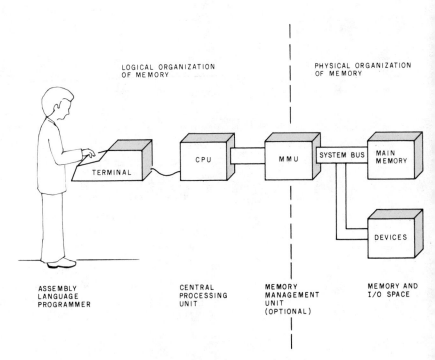

Figure 2.15: Memory organization—physical and logical.

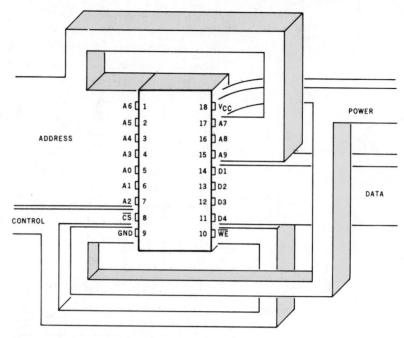

Figure 2.16: Pinouts for a typical memory chip.

If the data subbus on a memory chip is only 1 bit wide, then it takes eight chips connected in parallel to make a full byte and 16 chips to make a word; if the data subbus is 4 bits wide, then it takes only two chips to make a byte and four chips to make a word; and if the data subbus is 8 bits wide, it takes only one chip for a byte and two for a word (see the figure below).

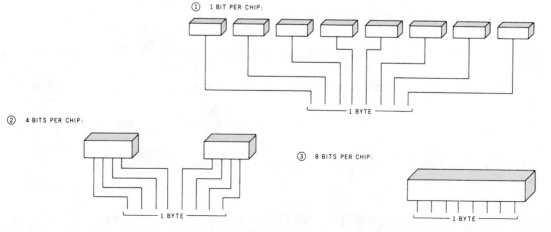

Figure 2.17: Making bytes out of memory chips.

If the address bus has n signal lines (possibly *multiplexed* through a fewer number of pins), then it will allow addressing of two to the nth power possible cells. For example, if there are 10 address lines, then an addressing range of 2^{10} or 1024 cells is possible. As far as each chip is concerned, the addressing starts at 0 and ends at $2^n - 1$.

Memory chips are placed on boards to create longer and wider sections of memory. The chips are usually laid out on the board in a rectangular "array" (see the figure below). The various columns may correspond to the different bits of the byte or word and the various rows may correspond to different addressing *ranges*. For example, if you have 8 rows of chips, each of which has 10 addressing lines, then you will have 8 times 1024, or 8192, possible addresses for memory bytes on that board.

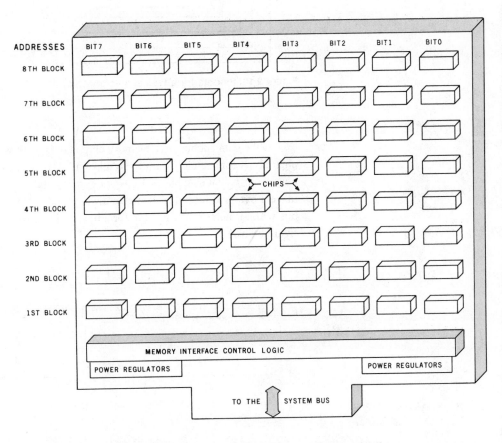

Figure 2.18: Layout for a typical memory board.

Usually there are switches on the board which will allow you to place or "map" the memory on the board to a section within the larger addressing space of the entire computer (see the figure below). Thus, you will often need several memory boards. Of course, as memory chips become more dense, you will be able to fit more memory on one board and need fewer boards for the same amount of memory. Presently, there are a number of 64 K-byte boards available for many microcomputer systems and, just recently, some 128 and 256 K-byte boards. However, memory addressing spaces have been growing larger, so some people will probably still need several boards no matter how much they can put on one board. It should be pointed out, on the other hand, that even though the memory is organized as long lines, not all of such a line needs to be filled in with "live" memory; that is, there can be gaps. If you don't fill in possible addresses with memory, then any memory read from the unfilled address will return "all 1s" (or perhaps "all 0s").

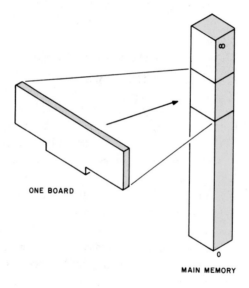

ONE BOARD

MAIN MEMORY

Figure 2.19: Mapping memory from a board into the larger system.

Sometimes a system will have more memory than can be accommodated by the normal, system-addressing range. For example, an 8080, 8085, or Z80 CPU can address only 64 K bytes of memory, but some people have put as much as 400 K bytes in such systems! This is done by breaking the total amount into *pages,* each of which will "fit" into the normal addressing space. There is an extra set of addressing lines to select among the various different memory pages. This scheme is called *physical paging.* Often, however, sending the page address is much slower than sending the normal address. Hence, the page address will be adjusted relatively infrequently, and the user will normally work within the same page for long stretches.

One such paging scheme which is sometimes used by 8-bit computers is to send the page-selection information over an I/O port to the memory boards in the system. Logic on each memory board then decodes these identifiers and enables or disables the memory on the board accordingly. In this way most 8-bit processors can have many times more than the usual 64 K in the addressing space.

Logical Memory Organization

We have just described two ways memory is normally physically organized: 1) as one, long, linear-addressing space or 2) as a collection of pages which each form a linear addressing space. These are the ways that the memory appears to any other device on the system bus. Now let's look at how the memory may be organized from the programmer's point of view. This is called the logical organization of memory.

In the simplest case, the memory's logical organization is the same as its physical organization. This is the normal situation for 8-bit microcomputers. However with their larger addressing space and multitasking applications the newer 16-bit processors require more elaborate logical schemes. The two methods we shall discuss are *segmentation* and *paging*.

Basically, *segmentation* is a method for accessing memory in which each memory access by the processor involves two separate addressing quantities: an *offset* and a *segment identifier*. The segment identifier points to a general area or section of memory (the segment), and the offset points to addresses within that segment. In the segmentation system, the physical memory is actually organized along one continuous number line and each cell has a unique physical address which is computed from the segment identifier and the offset by methods we shall discuss later. The offset is generally what appears in programs as the address of a piece of data, label, or instruction within a given program; whereas the segment identifier appears only when a new segment needs to be specified. That is, usually the choice of segment is set, and then the programmer and the processor both remember the current choice of segment for a whole sequence of memory accesses until a new area of memory is needed. At that time, the new segment identifier is trotted out. Normally, this happens only at the beginning of programs, when different areas of data have to be accessed, or when control is passed from one section of code to another.

With 8-bit, assembly-language programming, the single addressing quantity for each memory-access corresponds to just an offset, and the whole memory is just one big segment. With 16-bit processors, the addressing space is now so large that the addressing range available to the programmer (sometimes only 64 K) is often inadequate to cover all of the available memory. Segmentation provides a way for you, as a programmer, to specify your own addressing ranges within the larger actual addressing space. Instead of just one such range, you may want to set up several addressing ranges. We shall see that with the Intel 8086/8088 CPU there are automatically four such areas in memory called *segments*.

There are several prevailing attitudes toward segmentation: 1) It is a bad idea, 2) It is a good idea, 3) Whose idea was it?, and 4) I don't have any idea.

Motorola has presented the first view. They feel that segmentation causes a great deal of unnecessary overhead in processing. On the other hand, both Intel and Zilog have opted for segmentation, mainly because of its advantages in a multiprogramming environment. It tends to improve program and system design by encouraging the modern modular approach to programming, and it assists in multiprocessing environments by making it extremely easy to write modules which are completely relocatable. In fact, each module can be written in assembly language and translated into machine language as though it begins at the address zero! At *run time* the actual memory address is set via the segmentation hardware.

The Intel and Zilog implementations of segmentation are quite different. Zilog's requires an additional memory management unit (MMU) chip, while Intel's does not. Zilog has two versions of its Z8000 microprocessor chip: one without segmentation and one with. The version with segmentation requires an MMU chip to recombine the two parts of the address from the CPU to get the actual address. In other words, the segmented version of the Z8000 supports the separating of memory addresses into two parts, but it does not specify how these parts should be combined.

In contrast, Intel has placed a simple memory management scheme on the CPU chip itself. The 8086/8088 CPU chip has four special registers called *segment registers:* one for code (instructions), two for data, one for the stack (special temporary storage). The contents of these registers (the segment identifiers) are multiplied by 16 and added to the addressing information coming from the rest of the CPU (the offset) to compute actual memory addresses (see the figure below). With the 8086/8088, segments can actually start on any 16-byte boundary and end anywhere (up to 64 K bytes later). Future versions of the 8086/8088 (the iAPX 286) *will* allow segments to start at *any* address in memory. There are special instructions to load these segment registers with the proper segment identifier information. We will cover the details in Chapter 3 on the 8086/8088 CPU chips.

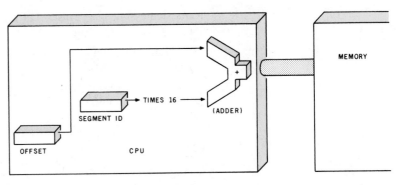

Figure 2.20: Intel segmentation/memory management.

We have just seen how segmentation produces two-part addressing information. The other possible scheme which we shall discuss is called *paging*. Paging also uses two-part addressing information. With logical paging the memory is logically divided into separate *pages,* each containing a few thousand memory cells. Each memory access has a *page identifier* to select the proper page and an offset to locate the particular cell within the page. Logical paging can be done even if the memory is physically organized as one long line. But if the memory is physically paged, then it is usually a good idea to use the same logical as physical pages because of possible delays and extra overhead caused by changing the physical page except when the logical page is changed.

There are several differences between paging and segmentation: 1) pages have fixed length, whereas segments have variable length, 2) segmentation allows segments to begin and end essentially anywhere in memory, whereas pages begin and end at fixed block boundaries, 3) segments can overlap each other, whereas pages never overlap, 4) segmentation often requires the assembly language programmer to be aware of segment boundaries, whereas paging is often done automatically either by the operating system or by the hardware.

In general, segmentation is a much more flexible scheme, but it often requires a different way of thinking. The programmer must remember that each piece of code or data belongs to some logical segment which will get translated to some physical stretch of memory. The Intel development tools actually require that the program declare the beginning and ending of each segment. This may seem like a bother at first, but it definitely makes the programmer conscious of the modern modular approach to programming.

Memory Management

Memory management provides the interface between the logical addressing scheme and the physical memory organization in that it involves the computation of a physical address in memory from the logical addressing information supplied by the programmer. Memory management is used in both segmentation and paging systems.

Memory management is needed because the memory may be huge, like a giant river, with traffic for any particular user contained only in certain sections, often far removed from each other. With several such users in a system, you need memory management to act as a controller or policeman for all this traffic. In particular, you need to protect the users from bumping into each other and the operating system. Before the days of memory management, some very strange system crashes happened as soon as assembly-language programmers got onto a system. It turned out that these assembly-language programmers were destroying words here and there within the operating system! In a more modern computer such as a PDP-11 or even some of the newer microcomputers, protection schemes prevent such occurrences. We will discuss some of these schemes in the first two appendices where we cover the iAPX 286 and the iAPX 432 processors.

In the last section we discussed how Intel has implemented a memory management system on the CPU chip itself. Now let's see how memory management is done by separate memory management unit (MMU) chips.

A memory management unit for a segmentation system contains a set of registers, called segment registers, each of which contains the beginning address of a different segment (stretch of memory). When the MMU receives a two-part address (offset and segment identifier) from the CPU, it uses the segment identifier to select one of its segment registers, and then it adds the contents of that segment register to the *offset* (supplied by the CPU) to compute the actual address (see the figure below). The difference between this and the Intel 8086/8088 scheme is that the MMU has an additional look-up for the segment starting address rather than just a multiplication by 16. A future version of the 8086 (the iAPX 286) will use such a look-up procedure and will not multiply the segment identifier by 16, so that a segment can start anywhere in memory.

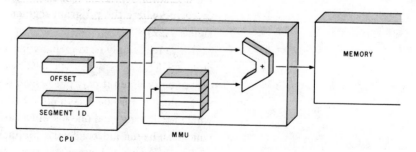

Figure 2.21: Memory management with segmentation.

The new 32-bit Intel iAPX 432 uses a double look-up scheme. That is, the segment identifier is used to look up another identifier which is in turn used to look up the actual address. This was developed to increase security within computer systems. Many of today's computers contain highly sensitive financial, personal, and military information, and yet are connected to telephone lines. Thus, with very little equipment and the right information most anybody can gain access to information which should not be modified or even just read. Special software and hardware support such as double look-up schemes is necessary to protect this information.

It is important to note that memory management requires a certain amount of overhead. In fact, the MMU segment registers must be previously loaded with the proper address information for memory management to work successfully.

When memory management is used with a paging system, the MMU registers are called page registers and they contain page numbers. When the MMU receives a two-part address (offset and page identifier this time) it uses the page identifier to select one of the page registers which then contains the page number of the particular memory cell. The offset just goes straight through to determine the offset of the memory cell within the page.

In some systems such as those used by the Digital Equipment Corporation PDP-11 minicomputers and Motorola MC68000, the user deals with addresses as single numbers instead of two. The upper part of the address is split off and used by the memory management unit as a page or segment identifier and the lower part is the offset.

One great advantage to memory management is that each user can appear to have the machine entirely to him/herself, even though many people are sharing it. This requires some special software called a *run-time system*. The run-time system assigns a separate set of segment registers to each user (in contrast to the Intel scheme in which a separate segment register is assigned to each type of access: code, stack, or data). Each user then uses offset addresses (starting from address 0) and segment identifiers as though there were no other users, never knowing or caring where the program segments actually reside in memory (see figure 2.22).

You really only need memory management when you want to have multitasking, that is, when you have several jobs running in the computer concurrently. Even if only one person is using the system, this can be very valuable, for one person often has many different computing jobs which need doing, and one job often can be broken up into smaller tasks which can be run independently. Multitasking can then use the resources of the computer much more effectively than can a straight sequential submission of jobs. For example, editing text and programs normally uses the full resources of the computer for only a small fraction of the editing session. Of course, during those times when the full power of the

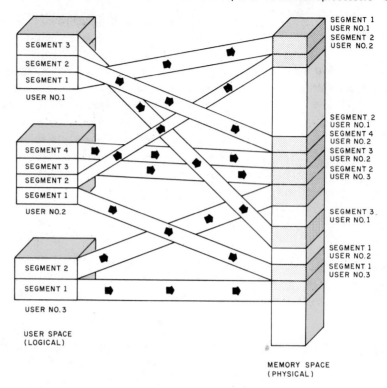

Figure 2.22: Multiuser environment with memory mapping.

computer is needed, it really should be immediately available. However, the slack times should be taken up by other tasks. A smart operating system can properly schedule tasks, assigning and maintaining priorities, making the system responsive to the user, and yet use the CPU to the fullest extent.

Eight-bit microcomputers can use memory management, especially with paging schemes described earlier. However, the processor has no built-in methods for handling page or segment identifiers. These identifiers can instead be kept track of by software and sent by the operating system via an I/O port to the memory boards in the system. This type of memory management with paging is relatively straightforward for 8-bit processors. Memory management using segmentation would be much more complicated with 8-bit processors, and is better left for those 16-bit processors designed to handle it.

There are operating systems now on 8-bit microcomputers in which it is possible to do multitasking. However, remember that supporting several jobs at once in a system puts a strain on the resources of a CPU, and thus it makes more sense to invest the time, effort, and money to develop multitasking on the more powerful 16-bit processor-based systems as long as the additional costs for the 16-bit system are not excessive. Present trends strongly indicate that the price of hardware is going to be quite small compared to the cost of labor. Thus, hardware that is easy to use will be less expensive in the long run.

Coprocessing and Multiprocessing

An important trend in computing is the use of several processors within a single computer system. For example, your printer, terminal, or digital plotter may have its own microprocessor built in. (In fact, sometimes the main computer has a less powerful microprocessor than a peripheral device such as a printer has. To use an example from the early days of microcomputing, a SOL-20 with an 8080 CPU might use an Anderson Jacobson converted IBM Selectric which is outfitted with the more powerful Z-80 CPU!)

The idea of multiprocessing is to place several processors within the computer itself so as to increase the total computing power (two brains are better than one). One approach to this is to have several equal or identical central processors within the same computer. This is the approach taken with the new Intel 32-bit iAPX 432 processor. The iAPX 432 is designed to run in parallel with as many as 256 copies of itself! The secret to doing this so that all are contributing effectively to the whole is to divide the programs into process*es* to be run on the process*ors*. This approach involves the idea of orthogonality discussed earlier in conjunction with the S-100 bus and the storage of data types, only on a much high level. Going back to the bus, imagine that the process*ors* are like the conductors on the bus (they conduct the business), and that each job is like a connector (each job has various processes each of which is run on, or uses, a different processor). This way a particular piece of code has a chance of being run on almost any processor. The actual choice of processor for that code depends upon which particular processor is free at the time rather than which one is better or more suitable. Each time such an allocation is made between process*es* and process*ors,* a mapping is said to have been created between these two types of objects. See the figure below:

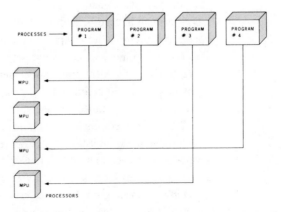

Figure 2.23: Processors and processes.

Another way to get higher performance from multiple processors is to assign *slave* or *peripheral* processors under the control of one central processor. Among the types of chips discussed in this book there are two methods, coprocessing and multiprocessing.

In a *coprocessing* system two or more processors share the same *instruction stream*. That is, they both follow the same program, but take turns executing instructions. Certain instructions are best performed by one processor and some are best done by another. Because of limitations of today's technology, the circuitry for all these processors cannot be placed on the same chip. We shall study the Intel 8087 Numeric Data Processor as an example of this in Chapter 4.

In a *multiprocessing* environment two or more processors share common memory, but operate on different instruction streams. One processor might be in charge, directing the other through messages placed in memory, but once started, each processor executes its own program. We shall study the Intel 8089 I/O Processor as an example of this in Chapter 5.

The big advantage to coprocessing and multiprocessing is that the central processor is relieved of a great deal of overhead, so that it can concentrate on running the system as a whole. It just turns other jobs over to other, more specialized processors which are better designed to handle these jobs. For example, the 8089 IOP is much better at handling I/O transfers than the CPU, and the 8087 NDP is much better at handling the longer, more complicated data types than the CPU. Most any application would benefit from such a larger (more instructions and more *specialized* instructions), more powerful (faster) system. With the use of the 8089 IOP certain transfers can be made up to six times faster, and using the 8087 NDP system performance can be increased by a factor of 10 to 100 times!

It takes special instructions to enable a processor to cooperate with other processors in coprocessing and multiprocessing systems. For example, to have coprocessing, the instructions must be divided into sets for the different processors in the system. If a processor receives an instruction not intended for it, it must not try to execute that instruction. It must, in fact, yield any rights to the system so that the processor for which the instruction was intended can work. Thus, for any given processor in the system, there must be one or more sets of dummy instructions. We will look at an example of how this works when we study the 8087 Numeric Data coProcessor in Chapter 4. The 8086/8088 dummy instruction called the ESCape instruction is used to form the 8087 instruction set, and of course, the entire rest of the 8086/8088 instruction set is dummy for the 8087 NDP! The situation is actually a little more complicated in that the 8086/8088 helps the 8087 NDP by fetching operands for it which are specified as a part of this dummy ESCape instruction.

You might wonder if coprocessing is possible with 8-bit

microprocessors. It is true that some 8-bit processors have dummy instructions. Unfortunately, because these are largely undocumented and thus unsupported a manufacturer can change the design of the processor from one batch to the next in ways that cause these instructions on some versions of the processor to perform undesirable actions. It is not a good idea to attempt to design a coprocessing system around an existing 8-bit processor.

Another special instruction is often used in a coprocessing system to synchronize the processors in the system. This is necessary because the two processors are both working on the same instruction stream. With an 8086/8088/8087 system, the WAIT instruction causes the 8086/8088 CPU to wait until the 8087 NDP finishes executing its current instruction. This requires an extra hardware signal line from the 8087 NDP to the 8086/8088 CPU which indicates when the 8087 NDP has indeed finished. Synchronization of coprocessors could be done entirely in hardware, instead of this hardware/software combination, but in either case the older 8-bit processors are ill equipped for the job.

Multiprocessing requires special, more subtle, processor instructions. Such an instruction is called *LOCK* for the 8086/8088. It causes a signal to be sent to all other processors in the system telling them not to use the bus until the next instruction has been completed. The reason this is necessary is that in a multiprocessing system there must be a way of protecting data and programs from being accessed at the same time by two or more different processors. Suppose, for example, two different processors attempt to update the same item of data. Each processor will read the data into one of its internal registers, operate on it, and then put it back into memory. However, the order in which the two different processors perform these events is important. Suppose processor A reads the data, and then processor B reads the same location before processor A puts the data back. Both processors will contain the original value. Now suppose that they both operate on the data in their internal registers, and they each put the data back with processor A first, and then processor B last. The final result will be as though only processor B had done its job, and that the entire action of processor A had been ignored (see the figure below). This is terrible, making it hard to detect errors in the data. Much more dramatic results happen if one processor tries to update or load a new program in an area of memory with instructions currently being read by another processor. Think about what that can do!

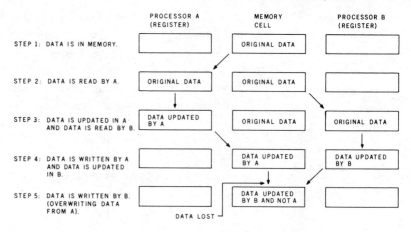

Figure 2.24a: Unprotected data accessed by two different processors.

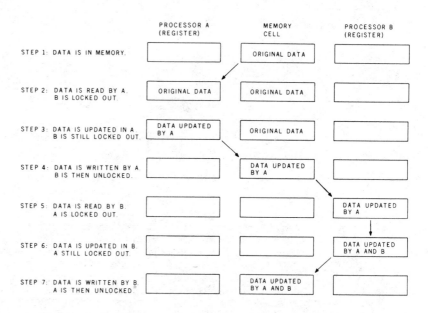

Figure 2.24b: Protected data accessed by two different processors.

To prevent such conflicts between processors, each block of memory which is used for data or programs for any one of the processors in the system contains a special "busy byte". Any processor which wants to use this block must first check this *busy byte* to see if the block is busy. If the block is not busy, then the processor sets this busy byte equal to "busy" before using the block. When the processor is finished with the block it sets the busy byte equal to "not busy". The only problem occurs at the very time that the busy byte is being updated. If the two processors attempt to check and update the busy byte at the same time, a conflict such as we just described could happen. As a result we could still have both processors accessing the same block. The solution is to use the LOCK instruction each time the busy byte is accessed. The LOCK instruction will keep other processors from doing anything with any memory bytes until the first processor puts a ''busy'' into the busy byte. This should happen within one processor instruction, perhaps using an eXCHanGe instruction. If the block was free, the processor goes ahead and uses the block, and if the block was busy, no harm was done, and the processor waits, and then checks later (see the figure below).

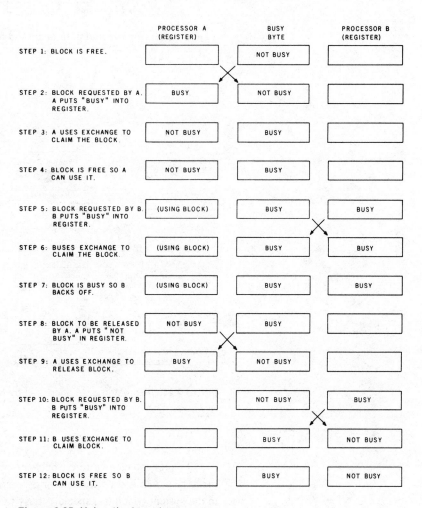

	PROCESSOR A (REGISTER)	BUSY BYTE	PROCESSOR B (REGISTER)
STEP 1: BLOCK IS FREE.		NOT BUSY	
STEP 2: BLOCK REQUESTED BY A. A PUTS "BUSY" INTO REGISTER.	BUSY	NOT BUSY	
STEP 3: A USES EXCHANGE TO CLAIM THE BLOCK.	NOT BUSY	BUSY	
STEP 4: BLOCK IS FREE SO A CAN USE IT.	NOT BUSY	BUSY	
STEP 5: BLOCK REQUESTED BY B. B PUTS "BUSY" INTO REGISTER.	(USING BLOCK)	BUSY	BUSY
STEP 6: BUSES EXCHANGE TO CLAIM THE BLOCK.	(USING BLOCK)	BUSY	BUSY
STEP 7: BLOCK IS BUSY SO B BACKS OFF.	(USING BLOCK)	BUSY	BUSY
STEP 8: BLOCK TO BE RELEASED BY A. A PUTS " NOT BUSY" IN REGISTER.	NOT BUSY	BUSY	
STEP 9: A USES EXCHANGE TO RELEASE BLOCK.	BUSY	NOT BUSY	
STEP 10: BLOCK REQUESTED BY B. B PUTS "BUSY" INTO REGISTER.		NOT BUSY	BUSY
STEP 11: B USES EXCHANGE TO CLAIM BLOCK.		BUSY	NOT BUSY
STEP 12: BLOCK IS FREE SO B CAN USE IT.		BUSY	NOT BUSY

Figure 2.25: Using the busy byte.

You can see that such a system requires a certain amount of hardware (for the signal lines to stop the other processors) as well as a special instruction. It is possible to rig up such a system for the older 8-bit processors. For example, the LOCK instruction could be effected by sending a signal out a special I/O port to some logic which would make the memory look temporarily not ready to the other processors in the system. Thus, 8-bit multiprocessing is a reality but at a small extra cost. If, however, dynamic memory is being used which requires refreshing by processors in the system, there could be serious problems. Because the LOCK machinery is built in, using multiprocessing with the newer 16-bit processors is easier and less expensive. The only additional cost is for the additional 16-bit processors. However, the cost of 16-bit processors is dropping, and they probably will soon be nearly as inexpensive as the older 8-bit processors.

Instruction Queues

A *queue* (pronounced like the letter ''Q'') is a waiting line such as at the checkout counter of a supermarket. Several of the newer 16-bit microprocessors such as the Intel 8086/8088 and the Motorola MC68000 use such a ''waiting line'' for their instructions. That is, they bring the instructions into the processor before they are to be used (see the figure below). The advantage to this queuing approach is that new instructions can be fetched while old instructions are being executed. This saves a significant amount of time, for example, allowing instructions in which data is included within the instruction (immediate data) to be executed at nearly the same speed as instructions using data entirely contained within CPU registers! This is also quite useful when the processor is used with slow memories such as erasable programmable ROMs (EPROMs).

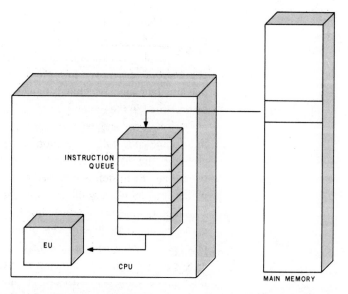

Figure 2.26: An instruction queue.

Instruction queues are typically very short, perhaps 4 to 6 bytes. In fact, for the 8086 CPU it is 6 bytes (3 words) and for the 8088 CPU, it is 4 bytes long. These two processors are each actually divided into two separate *subprocessors,* the bus interface unit (BIU) and the execution unit (EU). The BIU handles all traffic between the CPU and the outside world, while the EU actually performs all arithmetic and logical operations. In particular, the BIU fetches new instructions for the instruction queue at the same time the EU is executing previous instructions.

DEEPER-LEVEL MICROPROCESSOR PROGRAMMING

Today, when you start out programming a digital computer, you probably write programs in BASIC and are told that BASIC is a higher level programming language. This means that BASIC is an "English-like" computer language which is easy for humans to understand, does not vary too much from machine to machine, and rests upon other structures in the machine. Furthermore, it works on each computer by calling more primitive machine-dependent structures.

Next, a newcomer to computers might learn that there are what are called lower level programming languages. In particular, assembly language provides a way of getting *direct control* of the CPU in the computer, something BASIC can do only with great difficulty (using PEEK, POKE, and CALL or USR). Unfortunately, with this added control comes more dependence upon the particular CPU. That is, what is developed for one CPU will not work on another. (All assembly languages differ, but all BASICs are very similar since they are all "dialects" of the same language.) Almost every line (except the comment lines) of assembly language consists of the name of a processor instruction (the mnemonic) together with the name of where to locate some data (the operands) for that instruction. In addition, some lines of assembly language begin with a label to identify the line so that it can be used for such purposes as the start of a procedure or beginning of a loop.

Assembly language actually is designed to give you an easy way to get control over an even lower level, a programming language called machine language. Machine language consists of a sequence of numerical codes stored in the memory of the computer. The CPU reads these numerical codes and executes corresponding actions. A typical program in machine code will move information byte by byte or word by word around in the machine and perform primitive logical and arithmetic operations. Each step is specified by a small string of binary numbers which correspond very directly with the lines of assembly language.

You might think that machine language is the lowest level you can go to, but there are lower levels of programming and design within the processor. Each time you give the CPU an instruction (such as a MOVe) as a sequence of binary numbers in machine language, the microprocessor actually performs a short, built-in program written in a language called *microcode.* To distinguish between these two levels, we shall call the external machine code *macrocode* and the internal, next-lower-level-down code microcode. Microcode is actually a type of machine language for a CPU within the CPU. Microcode is stored in a ROM *within* the CPU. A typical microcode program might execute a memory-to-register MOVe instruction by first placing the address of the source on the address bus, then sending the control signals for a memory-read out over the control bus, then receiving the data over the data bus, and finally putting the data into the selected internal register. After this "program", the processor will execute another microcode program to fetch the next instruction. Each microcode program will take several clock cycles to execute.

On some processors such as the Motorola MC68000, there is an even deeper level of programming language called *nanocode*. At this level each individual step of microcode is executed by a separate nanocode program. This makes it easy to change the instruction set of the microprocessor. Each microcode program consists of a sequence of pointers to various nanocode programs inside the processor (see the figure below).

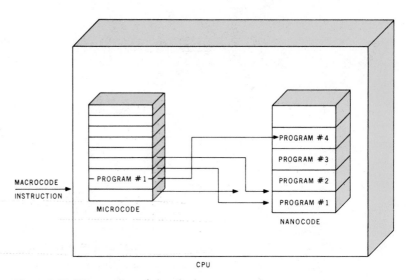

Figure 2.27: Microcode and nanocode.

The microcode (or in the case of the Motorola, the nanocode) usually consists of sequences of instruction codes where each instruction code is a bit pattern with many more bits than are used for the higher-level, external macrocode. Very roughly, each bit position in the microcode instruction corresponds to a control signal within the CPU (see the figure below). These control signals control such things as loading a register from a bus, performing an arithmetic operation, or loading an address onto a bus. Because each bit corresponds to a different control signal, several control signals can be initiated at once. With some variations of this theme, certain control signals are grouped together and encoded (converted to numbers) so that they take up a smaller number of bits. In such a case, control signals within the same encoding group cannot be simultaneously expressed and therefore not simultaneously activated, but two or more signals from different groups can be activated at once.

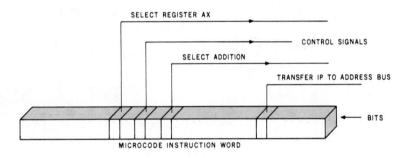

Figure 2.28: Microcode and control signals.

Within the CPU, control signals go to *gates* which are the lowest logical level of the computer. These gates perform all the basic, logical functions: AND, OR, XOR (exclusive OR), and NOT. Gates have one or more signal lines as inputs and one signal line as an output (see figure 2.29). Circuits consisting of a dozen or more gates perform such functions as: registers, encoding and decoding circuits, logical functions, and arithmetic functions. Included within the circuits to perform each such function are control gates to enable and disable these functions. The control signals from the microcoding scheme are routed to these control gates. The gates actually have three possible outputs: true, false, and not connected. This last state is often called "the third state" or the "high impedance state." It makes the gate look like its output is not connected to the system, thus completely disabling any signal coming through it and preventing such a signal from conflicting with any other signal in the system.

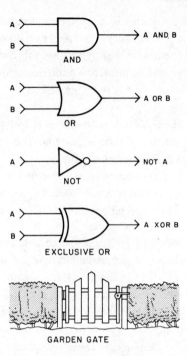

Figure 2.29: Some gates.

At a lower level than gates are the electrical components such as transistors. A transistor can be thought of as an amplifier with perhaps several input signals controlling the output. Each gate usually consists of several transistors. Below transistors is semiconductor physics with molecules, atoms, electrons, and finally quarks which we still haven't learned how to program.

DEVELOPING ASSEMBLY PROGRAMS FOR 16-BIT PROCESSORS

Developing assembly-language programs is a more complicated process than developing programs using a BASIC interpreter, but the results are well worth the effort. Fortunately, this process is almost identical to the process of developing programs using a compiler for a language such as FORTRAN, BASIC, or Pascal. In fact, an assembler is often intimately connected with some compilers. The nice thing about the newer 16-bit microprocessors is that their assembly-language works at a higher level than the assembly language for the older 8-bit machines. The trend is to produce machines that work on even higher levels. For example, the newer Intel 32-bit iAPX 432 has the very high-level language called Ada as its assembly language!

In developing a program in assembly language, the first step is to write what is called *source code*. The source code contains a sequence of mnemonics (names of instructions) and operands (data references) which the programmer has arranged to do something special. Source code is usually written with the aid of a program called a *text editor*. Source code is stored in memory, on tape, or on disk in a file called a *source file*.

The next step is to translate this code into what is called *object code* which contains the actual numerical codes for the machine. This translation process is accomplished with the aid of a program called an *assembler*.

There is often another step in which several modules of object code are combined to form a *load file*. This process, linking, is accomplished with the aid of a *linker* program.

The last step consists of loading the machine code into memory and running it. This is accomplished either by the facilities of the operating system or a special program called a *loader*.

Formats for The Source Code

Assembly language source code comes in a variety of formats according to which assembler you use. In general, assembly-language source code is arranged in four columns when it is printed out or displayed on the video screen. The first column contains *labels* which define target locations for jumps and subroutine calls as well as identifying the location of data. The second column contains instruction names (mnemonics). These are called *operation codes*. The third column contains the *operands* which specify the data. The last column is reserved for *comments*. The columns divide the lines into what are called *fields*. That is, a typical line consists of a *label field,* an *operation code field,* an *operand field,* and a *comment field*. Not all lines are typical in that they may be missing one or more of these fields. For example, some lines contain only a comment field. Later in this chapter you will see an example of such a format.

When an assembly-language programmer types in the source code, he/she usually does not need to be careful about lining everything up in its proper column. Assembler and editor programs will often do this with very little help. The programmer simply separates the fields by a *delimiter* (usually a tab or space).

In addition to instructions which are to be translated into machine language for the CPU, assembly-language source code contains instructions for the assembler. These are called *assembler directives* or *pseudo ops*. These instructions tell the assembler such things as the tab settings for the columns or how much storage in memory to leave for data.

The 16-bit Assembly Process

Now let's look at what a 16-bit assembler does. The 16-bit assembly process is essentially the same as the 8-bit process. At least that's true as far as the user is concerned. As far as the computer is concerned, the process is actually easier because many of the concepts such as relocation are difficult to implement on 8-bit processors, but relatively easy for the new, more powerful 16-bit processors. In fact, it is amazing that some of those concepts such as relocatable object code were ever implemented on the 8-bit machines.

An assembler usually makes two passes through the source code. In the first pass, address reference tables (called symbol tables) are constructed, and in the second pass, the code is actually translated.

Assembly code contains numerous references from one part of the source code to another. Before it can do a decent job of translating the assembly source code, an assembler needs to construct a table of all such references. Such a table is called the *symbol table* because it stores a list of all important symbols (identifiers) in the program and tells how they can be located. Some references are to locations inside the module that is currently being assembled. These are called *local references*. Other references are to code which is not currently being processed. These are called *external references*. All local references can be resolved during assembly, but the external references must be specially handled. Certain labels within the current module are also designed to be referenced from other modules. These are made *public* or declared *global* by the programmer. The assembler stores these in special *global symbol tables*. These tables are transmitted to the linker (if present) by special *linker instructions* which are placed in the object code by the assembler.

In the second pass, the object code is written into an *object file*. At the same time that the object file is being produced (second pass), a *listing file* can be generated. The listing file shows both the source code and the corresponding machine code. Usually, the source code is on the right and the machine code is on the left. One can usually also get a listing of a symbol table at the end of the listing of the codes.

The two passes require about the same amount of work by the assembler because the various CPU instructions require different numbers of bytes of machine code (and hence space in memory), and this can only be determined by looking closely at each instruction.

Types of Object Code

There are two types of object code. The first type is called *absolute code*. It is complete *machine code*, ready to be loaded into memory and run. In other words, a *linker* is not needed for this type of code. Absolute code can be stored in a variety of formats. The ASM assembler which is part of the CP/M operating system produces one format for this kind of code. We will look at this format in a moment. The second type of object code is called *relocatable code*. Relocatable object code requires further processing by a program called a *linker*. This is the type of object code produced by XM86, the Microsoft cross-assembler for the 8086. We will use both ASM and XM86 in Chapter 7 to help assemble and run our 8088 assembly-code language examples. ASM will be used to generate the "launcher" program for these examples, while XM86 will be used to actually assemble the 8088 code.

Now let's look in more detail at the kind of code produced by ASM. It is encoded in what is called the Intel HEX format. The major features of this format are that 1) it uses ASCII code to encode all its information,

2) it includes *load addresses* for its data, and 3) it includes *checksum* bytes for error detection and recovery. A file in this format can be displayed on a video screen or printed out and can easily be deciphered by a knowledgeable user because it is entirely composed of ASCII characters. The Intel HEX format can be used to store any kind of data which is to be loaded into the memory of a computer. Such a HEX file is divided into a number of records, each of which conveniently fits on one line of text and contains a number of bytes of data together with a load address for that data. The load address tells where the data in that record is to be loaded into the memory of the computer. It gives the address of the first byte of the record — all the rest are loaded into successive locations. Because each record has a separate load address, a HEX file (containing several records) can contain data which is to be loaded at widely spaced (but definitely determined) locations in memory.

It is interesting to see how a HEX file can contain all this information, so let's look extremely closely at the HEX file format. Each record of a HEX file starts with a colon, then a two-digit (ASCII) hexadecimal number which specifies the number of bytes of data in the record, then a four-digit hexadecimal number which gives the load address, then a two-digit file type which is hardly ever used, then the actual data bytes — each encoded as a two-digit hexadecimal number — and then finally a two-digit checksum for error detection. Again, it is important that the data bytes of a HEX file be loaded directly into memory at the specified (load) address without any further processing except conversion from hexadecimal representation to binary.

Besides the Intel HEX format, there are several other formats for storing absolute machine code. In some of these other methods, the load addresses, data, and checksums are all represented in straight binary instead of using ASCII characters and the hexadecimal numbering system.

In the CP/M operating system, binary data can be stored in a file directly. However, in this case there is no load address information included in the file. If you load such a binary file, then it will always be placed in memory starting at CP/M's favorite location which is 100H.

The CP/M operating system has a couple of ways to convert the hexadecimal HEX files into binary machine language. One way is through dynamic debugging tool (DDT). DDT will convert any HEX file into binary numbers, storing them directly into their designated memory locations. The other way is through the LOAD program which instead produces a file of the binary numbers. In Chapter 7, we will show you how to use DDT to load and start our example programs.

Now we look at the second type of object code, namely *relocatable code*. This is the type of object code produced by the Microsoft assemblers including its 8086 cross-assembler which we will use in Chapter 7. Files of this kind of code are meant to be combined by a *linker* with other files (which are also this same kind of relocatable object code) to make the final, machine-language program. The load address (in memory) of relocatable object code is not determined by the *assembler,* but instead is determined by the linker as it puts all the pieces together to form the final program. Perhaps a better name for this type of code would be locatable rather than relocatable code because it is usually not really "located" to begin with (unless you set it into a special absolute mode). Relocatable code contains a mixture consisting of two types of information. The first consists of bytes of machine code and the second consists of special instructions to the linker. The machine code in such files is incomplete because the address references are either missing or incomplete. The linker instructions are provided to give the linker information necessary to complete these missing address references in the machine code. These address reference instructions tell the linker such details as *entry points, common areas, external symbols,* and program size, allowing it to build tables of these quantities, and use these tables to fill in the missing information.

Using a Linker

Using a *linker* in addition to an assembler is important when several different languages are used in writing a program. For example, often programs will be written mainly in FORTRAN with some subroutines in assembly language. Other higher-level languages such as BASIC, Pascal and PL/1 have been packaged so that they can also be used in this way.

When such a multi-language approach is used, the program is often written in small sections or *modules*. Each module usually is designed to perform one task. Each module is written in source code in a chosen language and then translated into a common language, namely the relocatable object code. For assembly code modules, the translator is the *assembler,* and for FORTRAN modules, the translator is called a *compiler*. After all this translation has taken place, the result is a lot of pieces of program in the object-code language. These pieces have to be gathered together by a linker to form the final program. Again, the final location in memory of the machine code is not known at the time of writing the source code or even at the time of translation to object code. In fact, some of the modules may be fetched from special files called library files. These modules were written for general use and are also in relocatable format.

Clearly, no two modules which are to be *simultaneously* in memory should overlap or bizarre results will occur. However, during the running of a program, the same area in memory might be loaded with different tables of data or different modules of code at various times. This is called *overlaying*. It is possible to force overlaying to happen by specifying *absolute* addresses either in the *source code* or during the linking process, but normally you must make sure not to overlay two modules. If you just relax, stay in relocatable format, and let the linker do its job, then all such matters will be taken care of for you.

One of the main reasons you need a linker with this multi-module approach is that there normally will be references from one module to another. For example, certain variables might be shared by several different modules or one module might be a subprogram which is called by several other modules. Some of the linker instructions tell *where* these references occur in the "incomplete" machine code, and if everything is working fine, then other linker instructions will tell the linker *how* to fill in the address for each reference. Since the "where" is in one module, and the "how" often comes from other modules, an assembler which looks at one module at a time cannot fill in these references by itself.

The end result of a linker is the complete machine language. This may be saved in a file called a *load file*. Each time you want to run the program, you just ask the operating system to load this file into memory and start executing the program. The Microsoft linker, called L80, running on CP/M stores its load files in binary with no load addresses. In fact, the format is exactly the same as that produced by the LOAD program or the SAVE command in CP/M.

Naming Conventions for Files

You can see that a particular application will generate several different files, so there must be some way of naming these files so that the operating system and the user can identify both the particular application and the type of code for each file. Some disk operating systems such as Digital Research's CP/M or Digital Equipment's RSTS and RSX have several parts to the name of each file to help solve this problem. There may be as many as four parts, any one of which may be present or absent. One part, an account number, would be needed in multiuser systems for which each user has one or more account numbers. The account number is often surrounded by parentheses like (178,34) to set it off from the rest of the name. Another part of the name is the name of the device where the file is located. The device name often comes after the account number, but before the rest of the name. Device names usually end with a colon. Some possible device names are KB: (the keyboard), DKO (disk drive 0 on a PDP-11), or A: (disk drive A in CP/M). Next usually comes the main part of the file name. You can usually choose any combination of letters and numbers, provided that you do not have too many symbols (eight is the limit for CP/M). In some situations on some operating systems it is better not to start the main part of a name with a number, and in some cases you are allowed to use other symbols besides numbers and letters in the name. The main part of a name is usually used to identify a particular file independent of its form or format. (More on this in a moment.) The last part of a file name is often the file extension. File extensions are recognized and generated by various programs in the operating system, including compilers, assemblers, and linkers. The file extension usually indicates the type or format of the file, usually consists of three symbols which can be letters or numbers, and is usually separated from the main part of the name by a period.

To make things more concrete, let's look at some examples.

B:SORT.FOR could be a file name in the CP/M operating system on disk drive B. The file extension is FOR, which is used to identify files which contain FORTRAN source code (a program). The main part of the name is SORT. It is most likely that this is the name assigned to the FORTRAN program. As you can see, the main part of the name provides a clue as to what the program does.

A:L88.ASM could could be an assembly source code for a program module called L88 stored on disk A under the CP/M operating system. Unless you set it otherwise, the CP/M operating system assumes that any file without an explicit device name is on drive A. Thus, we could also specify this file with the name "L88.ASM". This is the name of one of the files (the launcher program) which will be discussed in Chapter 7. The file extension ASM is used for source code files for the ASM assembler which comes with the system.

L88.HEX is the name of the object file (on drive A) produced by assembling the file L88.ASM discussed above. The file extension HEX is automatically attached by the ASM assembler to the (absolute) object code file which it produces. The ASM assembler will also produce another file L88.PRN, called a print or listing file. This file contains a side-by-side display of both the machine code and the source code for this program.

L88.COM is the name of the file produced by using the LOAD command on the file L88.HEX discussed above. When the CP/M LOAD program transforms a HEX file into binary format, we always get a file with the same main name but with COM file extension. COM stands for COMmand and the existence of such a file literally adds a command to your system which can be used just like other commands in your system. In this case we have a new command called "L88" which will help launch our 8088 code.

The Microsoft Assemblers and Compilers

Microsoft makes a FORTRAN and a BASIC package that run under CP/M. They include an assembler and a linker. Under these systems, the file extension FOR designates a FORTRAN source code file, BAS designates a BASIC source code file, MAC designates assembly language source code files for its 8080 MACRO assembler, REL designates relocatable MACRO object files produced by these compilers and the assembler, and COM designates absolute binary files produced by the linker. REL stands for RELocatable object code, the second type of object code. The COM files are compatible with the COM files produced by the LOAD program.

Microsoft also makes an assembler for the 8086/8088 CPU called XMACRO-86. This assembler runs under the CP/M-80 operating system using an 8080, 8085, or Z80 CPU. Because this assembler produces code for a different CPU than the one it is run on, it is called a *cross-assembler*. The Microsoft cross-assembler expects source files with the file extension MAC (created with an editor), and produces object files with the file extensions REL. These REL files can then be further processed by the same linker (L80) that works with the 8080 MACRO assembler. From this we see that the linker does not have to know anything about the machine language except the raw addressing information as specified by the linker instructions contained in the REL file. That is, the rest of the machine code is just some kind of data as far as the linker is concerned. We will use this cross-assembler and linker in conjunction with the examples in Chapter 7 of this book. A future version of an 8086/8088 Assembler that runs on an 8086/8088 using CP/M-86 is coming from Microsoft. This will work even better in that the whole process will be done on one processor.

A Short Example of 16-Bit Assembly Language

Now let's look at a short example program and see how it might appear in the higher-level language BASIC and then how it might be translated into the lower level of assembly language. Then we shall see how to tune this program to run very efficiently, one of the more enjoyable aspects of programming 16-bit microcomputers.

We start out with a BASIC program. This program is designed to print out the Fibonacci sequence:

1, 1, 2, 3, 5, 8, 13, ...

Recall that in this magic sequence each number is the sum of the two previous numbers. The Fibonacci sequence has many applications to the arts and science, including very pleasant musical scales, the growth of tree leaves, and the reproduction of rabbits. Here is the BASIC source code:

```
100 REM - FIBONACCI
110 REM
120 X% = 0
130 Y% = 1
140 PRINT Y%;
150 Z% = X% + Y%
160 PRINT Z%;
170 X% = Y%
180 Y% = Z%
190 GOTO 150
```

Figure 2.30: BASIC program for Fibonacci sequence.

On many compilers there is an option which allows you to obtain a translation from higher-level language source code into assembly language. With the exception of the way the output is handled and special error handling procedures, this translation of source code into 8086/8088 assembly language is typical:

```
; Fibonacci  Sequence
;
X         DW       0       ; Storage for X
Y         DW       0       ; Storage for Y
Z         DW       0       ; Storage for Z
;
L00100:   ;  Program begins here
L00110:
L00120:   MOV      X,0      ; Let X = 0
L00130:   MOV      Y,1      ; Let Y = 1
L00140:   MOV      AX,Y     ; Get Y
          CALL     OUTPUT   ; Print it
;
L00150:   MOV      AX,X     ; Get X
          ADD      AX,Y     ; Add Y to it
          MOV      Z,AX     ; Store the result
L00160:   MOV      AX,Z     ; Get it
          CALL     OUTPUT   ; Print it
L00170:   MOV      AX,Y     ; Move Y to X
          MOV      X,AX
L00180:   MOV      AX,Z     ; Move Z to Y
          MOV      Y,AX
L00190:   JMP      L00150   ; Next term
;
```

Figure 2.31: Translation of BASIC program to assembly language.

The procedure for printing out the values is called OUTPUT, and it is located somewhere else. This program uses just the 8086/8088 MOV, ADD, CALL, and JMP instructions which we will study in detail in Chapter 3. Each line with these CPU instructions translates into several bytes of machine code.

The instruction DW which appears in the first three lines is not a CPU instruction. It is an instruction to the assembler (assembler directive) to leave a memory cell (in this case 1 word = 2 bytes) for the indicated variable. Here we leave a separate word for each variable X, Y, and Z. Notice the very strange labels. They correspond in a rather machine-like way to the statement numbers of the BASIC program. For example, L00150 corresponds to the BASIC line number 150.

As you can see, the program uses the same *algorithm* (method for computing) as the BASIC program, moving words around among the memory locations labeled X, Y, and Z and the CPU register called AX.

This translation approach is by no means the most efficient way of programming in assembly language. The reason why such a translation is generally less efficient is that the compiler produces pretty much a line-by-line translation of the higher-level language source code into assembly or machine code. By carefully mapping out usage of the CPU registers, it is possible to write much more efficient assembly language code. Suppose we use register BX for the variable X, register CX for the variable Y, and register AX for the variable Z instead of putting the variables in RAM. Then the program can be written as:

```
; Fibonacci  Sequence
;
ENTER:  MOV     BX,0    ; Let X = 0
        MOV     CX,1    ; Let Y = 1
        MOV     AX,CX   ; Get Y
        CALL    OUTPUT  ; Print it
;
LOOP:   MOV     AX,BX   ; Get X
        ADD     AX,CX   ; Z = X + Y
        CALL    OUTPUT  ; Print it
        MOV     BX,CX   ; Move Y to X
        MOV     CX,AX   ; Move Z to Y
        JMP     LOOP    ; Next term
```

Figure 2.32: Optimized assembly-language program.

Further perfecting is possible by taking advantage of certain instructions unique to the 8086/8088. With the eXCHanGe instruction you can use even fewer steps, thus making a program which will run significantly faster and take up much less memory than the original created by the BASIC compiler.

```
; Fibonacci  Sequence
;
ENTER:  MOV     BX,0    ; Let X = 0
        MOV     AX,1    ; Let Y = 1
        CALL    OUTPUT  ; Print it
;
LOOP:   XCHG    AX,BX   ; Exchange X and Y
        ADD     AX,BX   ; X = X + Y
        CALL    OUTPUT  ; Print it
        JMP     LOOP    ; Next term
```

Figure 2.33: Further optimized assembly-language program.

CONCLUSION

In this chapter we have introduced some basic 8- and 16-bit microprocessor concepts to help us get started with our study of the Intel 8086, 8088, 8089, and 8087 processors. We have given an introduction to such topics as the organization of a modern microcomputer and how chips simplify its design, the concepts of segmentation, multiprocessing, common data types and their storage, assembly language, machine language, microcode, and nanocode! We did this to prepare you to understand features on the new 16-bit microprocessors which were not available on 8-bit microcomputers.

We have dealt with the philosophical principle of orthogonality as it relates to such diverse topics as the S-100 bus, data storage, and multiprocessing environments.

In the next few chapters, we will present a more detailed discussion of the individual chips. We start in Chapter 3 with the two general-purpose, 16-bit, central processing units in the Intel iAPX 86 family. We will discuss how these relate to the earlier 8-bit microprocessors: the 8008, 8080, and 8085, and we will give an overview of their most important features. Next, in Chapters 4 and 5, we will cover the two special-purpose processors: the 8087 numeric data processor, and the 8089 input/output processor. We will show how these peripheral processors can work in conjunction with either of Intel's two general-purpose processors to achieve rather remarkable results. Next in Chapter 6, we will discuss some of Intel's controller chips and see how they can be used to delegate tasks to unburden the general-purpose and peripheral processors. In Chapter 7, we shall give a sequence of example programs which have been run on the Godbout 8085/8088 Dual-Processor Board. Finally, in Chapter 8, we will discuss the current scene, which is especially exciting because of large computer firms entering into the personal computing world with machines using the 8086/8088.

Chapter 3

The 8086 and 8088
General-Purpose Processors

The 8086 and 8088 are Intel's general-purpose, 16-bit microprocessors. Like many other manufacturers/designers of the new generation of microprocessor chips, Intel has several versions of its product. The 8086 is a full 16-bit processor with respect to both its internal structure and its external connections, while the 8088 is an 8-bit processor which is internally the same as the 16-bit 8086! In this chapter we will discuss the major features of these two processors and how the narrower-bused 8088 fits into a general scheme with Intel's other microprocessors.

Although Intel designed the 8086, 8088, and related chips, and is the prime as well as the premiere manufacturer of these chips, there are a number of other manufacturers who produce their own identical versions of these chips. These manufacturers are called second sources. Intel actually encourages second sources up to a point. The reason is that some chip consumers (such as the federal government) will not design or build anything using a chip which only has a single source. The 8086, 8088, and related chips are being second sourced by a number of companies (mostly Japanese), including Fujitsu. Intel has, in fact, granted Fujitsu a world-wide license to manufacture and sell the 8086, 8088, and 8089 chips. The license was nonexclusive and did not involve the exchange of any money between the two companies. All the other second sources for these chips (including such companies as Siemens, AMD, and NEC) will operate without a special license but with the blessing of Intel.

The 8086 and 8088 are just about identical except for the size of the external data bus. Intel accomplishes this internal conformity/external nonconformity by dividing each of the 8086 and 8088 processors into two subprocessors. That is, each consists of an execution unit (EU) and a bus interface unit (BIU). The execution unit is in charge of performing all the actual computations, while the bus interface unit is in charge of accessing data and instructions from the outside world. The execution units are identical in both processors, but the bus interface units are different in several ways which we will discuss later. This modular approach is an example of modular design. That is, the whole (the processor) is broken into parts (the two subprocessors), and each part or module forms a working unit to accomplish a certain subtask. This is a guiding principle in the modern theory of design of computer hardware and software, as well as the design of things entirely unrelated to computers. In this case,

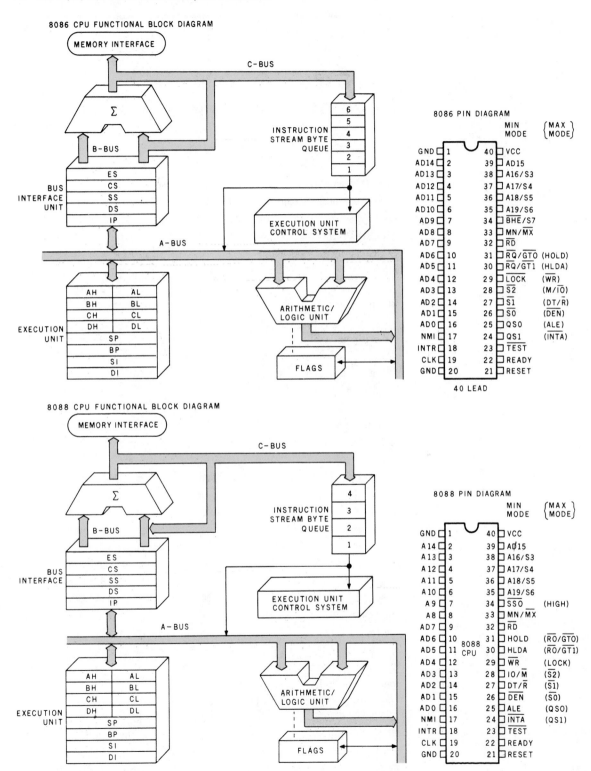

Figure 3.1: The 8086 and 8088 general-purpose processors.

the advantage to this modular approach is quite a saving of effort needed to produce the 8088 chip. Only one half (the BIU) of the 8086 had to be redesigned to produce the 8088!

WHY THE 8088?

As we have just discussed, the 8088 has a narrower (8-bit) external data bus. The reason for introducing the 8088 with this narrower data bus is to provide continuity between the 8086 and Intel's older 8-bit processors, the 8080 and 8085. This continuity is especially important to those who have substantial investments in the earlier type of equipment. By having the same size buses (as well as similar control and timing requirements), the 8088, which is internally a 16-bit processor, can replace one of these earlier 8-bit processors in an existent system. This greatly upgrades the performance of the system at a very small cost. For example, there are several 8088 CPU boards now available for the S-100 bus. If you already have an S-100 bus system, the cost of upgrading to 16 bits (internally) is confined to just the new CPU board ($300 to $500) and new software which, incidentally, is now becoming more expensive than the hardware.

Another advantage to the 8088 is that new systems which are small and inexpensive and yet very powerful can be designed around this chip. Because of the *price/performance* of a system designed around the 8088, it will be a natural choice for those who wish to design best-selling computers.

The first inexpensive and readily available 8-bit microprocessor on a chip, the 8080, became one of the all-time favorites, even though other processors like the 6502 and 6800 were also soon available and were actually less expensive. A great quantity of hardware and software was invested in systems based on the 8080. However, it had certain disadvantages, such as its requiring three different voltage supplies and two different clock signals. Later the 8085 was developed to overcome these problems. The 8085 requires only one voltage supply, produces its own clock signal (there are inputs for attaching a crystal), and runs at a higher clock speed than the 8080. Because of these improvements, the 8085 is not directly *hardware* compatible with the 8080, but it is 99 percent software compatible with it.[1]

---

[1]The difference is in two instructions, read interrupt mask (RIM) and set interrupt mask (SIM), which are included in the 8085 instruction set, but not in the 8080 instruction set. Besides their roles reading and setting interrupt masks, these instructions also can be used to receive and send data 1 bit at a time over a special, serial data line on the 8085.

8088 SIMILARITY TO THE 8085

The 8088 has many signals in common with the 8085, particularly those associated with the way the address and data are time multiplexed, although the 8088 does not produce its own clock signal as does the 8085. The 8088 and the 8085 have the same arrangement for running the 8-bit data bus over the same pins used by the lower 8 bits of the address bus, thereby requiring only 16 pins for address and data rather than 24. The 8085 and 8088 can, in fact, directly drive the same peripheral controller chips. Therefore hardware investments for both the 8080 and the 8085 systems are for the most part still usable for an 8088-based system! There are, of course, the same problems with the speed of the older equipment, but one can always run an 8088 at a slower speed by installing the appropriate clock generator crystal.

Because the 8086/8088 instruction set is so much more capable than that of the 8080/8085, software compatibility between the two is far from direct. The 8080/8085 registers form a subset of the 8086/8088 registers and most instructions on the 8080/8085 can be directly translated to instructions on the 8086/8088. However, this is best done with the source code rather than the machine code because the 8088 machine code is entirely different from that of the 8080. Intel offers such a translator program from 8080/8085 source code to 8086/8088 source code. This **program has to perform a number of jobs (see figure 3.2). Among** them are: 1) translate the various register names: for example, the 8-bit registers A, B, C, D, E, H, L become AL, CH, CL, DH, DL, BH, BL, respectively; 2) translate the flags: for example S, Z, AC, P, CY become SF, ZF, AF, PF, and CF, respectively; 3) translate the instructions: for example, MOV, MVI, LXI, LDA, STA all become various forms of the MOV instruction; 4) translate the operands: for example, an operand of a 16-bit 8080/8085 LXI instruction becomes a constant and an operand of either the 8080/8085 8-bit LDA or 16-bit LHLD instructions becomes a variable; and 5) translate the assembler directives. Intel's translator program requires source code which is compatible with Intel's 8085 assembler and produces code which is compatible for Intel's 8086 assembler. Chances are that if you have some 8085 source code which you want translated into 8086 source code, you will be using other assemblers whose code is not compatible with Intel's assemblers. For example, Microsoft's 8086 cross-assembler uses slightly different names for the instructions and handles data types differently than Intel does. Fortunately, Microsoft is now making such translator programs available which will work with their assembler formats.

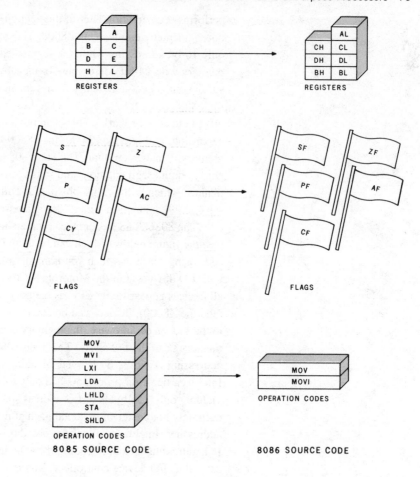

Figure 3.2: Translation from 8085 to 8086 source code.

MAJOR FEATURES OF THE 8086/8088 CPU: OVERVIEW

In this section, we shall quickly discuss the major features of the 8086 and 8088 CPU chips. In subsequent sections, we will expand on the topics covered very briefly here such as addressing modes, the register set, and the instruction set.

Addressing Capabilities

Both the 8086 and 8088 have a 20-bit-wide address bus, providing them with the capability of addressing a full megabyte of memory. For those of you who like a "bit" of mathematics, this is because:

$$2^{20} = 1,048,576 = 1 \text{ megabyte}$$

However, the address registers of the 8086/8088 chip are only 16 bits wide. This is equivalent to only 64 kilobytes. These processors use a rather clever method called *segmentation* to allows smooth access to the whole megabyte of address space. We will discuss how the 8086/8088 performs segmentation later in this section. Zilog has a segmented and nonsegmented version of its Z8000. The nonsegmented version supports only 16-bit addressing while the segmented version allows access to memory with 24-bit addressing (16 megabytes), but requires the use of a special chip called a memory management unit (MMU). The Motorola MC68000 has a full 32 bits in its address registers, but only sends out 24 bits to the outside world. This is an obvious opportunity for future expansion, and like the Z8000, the 68000 is designed to work with a memory management unit. The 8086/8088 does not need such an extra chip to do its segmentation, and future versions (the iAPX 286) are planned which will use a sophisticated built-in memory management scheme in conjunction with 24-bit addressing.

The 8086/8088 has another separate memory called the I/O space (see the figure below) which can be thought of as an extra memory addressing space in which you normally place (hardwire the addresses of) your I/O devices. On the Motorola MC68000 there is no extra I/O space; all devices appear to the CPU as memory locations. On the 8086/8088 (and the Z8000), devices can be connected to either the main memory or to the I/O space; likewise, the memory can either be connected to main memory or to the I/O space. The 8086/8088 I/O space uses 16-bit addressing (yielding 64 K bytes of address space for this I/O space). Intel's earlier 8-bit processors had only 8-bit addressing for their I/O, yielding only 256 bytes of I/O address space. This small amount was definitely not designed to contain actual memory. With the larger 16-bit addressing, Intel now invites the possibility of putting lots of things in the I/O addressing space, including the associated memory for the 8089 IOP, as well as I/O device controllers. You might think that putting all I/O in the I/O space (this includes the 8089 IOP and all the various device

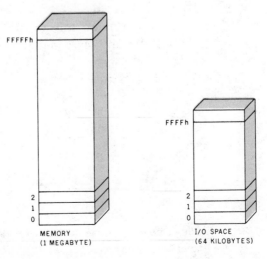

MEMORY
(1 MEGABYTE)

I/O SPACE
(64 KILOBYTES)

Figure 3.3: Memory and I/O space.

controllers it communicates with) might remove a substantial amount of traffic from the CPU-memory subsystem, but this is not true because both the main memory and the I/O space use the same set of address and data lines. Alas, only the use of control signals separates the memory and I/O spaces. It is, however, possible to place the controllers on a separate bus which then connects to the main processor's bus, thus relieving some of the traffic snarls. This requires the use of bus-interfacing chips such as those discussed in Chapter 6.

Register Set

The 8086 and the 8088 have the exact same set of fourteen, 16-bit, internal registers. Each register has a personality of its own, although many share traits in common. The 8086/8088 register set is an extension of the 8080 register set which in turn is an extension of the 8008 register set. To see this evolution, look at the figure below for comparison of the 8008, 8080, and 8086 register sets.

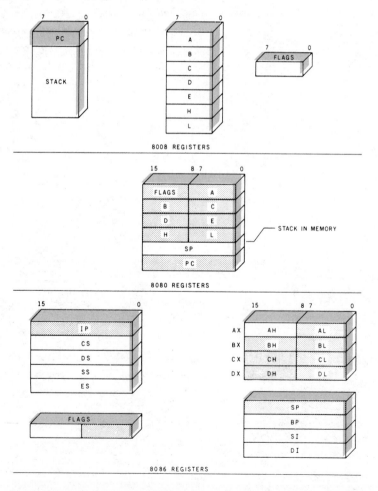

Figure 3.4: Comparison of 8008, 8080, and 8086 register sets.

Addressing Modes

The 8086/8088 has 25 different *addressing modes* or rules for specifying the location of data used during execution of an instruction. For example, in the simplest addressing mode the data is found in a specified register, and in one of the more complicated modes the contents of two registers are added together with an 8- or 16-bit quantity which is contained in the program to finally give the actual address of the data! We cover the addressing modes for the 8086/8088 later in this section.

Clock Signals

Like all the more recent microprocessor chips, the 8086/8088 requires a single clock signal. Unlike the 8085, these processors do not generate their own clock, but rather depend upon the 8284 clock generator which uses an attached crystal to determine the clock frequency. By changing this crystal you can select a different speed of operation. Intel has a 5 MHz and an 8 MHz version of both the 8086 and the 8088. These represent the fastest recommended speeds for these chips. The slowest recommended speed is 2 MHz for both versions. Depending upon your particular chip, faster or slower speeds might be okay or might cause errors. Proceed at your own risk!

For optimum performance the 8086/8088 requires a clock signal with a 33 percent duty cycle. This means that the clock is on one third of the time and off two thirds of the time. See the figure below.

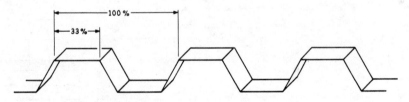

Figure 3.5: 8086/8088 clock signal.

Power Requirements

As is now standard, the 8086/8088 requires a single 5-volt power supply. All of Intel's 8000 series of chips of any interest to an 8086/8088 system have the same requirement.

Packaging

Today's 16-bit microprocessor chips generally come in 40-pin, 48-pin, or 64-pin packages. Both the 8086 and 8088 come in the smaller 40-pin package. Both Zilog and National Semiconductor have 40-pin and 48-pin versions of their products, but Motorola's MC68000 comes in a 64-pin package. However, in some configurations Intel's 8086 is designed to produce more signals than the greater-pinned Motorola 68000! The secret to doing this involves the techniques of time multiplexing and encoding which were discussed in the previous chapter. For those of you who were somewhere else, understand that *time multiplexing* means using the same set of lines, but different time periods to send different sets of signals, while *encoding* means converting a set of possible states into numbers and sending these numbers over just a few wires rather than using a wire for each different state. (For example, eight states can be encoded with the binary numbers 0 through 7 which can be sent over just three wires.)

Coprocessing and Multiprocessing

The 8086/8088 has special provisions to coordinate its activities with these other processors in *coprocessing* and *multiprocessing* environments. Coprocessing is a system in which two or more processors work in tandem on the same portion of a program and multiprocessing is a system in which two or more processors work on different programs, but share the same memory. The 8087 NDP uses coprocessing and the 8089 IOP uses multiprocessing. These concepts will be discussed in connection with the detailed discussions of the 8087 Numeric Data Processor and the 8089 I/O Processor in the next two chapters.

Instruction Set

The instruction set for Intel's 8086/8088 is comparable in many ways to the instruction sets for the other leading 16-bit contenders: Motorola's MC68000 and Zilog's Z8000. All three manufacturers have adopted extensive instruction sets making their 16-bit machines much more capable than their 8-bit counterparts. They have added new operations such as multiplication and division and have increased the efficiency of old operations such as jumping to an address calculated in the program. As we will discuss in the more detailed section on the instruction set, it's important to realize that the Zilog and Motorola processors are, in many respects, really 32-bit machines housed in 16-bit packages. The 16-bit 8086 and the 8-bit 8088 really compare quite favorably both in speed and flexibility for standard 8-bit and 16-bit operations to the Motorola and Zilog machines, but because of such things as slower multiplication and division operations and the lack of direct bit operations, the 8086 generally comes in behind the other two on benchmarks (speed tests) — behind, that is, only when it isn't teamed with its peripheral processors, the 8089 I/O Processor and the 8087 Numeric Data Processor. With them the Intel 8086 forms a combination much more powerful than either of the other CPUs working alone. Also, the 186, the next version of the 8086, is designed to speed up the instructions which now slow down the 8086.

PIPELINING ARCHITECTURE

Because the 8086's data bus is twice as large as the 8088's data bus, you might expect the 8086 to run twice as fast as the 8088. This does not actually happen for several reasons. One reason is that many applications require data to be passed 8 bits at a time. Another is that there is much more to be done by the processor than just passing data. The most important reason has to do with some design features which we have briefly introduced earlier, namely dual internal processors and a pipeline instruction queue.

Intel designed the 8086/8088 to perform major internal computing functions at the same time it is fetching instructions and passing data. To achieve this, the 8086 and the 8088 chips each consist of two processors linked together on the same piece of silicon (as seen in the figure below). One unit is in charge of fetching instructions and the other is in charge of executing them. Furthermore, the unit in charge of fetching instructions uses a method called *pipelining* or *queuing* to store new instructions until they are needed.

The main processor is called the execution unit (EU). It is in charge of decoding and executing all instructions. The EU is identical in both the 8086 and the 8088. The other processor is called the bus interface unit (BIU). The BIU is in charge of fetching instructions and transferring all data between the registers and the outside world. The BIU is more complicated in the 8088 because it has to transfer data between the internal 16-bit data bus and the external 8-bit data bus.

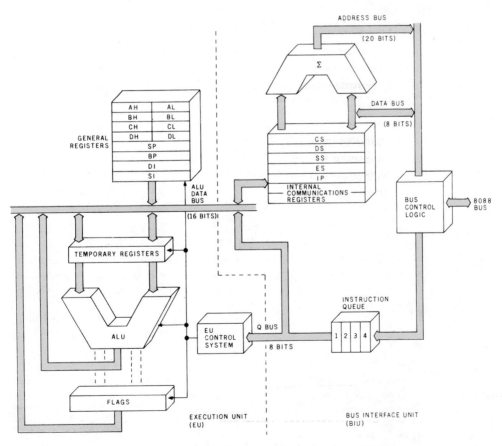

Figure 3.6: 8086/8088 with EU and BIU.

When the BIU fetches an 8-bit byte of machine code from memory, it places that byte in a special waiting line called the *instruction queue*.[2] On the 8086 this queue is 6 bytes long and the machine code is fetched from memory 2 bytes at a time; on the 8088 the instruction queue is only 4 bytes long and the machine code is fetched 1 byte at a time. The division of labor between the EU and the BIU causes a considerable saving of time and helps to make the performance of the 8-bit 8088 more comparable to that of the 16-bit 8086. Much like the tortoise and the hare, slow, steady progress often does as well as or better than short, rapid bursts of speed.

The situation is also very similar to that of a boss who has a secretary to handle telephone calls and correspondence. The secretary works at the same time the boss is doing other things, freeing the boss from many details of the outside world. Questions for the boss pile up and are dealt with one at a time, and in the order that the boss prefers.

REGISTER SET

The 8086/8088 contains fourteen 16-bit registers. Some of these registers belong to the EU and others belong to the BIU. The EU registers tend to be general-purpose registers, and the BIU registers tend to be used for addressing.

As you can see from figure 3.7, the EU has the following registers:

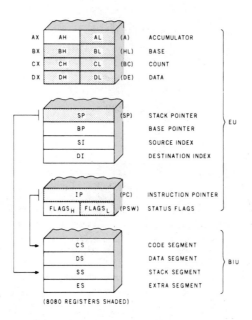

(8080 REGISTERS SHADED)

Figure 3.7: 8086/8088 register set.

___

[2]A queue is a way of storing data in which the first one in is the first one out — like a line at the supermarket.

• four 16-bit general registers, AX, BX, CX, and DX, which can be subdivided into (and separately addressed as) eight 8-bit registers, AH, AL, BH, BL, CH, CL, DH, and DL. In this case, the *X* stands for *extended* (16-bit), the *H* stands for *high,* and *L* stands for *low*. *A* stands for *accumulator, B* stands for *base, C* stands for *count,* and *D* for *data.*

• four 16-bit pointer and index registers, SP, BP, SI, and DI, which cannot be further subdivided. SP is the stack pointer, BP is the base pointer, and SI and DI name the source and destination index registers, respectively.

• a 16-bit flags register which contains various status bits for the processor. These include: zero flag (ZF), sign flag (SF), parity flag (PF), carry flag (CR), auxiliary flag (AF), direction flag (DF), interrupt flag (QF), overflow flag (OF), and trap flag (TF).

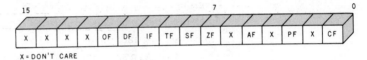

X = DON'T CARE

Figure 3.8: 8086/8088 flag register.

The BIU has the remaining registers:

• four segment registers, CS, DS, SS, and ES. These stand for the code, data, stack, and extra segment register respectively.

• one instruction pointer (IP).

Intel does not try to achieve a symmetric design for the register sets in its microprocessors as do other manufacturers of micro-, mini-, and maxi-computers. Each register has its own personality. This was true for the 8008, 8080, and 8085 and is still true for the 8086/8088. However, the registers in the 8086/8088 are more capable than those of the 8080. We see that the registers are given individual letter names and, in fact, individual names. This is in contrast to many other processors in which there are usually whole sets of registers such as R0, R1, ... , R7 or D0, D1, ... , D7.

While many instructions such as ADD, SUBtract, AND, and OR appear to treat the general registers AX, BX, CX, DX equally, there are certain choices of register which produce a radically different (usually shorter) machine code. For example, ADDing immediate data to most registers requires 2 bytes of instruction plus 1 or 2 bytes to store the data, but ADDing immediate data to AX (the accumulator) requires only 1 byte plus the bytes to store the immediate data. Thus, it is more efficient to use AX for calculations involving constants.

There are also instructions which use the personalities of these registers. For example, the LOOP instruction actually uses the count register (CX) to store the count for the number of iterations of the loop. The decimal adjust (DAA) instruction works only on AL, the lower part of the accumulator. The multiply and divide instructions use the accumulator register (AX) and data register (DX).

The AX register is the 16-bit accumulator. Using it sometimes causes the assembler to produce machine language which is encoded with fewer bytes. Its lower part, AL, corresponds to the 8-bit accumulator of the 8080.

The CX register is often used to store data for counting such things as loops (for LOOP instruction), the repeated string moves (more on this later), shifts, and rotates (just CL for these last two types of instructions). The CX register corresponds to the 8080 register pair BC.

The DX register is used to store 16-bit data. It can be thought of as an extension of the AX register for 16-bit multiply and divide operations. It corresponds to some extent to the 8080 register DE. However, the 8086 DX register cannot be used for indirect addressing like the 8080 DE register can with the 8080 LDAX and STAX instructions. The 8086 SI and DI registers take over the burden of indirect addressing. This poses some problems when you translate from 8080 code to 8086 code.

The BX (general-purpose base) register is distinguished because of its use as a base register in the addressing modes. The BX is a more powerful version of the 8080 HL register pair. Special-purpose registers such as the index registers source index (SI) and destination index (DI) and the base pointer (BP) are used as part of the addressing modes. That is, they are used to help "point" to data.

The instruction pointer (IP) and stack pointer (SP) registers are dedicated to their own program-control jobs. In fact most processors have corresponding registers which are dedicated similarly.

The segment registers in the BIU have special functions which we will explain in the section on segmentation later in this chapter.

It is interesting to compare this architecture with that of the MC68000 and the Z8000. Both of these other processors have uniform numbering systems for their registers. The Motorola MC68000 has address registers and data registers. These registers are all actually 32-bits wide, and the Motorola's instructions use these registers to hold 8-bit, 16-bit, and 32-bit data. On the other hand, the Zilog Z8000 has the same 16-bit width for its data bus, but its registers are 16-bits wide. To hold 32-bit data, the Z8000 must group its registers in pairs, thus making a 32-bit register out of two 16-bit registers. It can even form 64-bit registers by grouping four 16-bit registers together. This is similar to the way the Intel's 8080, 8085, 8086, and 8088 processors can make a 16-bit register out of two 8-bit registers. In general the Z8000 and 68000 have more registers and have general use of almost all their data registers.

SIGNALS AND PINOUTS

This next section is not really necessary for those of you who will stick entirely to programming the 8086/8088, because it contains a description of the various electrical signals coming in and out of the 8086/8088 through its pins. If you are so inclined, you might want to start reading again at the section on the interrupt structure of these chips. There are some important software concepts in that section.

Minimum and Maximum Modes

There are two ways to electrically connect the 8086/8088 in a circuit, minimum mode and maximum mode. The choice is made by connecting a pin (aptly named MN/MX) to ground or the voltage supply. The 8086/8088 must be in maximum mode to work in tandem with the 8087 Numeric Data Processor and the 8089 Input/Output Processor. In Chapter 2 we saw two model computers (the first using an 8086 and the second an 8088). In both of these computers, the CPU was placed in maximum mode, because they both use the 8087 NDP and 8089 IOP chips to form a small processor *cluster* with the CPU chip.

In the maximum mode the 8086/8088 depends upon other chips such as the 8288 Bus Controller to generate the full set of signals for the control bus. The minimum mode permits the 8086/8088 to perform in more of a stand-alone mode. See the figure below for a drawing of the 8086 in each mode.

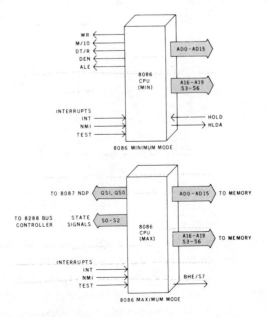

Figure 3.9: Minimum and maximum modes for 8086.

In either mode, the 8086/8088 signals (see figure 3.1 for the pinouts) can be arranged in the following groups:

power
clock
control and status
address
data

There are three pins for power: ground (GND) on pins 1 and 20 and a 5-volt supply (Vcc) input on pin 40. The ground is a ground for both power and signal.

There is one clock signal. This inputs to pin 19.

For both the 8086 and the 8088, there are 20 bits of address. The upper 4 bits of address share their pins with some status signals. On the 8086, the *lower 16 bits* are shared with the data bits, and on the 8088 only the *lowest 8* address bits have to share pins with data. This is, of course, because the 8086 has a 16-bit external data bus, and the 8088 has an 8-bit external data bus. At certain times address information is on these pins and at other times data and status. The 8282 latch is designed to grab the address information from these pins at the right moment and ignore the status and data.

There are several groups of control and status signals.

The MN/MX pin controls whether the processor is in minimum or maximum mode by ''tying'' either to ground or the 5-volt power supply line.

S0-S7 are status signals on pins 26, 27, 28, 38, 37, 36, 35, 34, respectively (note the slight ''twist'' to these assignments). They are output by the processor, but only at certain times. During other times different signals appear on these pins. By looking at the electrical state of these status signals, one can tell such things as the type of bus access (read vs. write and memory vs. I/O), the segment register presently being used, and the status of the interrupt system. S0, S1, S2 are only available in maximum mode, in which case they are fed into the 8288 bus controller chips. The 8288 bus controller then derives other important control signals from these. In the minimum mode the 8086/8088 produces some of the 8288 signals directly.

RD is a status signal which is output by the processor on pin 32. It indicates when the processor is doing a read (either memory or I/O).

The READY signal (pin 22) is an input *from* external devices (memory or I/O controllers). The READY signal is routed through the 8284 clock generator to synchronize it with the clock signal. See figure 3.10 for a diagram of how this is done. The READY signal works as follows: If an external device has been selected either for reading or writing and it is not ready to complete the data transfer, then it pulls down on the READY signal line forcing it towards 0 volts. The processor watches this signal and adds extra ''wait'' cycles until the READY line is brought up again to its normal 5-volt level indicating that the external device is ready to make the transfer. After the transfer, processor activities resume as usual.

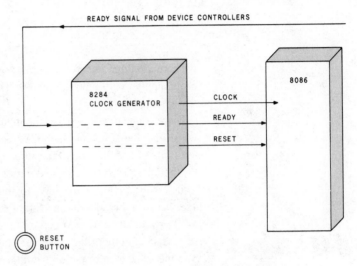

Figure 3.10: Signals routed through the 8284 clock generator.

The RESET signal (pin 21) is another input which is routed through the 8284 clock generator to synchronize it with the clock signal. The RESET is used to initialize the processor, as though it had been turned off and then on again. Resetting the processor using the RESET line is a lot easier on all the electrical components in the system than is turning it off and then on. Reset clears the instruction queue and certain registers (the flags; instruction pointer; and data segment, stack segment, and extra segment registers). In addition, upon reset, the code segment register is set to the value FFFFH. We will see later how this forces the processor to read the first byte of instruction from location FFFF0H.

NMI (Non-Maskable Interrupt — pin 17) and INTR (INTeRrupt Request — pin 18) are part of the 8086/8088 interrupt system. A pulse on the NMI line causes a special interrupt called *type 2 interrupt*. A signal on the INTR line will cause a *general* type of interrupt response. The term ''non-maskable'' refers to the fact that NMI-generated interrupt cannot be turned off and on under software command to the CPU. The more general INTR-generated interrupts can be turned off via software. See the section (below) on the 8086/8088 interrupt structure for a more complete discussion of this whole area.

In the minimum mode the following status and control signals are output: SS0 (S0 Status — pin 34), HLDA (HoLD Acknowledge — pin 30), WR (WRite control — pin 29), M/IO (Memory/IO Control — pin 28), DT/R (Data Transmit/Receive — pin 27), DEN (Data ENable — pin 26), ALE (Address Latch Enable — pin 25), and INTA (INTerrupt Acknowledge — pin 24). One signal is input: HOLD (HOLD — pin 31). On the 8088 the M/IO is inverted to make it compatible with the signals for the 8085, and on the 8086 the SS0 is not present (the 8086 uses this pin for BHE/S7). BHE (Bus High Enable — pin 34) is used in 16-bit addressing. Now let's look at these signals in more detail.

The SS0 (S0 status) pin on the 8088 is used in conjunction with Memory/IO Control (M/IO) and Data Transmit/Receive (DT/R) to give the complete status of the 8088, that is, exactly what state it is in (fetching code, writing to memory, reading from memory, writing to an I/O port, reading from an I/O port, etc.).

On the 8086 the BHE is used to help interface 8-bit devices to the 16-bit data bus. If address line 0 is 0 (indicating an even address), then BHE tells whether a whole word or just a byte is being addressed. If BHE is 0, then it's a word, and if BHE is 1, then it's a byte. If address line 0 is 1 (indicating an odd address), then the 8086 processor is addressing a byte and never a word. The BHE signal will always be 0 in this case.

We use the data enable (DEN) and the data transmit/receive (DT/R) signals to tell the 8286 data bus transceiver when there is data and which direction the data is going (in or out). The address latch enable (ALE) signal is used to tell the 8282 octal address latch when to grab the address.

The M/IO signal tells the system whether the 8086/8088 is requesting access to the system memory or to the I/O space. The WR signal is a *strobe* indicating that data is now ready on the data lines. The external devices (either memory or I/O controllers) can use this signal to help load the data into their registers. In the maximum mode, there is a separate *write strobe* for I/O and for memory. (These are generated by the 8288 bus controller.)

The hold (HOLD) and hold acknowledge (HLDA) signals are part of the 8086/8088 bus ownership control system. When another processor or a device such as a DMA controller wants to gain control of the bus, it sends a signal to the 8086/8088 over the HOLD line. When it is ready to do so, the 8086/8088 puts its address/data lines and most of its control lines into the tri-state condition (electrically disconnected from the bus). At the same time, the 8086/8088 sends out the HLDA signal indicating that the bus is now free. The other device can now use the bus. When it finishes with the bus, it sends a signal on the HOLD line. Soon after the 8086/8088 gets this signal, it resumes its use of the bus.

In the maximum mode the following signals are output: S2, S1, S0 (status — pins 28-26); QS1, QS0 (Queue Status — pins 25 and 24); RQ/GT1, RQ/GT0 (ReQuest/GranT — pins 31 and 30); and LOCK (pin

29). Actually, the ReQuest/GranT lines (RQ/GT) can also accept input signals as well. Now let's look at these more closely.

The two request/grant (RQ/GT) signals and the LOCK signal are useful for coordinating activities with other processors in the same *cluster*. A cluster is a subsystem consisting of one or more processors and interconnecting buses. A cluster is connected to the computer by connecting it to the *system bus* (main bus) via the bus interface chips discussed in the chapter on support chips. The RQ/GT signals work in the same way that the HOLD and HLDA lines work to transfer control of the bus (as described above).

The LOCK signal tells any other processors in the system when *not* to try to take over control of the system. This is important so that protection schemes written in the software can operate safely. These protection schemes require that a block of code which is to be accessed by two or more processors be protected from being changed by one processor while the other processor is reading it for another job. See the section in Chapter 2 on multiprocessing and the discussion of the busy byte in the chapter on the 8089 IOP for further enlightenment on this topic.

QS1 and QS0 are the instruction queue status signals. They are only available in maximum mode. The 8087 numeric data processor requires these signals to coordinate with the master 8086/8088 processor.

The TEST signal (pin 23) is used to hook the 8086/8088 to a coprocessor chip such as the 8087 numeric processor and to synchronize the main processor with its coprocessor. We will describe this in more detail in Chapter 4.

An *interrupt structure* is a way for a processor to provide rapid and uniform service for such things as I/O, debugging, and certain kinds of errors. In general, the processor continues about its usual business until an interrupt occurs, at which time it saves its current state (instruction pointer, code segment, and flags), executes a special service routine, and then returns to what it was doing before. You can think of an interrupt as a subroutine call and the interrupt service routine as the body of the subroutine. The major differences between subroutines and interrupts are: 1) subroutines are called only by software instructions, while interrupts can happen either as a result of software or hardware invocations; 2) subroutines only have to save the return address, while interrupts save both the return address and current condition of all the flags; and 3) subroutines need to have ways to pass data from the main program to the subroutine and back again, while interrupts do not.

Various devices can generate hardware interrupts for the 8086/8088, including the 8087 numeric data processor, the 8089 input/output processor, and the 8259 programmable interrupt controller. The 8086/8088 can even generate interrupts for itself! Details of how and when these other devices generate interrupts can be found in the sections on these devices throughout the rest of this chapter. The 8086/8088

INTerrupt (INT) can generate software interrupts.

The 8086/8088 interrupt structure uses a table of 256 four-byte locations starting at the absolute beginning of memory. Each of these locations in this interrupt table can be loaded with a pointer to a different routine in main memory. These pointers contain both the new contents of the code segment (2 bytes) and the instruction pointer (2 more bytes) for a routine that can be located anywhere in memory. In the section on segmentation we will explain why both of these quantities are needed. We will show how the actual address in memory is computed from these two quantities. Each of these 4-byte pointer locations is assigned a number from 0 to 255 according to its position in memory. This number is called its *type*. A type 0 interrupt is assigned to memory location 0, type 1 interrupt is assigned to location 4, and so on up to location 1020. In general, type *n* is located at address *4n* in memory. Not all of these locations have to be filled with pointers, but before an interrupt of a certain type can be used, the corresponding location in the interrupt table must be loaded with a pointer to its service routine. See the figure below.

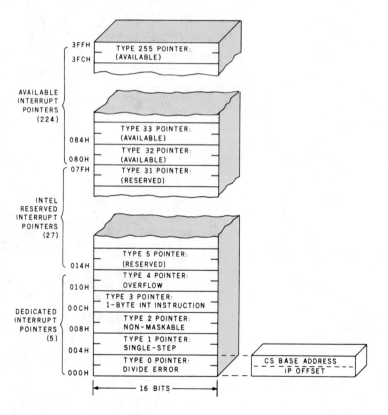

Figure 3.11: 8086/8088 interrupt pointer table.

Each interrupt type can be called either by hardware or by software. This makes it possible for each hardware interrupt to be easily tested by software. There is a control bit Interrupt Flag (IF) which controls whether or not the 8086/8088 will respond to external interrupts. This bit can be turned off and on with the software commands SeT Interrupts (STI) and CLear Interrupts (CLI). This opens and closes the door for interrupting the CPU. When the interrupt bit is cleared (interrupts disabled) it is like a "do not disturb" sign on this door.

Hardware interrupts work as follows: When an external device needs service, it signals the 8086/8088 on the interrupt request (INTR) line. If the 8086/8088 can respond (interrupts are on), then it soon puts out an acknowledge signal either directly (in the minimum mode) or via the 8288 bus controller (in maximum mode). The external device then puts a byte on the data bus indicating what *type* (location) of interrupt it is requesting. The 8086/8088 uses this number to locate the pointer in the 8086/8088 interrupt pointer table discussed above. The 8086/8088 then saves the condition of its flags and a pointer to the return address on the stack and loads its code segment and instruction pointer from the indicated 4-byte location in the interrupt table. This causes the processor to begin executing the service routine. At the end of the service routine there must be the Interrupt RETurn (IRET) instruction. This instruction causes restoration of the flags, the code segment, and the instruction pointer to the return address. The IRET must be used because the normal return instruction does not restore the flags and is quite unsuitable for this purpose. (Otherwise the stack gets broken.) At this point, the processor has resumed its normal operations.

There is a special kind of hardware-generated interrupt called a *non-maskable interrupt*. The term "non-maskable" refers to the fact that this kind of interrupt cannot be turned off by clearing the interrupt flag. This kind of interrupt will generate a type 2 interrupt; that is, its pointer is located at address $2 * 4 = 8$ in memory. The non-maskable interrupt should be reserved for emergency situations such as power failure or memory errors.

Special types of interrupts are generated in the case of division by zero, or overflow from division.

There are also special types of interrupts which are used for debugging. The single-step interrupt occurs after each instruction if the trap flag is turned on. Unfortunately, the procedure for turning the trap flag on and off is a little awkward. It involves pushing the flags onto the stack, changing their *image,* and popping them back into place. (By image we mean a *copy* of the flags as they sit in the flag word register, but not the actual flag bits themselves.) The single-step interrupt causes a type 1 interrupt. If you put a pointer at location $1 * 4 = 4$ to a routine which displays the contents of all the registers, then you can watch the progress of the processor as it steps through a program. Another kind of interrupt useful for debugging is the *breakpoint* interrupt. This is a special form of the software interrupt whose machine code has only 1 byte instead of the usual 2 bytes. This makes it easy to slip into place. It generates a type 3 interrupt. This kind of interrupt is used in the following way: The programmer selects an address where he/she wishes to stop the processor and examine what's happening with the registers and flags. The programmer inserts the byte-size machine code for this interrupt at the selected address and runs the program. When the processor gets to this breakpoint, it jumps to the type 3 service routine. This routine should turn control over to the programmer to do as he/she pleases, perhaps displaying contents of registers, perhaps dumping memory, or perhaps going off to something else. An example of this is included in Chapter 7.

ADDRESSING MODES

The 8086/8088 has 25 different *addressing modes* (see table 3.1) or rules for locating an operand for an instruction. The addressing modes for the 8086/8088 are somewhat complicated, but they can be viewed as special cases of two general cases: register references and memory references. Register references are simple in that the operand is simply located in a specified register. However, as many as four quantities may be added together to compute the address of an operand in memory. These four kinds of quantities are: 1) a *segment address,* 2) a *base address,* 3) an *index* quantity, and 4) a *displacement*. See the figure below, for a picture of the general case of a memory reference addressing mode.

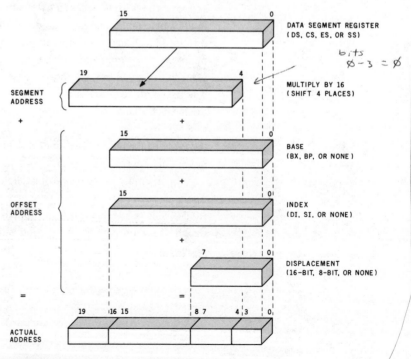

Figure 3.12: Pictorial view of the 8086 addressing modes.

The segment address is stored in a *segment register* (DS, ES, SS, or CS) in a manner which we shall describe in the next section. For now, understand that the contents of a segment register are always multiplied by 16 (shifted 4 binary digits to the left) before being used to form an actual address. For memory references a segment register is *always* used.

A *base* is a quantity which is stored in a *base register* (BX or BP). An *index* is a quantity which is stored in an *index register* (SI or DI). The addressing modes allow both, either, or neither of these quantities to be used in computing the actual address. A programmer can use both the base and the index in various ways to handle such things as two-dimensional arrays and the structures-within-structures which occur in modern programming practices.

Bases and indices are variable or dynamic because they are stored in very general purpose CPU registers. That is, they can be easily changed while the program is running. The names of these quantities imply that the base will vary more slowly than the index, but this is entirely up to the discretion of the programmer.

In addition to the segment, base, and index, a 16-bit, 8-bit, or 0-bit (nonexistent) *displacement* is used. The displacement is what is called a *static* quantity. It is fixed at the time of assembly (translation from source code to machine code) and thus cannot (and should not, even by devious tricks) be changed during execution of the program.

You use the displacement to make things like compiling data, organizing memory, and relocation easier and faster. For example, suppose you wish to access a byte variable which is always the fifth byte in a 40-byte table, and suppose this table is loaded into memory at different locations at different times (depending upon what else is in memory at the time), then each time you access this variable you will want to use an addressing mode with a *base* and an 8-bit displacement. The base will be equal to the current beginning address of the table, and the 8-bit displacement will always be equal to 5. Since the base is stored in a base register (usually BX), it can easily be changed as the location of the table is changed. Also, since the 5 is a constant, it can be stored as a never changing displacement.

In assembly language, special alphanumeric notation around the operand, such as parentheses or square brackets, indicates the addressing mode. This is translated into machine language in quite intricate ways, depending upon both the instruction and the addressing mode you choose.

mm	aaa	Offset part of Address
00	000	(BX) + (SI)
00	001	(BX) + (DI)
00	010	(BP) + (SI)
00	011	(BP) + (DI)
00	100	(SI)
00	101	(DI)
00	110	direct address
00	111	(BX)
01	000	(BX) + (SI) + 8-bit number
01	001	(BX) + (DI) + 8-bit number
01	010	(BP) + (SI) + 8-bit number
01	011	(BP) + (DI) + 8-bit number
01	100	(SI) + 8-bit number
01	101	(DI) + 8-bit number
01	110	(BP) + 8-bit number
01	111	(BX) + 8-bit number
10	000	(BX) + (SI) + 16-bit number
10	001	(BX) + (DI) + 16-bit number
10	010	(BP) + (SI) + 16-bit number
10	011	(BP) + (DI) + 16-bit number
10	100	(SI) + 16-bit number
10	101	(DI) + 16-bit number
10	110	(BP) + 16-bit number
10	111	(BX) + 16-bit number
11	000	register AX (word) or AL (byte)
11	001	register CX (word) or CL (byte)
11	010	register DX (word) or DL (byte)
11	011	register BX (word) or BL (byte)
11	100	register SP (word) or AH (byte)
11	101	register BP (word) or CH (byte)
11	110	register SI (word) or DH (byte)
11	111	register DI (word) or BH (byte)

Note: mm stands for the first two bits of the addressing byte, and
        aaa stands for the last three bits of the addressing byte.

Table 3.1: 8086/8088 addressing modes.

The following example gives a pictorial view of a general situation. In this case, the instruction is the INCrement instruction (INC) and its single operand is in memory and is being accessed using a based, indexed, addressing mode with an 8-bit displacement. In our case, the segment address is in the data segment, the base is in Base Register

(BX), the index is in Destination Index (DI), and the displacement is 6. In assembly language, this instruction would appear as follows:

```
INC     6[BX][DI]        ; Increment
                         ; contents
                         ; of BX+DI+6
```

Note that the comment only refers to the offset address. There are two reasons for this. The first one is that there is only so much room to put comments, and the second is that the programmer really should be thinking only in terms of the offset address once the various segments have been determined by setting the segment registers.

Now let's look at this reference entirely in terms of numbers. Suppose that BX contains 4000h (h = hex), DI contains 20h, and the DS contains 3000h. Then the offset is determined as follows:

$$\text{offset} = \text{displacement} + (BX) + (DI) = 6 + 4000 + 20 = 4026 \text{ (hex)}$$

As we shall see in the section on segmentation, the contents of the segment register (in this case, data segment register) are multiplied by 16 (decimal) before it is added to the rest. Since 16 decimal is 10h, this shifts it over one hexadecimal digit (4 bits) to the left. Combining this contribution with the offset gives us:

$$\text{actual address} = 10 * (DS) + \text{offset} = 3000 * 10 + \text{offset}$$

$$= 30000 + 4026$$

$$= 34026 \text{ (hex)}$$

Thus, 34026h is the actual location in memory where you will find this operand, whereas 4026 is the offset address which is in the programmer's mind.

As we have seen, this addressing mode scheme with its single static and dynamic duo of addressing quantities fits well with the modern modular or *boxes-within-boxes* approach to programming. The BX register may be constant within a large box (larger program module), the DI register constant within a smaller box (smaller program module) contained in the larger one, and the displacement might point to a particular location within the smaller box. This is useful for accessing such *boxes-within-boxes* data structures as arrays, records, records of records, arrays of records, or records of arrays, or whatever else a modern language such as Pascal might support or demand. (See *Pascal Primer* by David Fox and Mitch Waite, Howard Sams.)

On the 8086/8088 there is some penalty for having these addressing modes. That is, it does take time for the CPU to compute an address composed of several pieces. This is mainly due to the fact that the address computations in the 8086/8088 are programmed in microcode. In a future version of the 8086, called the iAPX 186, the address computations are *hardwired* into the machine and as a result take much less time.

MEMORY STRUCTURE AND SEGMENTATION

As we mentioned before, the 8086/8088 uses a clever scheme called segmentation to smoothly access a full megabyte of memory with only 16-bit address references. *(offsets)*

Let's now look at how this works. Any address inside the 8086/8088 has two parts, each of which is a 16-bit quantity. One part is called the *offset* and the other part is called the *segment paragraph address*. The 16-bit offset is in turn composed of several parts: a displacement (a fixed number), a base (stored in a base register), and an index (stored in an index register). The 16-bit segment paragraph address is stored in one of the four segment registers (CS, DS, ES, or SS). The processor uses these two 16-bit quantities to compute the actual 20-bit address by the following formula (in decimal):

actual address = 16 ∗ (segment paragraph address) + offset

As we saw before, since 16 decimal is 10 hexadecimal, multiplying by 16 decimal just shifts a hexadecimal number one place to the left. For example, if the segment paragraph address is 500h and the offset is 234h, then the actual address is 5234h.

Now let's look more closely at the segment paragraph address which is stored in one of the four 16-bit registers called segment registers. The segment registers have the following names: code, data, stack, and extra (CS, DS, SS, and ES, respectively). Instructions are fetched using the code segment, stack operations use the stack segment, and generally data is accessed using the data and extra segments.

For example, suppose that the processor is executing a program, and the Instruction Pointer (IP) contains 234H and the code segment register contains 800H. Then the above formula shows that the next byte of instruction will be located at the address

8234 = 800 ∗ 10 + 234 (hex)

in memory.

This segment paragraph address only determines where a segment is to begin in memory. It does not, however, in any way divide a segment into *paragraphs*.

There is a special *prefix* byte which allows you to *override* some but *not* all of these assignments. In particular, if the CPU uses the instruction pointer to help point to memory (that is, to fetch part of an instruction), then the code segment register is *always* used. And if the CPU uses the stack pointer to help point to memory (either for pushing or popping the stack), then the stack segment register is *always* used. The only other case where there is a restriction is the destination for string operations. The combination of the destination index (DI) and the Extra Segment register (ES) is *always* used to compute the address of the destination of any string operation. The prefix byte, however, can be used to cause *any* of the four segment registers to be used to compute the address of a string operation source address. The default value (that is, the value with no prefix byte) is the data segment register.

All 24 memory reference addressing modes (used for normal data access) can accept a prefix byte and override their default segment assignments to use *any* segment register. The default assignment is either the Data Segment (DS) or the Stack Segment (SS) register, and, in fact, the data segment is always used *unless* the addressing mode uses the Base Pointer (BP) in which case the stack segment register is used. Intel intends for you to use the base pointer to access data in the system's *stack,* usually in conjunction with subroutine calls. For example, just before calling a subroutine, you could push several, say *n,* 16-bit words of data on the stack for use by that subroutine during its computations. Then near the beginning of the subroutine, you would copy the contents of the stack pointer into the base pointer, and throughout the subroutine, you would use the BP (with a displacement) to access any of these words of data. See the figure below for a picture of how this works. You can also pass data back from the subroutine to the main program in a similar manner.

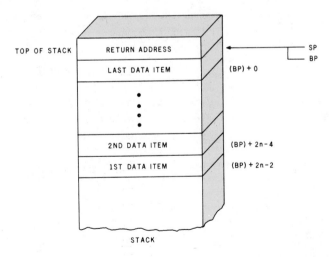

Figure 3.13: Using the base pointer to access data on the stack.

The use of these distinct segments can mean that there are separate *workspaces* for the program, the stack, and the data. Each workspace has a maximum size of 64 K bytes and a minimum size of 0. Since there are four segment registers, one each for program (CS) and stack (SS) and two for data — data segment (DS) and extra segment (ES) — the total amount of workspace can be as large as 4 * 64 K = 256 K bytes at any one time. This assumes that the workspaces for program, stack, and data do not overlap. This, however, is not necessary, for at the other extreme, it is quite possible and healthy to set all four segment registers equal. In that case, program, stack, and data all reside in the same 64 K workspace.

The programmer can select the location of these segments by loading the appropriate 16-bit segment registers with the appropriate segment paragraph addresses. Programmers normally do this at the beginning of the program, but can easily do it at any time while the program is running, *dynamically* changing the locations of these segments.

By varying the offset, the programmer can access locations within a segment. Think of the segment as just a stretch of memory which forms a workspace. The offset is the only part of the address which normally appears in the assembly-language programs during references to addresses in this workspace. In the section on addressing modes, we saw how this offset is computed by using as many as three quantities (base, index, and displacement).

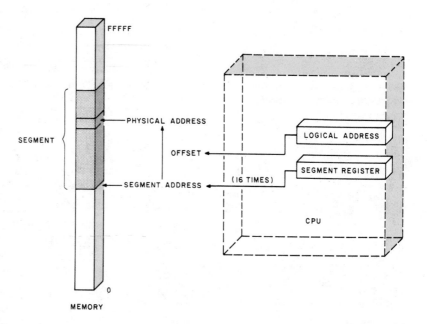

Figure 3.14: A segment.

We have seen that a segment address can begin at any multiple of 16. This is particularly easy to work with in hexadecimal arithmetic. For example, in hexadecimal notation the segment beginning addresses are 0h, 10h, 20h, 30h, on up to FFFF0h. Notice that these addresses occur at reasonably close intervals and yet run all the way up to FFFF0h, easily and densely covering the full 1 megabyte of addressing with 64 K possibilities. Notice that the content of the segment register is shifted 1 hexadecimal digit or 4 binary digits to the left before the offset is added. The figure below gives a pictorial representation of this.

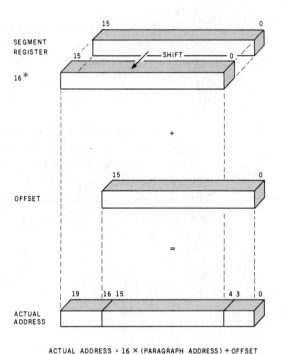

ACTUAL ADDRESS = 16 × (PARAGRAPH ADDRESS) + OFFSET

Figure 3.15: Computing an address.

There is a certain amount of overhead associated with this scheme, but it also has advantages. One of the chief advantages is that when it is used correctly, it encourages good programming practices. In particular, it encourages the development of small relocatable modules of code. *Relocatable code* is code which can run as is at *any* location in memory. Each module can be developed as though it starts at location zero. When it is to be run, it can be loaded starting at any address which is an even multiple of 16. Then the corresponding segment paragraph address can be loaded into the code segment via a special *intersegment jump* or call which then starts the code running. Once this code has been located, it is very easy to relocate it. In fact, the machine code can be dynamically relocated simply by moving the code (by an even multiple of 16) and changing the contents of the code segment accordingly.

This is very useful in multiprocessing environments where different jobs or parts of jobs need to be loaded in and out of memory, usually into different locations because other jobs are now located where they were. Many of the new operating systems will require this ability to quickly relocate small to medium size sections of code.

INSTRUCTION SET

We begin this section with a discussion of the 8086/8088 instructions by groups, and conclude with a comparison of the 8086/8088 instruction set with the instruction sets of the earlier 8-bit machines and the current generation of 16-bit processors. We will see how much more powerful the 16-bit processors are than their 8-bit predecessors, not only in the size data that they can accommodate, but also in other features, such as the new operations of multiplication and division and the new instructions to handle multiprocessing and coprocessing environments.

In general, 16-bit processor instructions can be classified in the following groups: 1) data transfer, 2) binary integer arithmetic, 3) logical operations, 4) shifts and rotates, 5) bit manipulations, 6) binary coded arithmetic, 7) string manipulation, 8) program control, and 9) system control. These categories are somewhat arbitrary, but they generally apply to all three of the current crop of 16-bit processors: The Intel 8086/8088, the Zilog Z8000, and the Motorola MC68000.

We shall use the Microsoft mnemonics for the 8086/8088 instruction set since they will probably be the most popular. With these mnemonics, many instructions have a way to indicate (as a part of their operation codes) whether the operands are in byte or word modes and a way to indicate when the source is immediate data. An extra *B* in the operation mnemonic indicates byte mode (8-bit data), while its absence indicates word mode (16-bit data). An extra *I* in the operation mnemonic indicates immediate data for the source. When the source is 8-bit immediate data, then both a *B* and an *I* appear (in that order) in the operation mnemonic. The use of the *B* and *I* as part of the *operation code* is not to be confused with the addressing modes (as described in the previous section) and how they affect the operands.

In this section, we shall not explicitly discuss the machine code for individual instructions. We will do this to some extent in the next section, and Appendix D has a table with the machine code for each variation of each instruction. Intel's *MCS-86 Assembly Language Reference Guide* is very useful for such details.

Note the syntax for the operands. Some instructions have no operands, some have one, and others have two. For two operand instructions, the destination is always written first, separated by a comma from the source. As the name implies, the destination is where the result is placed while the source is input only and unaffected by the operation.

Data Transfer Instructions

Data transfer instructions are those instructions which cause the CPU to move data from one place to another in the computer. These places include the main memory, the I/O space, and the CPU registers. In typical assembly-language programs, the most common instructions are data transfers. Data transfer instructions include the following:

MOV	destination,source	MOVe word from source to destination
MOVB	destination,source	MOVe Byte from source to destination
MOVI	destination,data	MOVe Immediate data to destination
MOVBI	destination,data	MOVe Immediate data to Byte destination
XCHG	destination,source	eXCHanGe contents of word locations
XCHGB	destination,source	eXCHanGe contents of Byte locations
PUSH	source	PUSH source onto stack
POP	destination	POP stack into destination
IN	source	INput from source to AX (word)
INB	source	INput from source to AL (byte)
IN		INput from location (DX) to AX (word)
INB		INput from location (DX) to AL (Byte)
OUT	destination	OUTput from AX (word) to destination
OUTB	destination	OUTput from AL (Byte) to destination
OUT		OUTput from AX (word) to location (DX)

OUTB		OUTput from AL (Byte) to location (DX)
XLAT		Translate (using a table)
LEA	register,source	Load Effective Address
LDS	register,source	Load DS and register
LES	register,source	Load ES and register

The MOVe instruction allows 8-bit (with the MOVB mnemonic) or 16-bit (with the MOV mnemonic) data to be moved: 1) from register to register, 2) from register to memory, 3) from memory to register, 4) from immediate data to register, and 5) from immediate data to memory. For types 2), 3), and 5), the memory reference can be made by any of the 24 CPU memory reference addressing modes. Types 1), 2), and 3) use the MOV (for 16-bit data) and the MOVB (for 8-bit data) mnemonics, and types 4) and 5) use the MOVI (for 16-bit data) and MOVBI (for 8-bit data) mnemonics.

Examples of the MOVe instruction are:

```
MOV     BX,CAT    ; is equivalent to
                  ; 8080 LHLD CAT
MOVI    BX,CAT    ; is equivalent to
                  ; 8080 LXI H,CAT
MOVB    AL,CAT    ; is equivalent to
                  ; 8080 LDA CAT
MOVBI   AL,3      ; is equivalent to
                  ; 8080 MVI A,3
MOV     BP,SP     ; make Base Pointer
                  ; point to stack
```

It is important to note that in certain special cases of the MOVe instruction, the assembler will produce (and the 8086/8088 will accept) completely different machine code than would be indicated by the general situation. These special cases are designed to optimize the performance of the 8086/8088 for very commonly used situations by running faster and using fewer bytes than the standard machine code. This is similar to the way natural languages such as English optimize certain verb forms. For example, using "did" instead of "doed" or "had" instead of "haved" requires fewer letters to write and is easier to say. These forms evolved as English developed. The special forms in the 8086/8088 machine language were, however, designed into the language by the Intel engineers.

For the MOVe instruction on the 8086/8088, the optimized forms are those which move data between the accumulator (AX for 16-bit or AL for 8-bit) and memory, using only one addressing mode for that memory reference. With this one addressing mode, you cannot have a base or an index, only a *displacement*. The displacement is simply included as part of the instruction just like the displacement is on the fancier addressing modes. To get the actual address the contents of the segment register (multiplied by 16) are added to this offset-displacement as usual.

There are also forms of the MOVe to transfer data to and from the segment registers.

All of these different possibilities create a myriad of machine codes. However, the assembly language is quite simple. The assembler analyzes the selection of source and destination and automatically chooses the optimal machine code. To do this, it has to quickly scan a series of tables.

The eXCHanGe instruction can be used to exchange the contents of two registers or a memory location with a register. Both 8-bit (XCHGB) and 16-bit (XCHG) are available. An example is:

```
XCHG      BS,DS     ; is equivalent to
                    ; the 8080 XCHG
                    ; instruction
```

A special optimized form provides a 1-byte machine code for exchanges between the accumulator and register. However, this is restricted to 16-bit register exchanges.

The PUSH and POP instructions are used to move data to and from the system stack. Only 16-bit data can be made to PUSH or POP. Examples are:

```
PUSH      AX        ; PUSH contents of
                    ; AX onto stack
POP       3         ; POP from stack
                    ; into mem location 3
```

Although any addressing mode can be used with these instructions, there are optimized forms for the case when the operand is a register. There are also special forms for making segment registers PUSH or POP. A discussion of how a stack works can be found in the chapter on the 8087 NDP, although the NDP's stack is internal, while the CPU stack is in memory and uses the stack pointer and stack segment register to form a pointer to the top of stack. For now, understand that a stack is like an in-box, in that the last item in is the first item out, and the PUSH puts data onto the stack and POP takes data from the stack.

The IN and OUT instructions transfer data to and from the CPU and I/O device controllers (and memory cells) whose addresses are located in the system's I/O space. These instructions actually have two forms: a static form in which the I/O port address is given as part of the instruction and a dynamic form in which the port address is located in the DX register, and thus can be changed as the program is running. The dynamic form allows a 16-bit address for the port, but the 8-bit version only allows an 8-bit address for the port (as is the case for the 8-bit 8080 and 8085 processors). The CPU accumulator (AX for 16-bit data and AL for 8-bit data) is the destination for the IN instruction and the source for the OUT instruction. Examples are:

```
INB       10H      ; transfer Byte from
                   ; Port 10H to AL
OUTB      11H      ; transfer Byte from
                   ; AL to Port 11H.


MOVI      DX,10H   ; set up for Port 10H
MOV       AX,BX    ; get data ready
OUT                ; transfer the data
                   ; to I/O Port
```

The XLAT (translate) instruction performs a lookup table translation. The table must be loaded into memory and its beginning address (base) must be placed into the BX register before this instruction can be used. If the byte entries of this table are a(0), a(1), a(2) ... , a(255), then a value of i in the AL register prior to the instruction will be replaced by a value of $a(i)$ after the XLAT has done its work. The mechanics of how the instruction works are as follows: The contents of the BX register and the AL register are added together to give the address of a memory location, and the contents of this memory location are copied into the AL register. The XLAT instruction only translates 8-bit data (held in AL) and is thus limited to a range of 0 to 255. Here is an example:

```
MOVI      BX,TABLE   ; Point to
                     ; table
MOVBI     AL,'*'     ; get a '*'
                     ; (now in
                     ; ASCII)
XLAT                 ; now AL has
                     ; its new
                     ; code
```

The Load Effective Address (LEA) instruction is used to load the offset of any operand specified by any one of the 24 memory reference addressing modes. It places this offset into a destination register. The 16-bit Motorola and Zilog processors both have an equivalent instruction, although the 8-bit processors such as the 8080/8085, Z80, and 6502 do not. An example is:

```
LEA        BX,COLOR[DI]      ; BX gets
                             ; address
                             ; of COLOR
                             ; + (DI)
```

The Load Data Segment (LDS) instruction is used to load the data segment and any 16-bit nonsegment register with data from memory. The contents of the source are placed in the selected register (destination register) and the contents of the next register are placed in the data segment register. The Load Extra Segment (LES) instruction works in a similar manner, except that the extra segment register is used instead of the data segment register. Examples are:

```
LDS        SI,SPOINTER       ; get source
                             ; pointer
                             ; from memory
LES        DI,DPOINTER       ; get
                             ; destination
                             ; pointer
                             ; from memory
```

Binary Integer Arithmetic

Binary integer arithmetic operations allow the CPU to compute both signed and unsigned integer operations using two's complement representation for signed arithmetic. These instructions include:

NEG	destination	Take NEGative of destination
NEGB	destination	Take NEGative of Byte destination
ADD	destination,source	ADD source to destination (word)
ADDB	destination,source	ADD source to destination (Byte)
ADDI	destination,data	ADD Immediate data to destination (word)

ADDBI	destination,data	ADD Immediate data to destination (Byte)
ADC	destination,source	ADd source + Carry to destination (word)
ADCB	destination,source	ADd source + Carry to destination (Byte)
ADCI	destination,data	ADd data + Carry to destination
ADCBI	destination,source	ADd data + Carry to Byte destination
SUB	destination,source	SUBtract source from destination (word)
SUBB	destination,source	SUBtract source from destination (Byte)
SUBI	destination,data	SUBtract data from destination (word)
SUBBI	destination,data	SUBtract data from destination (Byte)
SBB	destination,source	SuBtract source + Borrow from destination
SBBB	destination,source	SuBtract source + Borrow from Byte dest.
SBBI	destination,data	SuBtract data + Borrow from destination
SBBBI	destination,data	SuBtract data + Borrow from Byte dest.
MUL	source	unsigned 16-it MULtiply
MULB	source	unsigned 8-bit MULtiply
IMUL	source	signed 16-bit MULtiply
IMULB	source	signed 8-bit MULtiply

DIV	source	unsigned 16-bit DIVide
DIVB	source	unsigned 8-bit DIVide
IDIV	source	signed 16-bit DIVide
IDIVB	source	signed 8-bit DIVide
CBW		Convert from Byte to Word
CWD		Convert from Word to Double word
INC	destination	INCrement destination (word)
INCB	destination	INCrement destination (Byte)
DEC	destination	DECrement destination (word)
DECB	destination	DECrement destination (Byte)

The NEGate instruction takes the negative of its destination using two's complement arithmetic. This instruction has both 8-bit (NEGB) and 16-bit forms (NEG). Examples are:

```
NEG      AX      ; two's complement
                 ; negative of AX
NEGB     AL      ; two's complement
                 ; negative of AL
```

The ADD and SUBtract instructions perform either *signed* (two's complement) or *unsigned* arithmetic operations on their operands. With **ADD**ition the source is always added to the destination, and with SUBtraction, the source is always subtracted from the destination. Examples are:

```
ADDB     AL,CL   ; is equivalent to
                 ; 8080 ADD C
ADD      BX,DX   ; is equivalent to
                 ; 8080 DAD D
ADBBI    AL,5    ; is equivalent to
                 ; 8080 ADI 5
ADCBI    AL,7    ; is equivalent to
                 ; 8080 ACI 7
```

All the 8086/8088 arithmetic operations handle *six* different data types with 8- and 16-bit signed and unsigned integers as well as two types of binary coded decimal (to be covered later). Multiplication and division as well as the usual operations of addition and subtraction are fully supported throughout all six types of arithmetic on the 8086/8088 (including binary coded decimal).

Because of the way two's complement arithmetic works, the actual arithmetic operation (addition or subtraction) is the same for both signed and unsigned numbers. The only difference is where the overflow occurs, and this can be monitored by the programmer by watching the flags. With unsigned arithmetic, overflow occurs whenever there is a *carry* out of the leftmost (most significant) binary digit, and thus the *carry flag* (CF) is set to a value of 1 by the CPU whenever this *unsigned* overflow occurs. For example, look at the 4-bit binary additions:

```
        0101                          1011
       +0110                          0111
       ------                        ------
        1011                          0010


     no carry                         carry
```

In the first case, we have added 5 to 6 and got 11 (decimal) which is fine because there was no carry out of the leftmost digit, and hence a clear carry flag. In the second case, we added 11 to 7 and got 2 (decimal) which is quite wrong because we lost the end carry. (It went into the carry flag causing it to be set.) Thus, the carry flag would tell us that the first addition was correct, but the second was not.

With signed numbers, the situation is more complicated, but the *overflow flag* (OF) is used in this case. Essentially a signed arithmetic error occurs whenever the sign comes out wrong. For example, suppose you wish to ADD to positive numbers. If the resulting sum is too large, then it will appear (as a signed number) to be negative! The CPU has circuits which recognize this situation and set the overflow flag accordingly. Let's look at these same 4-bit additions as signed numbers.

```
        0101                          1011
       +0110                          0111
       ------                        ------
        1011                          0010


     overflow                       no overflow
```

In the first case, $+5$ added to $+6$ yields -5 (decimal). This is clearly wrong. The tip-off is that neither of the two terms is negative while the result is negative. In this case the overflow bit is set. In the second case, we get 2 from adding −5 and 7 (decimal) which is correct. If the two terms have different signs, then the overflow is never set. There cannot be an error in that case.

The ADd with Carry (ADC) and SuBtract with Borrow (SBB) work the same as the corresponding ADD and SUB instructions, except that the contents of the carry flag are input into the computation. These instructions are used in software routines to perform multidigit operations, such as when an 8-bit machine is forced to do 16-bit arithmetic.

The ADD, SUB, ADC, and SBB allow for 8-bit or 16-bit operands with: 1) register source and a register destination, 2) register source and a memory destination, 3) memory source and a register destination, 4) immediate data for the source and register destination, and 5) immediate data for the source and memory destination. The memory reference in 2),3), and 5) can use any of the 24 memory reference addressing modes. Unlike the MOVe instruction, the segment registers can never appear as operands, but like the MOVe instruction, there are special optimizations for the machine code in certain well-used cases. For these instructions, the case of immediate data with the accumulator register, a subcase of 4), is optimized, taking 1 less byte than the machine code for the more general case of immediate data with *any* data register. There is also a special mode of 4) and 5) in which 8-bit immediate data is automatically converted to 16-bit data before it is used.

There are two versions of the MULtiply instructions. MUL is used for signed arithmetic and IMUL is used for unsigned arithmetic. To see the difference, consider a 4-bit example. Suppose we wish to multiply binary 1111 by 1101. The usual algorithm for multiplication looks like the following:

```
          1111
          1101
         ------
          1111
          0000
          1111
         1111
       -----------
        11000011
```

With unsigned numbers, the binary 1111 represents decimal 15, the binary 1101 represents decimal 13, and the resulting binary 11000011 represents the decimal 195, which is correct. However, with two's complement signed numbers, the binary 1111 represents the signed decimal −1, the binary 1101 represents the signed decimal −3, and the resulting binary 11000011 represents the signed deciaml −61, which is certainly not correct. There are several ways to fix this. One way is to

sign extend both 4-bit factors to the size of the result (8-bit) before
multiplication, and use 8-bit arithmetic from then on:

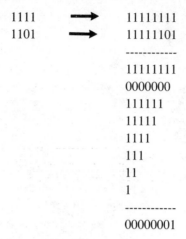

```
    1111    ━━▶    11111111
    1101    ━━▶    11111101
                   ------------
                   11111111
                   0000000
                   111111
                   11111
                   1111
                   111
                   11
                   1
                   ------------
                   00000001
```

In this case the result is binary 00000011, representing the signed
decimal 3, which is correct. Notice that both factors were negative. They
were extended by placing all 1s in the upper digits. Nonnegative numbers
are extended by placing 0s in the upper places. For example with a
positive and a negative number:

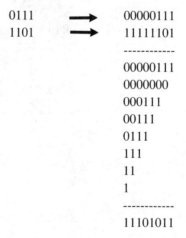

```
    0111    ━━▶    00000111
    1101    ━━▶    11111101
                   ------------
                   00000111
                   0000000
                   000111
                   00111
                   0111
                   111
                   11
                   1
                   ------------
                   11101011
```

This time we got 7 times −3 equals −21 which is also correct.
   For both signed and unsigned multiplication the source is multiplied
by the destination and the result is placed in the accumulator (extended if
necessary to the DX register). More precisely, there are word and byte
modes for both the signed and unsigned versions. In the byte (8-bit)
mode the result has 16 bits and is placed in the 16-bit AX (accumulator)
register, and in the word mode (16-bit), the result has 32 bits with half
placed in the AX register and the other half placed in the DX register!
We see that the result has twice the *precision* (number of digits) of the

factors, and thus we can say that the result has *double precision*.

The DIVide instruction also has signed and unsigned versions and byte and word modes. The DIVision returns two results, a quotient and a remainder. With the signed version, the remainder has the *same* sign as the divisor. This is especially important for so-called modular or clock arithmetic in which the remainder must be between 0 and the divisor or *modulus*. With both versions of the division, the divisor is a source and uses any of the usual 25 addressing modes (including register). However, the dividend (the number you are dividing into) is a double precision number which must be placed in the accumulator (extended to the DX register in the word mode) beforehand and the results will be placed in the accumulator (and DX register in the word mode) afterwards. More precisely, in the byte mode, the dividend is a 16-bit quantity placed in AX beforehand, and the resulting quotient is found afterward in AL and the remainder in AH; and in the word mode, the dividend is a 32-bit quantity half of which is in AX with the other half in DX beforehand, and the resulting quotient is found in AX and the remainder in DX (see the figure below).

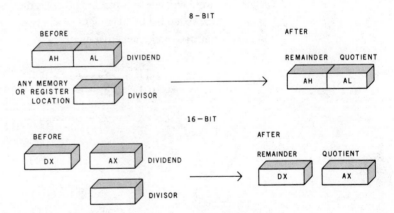

Figure 3.16: Registers used for division operation.

Examples of multiplication and division are:

```
MOVBI   AL,3        ; start with 3
MOVBI   CL,5        ; and 5
MULB    CL          ; now the answer of
                    ; 15 is in AX
MOVBI   CL,6        ; divisor will be 6
DIVB    CL          ; quotient of 2 is
                    ; in AL
                    ; remainder of 3
                    ; is in AH
```

The convert byte to word (CBW) and the convert word to double word (CWD) instructions are used to extend from smaller word sizes to larger word sizes, as indicated by the names given to these instructions. According to one of the developers of the 8086, Stephen Morse, these instructions were originally named SEX for Sign EXtend. The more conservative current name choices were made before going public. The chief purpose of these instructions is to prepare numbers for division. For example, if you wish to divide a 16-bit number NUMBER by a 16-bit number DIVISOR, then you can place DIVISOR almost anywhere (except perhaps in AX, DX, IP, or a segment register), but you must put NUMBER (the dividend) in AX. Then you must properly extend NUMBER to a 32-bit number with the lower half in AX and the upper half in DX. If NUMBER is positive, then all bits of the upper half extension in DX should be 0, and if NUMBER is negative, then all bits of DX should be set equal to 1. The CWD automatically does this extension for you. The CBW does the corresponding extension from the 8-bit AL register to the 16-bit AX. Here is an example:

```
MOVB     AL,XCRD  ; get X coordinate
CBW               ; extend to 16 bits
MOVBI    CL,FAC   ; get scale factor
IDIV     CL       ; signed divide by
                  ; scale factor
MOVB     XCRD,AL  ; put XCRD back again
```

The INCrement and DECrement instructions are used to add or subtract one from their destinations. Any of the usual 25 addressing modes can be used for this destination. The INCrement and especially the DECrement instructions are useful for counting the number of times a loop is to be executed, although the 8086/8088 has a special LOOP instruction which does this and more for you. Examples are:

```
INCB     AL       ; is equivalent to
                  ; 8080 INR A

INC      BX       ; is not equivalent
                  ; to 8080 INX H
                  ; because flags are
                  ; not preserved
```

Logical Operations

Logical operations are used to set (make equal to 1), clear (make equal to 0), and otherwise change or examine individual bits in the computer. The major reason for programming in assembly language is to get better control over the computer. You can see that the logical operations can really help in this respect. Applications for these instructions include examining status bits for I/O and system control, and setting control bits for I/O and system control. Another use for these operations is making an assembler. In this case the control bits control the CPU! In the next section we will look at the individual bits of machine language for the 8086/8088. The logical operations include:

NOT	destination	Take logical NOT of the destination (word)
NOTB	destination	Take logical NOT of the destination (Byte)
AND	destination,source	Logical AND of source and destination (word)
ANDB	destination,source	Logical AND of source and destination (Byte)
ANDI	destination,data	Logical AND of data and destination (word)
ANDBI	destination,data	Logical AND of data and destination (Byte)
OR	destination,source	Logical OR of source and destination (Byte)
ORB	destination,source	Logical OR of source and destination (Byte)
ORI	destination,data	Logical OR of data and destination (word)
ORBI	destination,data	Logical OR of data and destination (word)
XOR	destination,source	Logical XOR of source and destination (word)
XORB	destination,source	Logical XOR of source and destination (Byte)
XORI	destination,data	Logical XOR of data and destination (word)
XORBI	destination,data	Logical XOR of data and destination (word)

The logical operations for the 8086/8088 (as well as for all other known processors) work independently on each bit position of their operands using the truth tables in the figure below:

X	NOT X	X	Y	X AND Y	X OR Y	XX OR Y
0	1	0	0	0	0	0
1	0	0	1	0	1	1
		1	0	0	1	1
		1	1	1	1	0

Table 3.2: Truth tables for the logical operations.

On the 8086/8088 although these operations work on individual bits, their operands are whole bytes or words. That is, if you want to change a particular bit, you will first have to locate it within some byte or word in memory or a CPU register. Many times it is acceptable for a logical operation to modify all bits of a particular byte or word. For example, if you want to complement (reverse) each digit position of the 8-bit (binary) quantity 10110111 stored in the AH register, then you use:

```
     NOTB     AH        ; complement all 8
                        ; bits of AH
```

In this case, after this has been executed, AH would contain 01001000. Another example is the logical AND of the 8-bit quantities 11001100 and 10101010. This is obtained by making each digit of the first quantity AND with the corresponding digit of the second quantity, yielding 10001000. That is:

```
         11001100
    AND  10101010
         ------------
         10001000
```

In any case, the result of any logical operation is placed in the destination. By using combinations of logical operations or special patterns, you can actually change individual bits in a byte or word. For example, if you want to clear the second bit from the left of a word stored in AX, then you would use

```
                      ANDI      AX,1011111111111111B ; keep
                                                     ; all
                                                     ; bits
                                                     ; but
                                                     ; one
```

This can also be written as:

```
          ANDI      AX,0BFFFFH            ; all ones
                                          ; except
                                          ; second
                                          ; from left
```

The NOT instruction has a single operand, a destination which can be specified using any of the 25 addressing modes. There is no optimization of the machine code for special cases of this instruction. The AND, OR, and XOR instructions all have two operations and have almost exactly the same addressing structure as for the arithmetic operations ADD, SUB, ADC, and SBB described earlier. The only exception is that because these are logical operations, there is no 8-bit to 16-bit extension mode.

Shifts and Rotates

Shift and *rotate* operations allow you to move bits to the left or right in memory cells (in main memory or CPU registers) of the computer. There are no universally accepted definitions for naming the variety of variations possible with this basic theme, but the 8086/8088 mnemonics are a nice choice for shift and rotate nomenclature.

The figure below shows the 8-bit versions of each:

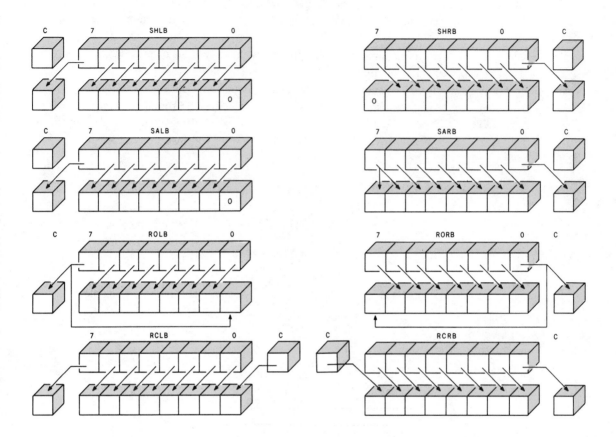

Figure 3.17: 8-bit shift and rotate operations.

Basically, a rotate moves the bits (left or right) in a *circular* pattern as though the word or byte was wrapped around a wheel, and a shift moves the bits in a straight *linear* pattern with no connection between the left and right ends of the word or byte. In each case, Intel has two varieties of each.

For the rotates, there is a plain rotate and there is a rotate which includes the carry bit as part of the rotating wheel. For the shifts, there is a *logical* shift and there is an *arithmetic* shift.

With a logical shift, bits shifted into the memory cell are 0.

With an arithmetic shift, a right shift performs a division by 2 and a left shift performs a multiplication by 2. That is, arithmetic shifts cause multiplication or division by the number base, namely 2, for the computer's arithmetic. You should recall that multiplying or dividing a decimal number by 10 just shifts its digits left or right. After making the distinction between arithmetic and logical shifts, let us now say that the arithmetic shift left is the same as a logical shift left. However, there is a difference between the two kinds of right shifts. The *arithmetic shift right* moves 0s into the leftmost (sign) bit if the original number was nonnegative and moves 1s into the left if the number was negative. This works out just right, preserving the sign of the number. After all, if you divide by a positive number (+ 2), you should preserve the sign. It is interesting to note that an arithmetic shift right *rounds down* the result. Thus shifting 3 yields 1, which is 3/2 = 1.5 rounded down, and shifting − 3 yields − 2, which is − 3/2 = − 1.5 rounded down. The fun starts when you arithmetic shift right a − 1. The answer is again − 1!

Now for the instructions:

SHL	destination	logical SHift Left one place
SHL	destination,CL	logical SHift Left CL places
SHLB	destination	logical SHift Byte Left one place
SHLB	destination,CL	logical SHift Byte Left CL places
SHR	destination	logical SHift Right one place
SHR	destination,CL	logical SHift Right CL places
SHRB	destination	logical SHift Byte Right one place
SHRB	destination,CL	logical SHift Byte Right CL places
SAL	destination	Arithmetic Shift Left one place
SAL	destination,CL	Arithmetic Shift Left CL places
SALB	destination	Arithmetic Shift Byte Left one place
SALB	destination,CL	Arithmetic Shift Byte Left CL places
SAR	destination	Arithmetic Shift Right one place
SAR	destination,CL	Arithmetic Shift Right CL places
SARB	destination	Arithmetic Shift Byte Right one place
SARB	destination,CL	Arithmetic Shift Byte Right CL places

ROL	destination	ROtate Left one place
ROL	destination,CL	ROtate Left CL places
ROLB	destination	ROtate Byte Left one place
ROLB	destination,CL	ROtate Byte Left CL places
ROR	destination	ROtate Right one place
ROR	destination,CL	ROtate Right CL places
RORB	destination	ROtate Byte Right one place
RORB	destination,CL	ROtate Byte Right CL places
RCL	destination	Rotate Left through Carry one place
RCL	destination,CL	Rotate Left through Carry CL places
RCLB	destination	Rotate Byte Left through Carry one place
RCLB	destination,CL	Rotate Byte Left through Carry CL places
RCR	destination	Rotate Right through Carry one place
RCR	destination,CL	Rotate Right through Carry CL places
RCRB	destination	Rotate Byte Right through Carry one place
RCRB	destination,CL	Rotate Byte Right through Carry CL places

As you can see, the 8086/8088 has the full set of shift and rotate instructions.

There are really two forms of each shift and rotate instruction: a *static*, one-step operation and a *dynamic*, multi-step operation. The number of steps (times the basic operation is performed) is called the *shift count*. In the first form, the only operand is destination, the quantity that is to be shifted or rotated, and the shift count has an implicit value of 1.

In the dynamic multi-step operations, the shift count is always contained in the CL register. For these forms, there are two operands: the first operand is the destination (as in the first form), and the second operand is explicitly the CL register.

Here are some examples:

```
ROR        DX          ; 16-bit rotate
                       ; right DX register
RCR        DX          ; 17-bit rotate
                       ; right DX and CF
RORB       AL          ; is equivalent to
                       ; 8080 RRC
RCRB       AL          ; is equivalent to
                       ; 8080 RAR

MOVBI      CL,4        ; set the shift count
ROR        AX,CL       ; now rotate 4 times
                       ; to the right
```

The arithmetic shifts are worthy of some more discussion. The Shift Arithmetic Left (SAL) is equivalent to a multiplication by a power of 2. The actual power is given by the shift count. For example, if the shift count is 3, then the destination is to be multiplied by 2 three times, and thus it will be multiplied by a total amount of:

$$2 * 2 * 2 = 2^3 = 8$$

The Shift Arithmetic Right (SAR) is equivalent to a division by a power of 2. Again, the power is given by the shift count. For example, if the shift count is 1, then the destination will be divided by 2 once. These operations should be used instead of multiplication or division whenever you multiply or divide by 2 because they run faster. Here are some examples:

```
SALB       AL          ; double the 8-bit
                       ; accumulator
SARB       AL          ; half the 8-bit
                       ; accumulator
MOVBI      CL,3        ; set the shift count
SAL        DX,CL       ; multiply DX by 8
```

Bit Manipulations

There are no true bit operations on the 8086/8088. A *bit operation* is an operation in which a *named* bit is modified (set, cleared, or complemented). Such operations can be obtained using logical operations. For example, if you wish to complement bit number 5 (remember to start counting from zero!!) of the AL register, then you could write:

```
XORBI      AL,32       ; 32 is 2 to the
                       ; fifth
```

Notice that the source is a binary 00010000 which has a 1 in bit position 5 and 0s in the other positions. You can see that this pattern is correct by looking at the truth table for the exclusive OR operation. In general, to obtain the corresponding pattern for the *ith* bit position, use the *ith* power of 2. That is, to modify bit 0, use $2^0 = 1$; to modify bit 1, use $2^1 = 2$; and so on.

With *macros* (user-defined assembly language instructions) you can write your own bit manipulation instructions for the 8086/8088. For example, a macro to complement any bit in a word could be defined as follows:

```
BITCOM    MACRO    X,I            ; define the
                                  ; macro
          XORI     X,(1 SHL I)    ; the
                                  ; assembler
                                  ; computes
                                  ; the pattern
          ENDM                    ; th-that's
                                  ; all, folks!
```

and used as:

```
          BITCOM   AX,5    ; is equivalent to
                           ; XORI AX,32
```

When the assembler sees this line, it substitutes the AX for X and 5 for I. The expression (1 SHL I) then becomes (1 SHL 5), which has a value of 32. Thus the new instruction BITCOM AX,5 becomes XORBI AL,32, which was described above.

Using macros in this way, you can get very close to the way the Zilog Z8000 does its bit manipulation operations. Motorola has a more elaborate (and more complete) set of bit manipulation operations than does Zilog. For one thing, Motorola always tests any bit (setting a flag accordingly) before modifying it. Doing this in software (perhaps using a macro) on the Z8000 or the 8086/8088 would take at least twice as long.

Binary Coded Decimal Arithmetic

Binary coded decimal arithmetic operations include:

AAA	ASCII Adjust for Addition
DAA	Decimal Adjust for Addition
AAS	ASCII Adjust for Subtraction
DAS	Decimal Adjust for Subtraction

AAM   ASCII Adjust for Multiplication

AAD   ASCII Adjust for Division

These operations are used in conjunction with the standard binary coded operations of ADD, ADC, SUB, SBB, MUL, IMUL, DIV, and IDIV to produce packed and unpacked binary coded decimal (BCD) results.

With *unpacked binary coded decimal*, a byte of data is restricted to the range of values from 0 to 9 and encodes a single digit of a decimal number. Thus, in this system you need several consecutive bytes to represent a decimal number (as many bytes as there are digits). With *packed binary coded decimal*, each byte is divided in half with the upper nibble encoding one decimal digit and the lower nibble encoding another decimal digit. You can read these values directly from the byte's hexadecimal representation. For example, if a byte contains a value of 34 hex, the upper nibble contains 3 and and the lower nibble contains 4, and thus the byte contains the packed binary coded decimal representation for the pair of decimal digits: 34.

Unpacked binary coded decimal uses the ASCII adjust for addition (AAA), the ASCII adjust for subtraction (AAS), the ASCII adjust for multiplication (AAM), and the ASCII adjust for division (AAD) operations. Packed binary coded decimal uses the decimal adjust for addition (DAA) and the decimal adjust for subtraction (DAS) operations.

Now let's see how these operations work. We start with unpacked BCD. Suppose we wish to add 7 + 5 as unpacked BCD numbers. Ordinary binary coded addition of a byte containing 7 with a byte containing 5 would yield a hexadecimal value of C. This is no longer a valid unpacked BCD quantity. The true answer is 2 with a carry of 1. The AAA instruction fixes things in the following manner. Assuming that the result of the binary coded addition is stored in the AL register, the AAA operation checks to see if the lower nibble of AL is too large (greater than 9). If it is, then 6 is added to AL, 1 is added to AH, and the upper nibble of AL is set equal to 0. In our example, the AAA causes the following sequence of events (using hexadecimal notation):

step 0)   AL contains C which is too large
step 1)   add 6 to AL so that it now contains C + 6 = 12
          (note: hexadecimal notation)
step 2)   increment AH
step 3)   clear the upper nibble of AL, giving the value 2 in AL. This is
          the correct value for the lower digit.

We have not shown how the AF and CF flags come into this because they can often be ignored in an actual application.

In Chapter 7, there is an example of how to use the AAA instruction with the ADD and ADC instructions to compute a multidigit operation. In that example, the next digit is fetched and placed in AH so that it may receive any carry from adjusting the current digit.

Now let's look at packed BCD. Suppose we have the two-digit numbers 34 and 29 stored in two different bytes in packed BCD form, and suppose we wish to add them. The standard ADD instruction will produce:

$$
\begin{array}{r}
34 \\
+\,29 \\
\hline
5D
\end{array}
$$

The result of this "ordinary" addition is no longer a valid, packed BCD number. The true answer is 63. The right nibble is too large by 16 and the left nibble is too small by 1. The DAA instruction fixes this by adding 6 to the "ordinary" answer. More precisely, the DAA executes the following microprogram on a quantity in the AL register:

If the lower nibble of AL is greater than 9,
      then add 6 to AL,
endif.

If the upper nibble of AL is greater than 9,
      then add 60 (hex) to AL,
           set the carry flag equal to one,
endif.

Again, we have mostly ignored the AF and CF flags (except at the end). In our example (34 + 29), we would have the following steps:

step 0)   AL contains 5D (hex)
step 1)   add 6 to AL so that it now contains 5D + 6 = 63
          (hexadecimal, which is the correct BCD).
step 2)   the upper nibble of AL is ok, thus we stop.

Notice that adding 6 automatically carries a 1 into the upper nibble!

In an actual application, you would have two multidigit numbers to add together. You would start from the right and work left just as in ordinary manual arithmetic, but you would do two digits at a time. For each set of double digits (byte) you would first use an ADC, and then a DAA. If the previous DAA instruction generated any carry, the ADC instruction would pick it up and add it in correctly to the current digit pair. Since the DAA only works on the AL register, you would have to move things in and out of the AL register as you worked your way down the digit pairs.

The AAS and DAS instructions work for subtraction in a similar manner. With multiplication and division, we only have unpacked versions (one decimal digit per byte). The ASCII adjust for multiplication instruction works as follows: The contents of AL are divided by 10 and the quotient is placed in AH and the remainder in AL. Believe it or not this is actually useful with unpacked multidigit multiplications, but we won't go into the details here. A couple of comments are worth making about this instruction. First, for numbers between 0 and 19, this instruction (AAM) has the same effect on AL and AH as the AAA instruction, but it takes much longer (83 clock cycles for the AAM and 4 clock cycles for the AAA), and so it is not a good replacement for the AAA. Secondly, the machine code for the AAM:

$$11010100 \ 00001010$$

has the second byte equal to 10! The current crop of 8086/8088s will support other numbers in its place, giving ASCII adjust operations for other bases as well as base 10 (however they work).

The ASCII adjust for division instruction multiplies the contents of AH by 10 and adds this to AL; then it clears AH. Since a multidigit division is fairly complicated we will not discuss how this instruction is actually used.

String Manipulation

Recall that a *string* is a sequence of data bytes or words. The 8086/8088 handles both byte strings and word strings. Technically, a string is a type of data which is stored in a type of storage called a *block* (see Chapter 2). However, the distinction between *types of data* and *types of storage* can often safely be blurred, especially in this case. Thus, for example, we can talk equally about moving a string *(string move)* as we can about moving the contents of a block of memory *(block transfer)*.

The 8086/8088 string operations include:

REP	REPeat
MOVC	MOVe string Characters (byte)
MOVW	MOVe string Words
CMPC	CoMPare string Characters (byte)
CMPW	CoMPare string Words
SCAC	SCAn string Characters
SCAW	SCAn string Words
LODC	LOaD string Characters
LODW	LOaD string Words
STOC	STOre string Characters

STOW	STOre string Words
CLD	CLear Direction flag
STD	SeT Direction flag

These string instructions are useful for quickly transferring blocks of memory, searching through tables or through text, or encoding data. The basic idea of string operations is similar to that of direct memory access (DMA). That is, certain parameters, such as source and destination pointers and a count, are set up using a short sequence of initializing commands. Then a command is issued to transfer a block of information. One difference is that the 8086/8088 string instructions only move blocks in the *main* memory of the computer and do *not* access the I/O space.

The REPeat instruction facilitates *block transfers* as well as *string scans* and *string compares*. We have already discussed block transfers. A block transfer (or string move) is simply an instruction which moves the contents of a whole block of memory in one shot. A string scan is an instruction which searches through a whole string for a match with a given byte or word of data. A string compare is an instruction which checks to see if two strings match byte by byte or word by word.

The REPeat instruction is actually a prefix byte used to modify a subsequent string instruction. It only modifies one instruction and that instruction must be a string operation which immediately follows this REPeat prefix. The prefix causes its subsequent string operation to repeat itself a varying number of times depending on the contents of the CX register (the repeat count) and any conditions that the string operation might be testing for. For example, a repeated scan operation will stop when it finds a match or when the count is up, whichever happens first. There are actually two versions of the REP. One version corresponds to the mnemonics REPeat (REP), REPeat while Zero (REPZ), and REPeat while Equal (REPE), and the other version corresponds to the mnemonics REPeat while Not Zero (REPNZ) and REPeat while Not Equal (REPNE). The two versions work the same except when they modify the CoMPare string Characters (CMPC), CoMPare string Words (CMPW), SCAn string Characters (SCAC), or SCAn string Words (SCAW) instructions. With these instructions the operation is repeated until either the count is reduced to zero or a match is found with the REP, REPZ, or REPE prefix or there is a *non* match with the REPNZ and REPNE prefix. The syntax for the REPeat prefix is simple. With the Microsoft cross-assembler, the REPeat can appear on one line of the assembly code, and the subsequent string operation can appear on the next line.

The string operations assume that the index registers, source index register (SI) and destination index register (DI), are properly initialized because SI will point to the source and DI will point to the destination. The string operations automatically increment or decrement these index registers to point to the next byte or word in memory. The direction flag

(DF) is used to control the direction of the motion. The CLear Direction flag (CLD) and SeT Direction flag (STD) can be used by the programmer to modify this flag. The data segment register is normally used with the source index register, but can be overridden, and the extra segment register (ES) is *always* used with the destination index register.

The MOVe string Character (MOVC), for byte mode, and MOVe string Word (MOVW), for word mode, instructions are used to make block transfers (in conjunction with the REPeat prefix). The data is MOVed from the source location, given by the source index register, to **the destination location, given by the destination index register,** and the source and destination indices are adjusted to point to the next positions. Here is an example of how this instruction can be used to transfer the contents of a block of data:

```
; Procedure to transfer block at OLDLOC to
new location NEWLOC
; The block is 1024 bytes long.
;
        MOVI     SI,OLDLOC         ; source is
                                   ; at OLDLOC
        MOVI     DI,NEWLOC         ; destination
                                   ; is NEWLOC
        MOVI     CX,1024           ; for a
                                   ; count of
                                   ; 1024 =
                                   ; block size
        REP                        ; this is
                                   ; the REPeat
                                   ; prefix
        MOVC                       ; now do
                                   ; the block
                                   ; transfer
```

The CoMPare string Character (CMPC), for byte mode, and CoMPare string Word (CMPW), for word mode, instructions compare two different strings. Set the flags according to the difference of the source and destination (destination minus source), but change neither the source nor the destination. We have already mentioned how the REPeat prefix bytes cause this instruction to be repeated either for a repeat count or until match (if you use REPZ or REPE) or until *no* match (if you use REPNZ or REPNE). Here is an example of how this instruction can verify whether two blocks contain the same data:

```
; Part of a procedure to verify block at
OLDLOC against block at NEWLOC
; The blocks are each 1024 bytes long
;
```

```
        MOVI      SI,OLDLOC        ; source is
                                   ; at OLDLOC
        MOVI      DI,NEWLOCK       ; destination
                                   ; is NEWLOC
        MOVI      CX,1024          ; for a
                                   ; count of
                                   ; 1024 =
                                   ; block size
        REPNZ                      ; this is
                                   ; the REPeat
                                   ; prefix
        CMPC                       ; now do
                                   ; the block
                                   ; compare
                                   ; if CX=0,
                                   ; the blocks
                                   ; are the
                                   ; same
                                   ; otherwise
                                   ; they differ
```

The SCAn string Character (SCAC), for byte mode, and SCAn string Word (SCAW), for word mode, instructions search through strings (pointed to by the destination index register) looking for a match with the contents of the accumulator (AL in byte mode and AX in word mode). They set the flags according to the difference of the string element and the contents of the accumulator (accumulator minus string element), but change neither. This instruction also works with the REPeat prefix in the same way as the CoMPare string instructions. Here is an example of how to use this instruction to skip spaces in a command line:

```
; Procedure to skip spaces
; DI points to current position in text
;
        MOVBI     AL,20H   ; ASCII code for
                           ; a space
        MOVI      CX,250   ; maximum size of
                           ; the buffer
        REPNZ              ; repeat until
                           ; not a space
        SCAC               ; scan through
                           ; the spaces
                           ; now DI points to
                           ; first non space
```

The LOaD string Character (LODC), for byte mode, and LOaD string Word (LODW), for word mode, instructions are used to load a string element from memory (using the source index register as the pointer) into the accumulator. This instruction is not normally repeated. Here is an example:

```
LODC            ; AL gets the
                ; character at (SI)
                ; now SI points
                ; to next byte
```

The STOre string Character (STOC), for byte mode, and STOre string Word (STOW), for word mode, instructions are used to store a string element into memory (using the destination index register as the pointer) from the accumulator. This instruction is not normally repeated. Here is an example of STOC:

```
STOC            ; store contents
                ; of AL into (DI)
                ; now DI points
                ; to next byte
```

The LOaD and STOre string operations are handy because they automatically bring data in and out of the accumulator, a place favored by the optimized versions of many arithmetic and logical operations.

Program Control

The term *program control* refers to controlling the *flow* of a program. This is done by manipulating the instruction pointer (IP) and/or the code segment register (CS). For example, a jump is accomplished simply by loading the IP (and possibly CS) with the address of the target loaction.

The 8086/8088 program control operations include:

JMP	target	JuMP direct within segment
JMP	target,segment	JuMP direct to new segment
JMPS	destination	JuMP Short
JMPI	destination	JuMP Indirect within segment
JMPL	destination	JuMP indirect Long (new segment)
JE	target	Jump if Equal
JZ	target	Jump if Zero
JNE	target	Jump if Not Equal
JNZ	target	Jump if Not Zero
JS	target	Jump is Sign (negative)
JNS	target	Jump if Not Sign (nonnegative)

JP	target	Jump if Parity (parity even)
JNP	target	Jump if Not Parity (parity odd)
JPE	target	Jump if Parity Even
JPO	target	Jump if Parity Odd
JL	target	Jump if Less than
JNGE	target	Jump if Not Greater than or Equal to
JNL	target	Jump if Not Less than
JGE	target	Jump if Greater than or Equal to
JLE	target	Jump if Less than or Equal to
JNG	target	Jump if Not Greater than
JNLE	target	Jump if Not Less than or Equal to
JG	target	Jump if Greater than
JB	target	Jump if Below
JNAE	target	Jump if Not Above or Equal to
JNB	target	Jump if Not Below
JAE	target	Jump if Above or Equal to
JBE	target	Jump if Below or Equal to
JNA	target	Jump if Not Above
JNBE	target	Jump if Not Below or Equal to
TEST	destination,source	TEST
TESTB	destination,source	TEST Byte
TESTI	destination,data	TEST against Immediate data
TESTBI	destination,data	TEST Byte against Immediate data
CMP	destination,source	CoMPare
CMPB	destination,source	CoMPare Byte
CMPI	destination,data	CoMPare against Immediate data
CMPBI	destination,data	CoMPare Byte against Immediate data
LOOP	target	LOOP
LOOPZ	target	LOOP if Zero
LOOPNZ	target	LOOP if Not Zero
LOOPE	target	LOOP if Equal
LOOPNE	target	LOOP if Not Equal
JCXZ	target	Jump if CX is Zero
CALL	target	CALL direct within segment
CALL	target,segment	CALL direct to new segment
CALLI	destination	CALL Indirect within segment
CALLL	destination	CALL indirect Long (new segment)

```
RET                          RETurn within segment
RET        number            RETurn and adjust stack
RETS                         RETurn from Segment
RETS       number            RETurn from Segment
                               and adjust stack
```

The unconditional JuMP instruction transfers control to a different area of the program, like a flea which crawls along and then suddenly jumps to another location on the dog.

The unconditional JuMP occurs in a number of variations which we will now describe.

JuMP (JMP) with one operand is a direct jump within the same segment to the target address given by the operand. The operand actually contains a relative address called a displacement. To get the true address you must add the value of the operand to the current value of the instruction pointer (IP). This can be a bit tricky because the instruction pointer points to the next instruction to be executed, not the actual jump instruction. Fortunately, the assembler does all the work for you. When you write in assembly language, you simply use the label of the target location as the operand for the jump, and the assembler will compute the proper relative address for the machine code. Relative addressing helps produce *position-independent code* which is code that will function properly when moved as a block to another location. In other words the block is *relocatable*. This form of the JuMP uses 16 bits to store the relative address (difference between target address and current contents of instruction pointer). Here is an example:

```
JMP        FUN1          ; jump to
                         ; function#1 in
                         ; same segment
```

JMP with two operands is a direct jump to a location in a possibly different segment. The offset is given by the first operand and the new contents of the code segment register are given by the second operand. Relative addressing is not used for this form for the offset, because it is not appropriate for a jump between two different segments. The contents of the code segment register take care of relocation considerations and the offset of the target is relative only to the beginning of its segment. Here is an example:

```
JMP        FUN1,SYS1          ; jump to
                              ; function#1
                              ; in segment
                              ; SYS1
```

JuMP Short (JMPS) is a shortened version of the JMP with one operand. It is a direct jump within a segment, using 8-bit relative addressing for the offset. Here is an example:

```
JMPS    FUN1      ; FUN1 must be in
                  ; same segment and
                  ; nearby
```

JuMP Indirect (JMPI) is an indirect jump within a segment. By *indirect* we mean that the operand (using any of the usual 25 addressing modes) contains the offset address of the target location. This is a far more sophisticated extension of the 8080/8085 PCHL instruction which exchanges the contents of the 8080/8085 program counter and the HL register. With the 8086/8088 JMPI instruction, you can shove the contents of any data register (or any memory location) into the 8086/8088 instruction pointer. Here is an example:

```
JMPI    BX        ; is equivalent
                  ; to 8080 PCHL
```

JuMP indirect Long (JMPL) is an indirect jump to a possibly different segment. Any of the 24 memory reference addressing modes can be used for the operand. In this case, the contents of the operand are placed into the instruction pointer and the next 2 bytes are shoved into the code segment register. Here is an example:

```
JMPL    [BX]      ; BX points to
                  ; 2 word target
                  ; address
```

The 8086/8088 has a full set of conditional jumps which depend upon a wide variety of conditions including single-flag conditions, signed, arithmetic relations, and unsigned relations. Table 3.3 below details them all. The conditional jump instructions use the same direct relative 8-bit addressing as the JMPS instruction described above. If you were to look at the machine code for these instructions (see Appendix D), you might observe that many of these conditional jumps translate to the same machine code as other conditional jumps. For example, JE and JZ are equivalent, as are JNE and JNZ.

Simple Flag Conditions

JE	Jump if Equal
JZ	Jump if Zero
JNE	Jump if Not Equal
JNZ	Jump if Not Zero
JS	Jump if Sign
JNS	Jump if Not Sign
JP	Jump if Parity
JNP	Jump if Not Parity
JPE	Jump if Parity Even
JPO	Jump if Parity Odd

Signed Arithmetic Relations

JL	Jump if Less than
JNGE	Jump if Not Greater than or Equal to
JNL	Jump if Not Less than
JGE	Jump if Greater than or Equal to
JLE	Jump if Less than or Equal to
JNG	Jump if Not Greater than
JNLE	Jump if Not Less than or Equal to
JG	Jump if Greater than

Unsigned Arithmetic Relations

JB	Jump if Below
JNAE	Jump if Not Above or Equal to
JNB	Jump if Not Below
JAE	Jump if Above or Equal to
JBE	Jump if Below or Equal to
JNA	Jump if Not Above
JNBE	Jump if Not Below or Equal to

Table 3.3: Conditional jumps.

The TEST and CoMPare instructions are normally used to determine conditions for conditional jumps. Both instructions have a source and destination but do not affect either, rather they merely set the flags. The TEST sets the flags according to the results of a logical AND of the source and destination, and the CoMPare sets the flags according to the results of a subtraction of the source from the destination.

Let's look more closely at how the CoMPare works with the

conditional jumps. Because the flag configuration produced by the CoMPare instruction is used by the jump instruction, the CoMPare instruction should be placed directly preceding the jump instruction; any other instruction intervening between them might mess up the flags. We will then have the sequence of instructions:

```
CMP            destination,source    ; first compare
Jcondition     target                ; then conditional
                                     ; jump
```

where "condition" is any of the conditions in the above table. To read this, say "If", then read the operands of the CMP, replacing the comma between them by the condition, then say "jump to", and finally read the target (operand of the conditional jump). For example:

```
CMP            BX,DX    ; if BX is
                        ; Greater
                        ; Than DX
JGE            GETIT    ; then
                        ; jump to
                        ; GETIT
```

It is interesting to note that the CoMPare on the 8086/8088 has the same order of subtraction as the usual subtraction operation, whereas the PDP-11/LSI-11 has the reverse order of subtraction for these two instructions. This is because the PDP-11/LSI-11 has the reverse order syntax for its double-operand operations, with the source preceding the destination. The order of subtraction had to be reversed on the PDP-11 CMP to make the CMP/conditional jumps read correctly.

The LOOP instruction is used to facilitate loop control. It is placed at the end of a loop. It essentially replaces the sequence:

```
DEC            count        ; decrement
                            ; and test
                            ; the count
JNZ            beginloop    ; loop if
                            ; count is
                            ; nonzero
```

in which a count is decremented and the loop is repeated as long as the count has not become 0. The differences between this and the LOOP instruction are as follows: 1) the LOOP does not affect the flags while the DEC does and 2) the LOOP instruction requires that the count be in the CX register (count register).

There are actually three versions of the LOOP instruction: LOOP, LOOPZ/LOOPE, and LOOPNZ/LOOPNE.

LOOP works as follows: the CX register is decremented and if CX is now not 0, a jump is made to the target. No flags are affected. Here is an example:

```
            MOVI    CX,24       ; set the count
                                ; equal to 24
START:      LODC                ; get the byte
            ANDI    7FH         ; strip off the
                                ; parity bit
            STOC                ; store the byte
            LOOP    START       ; loop for a
                                ; count of CX
```

LOOP if Zero (LOOPZ) and LOOP if Equal (LOOPE) work as follows: the CX register is decremented and if Zero Flag (ZF) is set equal to 1 and CX is now not 0, a jump is made to the target. No flags are affected.

LOOP if Not Zero (LOOPNZ) and LOOP if Not Equal (LOOPNE) work as follows: the CX register is decremented and if ZF is clear (equal to 0) and CX is now not 0, a jump is made to the target. No flags are affected. Here is an example (using the LOOPNZ):

```
START:      LODC                ; get the byte
            ANDI    7FH         ; strip off the
                                ; parity bit
            STOC                ; store the byte
            LOOPNZ  START       ; loop if count
                                ; is not zero
                                ; and byte is nonzero
```

The Jump if CX is Zero (JCXZ) is closely related to the LOOP instruction. It works as follows: If the CX is 0, then a jump is made to the target. This instruction is useful at the beginning of a loop to make sure that the loop is not executed if the count is 0. It is also useful in conjunction with the REPeat SCAn and REPeat CoMPare instructions to jump according to whether a match was made in a string. That is, after REP SCAC, REP SCAW, REP CMPC, or REP CMPW, if no match was made before the count was exhausted, then CX will be 0 and the JCXZ will cause a jump. On the other hand if a match was made, then the count will not be exhausted and, thus, JCXZ will not cause a jump.

The CALL and RETurn instructions control subroutine usage. The 8086/8088 uses the system stack (using the stack pointer) to save the return address for subroutines. Each time a subroutine is CALLed the return address is pushed onto the stack, and each RETurn causes the return address to be popped off the stack.

The CALL instruction has practically all the same versions as the unconditional jump except the short version.

CALL with one operand is used for subroutines within the same segment. It causes a direct jump to the subroutine using a 16-bit *relative* displacement to compute the offset. Here is an example:

```
CALL     ADDIT              ; within same
                            ; segment
```

CALL with two operands is used for subroutines within a possibly different segment. The first operand is the offset and the second operand is the new contents of the code segment register. Like the jump to another segment, the offset is *absolute* and *not* relative. Here is an example:

```
CALL     CDOUT,IOSEG        ; in
                            ; different
                            ; segment
```

CALL Indirect (CALLI) and CALL Long indirect (CALLL) are indirect calls. CALLI is used for subroutines within the same segment and CALLL is used for subroutines within a possibly different segment. In the first case, the operand can be specified with any of the 25 addressing modes. This operand contains the offset. In the second case, the operand can be specified with any of the 24 memory reference addressing modes, and it contains the offset while the next word contains the new segment address. Here is an example:

```
CALLI    AX                 ; AX has
                            ; address
```

RET is used to return from subroutines called from within the same segment, and RETS is used to return from subroutines called from other segments. Since the RETurn instruction is part of the body of the subroutine (the last instruction), these two different types mark a subroutine as either *local* (only called from the *same* segment) or global (must be called by the "long" calls). Here are some examples:

```
RET                         ; return to main
                            ; program

RETS                        ; return to main
                            ; program in
                            ; different segment
```

Both types of RETurns can either have no operand or one operand. The one-operand versions are used to help pass data to and from subroutines. If there is an operand, then its value is added to the stack pointer after the return address is popped. This then skips any data pushed onto the stack without actually popping it. Here is an example

```
RET     2          ; return and skip
                   ; 2 bytes of data
```

System Control

We have included a miscellaneous set of instructions under *system control*. These include the software interrupt instructions, the HLT and WAIT instructions, and flag manipulation instructions.

The 8086/8088 System Control operations include:

INT	INTerrupt
INTO	INTerrupt if Overflow
IRET	Interrupt RETurn
CLI	CLear Interrupt flag
STI	SeT Interrupt flag
HLT	HaLT
WAIT	WAIT
LOCK	LOCK
ESC	ESCape
NOP	NO Operation
CLC	CLear Carry
STC	SeT Carry
CMC	CoMplement Carry
SAHF	Store AH into Flags
LAHF	Load AH from Flags
PUSHF	PUSH Flags
POPF	POP Flags

The INTerrupt instruction can make software interrupts. It has one operand which is the "type" of interrupt. (See the earlier discussion of the 8086/8088 interrupt structure.) The INTerrupt on Overflow (INTO) is a special form which produces a "type 4" interrupt if the Overflow Flag (OF) is set. This is useful for such things as division errors. The Interrupt RETurn (IRET) is used to return from interrupt service routines. Since the INT calls its service routine in a different way than a CALL (INT pushes more stuff on the stack), the plain old RET cannot be used in place of IRET. The CLear Interrupts (CLI) and SeT Interrupts (STI) instructions are used to turn interrupts off and on. See Chapter 7 for an example of how to use the software interrupt instruction.

The HaLT instruction can stop the CPU. The CPU can be restarted either by an external interrupt or a reset. This is useful for when the CPU has finished all its work and needs more input before it can proceed.

The ESCape and WAIT instructions link the CPU with a coprocessor.

The ESCape instruction calls a coprocessor into action. It has a single operand which can use any of the 25 addressing modes. This operand is actually used by the coprocessor instead of the CPU. See Chapter 4 on the 8087 NDP for more details from the point of view of the coprocessor.

The WAIT instruction helps synchronize the CPU with a coprocessor such as the 8087 NDP. The WAIT instruction causes the CPU to stop activity until an input on the TEST pin gives a signal to proceed. The TEST pin of the CPU should be connected to the BUSY pin of the coprocessor. Again, see Chapter 4 for more details.

LOCK is really a prefix. It helps prevent conflicts in multiprocessing environments. It protects the bus from being accessed by another processor during the next instruction. This is important because software protection schemes (using busy bytes) have an Achilles heel at the moment they try to access their busy bytes. See the chapter on the 8089 IOP for further details.

The No OPeration (NOP) instruction does nothing except take up time and space. It is equivalent to exchanging AX with itself. Taking up time and space is important in several circumstances. For example, I/O routines in machine-coded programs often are followed by NOPs to allow the user more space for longer I/O routines than the original ones. Also, a few NOPs can help with a small timing problem.

The CLear Carry flag (CLC), SeT Carry flag (STC), and CoMplement Carry flag (CMC) are useful for directly manipulating this important flag.

The Store Accumulator High to Flags (SAHF) and Load Accumulator High with Flags (LAHF) can access the ZF, AF, PF, and CF flags. These are in the lower byte of the flags register. Here are some examples:

```
; the following is equivalent to the 8080
;PUSH PSW
        LAHF                ; move Flags into AH
        XCHG      AH,AL     ; for compatibility
                            ; with 8080
        PUSH      AX        ; now push AL and
                            ; Flags
```

```
; the following is equivalent to the 8080
;POP PSW
        POP      AX        ; first POP AL and
                           ; Flags
        XCHG     AH,AL     ; for compatibility
                           ; with 8080
        SAHF               ; move AH into Flags
```

To get at the entire set of flags, you need to use PUSH Flags onto stack (PUSHF) and POP Flags from stack (POPF). Here is an example:

```
        PUSHF              ; push flags onto
                           ; stack
        POP      AX        ; now you can find
                           ; them in AX
```

Comparison with Other Processors

Now we look at the 8086/8088 instruction set from a different angle, namely, its relation to the instruction sets of its 8-bit predecessors and its

much richer than that of its

ple, besides extending the original

a, it has new instructions such as:

vhole set of string operations; and

SCAPE, to handle multiprocessing

instruction set with its 16-bit

Zilog Z8000, must take into

the Motorola processors are really

at is, both the MC68000 and the

as 8-bit and 16-bit instructions),

milarly, the 8088 is really a 16-bit

act gives the 8088 a commanding

Motorola instruction sets with

ed would show that the

up except bit manipulation, but

with the use of "macros", can

alent results.

erally wins benchmark tests.

types of arithmetic and logical operations such as ADD or AND take fewer clock cycles on the 8086/8088 than on the Z8000 or the MC68000. On the other hand, since the MC68000 is designed to run in a two-clock system with a much faster clock speed for the processor than the one for its peripherals, an MC68000 system could be built with reasonably slow memory which executes a register-to-register ADD (not involving memory) instruction in less time than a single-clock speed 8086 system! This same trick can actually be done with any microprocessor, but a better method would be to increase the speed at which memory can be run. See the table below for a comparison of the number of cycles required for some typical cases of the 16-bit ADD instruction for these three processors.

| | (Cycles) | | | (Time in microseconds) | | | | | |
| | 8086 | Z8000 | MC68000 | 8086 | | Z8000 | | MC68000 | |
				5mhz	8mhz	4mhz	10mhz	4mhz	10mhz
Register to Register	3	4	4	.6	.375	1.00	.4	1.00	.4
Register to Direct Address	22	-	21	4.4	2.750	-	-	5.25	2.1
Direct Address to Register	15	9	16	3.0	1.875	2.25	.9	4.00	1.6
Immediate to Register	4	7	8	.8	.500	1.75	.7	2.00	.8
Immediate to Direct Address	23	-	25	4.6	2.875	-	-	6.25	2.5

Note: - means that the particular variation is not available.

Table 3.4: Comparison of speed for addition.

Acquiring multiply and divide instructions is an important reason for upgrading the processor in your system from 8 bits to 16 bits. The 8086/8088 has both 8-bit and 16-bit signed and unsigned multiply and divide, but the Z8000 has *only* signed multiply and divide, and neither the Z8000 nor the MC68000 have 8-bit versions of their multiply or divide instructions. However, the 16-bit versions of the multiply on the Z8000 and MC68000 tend to execute at the same speed as the 8-bit multiply on the 8086, and the 8086 is definitely the slowest on 16-bit multiply and divide. Intel plans to correct this with their 186. See the following tables for a comparison of the multiplication and a comparison of the division instructions.

| | (Cycles) | | | (Time in microseconds) | | | | | |
| | 8086 | Z8000 | MC68000 | 8086 | | Z8000 | | MC68000 | |
				5mhz	8mhz	4mhz	10mhz	4mhz	10mhz
Signed 8-bit									
Register to Register	90	-	-	18.0	11.250	-	-	-	-
Direct Address to Register	96	-	-	19.2	12.000	-	-	-	-
Signed 16-bit									
Register to Register	144	70	70	28.8	18.000	17.50	7.4	17.50	
Direct Address to Register	150	71	78	30.0	18.750	17.75	7.1	19.50	
Unsigned 8-bit									
Register to Register	71	-	-	14.2	8.875	-	-	-	-
Direct Address to Register	77	-	-	15.4	9.625	-	-	-	-
Unsigned 16-bit									
Register to Register	124	-	70	24.8	15.500	-	-	31.00	7.0
Direct Address to Register	130	-	78	26.0	16.250	-	-	32.50	7.8

Note: - means that the particular variation is not available.

Table 3.5: Comparison of speed for multiplication.

| | (Cycles) | | | (Time in microseconds) | | | | | |
| | 8086 | Z8000 | MC68000 | 8086 | | Z8000 | | MC68000 | |
				5mhz	8mhz	4mhz	10mhz	4mhz	10mhz
Signed 8-bit									
Register to Register	112	-	-	22.4	14.000	-	-	-	-
Direct Address to Register	118	-	-	23.6	14.750	-	-	-	-
Signed 16-bit									
Register to Register	177	95	158	35.4	22.125	23.75	9.5	39.50	15.8
Direct Address to Register	183	96	166	36.0	22.875	24.00	9.6	41.50	16.6
Unsigned 8-bit									
Register to Register	90	-	-	18.0	11.250	-	-	-	-
Direct Address to Register	96	-	-	19.2	12.000	-	-	-	-
Unsigned 16-bit									
Register to Register	155	-	140	31.0	19.375	-	-	35.00	14.0
Direct Address to Register	161	-	148	32.2	20.125	-	-	37.00	14.8

Note: - means that the particular variation is not available.

Table 3.6: Comparison of speed for division.

The 8086/8088 string instructions are quite complete. The Z8000 has a full set of these operations, but the MC68000 uses standard instructions with fancier addressing modes to accomplish nearly the same results. Generally, the Z8000 requires the least and the MC68000 requires the most clock cycles for such operations (including the repeat). For example, on the 8086/8088 a multiple string scan (REP SCAS) instruction takes $9 + 15n$ clock cycles (where n is the number of repetitions), while a corresponding instruction: ComPare, Decrement, and Repeat (CPDR), takes $11 + 9n$ clock cycles on a Z8000. The MC68000 accomplishes the same action by using the CoMPare (CMP) instruction with the "indirect with predecrement" addressing mode followed by a loop instruction (DBNE). This should take approximately $2 + 18n$ clock cycles. As you can see from the figure below, $2 + 18n$ grows bigger than $9 + 15n$ (8086) or $11 + 9n$ (Z8000) as n increases, thus the 68000 is the slowest for multiple searches. With this chart, as in the game of golf, the lower your score the better you do.

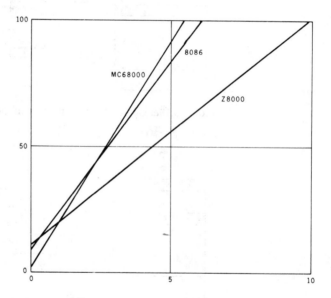

Figure 3.18: Speed comparison of multiple string searches.

Most 8086/8088 instructions do not allow moving data from memory directly to memory as you can on many minicomputers and maxicomputers. You must move the data into a CPU register first (see the figure below). String operations, however, will allow memory-to-memory moves and other kinds of instructions which move immediate data to memory. (Immediate data is data which is part of the program.) The other two processors have much the same problem. For example, with the ADD instruction, both the 8086/8088 and the

MC68000 can add from register to register, from register to memory, from memory to register, from immediate to register, and from immediate to memory; while the Z8000 can just add from register to register, from memory to register, and from immediate to register.

On a minicomputer such as the PDP-11 (and the micro LSI-11), you can actually add from memory to memory, which is very nice! It is said that Digital Equipment's PDP-11 has provided much of the inspiration for the current crop of 16-bit processors, although none of them has its full addressing power. It is also interesting to note the similarities between the PDP-11 operating systems and utilities and CP/M, the current "standard" operating system for the 8080, 8085, Z80, 8086, and 8088 processors (see Murtha, Stephen M.; Waite, Mitchell. *CP/M Primer* Indianapolis, Indiana: Howard W. Sams & Co., Inc.).

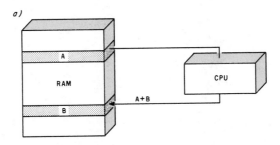

Figure 3.19a: Operation from memory to memory.

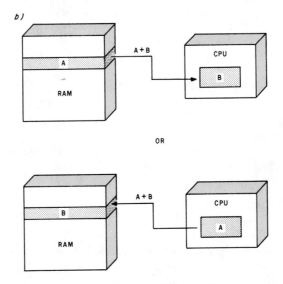

Figure 3.19b: Operation based in the CPU.

The 8086/8088 instruction encoding is byte oriented. This is in contrast to some of the other 16-bit processors such as the MC68000, Z8000, and LSI-11. With these processors, instructions come 16 bits at a time. On Intel's newest offering, the 32-bit iAPX 432, the instructions are coded in groups of bits of sizes according to just what is needed to specify each instruction. That is, there is no fixed instruction size, as there is for these 16-bit machines.

Overall, by itself, the 8086/8088 appears to be less powerful than the other two processors in several ways: it handles just 8- and 16-bit data while the others will handle 8-, 16-, 32-, and even some 64-bit integer operations; it takes more clock cycles than the Z8000 for string operations; and it has a smaller addressing space (20 bits) than these two other processors. The 8086 and definitely the 8088 are actually in a different class than the other processors and will probably fit into different areas of the price/performance curve. In particular, the 8088 is now beginning to take a leadership role in the 8-bit market, because it brings 16-bit performance to the 8-bit market and because its price is beginning to drop to a competitive level with the original 8-bit microprocessors. Apparently, the 8086 is just the beginning of a line of high-performance 16-bit processors. Remember that the 8086 was the first of this new generation of 16-bit microprocessors, and, thus, the testing ground for some new ideas. Some of these ideas now need tuning and expanding, so Intel is planning to do this with the iAPX 186 (mainly tuning) and iAPX 286 (expanding in the area of memory management). The battle is just beginning.

When an 8086/8088 is used in conjunction with the 8087 Numeric Data Processor and the 8089 Input/Output processor, the picture changes radically, and the 8086 and 8088 rise to new levels of processing power.

With the 8087 NDP, suddenly very high-precision, floating-point numbers (80 bits) can be handled at roughly the same kind of speeds that an integer multiply or divide is performed by any one of these CPU chips alone! On the other hand, the 8089 IOP is able to perform string-like operations (including using a translation table) extremely fast. For example, a block transfer using a translation table and a test for termination takes 15 clock cycles per byte on an 8089 IOP and 25 clock cycles per byte on a Z8000. Furthermore, while the 8089 is doing this, the 8086/8088 CPU and the 8087 Numeric Data Processors in the system can be doing other things! Each of these auxiliary processors has a chapter devoted to it.

MACHINE LANGUAGE FOR A TYPICAL INSTRUCTION

Let's consider how one particular instruction gets implemented in machine language. We will use the ADD instruction because it works exactly the same as seven other instructions: OR, ADC, SBB, AND, SUB, XOR, and CMP. All of these instructions have two operands, one of which is a source, and the other a destination. In each case, the contents of the source and destination are combined according to the particular instruction and then placed in the destination location.

There are several major assemblers available at the present time for the 8086/8088. Among these are Intel's own ASM86 assembler and a cross-assembler by Microsoft. Recall that a cross-assembler is an assembler which is run on one machine, the host, but produces code for another machine, the target. In this case, the host is an 8080, 8085, or Z80 running CP/M and the target is an 8086 or 8088.

The Microsoft 8086 cross-assembler has the following variations of the symbolic code for this instruction:

ADD	destination,source	ADD source to destination (word)
ADDB	destination,source	ADD source to destination (Byte)
ADDI	destination,data	ADD data to destination (word)
ADDBI	destination,data	ADD data to destination (Byte)

The additional I and B are used by the Microsoft assembler to help indicate information which is automatically determined by the Intel assembler as it looks at the data. The I means that the source data is immediate; that is, it is given as a part of the instruction. The B means that both the source and destination are bytes (8-bit quantities). The absence of the B implies that both the source and destination are words (16-bit quantities).

The mnemonics ADD and ADDB get implemented in machine language in different ways depending upon 1) the locations of the source and desintation, e.g., to register from register, to register from memory, and to memory from register; 2) the size of the data; 3) the size of the displacement; 4) the base and index registers used; and 5) the data registers used.

In any case, the first byte of the machine code is:

$$00ccc0dw$$

This first byte mainly tells the operation, but it also tells how big the operands are and a little bit about where they are. Specifically, it is encoded as follows: the $ccc = 000$ is a 3-bit binary code indicating the ADD instruction. The d is a 1-bit binary code indicating the direction. If the destination is memory and the source is a register, then $d = 0$, and if the destination is a register and the source is memory, then $d = 1$. The w is a 1-bit binary code indicating the data size. If the data size is 8-bit (byte), then $w = 0$ (in this case you would use a B with the Microsoft assembler), and if it is 16-bit (word), then $w = 1$ and you would not use the B.

The second byte is:

mm rrr aaa

This byte gives information about the operands (including the addressing mode). Specifically, the *mm* is a 2-bit binary code indicating part of the addressing mode information. The *aaa* is a 3-bit binary code which gives the rest of the addressing mode information. The *rrr* is a 3-bit binary code indicating a register. If $d = 0$, then *rrr* indicates the source register and the other addressing information determines the destination, and if $d = 1$, then *rrr* indicates the destination register and the other addressing information determines the source.

Depending upon *mm* and *aaa*, there may be more bytes which indicate values for the address displacement. See table 3.1 for details.

To put this all together consider the following example. The assembly source code is:

```
ADD        6[BX][DI],DX    ; add DX to
                           ; location
                           ; DI+BX+6
```

Here, we are adding the contents of DX to the location described by the same addressing mode used as an example in the section on addressing modes, namely based (using BX), indexed (using DI), with an 8-bit displacement equal to 6. Since the source is a register and the destination is memory, we must have $d = 0$. Since DX indicates a 16-bit register, we know the data size is 16 bits. Thus $w = 1$. Since the displacement is 8-bit, we see from the addressing mode chart (table 3.1) that *mm* = 01. Also from the addressing mode chart, we see that *aaa* is 001. The code for register DX is *rrr* = 010. Only 1 extra byte will be needed for the (8-bit) displacement. ''Assembling'' all of this gives us:

```
ADD 6[BX][DI],DX
=> 00 000 001   01 010 001    00000110
=>        01          51           06 hex
```

Under normal conditions, the assembler does all this work for you, but it is important to understand exactly how this is done when you have to debug code that refuses to perform properly.

Most of the time the operands are not so complicated. For example:

```
ADD        AX,[SI]         ; add
                           ; location
                           ; (SI) to
                           ; register AX
```

In this case, the source index points to the source, and the destination is the AX register. The machine code for this would be:

$$00\ 000\ 011 \quad 00\ 000\ 100$$

Here we have $w = 1$ (word data), $d = 1$ (from memory to register), $mm = 00$ (no displacement), $aaa = 100$ (index mode using SI to point to data), and $rrr = 000$ (register AX for other operand). Since there is no displacement, there are no other bytes.

Next we look at the mnemonics ADD Immediate word (ADDI) and ADD Immediate Byte (ADDBI). These are translated into machine code in two distinct ways. This is typical of the way the 8086/8088 is designed to optimize certain frequently used combinations, especially those using special registers such as the accumulator (AX or AL).

The more general form has immediate data as the source and a general register or memory location as the destination. The first byte is:

$$100000sw$$

Here, the s is a 1-bit binary code which indicates the size of the immediate data, and w is a 1-bit binary code which indicates the size of the destination data. If sw is 00, then both the source and destination are **8 bits wide**; if sw is 11, then both the source and destination are 16 bits wide, and if sw is 01, then the source is 8 bits wide and is extended (using two's complement integer arithmetic) to 16 bits before it is added to the destination. (Whew!)

The second byte is:

$$mm\ 000\ aaa$$

The mm and aaa indicate the addressing mode of the destination as described above. Notice the 000 in the middle of this byte. This is no longer a register designator, instead, it is part of the operation code, and helps specify that we are "ADDing".

Depending upon mm and aaa, there may be more bytes which indicate values for the address displacement (see the table above for the details). After all the addressing information comes the immediate data. If $w = 0$, there is 1 byte for the data, and if $w = 1$, then there are 2 bytes.

Here is an example of this form. The assembly source code is:

```
ADDBI    6[BX][DI],5     ; add 5 to
                         ; location
                         ; BX+DI+6
```

The source and destination are both 8 bits wide, and thus *sw* is 00. The destination has the same addressing mode as above. Thus, the machine code is:

$$100000\ 0\ 0 \qquad 01\ 000\ 001 \qquad 00000110 \qquad 00000101$$

Notice that just the last byte is the immediate data.

The special form for immediate data is only used when the destination is the accumulator (AX or AL). The first byte is:

$$0000010w$$

Here, the *w* indicates the data size. If the data is 8 bits, then $w = 0$, and if the data is 16 bits, then $w = 1$.

Next comes the immediate data. If $w = 0$, there is 1 byte for the data, and if $w = 1$, then there are 2 bytes.

Here is an example of this last form. The assembly code is:

```
ADDI      AX,7                         ;add 7 to AX
```

The AX register is 16 bits wide, so we know that $w = 1$. Thus, the machine code is:

$$0000010\ 1 \qquad 00\ 000\ 111 \qquad 00000000$$

Notice that the last 2 bytes are the immediate data.

SAMPLE PROGRAMS

In this section, we will give a short sample program for the 8086/8088 (see the figure below). We will actually assume an 8088 because we will be using an 8-bit data bus. This program is used as a subroutine to plot a single point (x,y) on a video screen.

XMACRO-86 3.36   1

```
; ROUTINE: DOT
;
; THIS ROUTINE PLOTS A POINT (X,Y) ON THE VIDEO SCREEN.
; THE SCREEN IS MEMORY MAPPED AND IS IN A MODE WHICH
; HAS 256 HORIZONTAL BY 240 VERTICAL PIXELS WITH
; 4 BITS PER PIXEL FOR COLOR ENCODING.
;
; THIS ROUTINE DESTROYS THE BX, DI, AND AL REGISTERS.
;
; THE SCREEN RAM OCCUPIES THE FIRST 32K BYTES OF A 64K SEGMENT OF
; SYSTEM MEMORY. THE QUANTITIES: XCRD (X-COORDINATE), YCRD
; (Y-COORDINATE), MASK, AND COLOR ARE STORED IN THE SECOND
; HALF OF THIS SAME SEGMENT. MASK AND COLOR ARE NEEDED TO
; PLACE THE CORRECT CODE IN THE SCREEN RAM BYTE. MASK AND
```

```
                            ; COLOR ARE ACTUALLY SMALL LOOKUP TABLES WHICH ARE SET UP
                            ; BY THE SETCOLOR ROUTINE.
                            ;
                            ;   MASK[0] CONTAINS BINARY 11110000 (USED TO CLEAR LOWER NIBBLE).
                            ;   MASK[1] CONTAINS BINARY 00001111 (USED TO CLEAR UPPER NIBBLE).
                            ;   COLOR[0] CONTAINS THE CODE FOR THE COLOR IN THE LOWER NIBBLE.
                            ;   COLOR[1] CONTAINS THE CODE FOR THE COLOR IN THE UPPER NIBBLE.
                            ;
                                    EXTERNAL        XCRD,YCRD,MASK,COLOR
                            ;
0000'   8A 3E 0000*         DOT:    MOVB    BH,YCRD         ; GET THE Y-COORDINATE
0004'   8A 1E 0000*                 MOVB    BL,XCRD         ; GET THE X-COORDINATE
0008'   8B FB                       MOV     DI,BX           ; SAVE IN DI ALSO
000A'   D1 FB                       SAR     BX              ; NOW BX HAS THE BYTE POSITION
000C'   81 E7 0001                  ANDI    DI,1            ; NOW DI HAS THE BIT POSITION
0010'   8A 07                       MOVB    AL,[BX]         ; GET THE BYTE FROM SCREEN
0012'   22 85 0000*                 ANDB    AL,MASK[DI]     ; MAKE A HOLE USING SHIFTED MASK
0016'   0A 85 0000*                 ORB     AL,COLOR[DI]    ; DROP IN THE PIXEL USING SHIFTED
                                                            ; COLOR
001A'   88 07                       MOVB    [BX],AL         ; PUT THE BYTE BACK
001C'   C3                          RET                     ; NOW RETURN
                                    END


        XMACRO-86 3.36   S



Macros:

Symbols:
COLOR   0018*   DOT     0000'   MASK    0014*   XCRD    0006*
YCRD    0002*



No   Fatal errors(s)
```

Figure 3.20: Sample program.

We assume that the video screen occupies 32 K of the system's RAM with 30720 bytes actually mapped to the screen, and has been initialized into a mode with a resolution of 256 horizontal dots (pixels) by 240 vertical dots and with 4 bits per pixel for encoding any one of 16 colors. The screen RAM is mapped to the screen in a very straightforward manner. Each nibble (4 bits) is mapped into a different dot (pixel) on the screen in the same order that you would read a page of print: from left to right, from top to bottom (see the figure below). The color that appears in a pixel depends upon the value stored in the corresponding nibble. The color coding scheme is determined by hardware switches and cables.

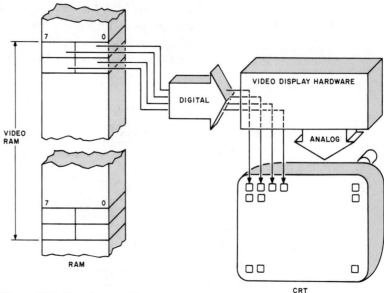

Figure 3.21: Mapping to video screen.

The subroutine must compute the address of the appropriate nibble in the screen RAM and drop the correct color code in it. Because the memory is byte-oriented, the process is somewhat complicated.

The subroutine first computes the position of the appropriate nibble counting from the beginning of the screen RAM. This is Y times the number of pixels per line (256) plus X. We actually get this by moving Y into BH (the upper byte of BX) and X into BL (the lower byte of BX). Dividing this total nibble count in half gives the offset for the byte address. Notice that shift arithmetic right (SAR) is used to perform the division. *Don't use the DIVide instruction for such purposes because it would take much longer.* The byte offset ends up in the BX register. The data segment is assumed to point to the beginning of the screen, and so the addressing mode [BX] can be used to access the correct byte.

The nibble can be in two possible positions within the byte. If the nibble count is even, then the nibble will be in the lower half of the byte, and if it is odd, then the nibble will be in the upper half of the byte. By ANDing the nibble count with 1, we get the nibble position within the byte (0 = lower and 1 = upper). This position number ends up in the DI register which is used as an index for two lookup tables, MASK and COLOR. The MASK and COLOR tables are set up previously by the SETCOLOR routine (not shown) which sets the color for subsequent plotting. There are two steps to putting the color code into place. First the appropriate nibble must be cleared. This is done by ANDing it with the correct mask: binary 11110000 for the lower nibble and 00001111 binary for the upper nibble. These are contained in MASK[0] and MASK[1], respectively. Next it must be ORed with the shifted color code. This is contained in the appropriate entry of the COLOR table. For example, if the color code is 5, then COLOR[0] will contain 00000101 and COLOR[1] will contain 01010000. See the figure below for an example.

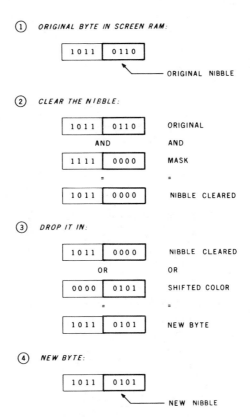

Figure 3.22: Putting color code into place.

The program is somewhat tricky because the Y value is not actually multiplied by 256; instead it is put into the upper byte of BX. This trickiness is excusable because the program must run as fast as possible to be able to draw pictures as fast as possible. The subroutine will take about 107 clock cycles. However, it might actually take more clock cycles because the BIU might not be able to fetch instructions as fast as the EU can process them. With a clock frequency of 5 megahertz, this is about 21.4 microseconds. About 46729 points can be plotted per second. There will be other software involved, so this is only a maximum rate. If a picture contains 50 line segments of 100 points each, then the overhead associated with this point plotting would be .11 seconds.

It is possible to improve this program by about 10 percent by loading both X and Y at the same time with the disadvantage of making it even trickier. This can be done by replacing the first two instructions by the instruction:

```
MOV        BX,XCRD
```

provided that YCRD is the next byte in memory after XCRD.

The figure below shows an equivalent 8080/8085 subprogram. The MASK and COLOR tables are merged to improve the speed. This was not necessary with the 8086/8088 program (perhaps we could have saved a couple of clock cycles). It will take about 161 clock cycles, which is about 32.2 microseconds with the same clock frequency of 5 MHz. This means that the 8080/8085 is approximately 50 percent slower than the 8086/8088. In this case, only 31056 points can be plotted per second. The 8080/8085 requires 33 bytes of memory as opposed to 29 bytes for the 8086/8088 program. Thus, the 8080/8085 takes up 14 percent more room.

Notice how much harder it is to program the 8080/8085. Both the 16-bit shift right and the 16-bit addition are much more awkward. The real saving with the 16-bit machines will be in programmer effort and translator efficiency. The 8086/8088 assembly language works at a slightly higher level than 8080/8085 assembly language, producing many more bytes per instruction as well as accomplishing more per instruction. This is partly due to the more extensive addressing modes available on the 8086/8088.

```
0000              0000              ORG    3000H
3000 00           0010 XCRD    DB     0
3001 00           0020 YCRD    DB     0
3002              0030 MASK    DS     4
3006    F800      0040 SCREEN  EQU    0F800H
3006              0050                           ; ROUTINE: DOT
3006              0060                           ;
3006              0070                           ; THIS IS AN EQUIVALENT 8080/8085
3006              0075                           ; ROUTINE
3006              0080                           ;
3006 AF           0090 DOT     XRA    A          ; CLEAR THE CARRY
3007 3A 01 30     0100         LDA    YCRD       ; GET Y-COORDINATE
300A 1F           0110         RAR               ; DIVIDE BY 2
300B 67           0120         MOV    H,A        ; UPPER HALF OF BYTE OFFSET
300C 3A 00 30     0130         LDA    XCRD       ; GET X-COORDINATE
300F 4F           0140         MOV    C,A        ; SAVE IT
3010 1F           0150         RAR               ; DIVIDE BY 2
3011 6F           0160         MOV    L,A        ; LOWER HALF OF BYTE OFFSET
3012 11 00 F8     0170         LXI    D,SCREEN
3015 19           0180         DAD    D          ; ADD TO SCREEN ADDRESS
3016 EB           0190         XCHG              ; DE POINTS TO BYTE IN VIDEO RAM
3017 79           0200         MOV    A,C        ; GET NIBBLE COUNT AGAIN
3018 E6 01        0210         ANI    1          ; JUST LOWEST BIT
301A 87           0220         ADD    A          ; DOUBLE IT
301B 4F           0230         MOV    C,A        ; LOWER PART OF BC
```

```
301C  06 00      0240        MVI    B,0      ; UPPER PART OF BC
301E  21 02 30   0250        LXI    H,MASK   ; ADD TO MASK ADDRESS
3021  09         0260        DAD    B        ; HL POINTS TO MASK
3022  1A         0270        LDAX   D        ; GET BYTE FROM MEMORY
3023  A6         0280        ANA    M        ; PUT A HOLE IN IT
3024  23         0290        INX    H        ; HL POINTS TO COLOR
3025  B6         0300        ORA    M        ; INSERT THE COLOR
3026  12         0310        STAX   D        ; PUT IT BACK
3027  C9         0320        RET             ; RETURN
3028             0330        END
```

ERRORS THIS ASSEMBLY   0000

Figure 3.23: Equivalent 8080/8085 program.

CONCLUSION

We have explored many facets of the 16-bit Intel 8086 and 8088 microprocessor chips. We have seen their relationship to each other and to the earlier 8-bit Intel 8080 and 8085 processor chips. We have also compared them with their 16-bit rivals, the Motorola MC68000 and the Zilog Z8000. We have described their internal structure including their pipelining architecture, their dual processors on a single chip design, and their 16-bit register set. We have shown how these chips are "wired" to the outside world (signals and pinouts). Finally, we have discussed their common instruction set which includes 8-bit, 16-bit, and binary-coded decimal arithmetic and logical operations (with signed and unsigned multiplication and division); a complete set of string operations; and special instructions (LOCK and ESCAPE) for multiprocessor and coprocessor environments. We have given some short example programs here, and in Chapter 7 we give a whole sequence of example programs.

In the next three chapters we will discuss the various chips needed to make a high-performance microcomputer based on the 8086 and 8088 processor chips. We will start with the powerful 8087 Numeric Data Processor in Chapter 4 and the amazing 8089 Input/Output Processor in Chapter 5.

Chapter 4

The 8087 Numeric Data Processor

In this chapter, we discuss the 8087 Numeric Data Processor (NDP). The figure below shows its pinouts and internal structure and how it may be attached to an 8086/8088 CPU. In Chapter 2 we saw how it fit into a block diagram of both a 16-bit 8086-based and an 8-bit 8088-based computer.

The 8087 NDP extends the 8086/8088 instruction set to provide serious ''number crunching'' capability. It serves as a coprocessor attached to an 8086/8088, effectively adding eight 80-bit floating-point registers to the 8086/8088 register set. It uses its own instruction queue to monitor the 8086/8088 instruction stream, executing only those instructions intended for it and ignoring the instructions intended for the 8086/8088 CPU. It requires the same type of timing, power, and bus structure as the 8086/8088/8089 in maximum mode so that it can, indeed, share a bus structure with an 8086/8088 CPU in maximum mode. The 8087 NDP instructions include a full set of arithmetic functions as well as a powerful core of exponential, logarithmic, and trigonometric functions. It uses a common 80-bit internal floating-point number format to handle seven different useful external formats. (Compare this to the popular 9511 Arithmetic Processing Unit which has a maximum size of 32 bits for its floating-point data.) We shall begin with a discussion of how numbers are represented in a computer, and then we shall detail how the 8087 NDP handles these representations.

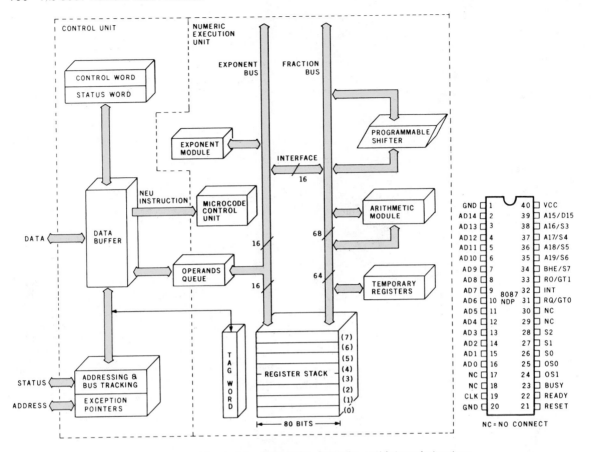

Figure 4.1a: 8087 NDP—pinouts and internal structure.

DEALING WITH NUMBERS

There are two types of numbers which normally occur in a computational environment: integers and real numbers. Although integers are a subset of the reals, a computer has to deal with these two types of numbers in fundamentally different ways. Integers are relatively easy for computers to deal with. Today's general-purpose microprocessor chips are all designed to handle integers using the popular two's complement binary number representation. They can even easily deal with very long integers by breaking them into smaller units. This is called multiple precision arithmetic. Real numbers, however, are more difficult. For one thing, most of them can never be accurately represented! Floating point representation provides an excellent practical *approximation* scheme for real numbers. Floating-point representation is really just a variation of the scientific notation you see on calculator displays and computer readouts. With this system, there are three parts to the representation of a number: the sign, the exponent, and the mantissa. We will first explain why this is necessary, and then show how it works. For starters, consider the following example of scientific notation:

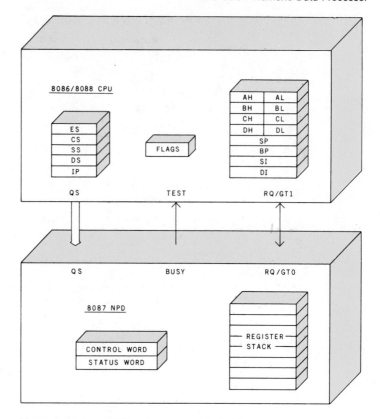

Figure 4.1b: 8087 NDP—connections to CPU.

4.1468E2

In this example the sign is positive (a missing sign indicates that it is positive), the mantissa is 4.1468, and the exponent is 2. The true value associated with this representation is obtained by the following expression:

$$4.1468 \times 10^2 = 414.68$$

Two Major Considerations   There are two essential problems in representing numbers: precision and range.

Precision is the accuracy of a representation. In the floating-point system, the mantissa is in charge of precision. It holds the *significant* digits of the number no matter where the decimal place is located. (In fact, this part is often called the significand.) To make a floating-point representation scheme more precise, you just allot more digits to the mantissa.

Precision is not a problem with integers, because every integer is precisely represented by two's complement arithmetic. Representing real numbers precisely is a problem because most of them (even most ''small'' real numbers) have an infinite number of digits, thus requiring a machine with an infinite number of components! Since our machines only allot a finite number of digits for precision, representations for real numbers are necessarily *approximations*.

There are further complications. Numbers such as the square root of 2, e, and pi have an infinite number of digits in any base, and thus never can be represented precisely. However, there are other numbers which require a finite number of digits in one base but not in another. For example, 2/3 in base 10 arithmetic is:

0.666...

which goes on forever, but in base 3 arithmetic, it is just:

0.2

which can be represented by one digit. A real problem is the number 1/10 which can be precisely represented as .1 in the base 10 arithmetic used by programmers, but requires an infinite number of digits in the binary used by the computer. The programmer will lose precision on a number which is entered precisely!

Range has to do with how large or small a number you can represent. With integers, the range depends on the number of bits you use. For example, if you only have 16 bits, then the smallest and largest numbers you can represent in two's complement arithmetic are −32768 and + 32767, respectively. To represent all integers would require an infinite number of digits, and hence this also would require a machine with an infinite number of components.[1] Thus, even integers have to have a restricted range. In the floating-point notation, the exponent is in charge of range. By separating problems of range from problems of precision, floating-point notation is able to obtain very large ranges with reasonable precision. The range is still finite because only a finite number of digits can be allotted to the exponent, but these digits can indicate an extremely large range in a very compact manner.

We have seen that since a computer can allot only a finite number of bits for the mantissa and the exponent, the precision and the range will be

---

[1]You would need to build a computer which could construct its own memory cells as it needed them, but even then it would take an infinite amount of time to ''construct'' just one real number such as pi or e.

both restricted. A third part of the representation is the sign. In the floating-point system, the sign is separate and no longer meshed in with the digits of the number as it is in two's complement arithmetic.

Implementing Floating-Point Notation

There are a number of schemes for implementing floating-point arithmetic. Intel uses the same method as the proposed IEEE standard.[2] To see how this works, let's look again at decimal scientific notation. For example, in decimal scientific notation the number 414.68 is *normally* written as:

4.1468E2

and the number − .00345 is *normally* written as:

− 3.45E − 3

In each case the number consists of a sign (not present, but understood for positive numbers), a mantissa, and an exponent. The E is short for "exponent" and can be read as "times ten to the ."

The *normal* position for the decimal place in the mantissa is to the right of the first significant digit. When it is in this position, the number is said to be in *normalized form*.

Sometimes calculations with these numbers produce results which are not in normalized form. *Normalization* can be accomplished by shifting the decimal point and at the same time incrementing or decrementing the exponent. For example, multiplying the above two numbers yields:

(4.1468E2)(− 3.45E − 3) = 14.30646E − 1

For this example, we shift once to the left and, at the same time, increment the exponent once:

14.30646E − 1 = 1.430646E0.

Zero is a special case, for there is no way to normalize it. It can be represented by a zero mantissa. The exponent in this case is quite arbitrary, although there are certain conventions depending upon the particular implementation.

In contrast to our usual scientific notation which uses a base of 10,

[2]"A Proposed Standard for Binary Floating-Point Arithmetic," *Computer* (March, 1981), IEEE.

computers use a base of 2 both for the base of the exponential expression and for the numerical representation of the mantissa and the exponent. For example, the decimal number 5.325 which can be written in powers of 2 as:

$$4 + 1 + 1/4 + 1/8 = 101.011 \text{ (in binary)}$$

is written in "binary" scientific notion as:

$$+ 1.01011E2$$

This time the E should be read "times 2 to the", and incrementing or decrementing the exponent will shift the binary point appropriately.

When a binary floating-point number is stored in the machine, 1 bit is used to store the sign, several bits to store the mantissa, and several bits to store the exponent. It is customary to store the sign bits first, followed by the exponent bits, followed by the bits of the mantissa. Since the exponent can be either a negative or a nonnegative integer, you might think that it is stored in two's complement form. This, however, is not usually the case. The standard way is to add a special constant called a *bias* before storing the exponent. The number actually stored is called the *biased exponent*. Conversely, if you are given the representation (the biased exponent), then to get the true value you must subtract this bias. The bias is a number about halfway through the range of possible representations for exponents. This way, there are about as many possible negative as positive exponents.

As an example of all this let's look at how Intel represents real numbers in the 8087 NDP registers. This particular format is called *temporary real* by Intel. It is the way all of its data types are stored inside the NDP. See the figure below for a picture of this format.

The temporary real format requires 80 bits: 1 bit for the sign, 15 bits for the exponent, and 64 bits for the mantissa, giving it 64 bits of precision. The bias is $2^{14} - 1 = 16383$. The smallest possible positive number is 2^{-16382}, which is approximately 3.36×10^{-4932}, and the largest possible positive number is about 2^{16384}, which is approximately 1.19×10^{4932}.

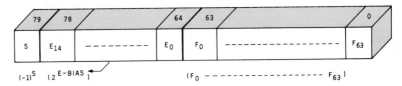

Figure 4.2: The internal format used by the 8087 NDP.

To get some idea of the magnitude of the range for the 8087 NDP's floating-point number system, consider that the size of the universe has, according to fairly recent theory, a radius of roughly 13 billion light years. This is a radius of about 1.23E28 centimeters or a volume of about 7.77E84 cubic centimeters. It would take about 1E122 electrons to fill this whole volume. These numbers are tiny in comparison with the range available with the NDP temporary real format. In contrast, mathematicians can easily come up with numbers which would strain the capabilities of the 8087 NDP number representation. For example, many calculators have a *factorial key* which is often labeled with the symbol n!. This function gives the total number of different ways (permutations) that n things can be arranged in order. Most calculators can only handle up to 69!. With the 8087 NDP, you can "only" go as high as 1754! ! It would take the 8087 less than a tenth of second to actually compute this directly (less time than required by a calculator to do 69!).

It is also important to understand the degree of precision available to the 8087 NDP. With 64 binary digits, you have accuracy of one part in 2^{64}. This is about the ratio of the diameter of a hydrogen atom to the circumference of the moon's orbit around the earth. Of course, such accuracy is not usually needed for final results, but it may be essential during intermediate steps of a lengthy calculation, because accuracy is usually lost at every step of such calculations.

If you look very carefully at the specifications for the temporary real format on the 8087 NDP, you will find that larger and smaller numbers can be represented than indicated. Intel has reserved these very large and very small "numbers" for other purposes. Some of them are even called NANs which stands for "not a number"! There will be more on this in the section on the NDP data types.

The rules or algorithms for performing floating-point arithmetic operations are much more complicated than those for two's complement operations. Even addition and subtraction require many more steps because the numbers have to be adjusted so that they have the same exponent before they can be added or subtracted, and the result has to be normalized before completion of the process. Intel has developed software packages which perform these operations using an 8080, 8085 or 8086/8088 CPU, but these run fairly slowly. For example, it takes about 1600 microseconds for an 8086 to perform an 80-bit, floating-point multiplication in software. Intel introduced a board (the iSBC 310 High-Speed Math Unit) which performs about ten times faster, and a single-chip arithmetic processor (the 8232) which then reduced the size, but achieved about the same performance as the single board version. The 8232 running at 5 megahertz would take about 40 microseconds to do a 32-bit or 64-bit floating-point multiplication. It has now introduced its new 8087 Numeric Processor to achieve another order of magnitude of performance. In the case of floating-point multiplication, the improvement is by about a factor of 2 with about 19 microseconds for such a multiplication on the 8087 NDP.

By putting such power in such a small package, Intel has opened up the way for some interesting applications such as position and orientation control of robots, and powerful graphics terminals with their own built-in, picture-transformation capabilities.

THE 8087 NDP AS A COPROCESSOR

The 8087 Numeric Data Processor acts as a coprocessor. That is, it shares: 1) the same bus and 2) the same instruction stream with the CPU.

Since the NDP requires the same type of timing, power, and bus structure as the 8086/8088/8089 in maximum mode, it can, indeed, share a bus structure with an 8086/8088 CPU in maximum mode. We will show later how to hook these two together (and an additional 8089 IOP).

The NDP instructions are mixed in, like raisins in bread, with the CPU instruction stream. However, like a pair of picky children, the CPU only eats the bread and the NDP only eats the raisins. The NDP knows which instructions to "eat" because all its instructions begin with a form of the 8086/8088 ESCAPE instruction (not to be confused with the ASCII escape code). The ESCAPE instruction is a dummy instruction for the 8086/8088 with a dummy operand which can be specified with any of the 24 addressing modes, and another dummy operand which is a register. The first byte of the ESCAPE instruction always has the same upper 5 bits (11011), but the lower 3 bits contain code for the NDP. The next byte contains 3 more bits of code (bits 3 through 5 which is the dummy register reference) for the NDP. It also contains addressing information for a possibie operand. If there is no operand, then other bits in this byte can be used as part of the code for the instruction. The figure below shows a typical instruction for the NDP.

Every instruction read by the CPU is also read by the NDP. When one of these ESCAPE instructions is read by the CPU, the NDP realizes that it will soon have to operate. It grabs the lower 3 bits of the ESCAPE byte and lets the CPU fetch the next byte. The NDP grabs 3 more bits from this byte. It now knows exactly what operation to perform. It then lets the CPU get the first part (byte or word, depending on the size of the data bus) of the operand using the indicated addressing mode. Then the CPU finally turns the bus over to the NDP, which fetches extra bytes of data as necessary, does its computations, and puts data back on the bus.

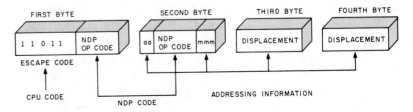

Figure 4.3: Typical NDP instruction.

**THE 8087 NDP AS
AN EXTENSION OF
THE 8086/8088
In Terms of Software**

The 8087 Numeric Data Processor is an extension of an 8086 or an 8088 in terms of software, architecture, hardware, and marketing.

The 8087 NDP extends the instruction set of the 8086/8088 to include floating-point operations. These new instructions implement Intel's floating-point package in hardware, thus providing a much better method for executing these floating-point algorithms. That is, these routines can now be executed at very high speeds. Intel estimates that the 8087 executes floating-point operations up to about *100 times* faster than possible by an 8086 CPU executing its software package. See the table below for a speed comparison of an 8087 against the 8086 running the software floating-point package. In both cases, the processors were running at 5 megahertz.

INSTRUCTION	APPROXIMATE EXECUTION TIME (MICROSECONDS)	
	8087	8086
ADD SIGN-MAGNITUDE	14	1600
SUBTRACT SIGN-MAGNITUDE	18	1600
MULTIPLY (SINGLE PRECISION)	19	1600
MULTIPLY (DOUBLE PRECISION)	27	2100
DIVIDE	39	3200
COMPARE	9	1300
LOAD (DOUBLE PRECISION)	10	1700
STORE (DOUBLE PRECISION)	21	1200
SQUARE ROOT	36	19600
TANGENT	90	13000
EXPONENTIATION	100	17100

Table 4.1: Speed comparison of 8086 with 8087.

**In Terms of
Architecture**

The 8087 NDP extends the register set of the 8086/8088 CPU. The CPU registers are on one chip (the 8086/8088) and eight 80-bit floating-point registers on the other chip (the 8087). See figure 4.4 for a programmer's view of this extended register set. These registers store numbers in the *temporary real* format discussed above.

The eight registers are organized as a stack. A stack is perhaps the best way to organize data for evaluating complex algebraic expressions. The 8087 NDP also has some more registers: a 16-bit status register, a 16-bit mode register, an 8-bit tag register, and four 16-bit registers to save instruction and data pointers for exception handling. Exception handling will be explained later.

iAPX 86/20, 88/20

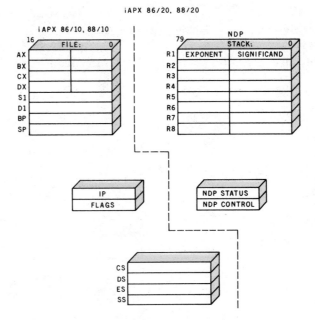

Figure 4.4: Extended register set of the iAPX 86/20.

In Terms of Hardware

The NDP is a hardware extension because it will not run by itself. That is, it needs to have an 8086 or 8088 to run the data, address, and control buses which feed it instructions and operands. Figure 4.5 shows how the 8087 NDP can be attached to an 8086/8088 CPU. In Chapter 2 we saw how it fit into a 16-bit 8086-based and an 8-bit 8088-based computer.

There are several lines running directly between the NDP and the CPU: the test-busy signal, a request/grant (RQ/GT0) line, and the queue status (QS1, QS0) signals. The exact purpose of these lines is as follows.

The test input pin of the 8086/8088 is connected to the busy output pin of the NDP. This allows the 8086/8088 to use the WAIT instruction to synchronize its activity with the NDP. The proper way to do this (at least with Intel's software) is for the assembler to automatically generate a WAIT instruction before each NDP instruction and for the programmer to put an FWAIT instruction in the program following each NDP instruction which deposits data in memory for immediate use by the CPU. If the software emulation package is being used instead of the 8087 NDP, then the numeric instruction is translated as a subroutine call (via an interrupt with no WAIT) and the FWAIT is translated as an NOP (no operation). If the 8087 NDP is being used, then the numeric instruction gets translated to the indicated NDP numeric operation (with the

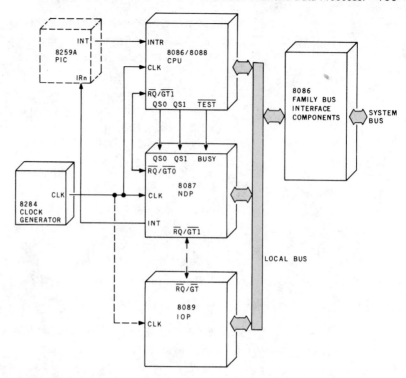

Figure 4.5: 8087 NDP—8089 IOP—8086 CPU cluster.

preceding WAIT) and the FWAIT instruction is translated as the CPU
WAIT instruction. While the 8087 NDP is executing a numeric
operation, it puts a 1 on its busy pin (hence the test pin of the CPU is
forced to a 1). While the 8086/8088 CPU executes a WAIT instruction, it
halts its activity until its test pin is returned to its normal state (0). Thus,
the sequence of an NDP numeric instruction followed by a CPU WAIT
will cause the CPU to call the NDP and then wait until the NDP has
finished before proceeding.

The request/grant line RQ/GT0 is used by the NDP to gain control
of the bus which is *shared* by the NDP and CPU. This request/grant on
the NDP line must be connected to one of the request/grant lines of the
CPU. This is a two-way communication line. A signal (request) from the
NDP to the CPU indicates that the NDP wants to use the bus. Before the
NDP can take the bus it must wait for a return signal (grant) from the
CPU. When the NDP finishes with the bus it sends a signal back to the
CPU on this same line to indicate that it is finished with the bus. In this
protocol, the CPU is the master and the NDP is the slave. That is, the
slave is always the one which requests the bus, and the master is always
the one which grants the bus as soon as it can after such a request.

There is another request/grant line (RQ/GT1) on the NDP which
may be used by other processors to request the bus from the CPU/NDP

combination! In this case, the extra device communicates with the NDP over the second request/grant line (RQ/GT1) and the NDP relays messages over the first request/grant line (RQ/GT0) to and from the CPU.

There are two queue status pins, QS1 and QS0. These help the NDP keep its instruction queue synchronized with the CPUs. The 2 bits are used to encode four possible states: 00 = no operation, 01 = first byte of instruction, 10 = empty the queue, and 11 = subsequent byte of an instruction.

In Terms of Marketing

The NDP must be considered an extension of the 8086/8088 because you cannot presently buy it alone. You must buy it as part of a two- or three-chip set. Intel uses the Intel Advanced Processor Architecture (iAPX) designation to specify its various processor chip sets. For example, iAPX 86/20 stands for the two-chip set consisting of an 8086 CPU and an 8087 NDP; iAPX 88/20 stands for the two-chip set consisting of the 8088 CPU and the 8087 NDP; and iAPX 86/21 stands for the three-chip set consisting of an 8086 CPU, an 8087 NDP, and an 8089 IOP. The table below shows how all of these chip sets are numbered.

		(includes)		
	8086 CPU	8088 CPU	8089 IOP	8087 NDP
iAPX 86/10	yes			
iAPX/86/11	yes		yes	
iAPX 86/20	yes			yes
iAPX 86/21	yes		yes	yes
iAPX 88/10		yes		
iAPX 88/11		yes	yes	
iAPX 88/20		yes		yes
iAPX 88/21		yes	yes	yes

Table 4.2: Numbering for Intel's chip sets.

8087 NDP DATA TYPES

The 8087 NDP is designed to deal with seven different data types. These include three lengths of integers, one type of signed, packed, BCD integers, and three types of floating-point representations. The real numbers are in accordance with the proposed IEEE floating-point standards. All seven types are stored internally in an 80-bit format Intel calls *temporary real* that was discussed above. All data types can be stored accurately in this format.

No matter what the format, every time a number is fetched from memory, it is converted from the desired format (word integer, short integer, long integer, packed BCD, short real, long real, or temporary real) in memory to the temporary real format used internally. Similarly, each time a number is stored, it is converted from the internal, temporary real format to the desired format in memory.

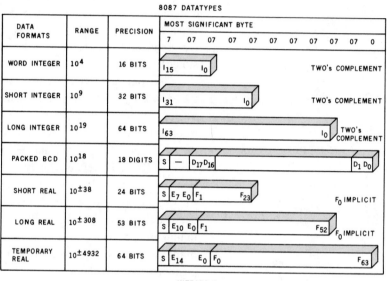

Figure 4.6: The 8087 data types.

The integer formats use two's complement representation. *Word integer* is 16 bits long, *short integer* is 32 bits long, and *long integer* is 64 bits long.

The packed BCD notation has 18 decimal digits and a sign. Each digit is encoded in a 4-bit nibble. This format is especially useful for business applications where decimal precision is essential. It allows completely precise representation of dollar amounts as high as $9,999,999,999,999,999.99 (one cent less than 10 thousand trillion dollars).

There are three different floating-point formats used by the 8087: short real, long real, and temporary real.

The short real format requires 32 bits: 1 bit for the sign, 8 bits for the exponent, and 23 bits for the mantissa. The bias is $2^7 - 1 = 127$. The biased exponents (stored representation of the exponents) range from 1 to 254. The smallest possible positive number is 2^{-126}, which is approximately 1.175×10^{-38}, and the largest possible positive number is about 2^{128}, which is approximately 3.40×10^{38}. There are actually 24 binary digits of precision, for the first significant digit (always a 1) is not stored. Only the 23 bits to the right of the point are stored. With 24 bits for the mantissa, you get about seven and a half decimal digits of precision. Zero is a very special case because it cannot be normalized, and a 0 mantissa is not possible because of the understood digit which is always 1. Instead, 0 is approximated by a very small number, smaller than the permissible range. In this case an exponent of -127 (biased exponent $= 0$) is used. The mantissa is chosen to be 1.0 which is represented by all 0s (remember that the first significant digit is not stored). The sign can be either positive or negative.

The long real format requires 64 bits: 1 bit for the sign, 11 bits for the exponent, and 52 bits for the mantissa. The bias is $2^{10} - 1 = 1023$. The biased exponent ranges from 1 to 2046. The smallest possible positive number is 2^{-1022}, which is approximately 2.23×10^{-308}, and the largest possible positive number is about 2^{1024}, which is approximately 1.80×10^{308}. There are actually 53 binary digits of precision, for the first significant digit (always a 1) is not stored. Only the 52 bits to the right of the point are stored. With this many bits, you get almost 15 decimal digits of precision. In this case also, 0 is represented by a minimum exponent (-1023 represented by a biased exponent of 0), the **mantissa is 1.0, which is represented by all 0s, and the sign is either** positive or negative.

We have already discussed the temporary real format. For completeness, let's also include it here. Recall that the temporary real format requires 80 bits: 1 bit for the sign, 15 bits for the exponent, and 64 bits for the mantissa. The bias is $2^{14} - 1 = 16383$. The biased exponent ranges from 1 to 16382. The smallest possible positive number is 2^{-16382}, which is approximately 3.36×10^{-4932}, and the largest possible positive number is about 2^{16384}, which is approximately 1.19×10^{4932}. This format is different from the others in that all bits of the mantissa are actually stored. The 64 bits of precision yield more than 18 decimal digits of precision. In this case 0 can be represented with a 0 **mantissa (and it is), but the exponent is also the minimum (-16383),** which when biased is 0. As with the other real formats, the sign for 0 can be positive or negative.

Associated with each data type are certain patterns which do not correspond to normalized real numbers. The patterns which do correspond to normalized floating-point representations are called *normals*. Among the ones which are not normal there are: denormals, unnormals, infinities, NANs (for ''not a number''), and indefinite. We will only briefly describe these here. Read the *Numerics Supplement* of *The 8086 Family User's Manual* for a more complete discussion. These special patterns either have maximum-size exponents, that is, one larger than allowed for real numbers, or minimum-size exponents (stored as a biased exponent 0). The unnormals and denormals correspond to underflow situations allowing the NDP to go through several stages of alert as it begins to compute numbers too small to handle. Infinity is handled in two different ways depending upon a bit in the control word. NANs are useful for debugging purposes. There are enough of them to leave quite a trail when something goes wrong. Indefinite is a useful answer with certain conditions such as 0 divided by 0. These extra ''numbers'' provide the NDP with a very powerful arsenal for handling all sorts of abnormal (or unreal) situations such as division by 0, overflow, and underflow.

It is interesting to compare the 8087 NDP with a large, mainframe computer such as a Control Data Corporation Cyber. The Cyber's central processor has three different types of registers (as shown in the figure below): address (A), index (B), and data (X). There are eight of each type. The address registers are 18 bits (as compared with the larger 20-bit addressing capability of the iAPX chips), the B registers are also 18 bits, and the data registers are 60 bits (as compared with the 80-bit NDP registers). The B registers are used to hold small numbers such as loop indices. The X registers hold either integer or floating-point numbers. The integer format is called *one's complement*. The rules are similar to, but slightly different from those for two's complement arithmetic. In particular, negatives are taken by a straight one's complement, and addition is done by adding as usual, and then bringing the carry out of the leftmost digit all the way around to add to the rightmost digit! The floating-point notation uses all 60 bits, with 1 bit for the sign, 11 bits for the exponent, and 48 bits for the mantissa. This is comparable to the 64-bit long real format on the 8087 NDP. Although the smaller and more modern Intel machine has larger addressing and data capabilities, the large mainframes still have a speed advantage. For example, a floating-point multiplication which takes about 19.4 microseconds on the 8087 NDP will take about 1 microsecond on the Cyber! However, a complete Cyber system might take up about 260 square feet of floor space (700 square feet if you include space needed for power, air conditioning, and things like spare parts), weigh about 23,000 pounds, require about 60,000 watts of power, and lease at about $9,500 per month with an additional $8,600 per month for maintenance. In comparison, a complete Intel NDP-CPU–based system might weigh about 120 pounds, take up about 15 square feet of floor space (or fit on a table top), consume a couple of hundred watts of power, and cost about $5,000.

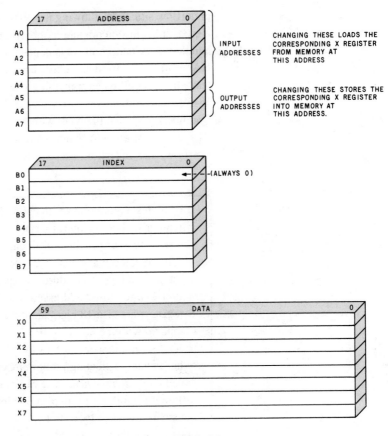

Figure 4.7: The registers for the CDC Cyber.

USING THE NDP STACK

A stack is like an in-box on a desk. It is a convenient way to temporarily store items that you are about to work on. In such a storage system, the last item *in* is the first item *out*. Calculators such as those manufactured by Hewlett Packard that use reverse Polish notation use a stack. One can quickly get used to working with such a system and can easily learn how to evaluate algebraic expressions from the inside out, "pushing" intermediate results onto the stack until they are needed.

A *stack* is a *data structure*. That is, there are rules for allotting storage to data and rules for accessing that data. With a stack, the data is stored in consecutively numbered locations (in this case consecutive NDP registers). Another location, called the stack pointer, contains the address of one of these data locations. The location "pointed to" by the stack pointer is called the *top of stack*. This location and the locations "beneath" it are considered part of the stack and locations "above" are considered not to belong to the stack. The locations are normally numbered in increasing order from the top of the stack toward the locations beneath it.

The basic operations for accessing data are called *push* and *pop*. Push works as follows: It has one operand which is a source. The stack pointer is first decremented so that it points to the location "above" the previous top of stack, and then data is transferred from the source to this new top of stack. Pop works as follows: It has one operand which is a destination. Data is first transferred from the top of stack to the destination, and then the stack pointer is incremented so that it now points to the new top of stack which is "beneath" the previous top of stack. The previous top of stack is no longer considered to be a part of the stack, and thus the stack has one less element. See the figure below for a picture of how these two operations behave.

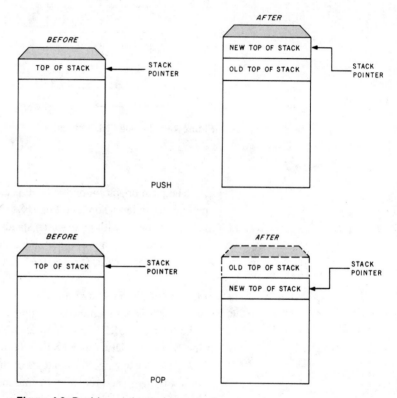

Figure 4.8: Pushing and popping a stack.

Just as it is dangerous to pile too many items on an in-box, there are hazards to pushing too many items on a stack because of memory limits. The NDP stack has only enough room for eight items. This is normally quite enough for its job. In fact, Hewlett Packard calculators have only four locations on their stack.

The stacks in the NDP and the RPN calculators are used for storing intermediate results while evaluating algebraic expressions. Stacks are used by other devices for other purposes. For example, the CPU uses a stack to save the return address during subroutine calls.

For the NDP, the stack is numbered relative to the top of the stack. The top of the stack is denoted by ST(0) or just ST, and the locations "beneath" are denoted by ST(1), ST(2), . . ., ST(7) down from the top. See the figure below.

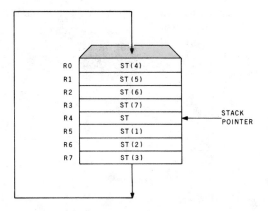

Figure 4.9: The 8087 NDP stack.

The push operation on the NDP is called LoaD (FLD) and the pop operation is called STore and Pop (FSTP). (Note: Every NDP instruction mnemonic begins with an *F* which stands, naturally enough, for *F*loating point.) There are plenty of other operations, so what we really have is an *extension* of the idea of stack in the strict sense described above. For example, there is an operation called STore (FST) in which the contents of the top of the stack are transferred to the indicated destination, but the stack pointer is not incremented. Some of the additional stack operations for the NDP are: eXCHange (FXCH), INCrement STack Pointer (FINCSTP), and DECrement STack Pointer (FDECSTP). EXCHange allows you to exchange the contents of the top of the stack with any other item in the stack, and the other operations allow you to adjust the stack pointer without actually transferring any data.

Operations such as addition, subtraction, multiplication, and division which require two *input arguments* come in several different forms. If they are specified with no operand, then the two *inputs* are the top two items on the stack, ST and ST(1). After the operation is performed with these two inputs, the stack is popped, and the result is placed in the new top of stack. In essence, the two operands are replaced by the one result. This is considered a classical stack operation. It is essentially what happens when a reverse polish calculator performs a two-operand operation.

If there is just one operand, then this operand is one of the inputs and the other input is the top of the stack. The result replaces the top of the stack.

If there are two operands, then they must both be NDP registers. One of them must be the top of the stack and the other can be any other NDP register. There are three different cases: 1) the source is ST and the destination is ST(i), 2) the source is ST(i) and the destination is ST, and 3) the source is ST and the destination is ST(i) and the stack is popped. In the first two cases the source is not affected, but in the third case, the source (ST) is destroyed in the subsequent pop. All of these are quite useful, making unnecessary most of the stack manipulation operations such as *roll up* and *roll down* which can be found on the reverse polish notation calculators.

Some of the most useful features are the special *reverse* forms of the subtraction and division algorithms. In the case of division, in the normal form, the source is divided *into* the destination, and in the reverse form, the source is divided *by* the destination. In both cases the result is placed in the destination. Having this feature cuts down on the need for the stack manipulation operation often called *swap* in which the top two items on the stack are exchanged. The overhead for running the reverse forms of these operations is only one or two clock cycles, while the exchange (the NDP's implementation of a swap) takes 12 clock cycles.

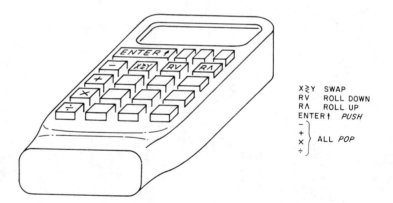

Figure 4.10: RPN stack operations.

8087 NDP INSTRUCTION SET

The 8087 NDP has 48 different instruction types. These instructions include data transfer and conversion, comparison, four basic arithmetic operations, square root, scaling, rounding, absolute value, trigonometric functions, exponentials and logarithms, special constants, and processor control. See table 4.3 for a summary of the 8087 NDP instruction set.

Table 4.3

MNEMONIC		DESCRIPTION
FLD	source	Floating point LoaD from memory to ST
FST	destination	Floating point STore from ST to memory
FSTP	destination	Floating point STore and Pop from ST to memory
FXCH	source	Floating point eXCHange ST(i) and ST
FCOM		Floating point COMpare ST(1) to ST
FCOM	source	Floating point COMpare memory to ST or ST(i) to ST
FCOMP		Floating point COMpare and Pop ST(1) to ST
FCOMP	source	Floating point COMpare and Pop memory to ST or ST(i) to ST
FCOMPP		Floating point COMpare and Pop twice ST(1) to ST
FTST		Floating point TeST ST
FXAM		Floating point eXAMine ST
FADD		Floating point ADDition from ST(1) to ST
FADD	source	Floating point ADDition from memory to ST
FADD	destination,source	Floating point ADDition from ST(i) to ST or from ST to ST(i)
FSUB		Floating point SUBtraction from ST(1) to ST
FSUB	source	Floating point SUBtraction from memory to ST

FSUB	destination,source	Floating point SUBtraction from ST(i) to ST or from ST to ST(i)
FSUBR		Floating point Reverse SUBtraction from ST(1) to ST
FSUBR	source	Floating point Reverse SUBtraction from memory to ST
FSUBR	destination,source	Floating point Reverse SUBtraction from ST(i) to ST or from ST to ST(i)
FMUL		Floating point MULtiplication from ST(1) to ST
FMUL	source	Floating point MULtiplication from memory to ST
FMUL	destination,source	Floating point MULtiplication from ST(i) to ST or from ST to ST(i)
FDIV		Floating point DIVision from ST(1) to ST
FDIV	source	Floating point DIVision from memory to ST
FDIV	destination,source	Floating point DIVision from ST(i) to ST or from ST to ST(i)
FDIVR		Floating point Reverse DIVision from ST(1) to ST
FDIVR	source	Floating point Reverse DIVision from memory to ST
FDIVR	destination,source	Floating point Reverse DIVision from ST(i) to ST or from ST to ST(i)
FSQRT		Floating point SQuare RooT of ST
FSCALE		Floating point SCALE of ST by ST(1)
FPREM		Floating point Partial REMainder
FRNDINT		Floating point RouND ST to INTeger
FXTRACT		EXTRACT Floating point components

Table 4.3

FABS	Floating point ABSolute value of ST
FCHS	Floating point CHange Sign of ST
FPTAN	Floating point Partial TANgent of ST
FPATAN	Floating point Partial ArcTANgent
F2XM1	Floating point power 2 minus 1
FYL2X	Floating point Y times Log base 2 of X
FYL2XP1	Floating point Y times Log base 2 of X+1
FLDZ	LoaD Floating point 0.0 into ST
FLD1	LoaD Floating point 1.0 into ST
FLDPI	LoaD Floating point Pi into ST
FLDL2T	LoaD Floating point Logarithm base 2 of 10 into ST
FLDL2E	LoaD Floating point Logarithm base 2 of e into ST
FLDLG2	LoaD Floating point Logarithm base 10 of 2
FLDLN2	LoaD Floating point Logarithm base e of 2
FINIT	INITialize NDP
FENI	ENable Floating point Interrupts
FDISI	DISable Floating point Interrupts
FLDCW	LoaD Floating point Control Word
FSTCW	STore Floating point Control Word
FSTSW	STore Floating point Status Word
FCLEX	CLear Floating point EXceptions
FSTENV	STore Floating point ENVironment
FLDENV	LoaaD Floating point ENVironment
FSAVE	SAVE Floating point state

FRSTOR	ReSTORe Floating point state
FINCSTP	INCrement Floating point Stack Pointer
FDECSTP	DECrement Floating point Stack Pointer
FFREE	FREE ST(i)
FNOP	Floating point No OPeration
FWAIT	CPU WAIT for NDP

Table 4.3: Summary of 8087 NDP instructions.

Notice that in all cases the instructions begin with a CPU ESCAPE instruction as previously discussed. Recall that the ESCAPE instruction (not to be confused with the ASCII escape code) is a dummy instruction for the 8086/8088 with a dummy operand which can be specified with any of the 24 CPU addressing modes. Let's look at the various fields within these instructions. In this context, a *field* is a group of consecutive bits used for a common encoding purpose. See the figure below.

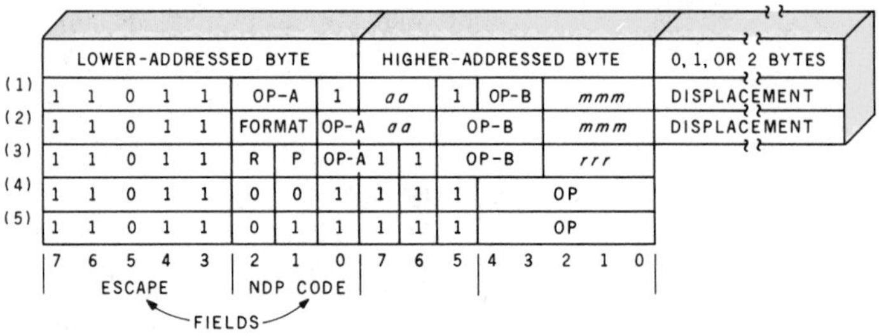

Figure 4.11: Instruction-encoding formats for the 8087.

The first byte of an NDP instruction always has the same upper 5 bits (11011 ESCAPE code), and the lower 3 bits contain code for the NDP. Thus, this byte has two fields: the ESCAPE field and the NDP code field. There are actually five different formats for NDP instructions depending among other things upon how many explicit operands there are. The instructions which do have an operand have their operation code split into two different fields: the first one is contained in the lower 3 bits of the first byte, and the second is contained in bits 3 through 5 of the second byte. This second field is normally the field reserved to designate a second operand (which must be a register) of two-operand CPU instructions. All NDP instructions have at most one (external) operand,

and so the field for the second operand is free to use as part of the operation code (as it is used with many CPU instructions which have only one operand).

Both NDP and CPU instructions which do not reference main memory have a binary 11 in the upper 2 bits of the second byte of the instruction. For CPU instructions, this pattern normally indicates the register addressing mode. That is, the operand is contained in a register. For NDP instructions, this will either mean that the operand or operands are contained in NDP registers, or that there are no operands. The figure above shows how these five possible formats are arranged.

We have already discussed the operations of addition, subtraction, multiplication, and division in the section about using the stack. Of particular note are the time-saving and step-saving reverse forms for the subtraction and division operations.

There is also a set of instructions which push upon the stack the well-used constants 0, 1, pi, and various standard logarithmic constants. To create these in memory and then bring them into the NDP would take vital time during commonplace calculations. Instead, the NDP stores them in silicon!

Although the NDP has 16-bit two's complement integer arithmetic, it is not advisable to use it to process a lot of these integers because it is considerably slower than the CPU with this type of arithmetic. For example, a 16-bit register-to-register addition takes 3 clock cycles on the 8086/8088 CPU, but 85 cycles on the NDP! The reason is, of course, that the NDP is using its 80-bit temporary real format to process these 16-bit quantities (and converting between integer and this format as well)! The real advantage in having the NDP handle such small integers is in mixed-mode computations, that is, computations which involve both real numbers and integers. In fact, because the NDP stores everything in the same internal format, any number of the seven different data types can be easily mixed within one calculation.

Many of the functions, such as SQuare RooT (FSQRT), absolute value (FABS), and the trigonometric and logarithmic functions, cannot have their operands in memory. In fact, they only work with the NDP's current top-of-stack register. This creates the usual bottlenecks associated with a register-oriented machine. However, it is not so bad, at least once the data is inside the NDP, because of the eXCHange (FXCH) instruction which will exchange any NDP register with the top of the stack. For example, to take the absolute value of any NDP register, first exchange that register with the top of the stack, then do the absolute value, and then exchange again. Nothing needs to be gotten rid of to do this; it just takes up a little more space, time, and effort. Thus, the stack can be viewed as a general operand storage area, that is, a scratch pad RAM inside the NDP.

Certain NDP operations such as the trigonometric functions deliver *partial* results, meaning that the operations provided by the NDP are only a *core;* to get the actual functions you must do some preprocessing and postprocessing. For example, the Partial TANgent (FPTAN) function takes its argument from the top of the stack (an angle) and produces two results: X and Y. Y replaces the top of the stack, and then X is pushed onto the stack. Thus, X and Y are now the top two items on the stack. The six standard trigonometric functions: sin, cos, tan, sec, csc, cot are all easily derivable from the quantities X and Y. For example, the tangent is Y/X, which is accomplished with a division operation, the sin is Y/SQR(X * X + Y * Y), and the cos is X/SQR(X * X + Y * Y) (using the Pythagorean theorem). The other three functions are reciprocals of these and can be obtained by reversing the division. There is a further complication: the argument for the FPTAN must be between 0 and pi/4 (0 and 90 degrees), and thus the original angle must be reduced to this range before the FPTAN can be applied. Our second sample program shows how to program these functions. It might be faster to use a lookup table to store values for these functions, but such a table would require a tremendous amount of memory to store all the values possible with this program.

Certain NDP operations are optimized so that they can be easily used to compute other functions. For example, the logarithm operation actually calculates the function Y * LOG 2 X, where X is taken from the top of the stack and Y is the second item on the stack. This is useful for computing arbitrary power functions X**Y (FORTRAN notation). This is computed by the formula:

X**Y = 2**(Y*LOG 2 X)

and thus this expression can be computed in just two steps. Other instructions have been perfected for accuracy. For example, the FYL2XP1 (Y log base 2 of (X + 1)) instruction is useful for getting accurate results for logarithms whose arguments are very close to one.

THE CONTROL AND STATUS WORDS

The *control word* is a 16-bit register in the NDP (see figure 4.12) which allows one to specify such things as the degree of precision, the type of rounding, and even how to treat infinity! The control word also specifies how *exception handling* (error recovery) is to proceed. Exception handling will be discussed in the next subsection. The control word is loaded into the NDP from memory by one of the NDP processor control instructions. Thus the CPU can set up these conditions by putting the appropriate image of the control word in memory and then calling the NDP to pick them up from this image.

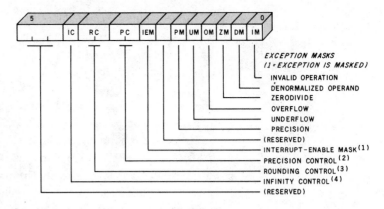

(1) Interrupt-Enable Mask:
    0 = Interrupts Enabled
    1 = Interrupts Disabled (Masked)

(2) Precision Control:
    00 = 24 bits
    01 = (reserved)
    10 = 53 bits
    11 = 64 bits

(3) Rounding Control:
    00 = Round to Nearest or Even
    01 = Round Down
    10 = Round Up
    11 = Chop (Truncate Toward Zero)

(4) Infinity Control:
    0 = Projective
    1 = Affine

Figure 4.12: 8087 NDP control word.

The *status word* is a 16-bit register in the NDP (see the figure below) which tells such information as the kind of problem that occurred during the last error, the quadrant of the angle for trigonometric functions, flags resulting from the comparison instruction, the stack pointer value, and the condition of the busy signal. The main use of the status word is to determine conditional branching after a comparison. The status word must be placed into memory (using the FSTSW STore Status Word instruction), and then picked up by the CPU to do this kind of testing and branching.

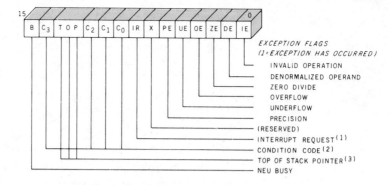

(1) IR is set if any unmasked exception bit is set, cleared otherwise.
(2) See Table 3 for condition code interpretation.
(3) Top Values:
    000 = Register 0 is Top of Stack.
    001 = Register 1 is Top of Stack.
    •
    •
    •
    111 = Register 7 is Top of Stack.

Figure 4.13: 8087 NDP status word.

EXCEPTION HANDLING

The 8087 NDP can interrupt the 8086/8088 when it finds an error. This is part of exception handling, the name for procedures that handle possible errors. For example, on the 8087 NDP there are six exceptions: invalid operation, unnormalized operand, zero divide, overflow, underflow, and inexact result. Using the control word, the programmer can choose to mask (ignore) any combination of these conditions. If the NDP produces any one of those not currently being masked, then the NDP causes an interrupt for the CPU either directly or through the 8259 Programmable Interrupt Controller. The CPU then stops what it (and the NDP) is doing and executes the proper service routine to handle the possible error. Such a routine will most likely require the use of the NDP to straighten things out. Thus, there are NDP instructions (such as: STore ENVironment FSTENV, LoaD ENVironment FLDENV, SAVE state FSAVE, and ReSTORe state FRSTOR) to save and restore the current state of the NDP including the contents of all eight of the NDP's data registers. These are also very useful to help determine exactly what went wrong at the time of the error. Before almost any useful NDP software can be run successfully, there has to be some sort of exception handling package. In Intel's *Numeric Supplement to the 8086 Family User's Guide,* there are examples of such routines.

SAMPLE PROGRAMS

This section gives two sample programs, a matrix multiply program and a program to compute trigonometric functions. In this chapter, we do not show the corresponding 8086/8088 programs because they would be much more lengthy. On the other hand, the corresponding program using the 8087 NDP software emulator program would have identical source code. That is, the same assembly-language programs would be calling software routines instead of hardware routines. We have already discussed how much slower this would be.

The first program consists of a routine to multiply a 4 × 4 matrix by a 4-vector. It is a key to unleashing 8087 NDP's power in the important area of computer graphics. Before we describe how the routine works, let's describe how it can be used. Suppose we have a three-dimensional scene drawn entirely with straight lines. Information to draw this scene may be stored in the computer as a list of points. If the scene is to be drawn in perspective, then each point is most conveniently stored as a 4-vector; that is, each point has four positional coordinates. This is because the *projective transformations* that are needed to show a scene from various perspectives are most easily represented by 4 × 4 matrix multiplication. More specifically, to compute the most general projective transformation we take any 3-vector (x, y, z) and form the 4-vector (x, y, z, 1). We then matrix multiply this 4-vector by the appropriate 4 × 4 matrix, yielding a 4-vector (x', y', z', w'). To convert this back to the correct 3-vector, we divide all coordinates by the fourth coordinate and discard the fourth coordinate. See the figure below for the formulas.

THE MATRIX:

$$
\begin{pmatrix}
a_{11} & a_{12} & a_{13} & a_{14} \\
a_{21} & a_{22} & a_{23} & a_{24} \\
a_{31} & a_{32} & a_{33} & a_{34} \\
a_{41} & a_{42} & a_{43} & a_{44}
\end{pmatrix}
$$

THE VECTOR:

$$
\begin{pmatrix}
x_1 \\
x_2 \\
x_3 \\
x_4
\end{pmatrix}
$$

THE TRANSFORMATION:

$$
x_1 \leftarrow \frac{a_{11}\,x_1 + a_{12}\,x_2 + a_{13}\,x_3 + a_{14}\,x_4}{a_{41}\,x_1 + a_{42}\,x_2 + a_{43}\,x_3 + a_{44}\,x_4}
$$

$$
x_2 \leftarrow \frac{a_{21}\,x_1 + a_{22}\,x_2 + a_{23}\,x_3 + a_{24}\,x_4}{a_{41}\,x_1 + a_{42}\,x_2 + a_{43}\,x_3 + a_{44}\,x_4}
$$

$$
x_3 \leftarrow \frac{a_{31}\,x_1 + a_{32}\,x_2 + a_{33}\,x_3 + a_{34}\,x_4}{a_{41}\,x_1 + a_{42}\,x_2 + a_{43}\,x_3 + a_{44}\,x_4}
$$

Figure 4.14: Using a matrix to compute a projective transformation.

   In terms of mathematical theory, it is much more natural to represent the entries of these matrices and vectors by floating-point numbers.

   In addition to positional information, each point may have a "fifth" coordinate to specify how to connect the point with the previous point. A value of 0 would mean, do not draw a line from the previous point, while a value of 1 would mean that these points are connected with a line. This is exactly the code used by many digital plotters to control the raising and lowering of the pen. More elaborate codes can be used, including the possibility of having different colored lines. These *connectivity* code numbers are usually represented by integers. The figure below shows how to draw a letter *A* with this notation.

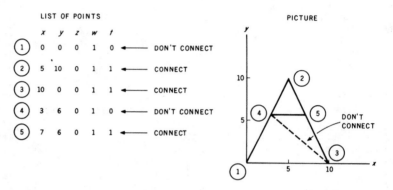

Figure 4.15: Drawing a letter *A*.

   Figure 4.16 shows an 8087 NDP floating point routine to multiply a 4-vector by a 4 × 4 matrix. Upon entry, the DI register *points to* (contains the address of) the original 4-vector, and the BX *points to* the 4 × 4 matrix. The entries of the matrix are stored in successive locations, row by row. The resulting 4-vector replaces the original 4-vector.

```
                    ; 8087 MATRIX MULTIPLY
                    ; ***********************
                              NAME    MATPROD
                              PUBLIC  PROD
                    MAT       SEGMENT
                    ;
     0004           RSIZE     EQU     4
                              ASSUME  CS:MAT
                    ;
0000                PROD      PROC    FAR
0000 1E                       PUSH    DS                         ;SAVE D SEG
0001 55                       PUSH    BP                         ;SAVE BASE POINTER
0002 8B EC                    MOV     BP,SP                      ;POINT TO STACK
0004 C5 7E 08                 LDS     DI,DWORD PTR [BP+8]         ;GET LOCATION OF VECTOR
0007 C5 5E 0C                 LDS     BX,DWORD PTR [BP+12]        ;GET LOCATION OF MATRIX
                    ;
000A 9B DB E3                 FINIT                              ;INITIALIZE NDP
000D 9B D9 45 0C              FLD     DWORD PTR [DI+3*RSIZE]      ;LOAD X4
0011 9B D9 45 08              FLD     DWORD PTR [DI+2*RSIZE]      ;LOAD X3
0015 9B D9 45 04              FLD     DWORD PTR [DI+1*RSIZE]      ;LOAD X2
0019 9B D9 05                 FLD     DWORD PTR [DI]             ;LOAD X1
001C B9 04 00                 MOV     CX,4                       ;4 ROWS
001F 9B D9 07       ROW:      FLD     DWORD PTR [BX]             ;GET FIRST ELEMENT OF ROW
0022 9B D8 C9                 FMUL    ST,ST(1)                   ;TIMES X1
0025 9B D9 47 04              FLD     DWORD PTR [BX+1*RSIZE]      ;GET SECOND ELEMENT OF ROW
0029 9B D8 CB                 FMUL    ST,ST(3)                   ;TIMES X2
002C 9B DE C1                 FADD                               ;ADD TO PREVIOUS
002F 9B D9 47 08              FLD     DWORD PTR [BX+2*RSIZE]      ;GET THIRD ELEMENT OF ROW
0033 9B D8 CC                 FMUL    ST,ST(4)                   ;TIMES X3
0036 9B DE C1                 FADD                               ;ADD TO PREVIOUS
0039 9B D9 47 0C              FLD     DWORD PTR [BX+3*RSIZE]      ;GET FOURTH ELEMENT OF ROW
003D 9B D8 CD                 FMUL    ST,ST(5)                   ;TIMES X4
0040 9B DE C1                 FADD                               ;HERE IS THE TOTAL
0043 9B D9 1D                 FSTP    DWORD PTR [DI]             ;STORE ONE ENTRY OF Y
0046 83 C7 04                 ADD     DI,1*RSIZE                 ;AND INCREMENT POINTER
0049 83 C3 10                 ADD     BX,4*RSIZE                 ;NEXT ROW
004C E2 D1                    LOOP    ROW
004E 5D                       POP     BP                         ;RESTORE BP
004F 1F                       POP     DS                         ;RESTORE DS
0050 CA 08 00                 RET     8                          ;RETURN AND SKIP 2 POINTERS
                    ;
                    PROD      ENDP                               ;END OF PROCEDURE
                    ;
                    MAT       ENDS                               ;END OF SEGMENT
                              END                                ;END OF MODULE
```

Figure 4.16: 8087 NDP program to matrix multiply.

The routine begins by loading all components of the vector into the NDP stack. Then it executes a loop four times, once for each row. The first row gets *squashed* against the vector to produce the first coordinate of the answer. The coordinates of the original vector are not lost, because they will be needed to squash against the next row to get the next coordinate of the answer, and so on.

Notice how the stack is used to help store intermediate results during each row loop. If you examine the machine code, you will see that each floating-point operation is automatically preceded by a CPU wait instruction (even though this is not explicitly coded in the source code). This is necessary for synchronization of the NDP with the CPU.

The next program (see the figure below) shows how to compute all six trigonometric functions. The key instruction is Floating point Partial TANgent (FPTAN). It is hard to find this instruction in the program because so much has to be done before and after to get the correct results.

Figure 4.17

```
                              ; 8087 TRIG FUNCTIONS
                              ; ********************
                              NAME TRIGMOD
                              PUBLIC TRIG
                              TRIGSEG SEGMENT
                                      ASSUME CS:TRIGSEG,DS:TRIGDAT
                              ;
                              ;
  0002                        C1      EQU     2
                              ;
  0000                        TRIG    PROC    FAR
  0000 1E                             PUSH    DS              ; DS MUST BE PRESERVED
  0001 55                             PUSH    BP              ; AND ALSO BP
                              ;
  0002 8B EC                          MOV     BP,SP           ; BP WILL POINT TO DATA
  0004 83 C5 08                       ADD     BP,8            ; BUT FIRST SKIP DS,BP
                                                              ; AND RET ADDRESS CS,IP
                              ;
  0007 B8 -- --                       MOV     AX,TRIGDAT
  000A 8E D8                          MOV     DS,AX           ; TRIGDAT IS NEW DS
                              ;
  000C 9B D9 06 02 00         TRIG0:  FLD     NEGTWO          ; GET -2
  0011 9B D9 EB                       FLDPI                   ; GET PI
  0014 9B D9 FD                       FSCALE                  ; MAKE PI/4
  0017 9B D9 C2                       FLD     ST(2)           ; ANGLE IS TOP OF STACK
                              ;
  001A 9B D9 F8               TRIG1:  FPREM                   ; REDUCE THE ANGLE
  001D 9B DD 3E 00 00                 FSTSW   STAT87          ; STATUS BITS C3, C1, C0
  0022 9B                             FWAIT                   ; TELL WHICH OCTANT
  0023 A1 00 00                       MOV     AX,STAT87
  0026 9E                             SAHF                    ; 87 STATUS INTO 86 FLAGS
  0027 7A F1                          JPE     TRIG1           ; LOOP UNTIL FULLY REDUCED
                              ;
  0029 9B D9 F2                       FPTAN                   ; X=R*COS(ARG) & Y=R*SIN(ARG)
                              ;
  002C 73 0C                          JNC     TRIG2           ; TEST C0
  002E 9B D9 E0                       FCHS                    ; FOR OCTANTS 4,5,6,7
  0031 9B D9 C9                       FXCH                    ; NEED BOTH SIGNS CHANGED
  0034 9B D9 E0                       FCHS
  0037 9B D9 C9                       FXCH
                              ;
  003A 75 06                 TRIG2:  JNZ     TRIG3           ; TEST C3
  003C 9B D9 C9                       FXCH                    ; FOR OCTANTS 2,3,6,7
  003F 9B D9 E0                       FCHS                    ; NEED SWITCH AND A SIGN CHG
                              ;
```

```
0042 F6 C4 02        TRIG3:   TEST    AH,C1           ; C1 IS NOT IN AN 86 FLAG
0045 74 0F                    JZ      TRIG4           ; TEST IT
0047 9B D9 C0                 FLD     ST              ; FOR OCTANTS 1,3,5,7
004A 9B D9 C2                 FLD     ST(2)
004D 9B DE C1                 FADD                    ; NEED X-Y AND X+Y
0050 9B D9 CA                 FXCH    ST(2)
0053 9B DE E9                 FSUB
             ;
                     TRIG4:                           ; COMPUTE R
0056 9B D9 C0                 FLD     ST              ; DUPLICATE X
0059 9B DC C8                 FMUL    ST,ST           ; SQUARE IT
005C 9B D9 C2                 FLD     ST(2)           ; GET Y
005F 9B DC C8                 FMUL    ST,ST           ; SQUARE IT
0062 9B DE C1                 FADD                    ; NOW HAVE X*X + Y*Y
0065 9B D9 FA                 FSQRT                   ; R = HYPOTENUSE
             ;
0068 9B D9 C1                 FLD     ST(1)           ; GET X
006B 9B D9 C1                 FLD     ST(1)           ; GET R
006E 9B DE F9                 FDIV                    ; X/R
0071 C5 5E 14                 LDS     BX,DWORD PTR [BP+20]   ; ADDRESS TO
0074 9B D9 1F                 FSTP    DWORD PTR [BX]  ; STORE COSINE
             ;
0077 9B D9 C2                 FLD     ST(2)           ; GET Y
007A 9B D9 C1                 FLD     ST(1)           ; GET R
007D 9B DE F9                 FDIV                    ; Y/R
0080 C5 5E 10                 LDS     BX,DWORD PTR [BP+16]   ; ADDRESS TO
0083 9B D9 1F.                FSTP    DWORD PTR [BX]  ; STORE SINE
             ;
0086 9B D9 C2                 FLD     ST(2)           ; GET Y
0089 9B D9 C2                 FLD     ST(2)           ; GET X
008C 9B DE F9                 FDIV                    ; Y/X
008F C5 5E 0C                 LDS     BX,DWORD PTR [BP+12]   ; ADDRESS TO
0092 9B D9 1F                 FSTP    DWORD PTR [BX]  ; STORE TANGENT
             ;
0095 9B D9 C1                 FLD     ST(1)           ; GET X
0098 9B D9 C1                 FLD     ST(1)           ; GET R
009B 9B DE F1                 FDIVR                   ; R/X
009E C5 5E 08                 LDS     BX,DWORD PTR [BP+8]    ; ADDRESS TO
00A1 9B D9 1F                 FSTP    DWORD PTR [BX]  ; STORE SECANT
             ;
00A4 9B D9 C2                 FLD     ST(2)           ; GET Y
00A7 9B D9 C1                 FLD     ST(1)           ; GET R
00AA 9B DE F1                 FDIVR                   ; R/Y
00AD C5 5E 04                 LDS     BX,DWORD PTR [BP+4]    ; ADDRESS TO
00B0 9B D9 1F                 FSTP    DWORD PTR [BX]  ; STORE COSECANT
             ;
00B3 9B D9 C2                 FLD     ST(2)           ; GET X
00B6 9B D9 C2                 FLD     ST(2)           ; GET Y
00B9 9B DE F1                 FDIVR                   ; X/Y
00BC C5 5E 00                 LDS     BX,DWORD PTR [BP+0]    ; ADDRESS TO
00BF 9B D9 1F                 FSTP    DWORD PTR [BX]  ; STORE COTANGENT
             ;
00C2 9B DB E3                 FINIT                   ; CLEAR THE STACK
             ;
00C5 5D                       POP     BP              ; RESTORE BP
00C6 1F                       POP     DS              ; RESTORE DS
00C7 CA 18 00                 RET     24              ; JUMP OVER DATA
             ;
```

```
----              TRIG    ENDP              ; END OF PROCEDURE
                  TRIGSEG ENDS              ; END OF SEGMENT
                  ;
----              TRIGDAT SEGMENT           ; DATA SEGMENT
0000 00 00        STAT87  DW      0
0002 00 00 00 C0  NEGTWO  DD      -2.
----              TRIGDAT ENDS              ; END OF DATA SEG
                  ;
                          END               ; END OF MODULE
```

Figure 4.17: 8087 NDP program to handle trigonometric functions.

Upon entry, the angle is on the top of the NDP stack. The first step is to reduce this angle to a number between 0 and pi/4 as required by the NDP for the FPTAN. A loop using the FPREM (Floating point Partial REMainder) instruction is used to make this reduction. The FPREM instruction (in this loop) works by subtracting pi/4 from the angle until the angle comes into range. The process stops, uncompleted, every once in a while, so that any CPU interrupts can be processed. You can tell when the instruction is completely finished by looking at a certain bit in the NDP control word. We examine this bit by loading the upper half of the control word into the upper byte of the CPU flags register. The *process-finished* bit just happens to "line up" with the parity flag, and so we loop until the parity flag says that we can continue on with the rest of the program.

The FPTAN produces two numbers, X and Y, as the top two items on the NDP stack. The next step is to adjust these for the various *octants* around the unit circle. That is, pi/4 divides the unit circle into eight octants and the trigonometric functions are various algebraic combinations of X and Y depending on which octant the original angle was in as well as which particular trigonometric function you wish. In our program, we even adjust the angle a bit as part of the process. The correct octant can be determined by certain bits in the NDP control word which was loaded into the CPU flags.

After X and Y are adjusted, we compute $R = SQRT(X * X + Y * Y)$. This is the hypotenuse of the right triangle whose sides are given by X and Y.

The last part of the program consists of taking various ratios of R, X, and Y to get the six trigonometric functions. These are stored in six separate locations and then pushed onto the NDP stack for return.

CONCLUSION

As we have seen, the 8087 NDP provides a powerful extension to the 8086/8088's capabilities, putting its performance in more of a category with the past generations of minicomputers (still running at many installations), and giving it greater precision than was normal for even large mainframes!

Attaching coprocessors to a system is a very nice solution to the problem of expanding or extending a CPU's capabilities, while maintaining upward software (and to some extent hardware) compatibility. Using this same idea it would be possible to add other chips besides the 8087 NDP (perhaps designed and made by other manufacturers) to extend the instruction set of the 8086/8088 in other ways to provide other types of capabilities.

Chapter 5

The 8089 Input/Output Processor

The figure below shows the 8089 Input/Output Processor's internal structure and pinouts. This device is a microprocessor whose job is to handle the input/output for the 8086/8088 CPU. The 8089 IOP executes its own instruction stream, communicating with an 8086/8088 CPU through a few signal lines and large blocks of information deposited in system memory and/or the system I/O space. In Chapter 2, we saw how the 8089 IOP fits into a whole computer system. In fact, we saw a 16-bit 8086-based system and an 8-bit 8088-based system, both of which use the one available version of the 8089 IOP! Before discussing *how* the 8089 IOP works, we shall explore *why* it is needed.

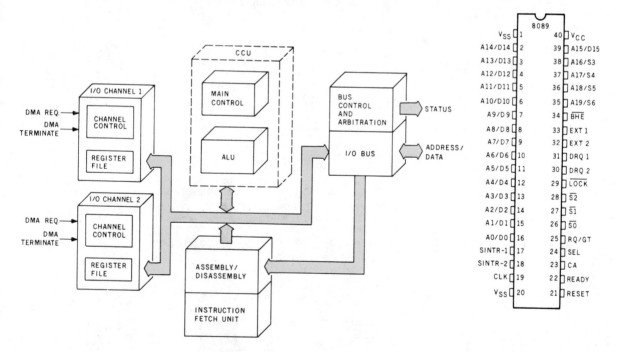

Figure 5.1: 8089 IOP—internal structure and pinouts.

DEALING WITH I/O

As applications for microprocessors have evolved from calculators to terminals and finally to complete computer systems, Intel's approach to the handling of input/output has grown more sophisticated. For a calculator, programs are short, mostly consisting of evaluating expressions typed in through the keyboard and then outputting the result on the display. In contrast, a modern microcomputer system usually runs lengthy, complex programs and may have over half a dozen different input/output devices. These devices may include several keyboards, floppy disks, tape drives, video text displays, video graphics displays, modems, printers, digitizer tablets, and digital plotters. See the figure below for a picture of the evolution from calculator to modern microprocessor.

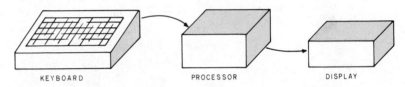

Figure 5.2a: I/O for a calculator.

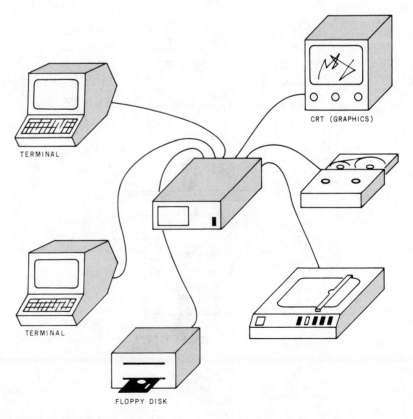

Figure 5.2b: I/O for a computer.

**Five Major
Considerations**

In dealing with I/O there are many important considerations. These include the speed of transmission, the way that the information is grouped, the degree of control required, the amount of translation or conversion required, and the type of error detection and correction used. Each I/O device has widely different requirements in regard to these factors as follows.

1. The speed of information transmission for a given input or output device varies from many orders of magnitude slower than the CPU to much faster than possible by the CPU. For example, if a CPU is directly monitoring a keyboard, then the CPU will usually have to wait millions of its cycles for the transmission of a single character! With this method the CPU spends more than 99.99 percent of its time waiting for the operator to type the next letter. Then once the command is fully typed in, the operator must wait for the CPU to do its work. This turns out to be quite a waste of time for both the CPU and the operator, neither of which is doing useful work while waiting for the other. At the other extreme, if a CPU is being used to directly control the rapid display of information on a video screen, then the display might appear sluggish because the CPU is not designed to push information around fast enough.

2. Data is usually grouped in packages of various sizes, often with smaller packages contained within larger packages. The smallest unit of data is a bit (binary digit). Next, a small number of bits (4 to 64) are normally grouped together to form what is called a *word*. A special case of this is the *byte*, which is a word that contains 8 bits. Finally, a number of words (0 to several thousand) are grouped together to form what is called a *block*. A full transmission might consist of a single bit at one **extreme or several blocks at the other. See Figure 5.3 for a picture** of these groupings. For example, a single bit might be used to control the opening or closing of a valve in a microprocessor-controlled automobile engine; a single byte might be sent to the display of a calculator to form a digit; a whole screenful (24 lines by 80 columns) of characters (bytes) might be sent to the terminal of a word processor; or a large disk file might be written that consists of a thousand blocks in which each block contains 128 bytes. This wide variation in length is true for input as well as output.

3. By *control* of I/O we mean programmed manipulation of input/output devices to cause the conversion between the electrical signals used by the computer system and the sensory signals used by the human operator. You can actually think of a transmission stream as a program which, when run, will cause a desired effect such as a printed page of text on a typewriter, a video screenful of information, or a picture on a digital plotter. Usually a transmission stream consists of a mixture of data and control words. You can think of the control words as "instructions"

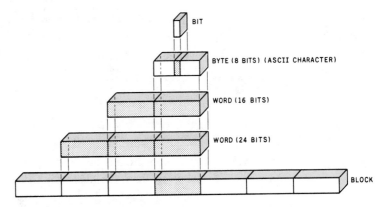

Figure 5.3: Data groupings.

which are mixed in with the "data" which is the information being transmitted. For example, in the transmission of text, such things as carriage return, linefeed, and end of message are sent as *control bytes* intermixed with bytes of text characters. Depending on the particular output device, control bytes cause different physical actions to be performed. For example, a carriage return causes a completely different action on a line printer than on a CRT terminal display. The amount of work required by the computer to "execute" these "programs" varies widely. For example, at one extreme it might consist of sending ASCII characters one by one out a port, or at the other extreme it may involve complicated line-drawing routines for a digital plotter. Many of today's I/O devices have their own microprocessors on board to perform these control functions. For example, some digital plotters execute their own line-drawing routines in response to simple graphics commands from the main computer. These are called *smart plotters*. In contrast, there are *dumb plotters* in which every tiny step of the pen-positioning apparatus has to be individually controlled by the main computer, causing the computer significant overhead.

4. By *data conversion* of I/O we mean transforming one transmission stream with one set of coding for its data and control words to another transmission stream with other coding rules. A typical type of data conversion might be translating from one code such as ASCII to another code such as EBCDIC. Here a simple lookup or translation table could be used. Usually, a register would contain the address of the beginning of this table. This is called the *base address*. The incoming code would simply be added to this base address to determine a location within this table. The outgoing code would be picked up from this location.

5. By *error detection and correction* schemes we mean methods to send digital information over noisy transmission lines in such a way that errors

introduced in transmission are either detected or eliminated at the receiving end. The amount of error detection and correction varies from a "cross your fingers" without any error detecting or correcting to elaborate parity checking schemes.

Typically, extra information is added to the message just before transmission. This information is used at the receiving end to detect and/or correct transmission errors.

For example, with the parity checking schemes, bits called *parity bits* are added to each word just before transmission to produce larger words called *code words*. These code words are sent over the transmission line. Only certain words of this larger word-size are actual code words. For example, if one extra parity bit is added to 7-bit ASCII code (using a very simple rule so that the sum of the digits in the resulting code word is always even or always odd), then the resulting code words will have 8 bits. There are 128 possible 7-bit ASCII code words to start with, and there are 256 possible 8-bit words. Thus, only half of all the 8-bit words could have come from an ASCII character in this manner. When a word is received at the other end of the transmission line, it is checked to see if it is a code word (for example, the sum of digits is even). If it is not, an error must have occurred and the transmission can be retried!

When you use more than just one parity bit, you can determine the most likely choice for the original word (character), and thus achieve error correction. Such parity schemes can only detect or correct a small number of mistransmitted bits in a word. For example, with a single parity bit, only single-bit errors can be detected in each word, and *no* errors can be corrected. That is, if 2 bits are erroneous in a word, the receiver will get a code word, but not the right one, and no error will be detected.

One popular scheme with more parity bits is called the Hamming code, named after Richard Hamming who is currently teaching at the Naval Postgraduate School in Monterey, California (see Hamming, R. W. *Coding and Information Theory,* Englewood Cliffs, N.J.: Prentice Hall. 1980). With the Hamming code the original message words (plain text) are 4 bits long, and to these, 3 parity bits are added, yielding 7-bit code words. This scheme has the ability to detect *double-bit* errors (2 bits wrong) and correct *single-bit* errors (1 bit wrong) in words.

The error correction works by selecting the *nearest* code word to the word actually received. Nearest is defined in terms of a way of measuring distance among the computer words called the *Hamming distance.* The Hamming distance between two words is the number of digit positions which are different in the two words. For example, the distance between the 7-bit binary words 1010111 and 1110110 is 2, because they differ in exactly two places. With the 7-bit Hamming code, every possible 7-bit word is either a code word or is precisely distance *one* from some unique code word. That is, given *any* 7-bit word *received,* there is always one and *only one* nearest code word (with 0 or 1 digit positions in error). Since this is the most likely code word sent, that is the one which is chosen during the correction process.

As you can see, parity checking schemes are good, but far from perfect. But since a small number of errors per word is usually much more probable than a larger number, this method turns out to be fairly reliable.

Another error-checking method commonly used with tapes or floppy disks is called the *cyclic redundancy check.* With this method there is a special *checker* byte at the end of each sector of data. If this does not check, then the sector is retried. There might be a whole sequence of retries with adjustments in between. This checker byte is computed by adding up all the bytes in the message, keeping only the lowest byte of this sum.

Bus-Oriented Architecture

The first step toward managing all these diverse devices with their diverse requirements is to have a central bus with each device attached to this bus via its own separate controller. See the figure below for a diagram of what this looks like. This is the philosophy behind Intel's bus-based architecture and its device controller chips such as the 8278 programmable keyboard interface and the 8275 programmable CRT controller.

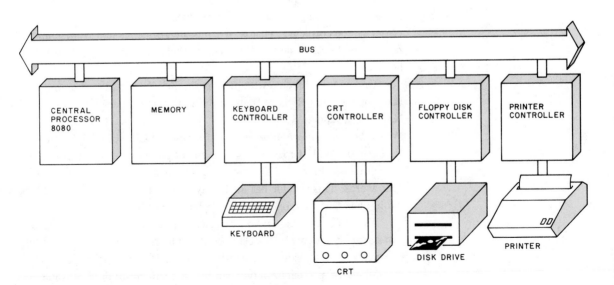

Figure 5.4: A simple bus for I/O.

Polled and Interrupt I/O

The two most common ways that I/O is handled on such a bus system are polled I/O and interrupt I/O. The essential problem with any I/O operation is the tremendous difference in speed between the processor and the input and output devices in the system. For example, an 8086 processor may operate at 5 megahertz, which is about 100,000 instructions per second. In contrast, input from keyboard typing usually produces only a few characters per second, and a telephone link might transfer at most 120 characters per second (faster—960 characters per second—if you get a special line or slower—11 to 30 characters per second—if you use an inexpensive modem).

With the polled I/O method, the processor has to wait for the transmission of each character before it can proceed to any other business. While it waits, the processor executes a tight loop in which it checks a special I/O byte called a status register. This status register is connected to the device controller circuitry in the computer. When this circuitry is ready for the transfer (either because the external device is now ready or because of the timing within the computer's circuitry), it sends a ''ready'' signal to the status port where the CPU can see it. The CPU then makes the transfer, and then and only then can the CPU leave the loop and do other things.

However, with the more efficient interrupt I/O method, the processor goes about its business, with *no* apparent checking of the I/O devices in the software. *Built into the hardware is a check for signals from the I/O device controllers*. When an I/O device controller indicates that it is ready for a transfer, it sends an interrupt signal either directly to the CPU or to the 8259 PIC (Programmable Interrupt Controller) which then signals the CPU. The processor finishes the current instruction, saves enough information so that it can return later and resume processing at that same point, and then jumps to a special *interrupt service* subroutine designed to make the transfer. The transfer is usually made between the device and a special area in memory called a buffer. After this transfer, the processor jumps back (using the information it saved) to what it was doing before it was interrupted. The processor can then access the data in the buffer as it is needed. Thus, the character-by-character transfer of information proceeds concurrently with other tasks. Of course, the processor will eventually finish all other jobs and will have to wait for new information from external devices before proceeding. The interrupt method is particularly appropriate and useful when a computer is handling several jobs at once. For example, in a time-sharing system, if one user's program is waiting for the next command line or is printing out its results, other users' jobs can be computing results. We shall use interrupt I/O in our model computer. See figure 5.5 for a picture of these two methods.

Some interrupts are more important than others. For example, a keystroke should be processed as soon as possible while a character to a

a)

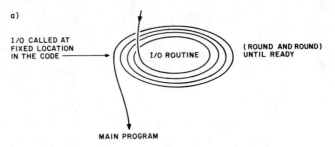

I/O CALLED AT
FIXED LOCATION
IN THE CODE

I/O ROUTINE

(ROUND AND ROUND)
UNTIL READY

MAIN PROGRAM

Figure 5.5a: Polled I/O.

b)

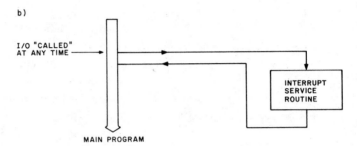

I/O "CALLED"
AT ANY TIME

INTERRUPT
SERVICE
ROUTINE

MAIN PROGRAM

Figure 5.5b: Interrupt I/O.

printer can usually wait for a fraction of a second. Thus, it is sometimes important to assign priorities to interrupts from various devices so that the most important things always get done first.

Using interrupt I/O can have certain disadvantages. It still requires that the CPU deal with the transmission of information byte by byte. Each time a new byte is to be transmitted, the processor has to stop what it is doing, save its working registers, make the transfer, restore its working registers, and then return where it left off. This can happen at any point in the program (except in those sections in which interrupts have been turned off), and can cause considerable overhead to the processor, slowing it down in an unpredictable manner. There are certain critical operations such as disk I/O which require uninterrupted service and, indeed, interrupts are purposely ignored or turned off in sections of code which handle these operations. While these sections are being executed, inputs from other devices are ignored. This is crucial to the operation of the computer. Another problem is that certain interrupts might happen so often (for example, every horizontal scan line (63 microseconds)) that there is little time for other processing by the CPU.

To solve some of these problems, there should be a processor which is *in charge* of I/O, but under the *direction* of the CPU. In fact it might be nice to have a processor in charge of each major I/O device! Intel has developed the 8089 Input/Output Processor to answer this need. It is a special-purpose processor with a special-purpose instruction set designed to handle just I/O operations. It even has two separate I/O channels to provide dedicated service to two different I/O devices concurrently, and it also allows for the existence of other IOPs attached to other I/O devices in the system.

PERIPHERAL PROCESSOR AND MULTIPROCESSING

The 8089 IOP is a microprocessor in its own right, but with a special-purpose instruction set and a very special initialization procedure. It belongs to the new generation of coprocessing and multiprocessing microprocessors, playing the role of a *peripheral processor*. The 8089 IOP is designed to be used as a *front end* for an 8086 or 8088. That is, all the I/O devices communicate with the 8089 which in turn communicates with the main processor. This teamwork approach can result in substantial improvement in performance of the whole system. The 8089 IOP is now the one to wait for an I/O device such as a keyboard while the CPU goes about its business, which is doing general computations and managing the whole system. The 8089 IOP is better able to handle I/O because it can make data transfers between memory and I/O devices with various kinds of data conversion and control in fewer clock cycles than the 8086/8088 CPU can. The use of front ending is quite common in the world of large, mainframe computers. Often a smaller computer such as a PDP-11 minicomputer will be used as a front end for a very large and fast computer such as a Cray.

In Figure 5.6, two 8089 IOPs front end for an 8086 CPU. Each IOP has two channels, one channel per I/O device. Each channel communicates directly with the device controller for the corresponding device. The top IOP is in charge of a keyboard on channel 1 and a CRT on channel 2, and the bottom IOP is in charge of a hard disk on channel 1 and a high-speed printer on channel 2. Both 8089 IOPs use the 8086's I/O space to store their data and programs. The 8086 directs the activities of these two IOPs by reading and writing information into blocks in this I/O space. The main RAM is reserved for use by the 8086 CPU. We do not show the bus structure of such a system. The model computers in Chapter 2 show how this is done.

In a system using the 8089 IOP, the CPU (an 8086 or 8088) supervises the whole system. It issues commands to the 8089 IOP in two ways: 1) via signal lines between the two processors and 2) via message tables in memory shared by the two processors. There are actually several signal lines between the CPU and the 8089 IOP. Some of these signal lines (the request/grant, RQ/GT lines) provide a method for the CPU and the IOP to efficiently share the same bus. These signals work as follows: One request/grant line runs between the CPU and the IOP. When the IOP needs to use the bus, it sends a pulse over this RQ/GT line. Soon the CPU relinquishes the bus, electrically disconnecting (tri-stating) its bus pins, and sends a pulse back over this same RQ/GT line. The IOP then

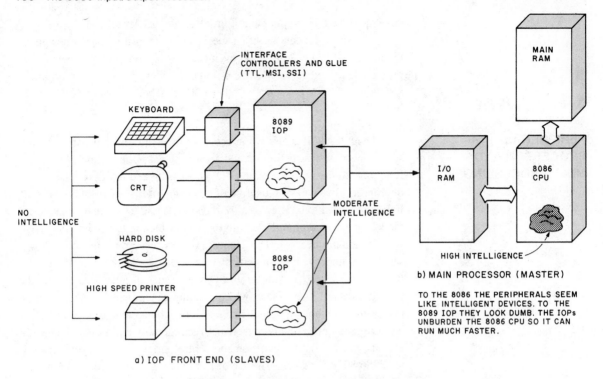

INTERFACE
CONTROLLERS AND GLUE
(TTL, MSI, SSI)

KEYBOARD

8089
IOP

MAIN
RAM

I/O
RAM

8086
CPU

CRT

NO
INTELLIGENCE

MODERATE
INTELLIGENCE

HARD DISK

8089
IOP

HIGH SPEED PRINTER

HIGH INTELLIGENCE

b) MAIN PROCESSOR (MASTER)

TO THE 8086 THE PERIPHERALS SEEM
LIKE INTELLIGENT DEVICES. TO THE
8089 IOP THEY LOOK DUMB. THE IOPs
UNBURDEN THE 8086 CPU SO IT CAN
RUN MUCH FASTER.

a) IOP FRONT END (SLAVES)

Figure 5.6: I/O front ending with the 8089 IOP.

takes over the bus, electrically connecting its bus lines, and makes its transfers. When it is finished, it electrically disconnects its bus lines and sends a pulse back to the CPU (over this same RQ/GT line). Upon receipt of the "relinquishing" pulse from the IOP, the CPU resumes its normal bus activity.

There is one line (the channel attention line) which allows the CPU to give a quick kick to the 8089 IOP to inform it that there is work to be done. The exact details of what has to be done and how to do it will have been previously loaded into special blocks in memory by the CPU.

In response to these commands the 8089 IOP performs the required I/O tasks using its own built-in and rather limited instruction set. These tasks involve initializing and monitoring the device controllers, giving them the necessary instructions so that it can transfer a complete unit or block of information between the I/O devices and the computer's memory. The key operation is the transfer instruction XFER which performs smart, DMA-like (more on this later) transfers between I/O devices and memory. These transfers are faster than can be done by the CPU, but allow for the same kind of control and data conversion that can be done by a CPU. Of all the CPU instructions, this 8089 transfer operation comes closest to being a general string operation. In fact, one use of an IOP is to do all block-move and string operations for the CPU as we do in our model computer. Once the 8089 IOP has done its job, each I/O device appears pretty much the same to the CPU, namely as a block of memory. In fact we can think of each such block as a file. Just like a disk file, you can open it, read or write, and close it.

LOCAL VERSUS REMOTE MODE

The 8089 can be configured in a computer system in two basic ways, *local* and *remote*. In *local* mode everything such as the CPU, IOP, device controllers, and main memory is attached to the system's main bus. This is the mode we shall use in our model computers. The 8086 or 8088 CPU acts as a master and the 8089 acts as a slave. Signal lines connect together a request/grant line (RQ/GT) pin on the CPU with one of the two corresponding pins on the IOP. As we have already mentioned, the request/grant signal line is a two-way communication signal line which provides a method for determining which of the two processors is to have control of the bus. The advantage to this local mode is low cost because it requires a minimum number of chips. The disadvantage is the burden that might be placed on the single bus. That is, any bus (like a highway) can take only so much traffic before everything comes to a halt (such as during rush hour). The figure below shows this local configuration.

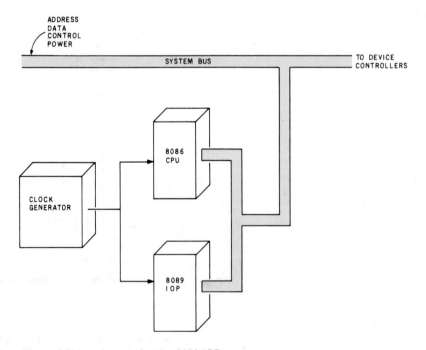

Figure 5.7: Local mode for the 8089 IOP.

In the remote mode, one or two IOPs form a small cluster with their own local bus. The I/O controllers are attached to this local bus. There is also a system bus to which this I/O processing cluster is attached. See the figure below for diagrams of two such systems. It is conceivable to have several such I/O clusters in a large system. In this way the I/O activity can be spread among several processors and several different buses. For example, each user might have a different cluster, and the system disk and printer might also each have its own clusters.

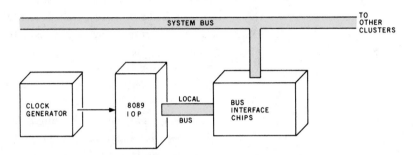

Figure 5.8a: Remote mode for the 8089 IOP—one IOP in a cluster.

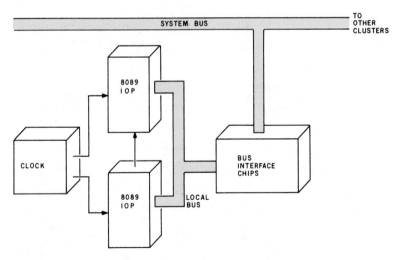

Figure 5.8b: Remote mode for the 8089 IOP—two IOPs in a cluster.

The 8089 has the same kind of voltage and timing requirements as the 8086/8088. It can be made to have an 8-bit data bus just like the 8088 or a 16-bit data bus just like the 8086. This is determined by a byte in memory which is read by the 8089 during initialization.

**HOW THE 8089
IOP WORKS**

The 8089 IOP can process two jobs (called *tasks*) at the same time. Each job could be the interface of a separate I/O device. Running more than one job at once is called concurrent processing. To run two jobs concurrently, the 8089 IOP is divided into two sections called channels, one for each I/O task. Each channel has its own register set, and its own program called a *task block* which resides in the system's memory or the I/O space. However, at any one instance, only one channel is actually executing. There is a common control unit (CCU) which coordinates the activities of the two channels. It will run the channel which has highest priority, or if both have the same priority, it will interleave the two tasks, alternately performing an instruction from each channel (see the figure below).

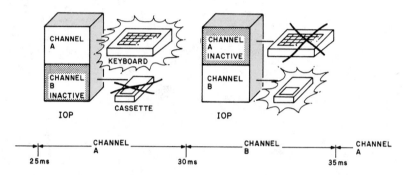

Figure 5.9: Interleaving the two channels of the 8089 IOP.

The 8089 IOP communicates with the main processor (8086 or 8088) through a somewhat elaborate series of tables in memory called blocks (see figure 5.10). These tables must be set up before the IOP begins operation. This can be done either directly by the CPU or by another IOP under the direction of the CPU.

When the 8089 IOP is reset, it begins by picking up 6 bytes of information starting from a special location in main memory (FFFF6h = 1048566 in decimal). This is right near the top of memory (FFFFFh) just above the few bytes allotted to the 8086/8088 CPU for its start-up point (FFFF0h). From this it computes the address of the next table, called the system configuration block. This table leads to another table, called the control block. The control block leads to two more tables which are called the parameter blocks, one for each channel. Each parameter block contains the address of the task block, which is the actual IOP program for that channel. Once the 8089 IOP is initialized in this manner, the system configuration block is no longer needed and may be used to initialize other 8089 IOP's in the system, but the control block, the parameter blocks, and the task blocks must be present for the two channels to operate properly. Both the main processor and the 8089

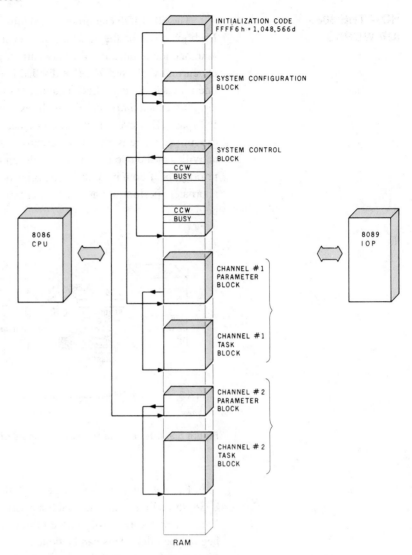

INITIALIZATION CODE
FFFF6h = 1,048,566d

SYSTEM CONFIGURATION
BLOCK

SYSTEM CONTROL
BLOCK

CCW
BUSY

CCW
BUSY

8086
CPU

8089
IOP

CHANNEL #1
PARAMETER
BLOCK

CHANNEL #1
TASK
BLOCK

CHANNEL #2
PARAMETER
BLOCK

CHANNEL #2
TASK
BLOCK

RAM

Figure 5.10: Control, parameter, and task blocks for the 8089 IOP.

IOP read and write information into the parameter blocks and control block. It is even possible for one IOP to help load programs and data into parameter and task blocks for other IOPs. There are special bytes, one for each channel, in the control block called busy bytes. These are checked each time a processor wants to access a channel block. It is important for the CPU and IOP never to access a task or parameter block at the same time. Disastrous results can occur if the IOP begins to execute one task and, before it is finished, is interrupted by the CPU starting to overwrite parameters and/or programs for this task with information for a new task (see figure 5.11).

TASK BLOCK

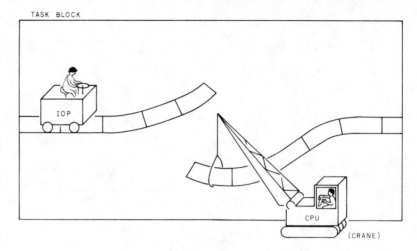

(CRANE)

Figure 5.11: IOP and CPU in conflict.

One type of job that the 8089 IOP is especially designed for is high-speed data transfer. The source and destination can be any of the following: a device controller, I/O memory, or main memory. This type of rapid transfer is often called direct memory access (DMA). See the section on the 8237 programmable DMA controller for more discussion of DMA. DMA can be used for quick, efficient movements of data from devices such as floppy disks or external computers to system RAM while the CPU either rests or does other things which don't use the system's buses.

An IOP channel can be thought of as having two modes, regular and DMA. The regular mode is useful for setting up various parameters in the IOP and its parameter block and initializing the controller chips for the actual transfer. Once this is done, there is a special instruction (XFER) to make a channel go into the DMA mode. In this mode one register points to the source and another register points to the destination. (The 8089 IOP registers will be explained in the next section.) If the source or destination is supposed to be a memory location, then after the transfer of each byte or word, its pointer is automatically incremented to point to the next location (in system memory or in the I/O space!) for the next transfer. If the source or destination is an I/O port, then the pointer stays where it is. There are bits in a special IOP register called the channel control register which determine which of these options is chosen for the source and the destination. For example, if you want to make a transfer from an input port to a block of memory, then during initialization you should set the bits in the channel control register so that the source is a port (nonincrementing) and the destination is memory (incrementing).

See the figure below.

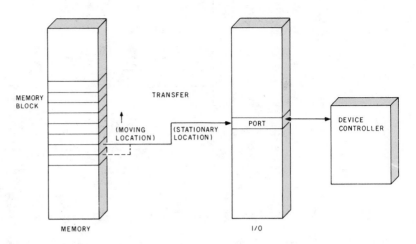

Figure 5.12: Memory versus I/O type transfers.

There are several ways that an IOP transfer can terminate. Again, there are bits in the channel control register which determine this. Termination of transmission can happen after a single transfer, for a specified byte count, on a masked compare, or upon external signal. These last three ways can be turned on or off independently. Then the transfer will terminate on the first one that occurs which is selected.

Translation can also take place during the transfer. That is, each incoming byte can be used as an index to a table of possible outgoing bytes which is called the translation table. If the translation table contains the bytes a(0), a(1), a(2), etc., then an incoming value of i will produce an outgoing value of a(i). One of the IOP registers is used to point to this table (which has to be set up previously either by the IOP or the CPU), and a bit in the channel control register turns this option on and off. This feature has many important uses, including translation from one code such as ASCII to another such as EBCDIC or biasing a color-intensity scheme for video graphics. The 8086/8088 has an instruction which also automatically does this (see Chapter 3). Since the IOP does this translation automatically, it results in a very efficient operation.

8089 IOP REGISTER SET

The 8089 IOP register set is illustrated in figure 5.13. Each I/O channel has a set of eight registers to itself. Four of these are 21-bit registers and four are 16-bit registers. The 21-bit registers are called general purpose A (GA), general purpose B (GB), general purpose C (GC), and task pointer (TP). These registers are designed to hold 20-bit addresses, giving the same 1 megabyte addressing space as the 8086/8088. Bit number 20 (extreme left bit) is called the tag bit. The tag bit determines whether an address belongs to the main memory or to the I/O space. When the 8089 IOP is addressing main memory, it uses all 20 bits of its address registers, and when it is addressing the I/O space it uses only 16 bits.

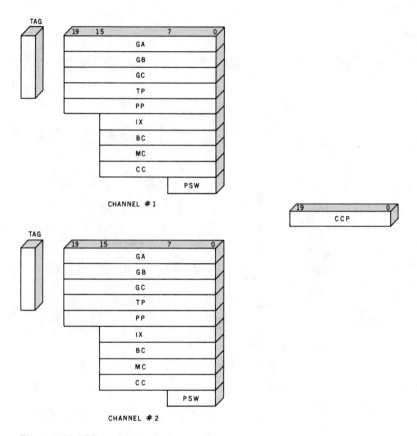

CHANNEL #1

CHANNEL #2

Figure 5.13: IOP register set.

During DMA transfers, registers GA and GB are used interchangeably as pointers to the source and destination locations, and register GC can be used to point to a translation or lookup table as mentioned above. The task pointer (TP) is the program counter for that channel. That is, it points to the next instruction of the channel's program. The four 16-bit registers are called index (IX), byte count (BC), mask/compare (MC), and channel control (CC). The index register is used for the two addressing modes of the IOP which use indexing. The byte count and the mask/compare registers are used to help control termination of DMA transfers. The mask/compare register also is used in the Jump if Mask/Compare is Equal (JMCE) and Jump if Mask/Compare is *Not* Equal (JMCNE) instructions. We will explain later how these work. The channel control (CC) register is used to specify many of the parameters for DMA transfers as seen in the figure below. When not being used in a special way, all of these registers may be used as general-purpose registers in conjunction with the regular mode of the IOP. See the table below for a summary of the function of the various channel registers.

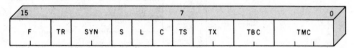

F	FUNCTION
00	PORT TO PORT
01	MEMORY TO PORT
10	PORT TO MEMORY
11	MEMORY TO MEMORY

TR	TRANSLATE
0	NO TRANSLATE
1	TRANSLATE

SYN	SYNCHRONIZATION
00	NO SYNCHRONIZATION
01	SYNCHRONIZE ON SOURCE
10	SYNCHRONIZE ON DESTINATION
11	RESERVED BY INTEL

S	SOURCE
0	GA POINTS TO SOURCE
1	GB POINTS TO SOURCE

L	LOCK
0	NO LOCK
1	ACTUATE LOCK DURING TRANSFER

C	CHAIN
0	NO CHAINING
1	CHAINED: RAISE TB TO PRIORITY 1

TS	TERMINATE ON SINGLE TRANSFER
0	NO SINGLE TRANSFER TERMINATION
1	TERMINATE AFTER SINGLE TRANSFER

TX	TERMINATE ON EXTERNAL SIGNAL
00	NO EXTERNAL TERMINATION
01	TERMINATE ON EXT ACTIVE; OFFSET = 0
10	TERMINATE ON EXT ACTIVE; OFFSET = 4
11	TERMINATE ON EXT ACTIVE; OFFSET = 8

TBC	TERMINATE ON BYTE COUNT
00	NO BYTE COUNT TERMINATION
01	TERMINATE ON BC = 0; OFFSET = 0
10	TERMINATE ON BC = 0; OFFSET = 4
11	TERMINATE ON BC = 0; OFFSET = 8

TMC	TERMINATE ON MASKED COMPARE
000	NO MASK/COMPARE TERMINATION
001	TERMINATE ON MATCH; OFFSET = 0
010	TERMINATE ON MATCH; OFFSET = 4
011	TERMINATE ON MATCH; OFFSET = 8
100	(NO EFFECT)
101	TERMINATE ON NON-MATCH; OFFSET = 0
110	TERMINATE ON NON-MATCH; OFFSET = 4
111	TERMINATE ON NON-MATCH; OFFSET = 8

Figure 5.14: The channel control register.

Register	Size	Points to	Use by Program	Use by DMA
GA	21	memory or I/O	general & base	source/destination pointer
GB	21	memory or I/O	general & base	source/destination pointer
GC	21	memory or I/O	general & base	translate table base pointer
TP	21	memory or I/O	program counter	jump table pointer
PP	20	memory	base	N/A
IX	16	N/A	general & index	N/A
BC	16	N/A	general	byte counter
MC	16	N/A	general and mask/compare	masked/compare
CC	16	N/A	don't use it	parameter storage

Table 5.1: Summary of channel register functions.

Besides these general purpose and DMA registers, each channel has a Parameter Pointer (PP) and a Program Status Word (PSW). The Parameter Pointer has 20 bits and contains the address of the parameter block for the channel. The program status word has 8 bits which keep track of various conditions. Neither of these registers is accessible to the channel program itself but is saved in memory when the IOP is given a command to suspend operations and is restored when the IOP resumes operations. The CPU can check and modify this location to monitor and control the IOP.

There is also a register called the Channel Control Pointer (CCP) which contains the address of the channel control block. Since there is only one channel control block per IOP, there is only one channel control pointer in an 8089 IOP.

8089 IOP ADDRESSING

There are five basic addressing modes used by the 8089 IOP: register, based, offset, indexed, and indexed auto-increment. In register addressing, the register contains the operand. In based addressing, a base register (GA, GB, GC, or PP) contains the address of the operand, thus acting as pointer to the actual data. In offset addressing, the address of the operand is obtained by adding a number to the contents of a base register. In indexed addressing, the address of the operand is obtained by adding the contents of a base register and the index register (IX). In indexed, auto-increment addressing, the operand is determined as in indexed addressing but the index register is incremented afterwards by an appropriate amount (1 or 2 depending upon byte or word mode).

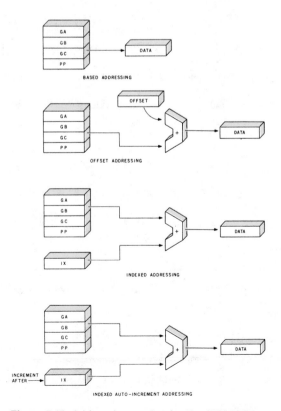

Figure 5.15: Addressing modes for the 8089 IOP.

IOP INSTRUCTION SET

The instruction set for the 8089 IOP includes instructions for data transfers, arithmetic and logical operations, conditional and unconditional branches, subroutine calls, bit manipulation and testing, a special DMA transfer instruction, and program control instructions. The table below contains a summary of the 8089 IOP instructions.

MNEMONIC		DESCRIPTION
MOV	destination,source	MOVe from memory to memory or from register to memory or from memory to register
MOVI	destination,data	MOVe immediate data to register or memory
MOVP	destination,source	MOVe Pointer from memory to register or from register to memory
LPD	register,memory	Load register with address from memory
LPDI	register,data	Load register with address from immediate data
ADD	destination,source	ADD register to memory or memory to register
ADDI	destination,data	ADD immediate data to register or memory
AND	destination,source	AND register to memory or memory to register
ANDI	destination,data	AND immediate data to register or memory
OR	destination,source	OR register to memory or memory to register
ORI	destination,data	OR immediate data to register or memory
NOT	destination	NOT contents of register or memory
DEC	destination	DEC contents of register or memory

INC	destination	INC contents of register or memory
JMP	target	JuMP unconditionally to target
JMCE	source, target	Jump if Masked Compare is Equal
JMCNE	source,target	Jump if Masked Compare is Not Equal
JZ	source, target	Jump if source is Zero
JNZ	source,target	Jump if source is Not Zero
JBT	source,bit,target	Jump if BiT is set
JNBT	source,bit,target	Jump if BiT is clear
CALL	save address,target	CALL target subroutine
CLR	destination,bit	CLeaR selected bit
SET	destination,bit	SET selected bit
TSL	destination,value,target	Test and Set while Locked
NOP		No OPeration
SINTR		Set INTeRrupt service bit
WID	source width,destination width	set bus WIDths
XFER		Enter DMA mode

Table 5.2: Summary of the 8089 IOP instructions.

Several instructions deserve special attention.

The Jump if Mask/Compare is Equal (JMCE) and Jump if Mask/Compare is *Not* Equal (JMCNE) instructions use the IOP's Mask/Compare register. These instructions have a source and a target. A match is made between the source and the MC register, and a jump to the target is made according to the results of the match. A match is made if the following happens:

For each bit of the mask byte which is set, the corresponding bits of the source byte and the compare byte are the same.

This gives a very general, powerful compare operation. Without modifying the data or any registers it is able to tell when a certain subset of bits matches a given pattern. For example, suppose you wish to jump if a data byte is the ASCII code for either lowercase or uppercase A and you don't care if the highest bit (bit number 7, the parity bit) is either on or off. Since the code for A is 41H = 01000001B and the code for a is 61H = 01100001B, bit number 5 can be either 0 or 1 and thus will not be included in the mask. If we also don't include bit number 7, then the mask will be 5FH = 01011111B (all ones except for bits 5 and 7). Only the bits which are 1 in this mask will be examined in the test, and the 0 bits (bit numbers 5 and 7) will be ignored. The compare byte can be any one of the following: 41H = 01000001B, 61H = 01100001B, C1H = 11000001B, or E1H = 11100001B, for any of these constitutes a valid match. See the figure below.

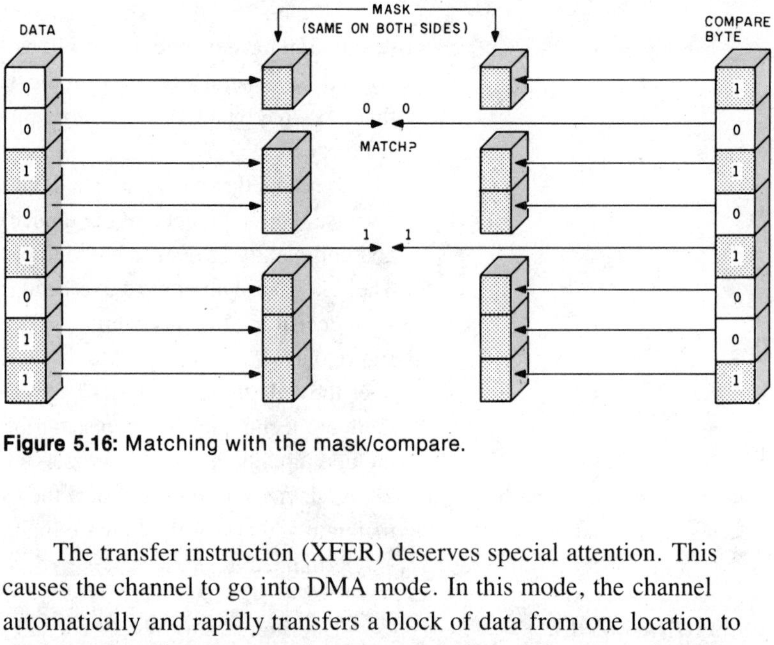

Figure 5.16: Matching with the mask/compare.

The transfer instruction (XFER) deserves special attention. This causes the channel to go into DMA mode. In this mode, the channel automatically and rapidly transfers a block of data from one location to another. These locations can be either memory or I/O ports and can be located in the main memory or in the I/O space. All of this can be independently set for both the source and the destination. Another interesting feature of this transfer is the ability to automatically convert between 8-bit and 16-bit data buses. The source or destination can independently be either 8 or 16 bits wide. The width instruction WID is used to set these data bus widths.

The address of the source is contained in either register GA or GB, and the address of the destination is in the other one. A bit in the channel control register determines which way it is. As we mentioned previously, the condition for terminating the transfer is also determined by bits in the channel control register. Termination of transmission can happen after a single transfer, or in three other ways: for a specified byte count (in the BC register), on a masked compare (using the mask/compare register), or upon external signal (using the EXT pin for that channel). These last three ways can be turned on or off independently. Then the transfer will terminate on the first one that occurs which is selected.

Translation (discussed previously) can also take place during the transfer. Again, a bit in the channel control register turns this option on and off. The GC register is used to point to the translation table if this option is selected.

The speed of execution for the transfer instruction depends on the bus sizes of the source and destination, whether or not the translation option has been selected, as well as other factors such as the manner of synchronization (not discussed here). The minimum number of clock cycles required is 8 per transfer. This happens when the source and destination have the same width and there is no translation. If translation is used, then 7 extra clock cycles are required, and if the source and destination have different bus widths, an extra 4 to 8 cycles will be needed. In general a transfer on the 8089 IOP will take much less time than possible by a CPU, but more time than a less intelligent DMA controller.

It seems that the smarter a device is, the slower it operates. This is because the intelligence of the device is directly related to the number and complexity of decisions required to select among various options. There is a large amount of overhead (of time) associated with making such decisions. In other words, a less intelligent device does not have to figure out what you want it to do when you call upon it for service, it just does the only thing that it has been designed to do. On the other hand, there are techniques for increasing the efficiency of devices. These include pipelining, parallel processing, and larger data paths (see Chapter 2). As devices become smarter, they will need to use these techniques to maintain and hopefully increase their performance over the older, more single-minded devices.

8089 IOP SAMPLE PROGRAMS

The figure below shows a small sample program which uses an 8089 IOP to initialize an 8155 Programmable Serial Interface Controller (PSIC) and input a block of data from it. The figure also shows an equivalent program written for the 8086/8088. The initialization routine sets the 8251 SIC transmission rate to either 300 or 1200 baud, depending upon a parameter called BAUDFG. In the 8089 IOP version, this parameter is stored in the parameter block and is accessed using the parameter pointer (PP) as a base with an offset. The PP is set when the IOP is initialized to point to the beginning of the parameter block. The IOP adds the offset to PP to get the address of BAUDFG within the parameter block. This offset is not specified at assembly time in our program; instead, its value is automatically filled in later by a linker program.

```
                    IOPORT  EQU     OECH
                    CMDPORT EQU     OEDH
                            EXTERNAL BUFFER,BUFFSZ,TPSAVE, BAUDFG
                    ;
                    ; BLOCK TRANSFER ROUTINE
                    ; ***********************

0000'  8B 9F 00* 1C  BEGIN:  CALL    [PP],TPSAV,XINIT ;INITIALIZE USART
0004'  11 30 00EC             MOVI    GA,IOPORT        ;DATA PORT
0008'  31 08 00000* 0000*     LPDI    GB,BUFFER        ;BEGINNING OF BUFFER
000E'  71 30 0000*            MOVI    BC,BUFFSIZ       ;SIZE OF BUFFER
0012'  F1 30 7F1A             MOVI    MC,07F1AH        ;STRIP PARITY
                                                       ;AND CK FOR CONTROL Z
0016'  D1 30 8A09             MOVI    CC,08A09H        ;CONTROLS FOR XFER
001A'  60 00                  XFER                     ;TELL IT TO TRANSFER
001C'  80 00                  WID     8,8              ;NOW DO IT
001E'  20 48                  HLT                      ;DONE SO STOP
                    ;
                    ; EXTERNAL I/O (USART) INITIALIZATION
                    ; ***********************************
0020'  31 30 00ED  XINIT:  MOVI    GB,CMDPORT       ;COMMAND PORT ADDRESS OF USART
0024'  08 4D AA            MOVBI   [GB],0AAH        ;DUMMY COMMAND TO USART
0027'  08 4D 40            MOVBI   [GB],40H         ;RESET COMMAND
002A'  02 AF 00*           NOTB    GA,[PP].BAUDFG   ;LD BAUD RATE INDICATOR
002D'  08 28 01            ANDBI   GA,1             ; AND USE IT TO CREATE
0030'  08 24 CE            ORBI    GA,0CEH          ; USART MODE INSTRUCTION
0033'  00 85               MOVB    [GB],GA          ;SEND MODE INSTRUCTION TO USART
0035'  08 4D 27            MOVBI   [GB],27H         ;COMMAND TO TRANSMIT & RECEIVE
0038'  83 8F 00*           MOVP    TP,[PP].TPSAV    ; RETURN
                    ;
                            END
```

Figure 5.17a: Small 8089 IOP program to initialize and use an 8251.

```
     XMACRO-86 3.36   1
                    ;
                            EXTERNAL       BUFFER,BUFFSZ,CKBRK,BAUDFG
                    ;
                    ; BLOCK TRANSFER ROUTINE
                    ; ***********************
0000'  E8 0018'   INBLK:  CALL    XINIT            ;INITIALIZE 8251 USART
0003'  8B 0E 0000*        MOV     CX,BUFFSZ        ;BUFFER SIZE
0007'  BF 0000*           MOVI    DI,BUFFER        ;POINT TO BEGINNING OF BUFFER
000A'  FC                 CLD                      ;FORWARD DIRECTION
000B'  E8 0025'   INBKLP: CALL    XINP             ;TEST FOR THE CHARACTER
000E'  75 FB              JNZ     INBKLP           ;LOOP UNTIL CHARACTER
0010'  3C 1A              CMPBI   AL,1AH           ;CONTROL Z?
```

```
0012'   74 06                        JZ        INBKRT        ;IF IT IS, THEN RETURN
0014'   AA                           STOC                    ;STORE CHARACTER
0015' \ E8 FFE8*                      CALL      CKBRK         ;KEY INTERRUPT?
0018'   E0 F1                        LOOPNZ    INBKLP        ;LOOP UNTIL KEY OR BUFFER FULL
001A'   C3             INBKRT: RET
                       ;
                       ; EXTERNAL I/O (USART) INITIALIZATION
                       ; **************************************
001B'   B0 AA          XINIT:  MOVBI     AL,0AAH       ;DUMMY COMMAND
001D'   E6 ED                  OUTB      0EDH          ;  SENT TO USART
001F'   B0 40                  MOVBI     AL,40H        ;RESET COMMAND
0021'   E6 ED                  OUTB      0EDH          ;  SENT TO USART
0023'   A0 0000*               MOVB      AL,BAUDFG     ;LD BAUD RATE INDICATOR
0026'   F6 D0                  NOTB      AL            ;  AND USE IT TO CREATE
0028'   24 01                  ANDBI     AL,1          ;  USART MODE INSTRUCTION
002A'   0C CE                  ORBI      AL,0CEH
002C'   E6 ED                  OUTB      0EDH          ;SEND MODE INSTRUCTION TO USART
002E'   B0 27                  MOVBI     AL,27H        ;COMMAND TO TRANSMIT & RECEIVE
0030'   E6 ED                  OUTB      0EDH          ;  SENT TO USART
0032'   C3                     RET
                       ;
                       ; EXTERNAL INPUT ROUTINE
                       ;***********************
0033'   E4 ED          XINP:   INB       0EDH          ;CHECK EXTERNAL INPUT STATUS WORD
0035'   F6 D0                  NOTB      AL            ;  FOR RAISED INPUT FLAG
0037'   24 02                  ANDBI     AL,02
0039'   75 06                  JNZ       XINEND        ;IF NONE THEN RETURN
003B'   E4 EC                  INB       0ECH          ;READ EXTERNAL INPUT
003D'   24 7F                  ANDBI     AL,7FH        ;STRIP OFF PARITY BIT
003F'   3A C0                  CMPB      AL,AL         ;SET Z BIT
0041'   C3             XINEND: RET
                       ;
                                       END
```

Figure 5.17b: Equivalent 8086 program.

Notice that 4 bytes are sent to the command port of the 8251 PSIC. The PSIC expects a mode byte and then a series of command bytes. The first byte we send (AAH) is a dummy command which is needed to synchronize with this sequence so that the next byte is a command byte. Then we reset the PSIC so that the next byte will be a mode byte (setting the baud rate among other things). Note that this mode byte is computed on the spot by dropping a bit from the variable "BAUDFG" into a bit pattern which is supplied as a constant. The final byte is a command byte enabling the 8251 to start working for us. The NOTB instruction deserves special attention. In this program, we used a special two-operand version which takes a byte from memory and puts its complement into a register.

In the IOP version, the one instruction XFER causes the transfer. It so happens that the actual transfer will not take place until the instruction *after* the XFER instruction. It will take about 8 clock cycles to process 1 byte. In the CPU version, there is a loop which takes more than 100 clock cycles per byte. However, the PSIC operates at 300 or 1200 BAUD

(300 or 1200 bits per second = about 160,000 to 40,000 clock cycles per byte). Thus, in this program, both the IOP and the CPU execution time is negligible.

The advantage to using the IOP in this case is that the CPU would be free to do other things instead of spending this incredible amount of time waiting for the 8251 PSIC.

We have seen that the 8089 IOP fills an important role, which is the dedicated transfer of blocks of data associated with I/O. It can also be used to increase the system's performance with regard to the so-called string or block transfer instructions which have traditionally been handled by the CPU. If an 8086 CPU uses an 8089 IOP to make its block transfers, then the results will exceed those possible by the Z8000 or the MC68000, especially when special control is needed to terminate the transfer.

The figure below uses the 8089 IOP to transfer a block of text from memory to memory. The beginning address of the source block is SOURCE, the beginning address of the destination block is DEST, and the maximum size of the block (in bytes) is given by the variable COUNT. All three quantities are stored in the parameter block. If any character (with the parity bit stripped off) is a carriage return, then the transfer is terminated. For contrast, the figure also shows a similar program written in 8086 code as if there was no IOP. The IOP program will transfer information at a maximum rate of 8 clock cycles per byte (if it has the bus to itself). With a 5-megahertz clock frequency, it will be able to move 64 K in about a tenth of a second. Since the CPU cannot accomplish what the IOP can do in a single instruction, it requires a loop. This loop executes in about 45 clock cycles, making the CPU almost six times slower than the IOP for this particular task.

```
0000'   03 8B 00*       BEGIN:  LPD     GA,[PP].SOURCE      ;ADDRESS OF SOURCE
0003'   23 8B 00*               LPD     GB,[PP].DEST        ;ADDRESS OF DESTINATION
0006'   63 83 00*               MOV     BC,[PP].COUNT       ;COUNT
0009'   F1 30 7F0D              MOVI    MC,07F0DH           ;STRIP PARITY
                                                           ; AND CK FOR CARRIAGE RETURN
000D'   D1 30 C209              MOVI    CC,0C209H           ;CONTROLS FOR TRANSFER
0011'   60 00                   XFER                        ;TELL IT TO TRANSFER
0013'   80 00                   WID     8,8                 ;DO IT
0015'   20 48                   HLT                         ;DONE SO STOP
                        ;
                                END
```

Figure 5.18a: Small 8089 IOP program to transfer memory.

```
XMACRO-86 3.36   1
                          ;
                                        EXTERNAL          SOURCE,DEST,COUNT

                          ;
                          ; BLOCK TRANSFER ROUTINE
                          ; ***********************
0000'   8B 36 0000*       BEGIN:  MOV      SI,SOURCE         ;ADDRESS OF SOURCE
0004'   8B 3E 0000*               MOV      DI,DEST           ;ADDRESS OF DESTINATION
0008'   8B 0E 0000*               MOV      CX,COUNT          ;COUNT
000C'   FC                        CLD                        ;FORWARD DIRECTION
000D'   AC                LOOP:   LODC                       ;GET THE BYTE
000E'   8A E0                     MOVB     AH,AL             ;SAVE IT
0010'   24 7F                     ANDBI    AL,7FH            ;STRIP PARITY
0012'   3C 0D                     CMPBI    AL,0DH            ;TEST OF CARRIAGE RETURN
0014'   8A C4                     MOVB     AL,AH             ;RETORE IT
0016'   AA                        STOC                       ;STORE BYTE
0017'   E0 F4                     LOOPNZ   LOOP              ;LOOP UNTIL DONE
0019'   C3                        RET
                          ;
                                  END
```

Figure 5.18b: Equivalent 8086 program.

CONCLUSION

In this chapter, we have presented a survey of the 8089 IOP. We have seen how the IOP works, executing its own programs in a multiprocessing environment under the direction of an 8086/8088 CPU to relieve the CPU of I/O overhead due to slow I/O devices, and how the IOP can *intelligently* transfer blocks of memory at speeds much greater than possible by the CPU.

There are a number of subtle points to know in using the 8089 IOP. In fact, Intel mentions that it expects that there will be specialists in I/O who will program with this device and hardly ever even look at CPU programs. If you wish to learn how to program the 8089 IOP you will have to study further. In particular, you will have to read thoroughly the appropriate sections of *The 8086 Family User's Manual.*

Chapter 6

The 8086/8088 Support Chips

In this chapter, we shall cover chips which supply three kinds of circuitry for an 8086/8088 computer system: clock-generator logic, bus-interface logic, and controllers. Though these chips are less glamorous than the processor chips just covered in the last three chapters, they do perform vital functions which include synchronizing the whole system, connecting the processors with the rest of the system, and connecting the computer with the outside world.

CLOCK-GENERATOR LOGIC

An 8086/8088-based system requires extra logic to supply the timing for the entire system. The Intel 8284 Clock Generator in conjunction with a crystal is designed to do this job. It is interesting to note that the 8085 CPU includes this circuitry within the processor chip. This will probably also be true for future versions of the 8086, starting with the iAPX 186.

The 8284 Clock Generator

The 8284 (see the figure below) is an 18-pin chip which may be used to economically generate the clock signal for the 8086, 8088, 8087,

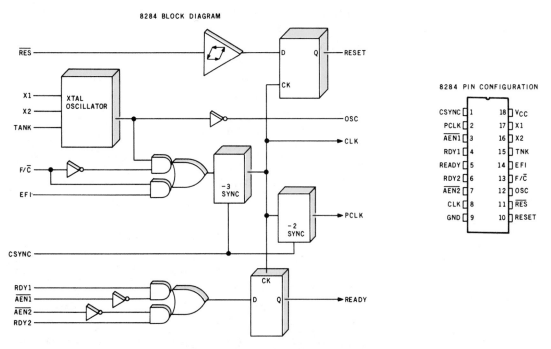

Figure 6.1: 8284 Clock Generator—pinouts and internal structure.

and 8089 processors and their peripherals. The clock signal determines the speed at which the system runs. The standard maximum speed for these processors is a clock frequency of 5 megahertz (meaning $1/(5 * 10^6) = .2 * 10^{-6} = 200$ nanoseconds per cycle), but selected chips are available which run at 8 megahertz ($= 125$ nanoseconds per cycle). Both the standard and selected versions specify a minimum speed of 2 megahertz, although it is possible to run these processor chips even slower.

The 8284 Clock Generator requires either a crystal or an external logic signal as a frequency source. The choice is selected by wiring a pin either to ground or to the 5-volt supply. This source is always three times the frequency of the resulting clock signal produced by the 8284 Clock Generator. By choosing different crystals the speed can be varied from about 4 megahertz to a little over 8 megahertz. If an external signal is used, the speed can be varied from one cycle at a time (under manual control) up to about 8 megahertz.

For optimum performance of the processors, the clock signal produced by the 8284 has a 33 percent duty cycle. This means that the clock attains its high level only 33 percent of the time. Because the source frequency is three times this output clock signal, it is easy for the clock generator to generate this type of shape for the clock signal. To see this, consider a tuba player in a band whose job is to play all the "oomps" in a waltz's familiar three-beats-to-the-measure "oomp-pa-pa" rhythm. The tuba player merely has to count 1, 2, 3 over and over again, just playing an "oomp" when the count is 1 and resting during the other two beats. The beats correspond to the crystal frequency and each three-beat measure corresponds to a full clock cycle. Like the tuba player, the 8284 Clock Generator only needs to be able to count to 3 over and over, but instead of "oomping" and resting, it turns on the clock signal during the time periods in which the count is 1 and turns it off during the time periods when the count is 2 or 3.

Normally, there are three signals which go from the 8284 Clock Generator to the processor. These are the CLK (the clock signal), RESET, and READY. These last two signals are routed through the clock generator to synchronize them with the CLK signal.

The function of the RESET signal is to restart the computer as though you turned it off and then on again. You will need to do this in situations such as an infinite loop or a power glitch which has affected parts of your program in memory. Turning the machine off and then on again is hard on the computer because it causes voltage surges which strain the electrical components. Pulling the RESET line is a much safer way to achieve the same logical result.

The function of the READY signal is used to synchronize the processor with slower external devices. The READY signal goes from the external device through the clock generator to the processor. When the processor requests access to a device which is not ready to make a transfer, the device sends a 0 over the ready line. When the processor gets this signal it spins its wheels until it gets a 1 on the ready line. Only then does it continue with the program.

The 8284 Clock Generator also produces a signal PCLK (peripheral clock) which is one half the frequency of CLK and has a 50 percent duty cycle. It can be used to drive logic which requires this older type of timing.

BUS-INTERFACE LOGIC

Bus-interface logic is needed for two reasons: 1) the signals from the processors may not be strong enough to drive the rest of the system, and 2) the signals produced by the processors may not directly correspond to those required by the rest of the system.

The 8288 Bus Controller, 8286 Octal Data Transceiver, and 8282 Octal Latch (see figures 6.2–6.4) are used to solve these interfacing problems for a maximum mode 8086 or 8088 system. In addition, the 8289 Bus Arbiter can be used to interface *processor clusters* to the main system bus in larger systems. Although some of these chips, in particular the 8286 Octal Data Transceiver and the 8282 Octal Address Latch, are used for many other purposes, we will only consider them in light of what they can do for us in this situation.

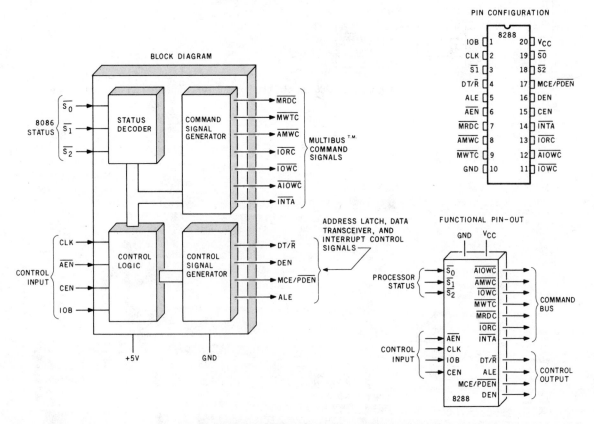

Figure 6.2: 8288 Bus Controller—pinouts and internal structure.

PIN CONFIGURATIONS   LOGIC DIAGRAMS

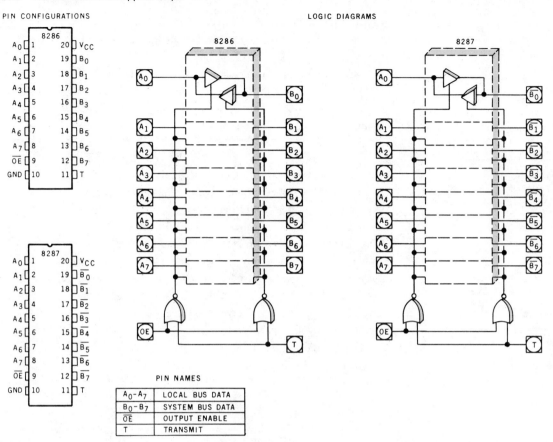

PIN NAMES	
A_0-A_7	LOCAL BUS DATA
B_0-B_7	SYSTEM BUS DATA
$\overline{OE}$	OUTPUT ENABLE
T	TRANSMIT

Figure 6.3: 8286 Octal Data Transceiver—pinouts and internal structure.

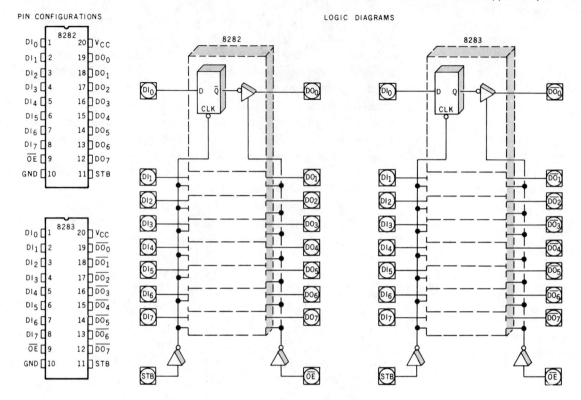

Figure 6.4: 8282 Octal Address Latch—pinouts and internal structure.

In addition to amplifying the 8086/8088/8087/8089 signals, these chips solve the problem of too many signals for the 40 pins on the 8086/8088/8087/8089 processors. They neatly wrap up the control logic needed to do this. Informally, they supply what is called glue to hold the system together. A system bus has four subbuses: power, control, address, and data. Let's ignore the first subbus, which requires such things as power supplies and regulators, and concentrate on just the last three. Each of these three chips neatly takes care of interfacing the processor chips with each of these three subbuses.

The 8288 Bus Controller

The 8288 Bus Controller is a 20-pin chip which is used to interface the processor to the control bus. It decodes the maximum mode 8086/8088 status signals S0, S1, and S2 to produce a whole array of useful control types of signals, including memory read control (MRDC), I/O read control (IORC), memory write control (MWTC), I/O write control (IOWC), address latch enable (ALE), and data enable (DEN). Some of these output signals, such as the read and write controls, are destined for a system bus and some, such as the address and data enable controls, are for the other chips which interface the processor to the other subbuses (the 8286 Transceiver and 8286 Octal Latch). There are also some inputs to the 8288 from these other devices. The tables below show the bus signals produced by the 8288 Bus Controller in response to the status signals from the processors.

S2	S1	S0	processor state	8288 bus commands
0	0	0	interrupt acknowledge	INTA
0	0	1	read I/O port	IORC
0	1	0	write I/O port	IOWC,AIOWC
0	1	1	halt	none
1	0	0	code access	MRDC
1	0	1	read memory	MRDC
1	1	0	write memory	MWTC,AMWC
1	1	1	passive	none

Table 6.1: 8288 decoding.

MRDC	Memory Read Command
MWTC	Memory Write Command
IORC	I/O Read Command
IOWC	I/O Write Command
AMWC	Advanced Memory Write Command
AIOWC	Advanced I/O Write Command
INT	Interrupt Acknowledge

Table 6.2: 8288 bus commands.

The 8286 Transceiver

The 8286 Transceiver is a 20-pin chip which is used to interface the processor to the data bus. It is used to buffer the data going to and from the processor. It is needed for several possible reasons. For example, sometimes the processor data lines cannot deliver enough current to drive a normal load of external devices and have to be amplified before going onto the system bus. Another use is to convert the two-way, bidirectional signals to one-way, unidirectional signals needed by some external data buses. A third possible use is to help extract the data signals from the address signals. Note that the data and address signals are *multiplexed* over the same pins on the 8086/8088.

The 8282 Octal Latch

The 8282 Octal Latch is a 20-pin chip which is used to interface the processor multiplexed address/data lines to the system's address bus. The 8282 Octal Latch waits until address information is on these pins and then grabs this information and holds it on the system's address bus. Using the address latch enable (ALE) line, the processor (minimum mode) or the 8088 Bus Controller (maximum mode) tells the Octal Latch when to do its grabbing.

All of these interface chips can be tri-stated (electrically disconnected from the bus) when other processors or controllers have control of the bus. See figure 6.5.

The 8289 Bus Arbiter

The 8289 Bus Arbiter (see figure 6.6) is used for larger 8086/8088 systems. It provides a connection or interface between an 8086/8088/8089 processor and a system bus which has other processors connected to it. The 8289 comes in a 20-pin package.

The 8289 works as follows: The 8086/8088/8089 issues signals as though the 8289 were not there. If the system bus is otherwise occupied with such activity as might be generated by other processors, then the 8289 issues a NOT READY signal to the processor which waits until it gets a READY signal back from the 8289, indicating that the system bus is available. (Recall that the READY signal is routed through the 8284 Clock Generator to synchronize it with the clock signal.) See figure 6.7 for a block diagram of how to use the 8289 Bus Arbiter in a circuit.

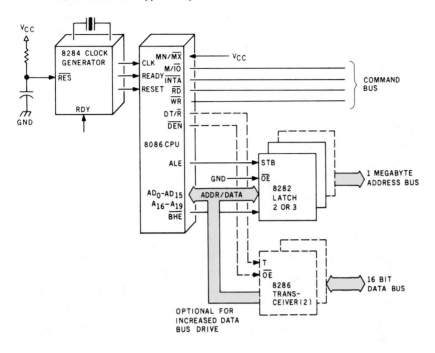

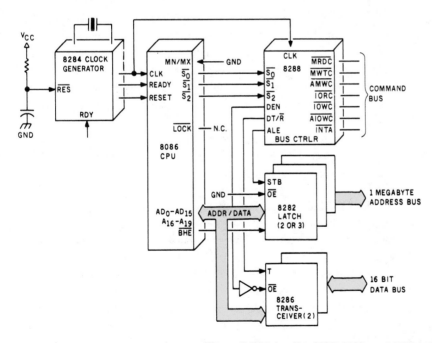

Figure 6.5: Using the 8288, 8286, and 8282 interface chips.

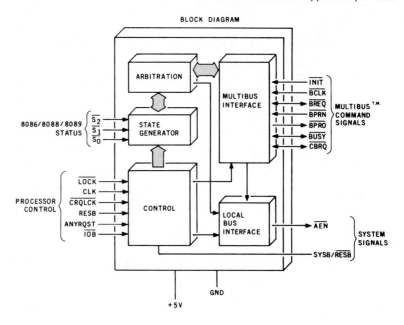

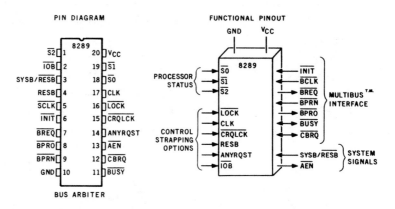

Figure 6.6: 8289 Bus Arbiter—pinouts and internal structure.

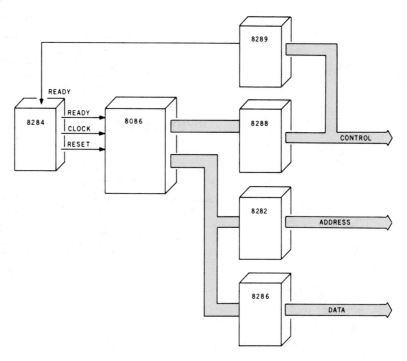

Figure 6.7: Block diagram showing how to use the bus arbiter.

The 8289 Bus Arbiter has several user-programmable schemes for deciding when to let its processor have access to the master bus. The three basic methods are: *parallel priority, serial priority,* and *rotating priority.* Each of these schemes involves the use of several bus arbiters, one for each local processor cluster.

With the parallel priority scheme, each bus arbiter sends a bus request signal to a central, bus-priority circuit. This circuit is set up so that it assigns different priority to each cluster. It determines which bus request has the highest priority and then tells the corresponding bus arbiter to go ahead and grab the bus.

With the serial priority scheme, signal lines connect one bus arbiter to another along strings like Christmas tree lights. The first in line has higher priority than the next and so on down the line. The bus priority out (BPRO) line of each is connected to the bus priority in (BPRN) line of the next lower priority bus arbiter. This scheme requires no special master circuitry.

With the rotating priority scheme, signal lines from each bus arbiter go to some central circuitry as in the parallel priority scheme. This time, however, a more complicated *dynamic* scheme decides which one should have the bus.

The figure below shows these three schemes.

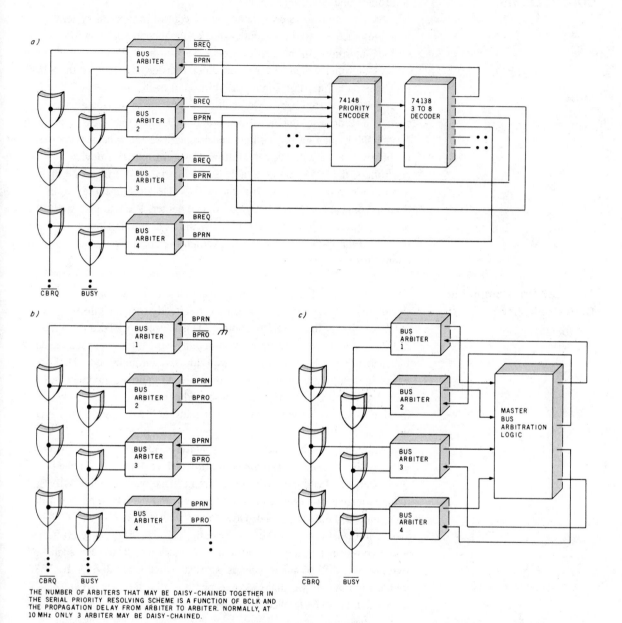

THE NUMBER OF ARBITERS THAT MAY BE DAISY-CHAINED TOGETHER IN
THE SERIAL PRIORITY RESOLVING SCHEME IS A FUNCTION OF BCLK AND
THE PROPAGATION DELAY FROM ARBITER TO ARBITER. NORMALLY, AT
10 MHz ONLY 3 ARBITER MAY BE DAISY-CHAINED.

Figure 6.8 a, b, c: Three bus arbitration schemes.

SYSTEM AND DEVICE CONTROLLERS

There are two types of controllers in a computer system, system controllers and device controllers.

System controllers provide automatic control for special system functions such as rapid transfers of blocks of data and coordination of various interrupts. In this section we shall cover the 8237 Programmable DMA Controller which performs the clock transfer function and the 8259 Programmable Interrupt Controller which coordinates interrupts.

Device controllers provide intelligent interface to outside devices such as disk drives, keyboards, and printers. Device controllers can be further subdivided into two kinds, general purpose and special purpose. In this section we will study the following general-purpose device controllers: the 8251 Programmable Serial Interface Controller and the 8255 Programmable Parallel Interface Controller. Both of these can be used to connect a variety of devices to a computer. We will also study the 8275 Programmable CRT Controller and the 8272 Single/Double Density, Floppy-Disk Controller as examples of special-purpose controllers.

The 8237 Programmable DMA Controller

DMA stands for direct memory access and a DMA Controller is a device which takes over the system bus to directly transfer information from one part of the system to another. This is necessary because often blocks of data have to be moved very rapidly, sometimes at speeds even faster than is practical if each byte were to move through the CPU. For example, displaying pictures on a video screen requires a complete scan (one *frame*) of the screen 30 times a second or a half scan (one *field*) every 60 seconds. (The two half scans (fields) are interlaced (interwoven) on the screen to form one frame.) Suppose we wish to display a black and white picture which has 256 horizontal by 240 vertical dots which are either on or off. Such a *medium-resolution* picture is usually scanned once every field and thus twice every frame. That way each dot will actually appear as a double dot on the screen, and the whole picture will be scanned 60 times a second. Now 256 by 240 dots will require 61440 bits of information or 7680 bytes. Scanning through all of these 60 times a second means that there is a little over 2 microseconds to scan each byte. $(1/60 = 16.67$ microseconds per scan which when divided by 7680 yields approximately 2 microseconds per byte.) Each time the byte is scanned it has to be fetched from memory. With a 5-megahertz clock, this allows approximately 10 clock cycles per byte. Since it takes an 8086/8088 CPU approximately 17 cycles to move one byte, it is impossible for the CPU to do this. Even if the CPU were to move 16 bits (2 bytes) at a time, it would spend about half its time shoveling bits for the video display. This would be a complete waste of time for the processing power of the CPU.

For the computer to be efficient, it needs special circuitry to read these bytes. One solution is to store these bytes in a special display memory with built-in scanning circuitry and an *arbitration scheme* between the memory accesses by the scanning circuitry and memory accesses by the CPU. This is sometimes called a *frame buffer*. The memory in such a system is said to be *dual ported* because there are two different ways to access it.

In contrast, one of the first low-cost systems (the Cromemco Dazzler) stored these bytes in regular memory (single ported) and the scanning circuitry consisted mainly of a device called a DMA controller which actually took over the bus and generated its own address and control information on the system's bus. The Dazzler actually had only about a third of the resolution in this example and it was designed to work with a clock speed of about 2 megahertz, but this presents a timing problem very comparable to the one in our example.

Because of the narrow or impossible timing constraints, DMA as described above is not recommended for direct scanning of regular memory for video display, but is the preferred method for making quick transfers of information. For example, DMA is often used when a picture or part of a picture needs to be moved quickly between a frame buffer and regular memory, or when the contents of buffers for a floppy disk need to be quickly transferred to new locations.

In general a DMA controller is used as follows: The DMA controller is told to make a transfer either by the CPU or some special circumstance; then the DMA controller makes a request to gain control of the bus from the CPU, other processors, or controllers which might currently be using the bus; these other devices then relinquish control of the bus by putting their lines into the tri-state condition (electrically disconnecting these lines); they then grant the bus to the DMA controller; and, finally, the DMA controller takes over the bus, generating its own address and control signals for the bus and causing the transfer of information. See the figure below.

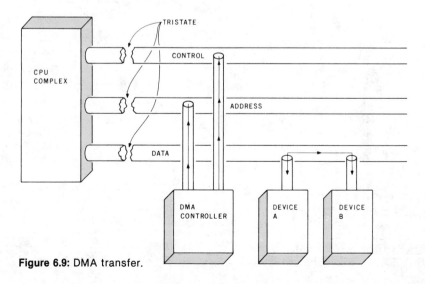

Figure 6.9: DMA transfer.

The Intel 8237 DMA Controller shown in the figure below is used to perform DMA transfers. It comes in a 40-pin package. The 8237 DMA Controller can provide service for a total of four different devices at once. For example, one 8237 DMA Controller might be handling transfers for two different CRT displays, a floppy-disk controller, and a

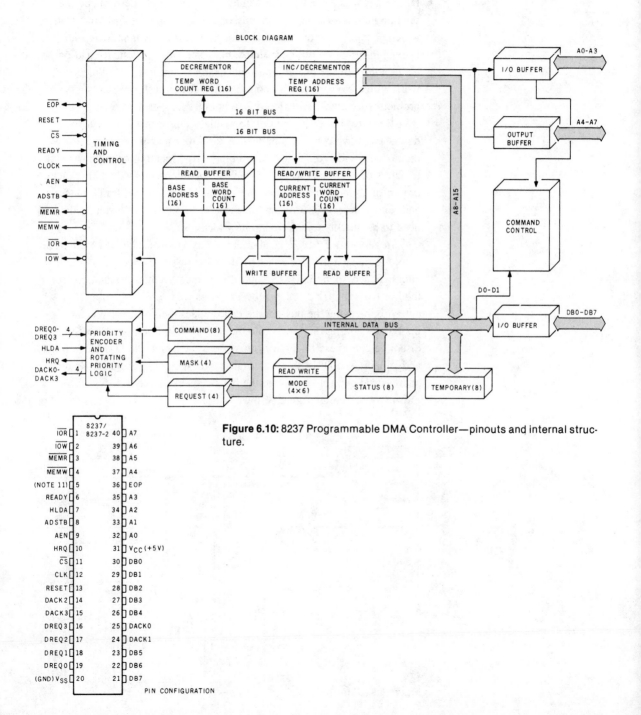

Figure 6.10: 8237 Programmable DMA Controller—pinouts and internal structure.

magnetic tape unit. Each device is assigned a *channel* in the 8237. By connecting several DMA chips together, any number of channels can be supported at once. The 8237 has registers to keep track of source and destination addresses, counts and masks, and commands and status. The 8237 is programmed by writing I/O bytes to special command and mode registers. Many options are available including timing; priority schemes; and location, size, and type of transfer.

A special, compressed timing mode is available in which transfers are made in just two cycles.

Priority schemes are important. For example, if a DMA transfer is being made for a video display, then the DMA transfer should always take precedence over the CPU. Otherwise, blank spots will frequently appear on the screen.

You can make transfers whose source or destination is either a fixed I/O port or a block of memory. If the source or destination is in memory, then the address is automatically incremented (or decremented) after each access (byte move). If the source or destination is an I/O port, then the address should remain constant during the transfer.

The 8237 has a very useful feature called *autoinitialization*. When you select this, you automatically restore parameters (such as beginning address and count) for a channel after the transfer is complete. This way you can repeat the same action without needing to update the old counter parameters in the chip.

The 8259 Programmable Interrupt Controller

The 8259 Programmable Interrupt Controller (PIC) (see figure 6.11) is used to directly handle interrupts for up to eight different devices, and up to 64 devices by hooking as many as eight 8259s together. In one mode, the 8259 is designed to work with the 8080/8085 processors, and in another mode it is designed to work with the 8086/8088 processors. The basic ideas behind interrupt I/O have been discussed in the section on the 8089 IOP earlier in this chapter.

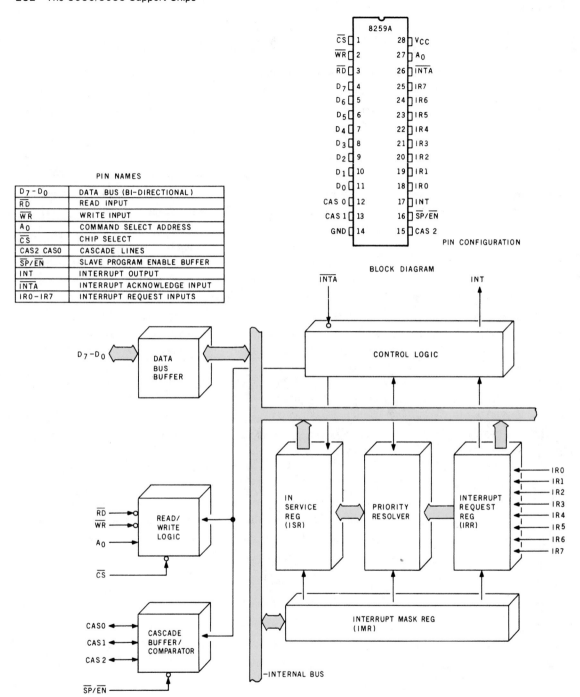

PIN NAMES

$D_7 - D_0$	DATA BUS (BI-DIRECTIONAL)
$\overline{RD}$	READ INPUT
$\overline{WR}$	WRITE INPUT
A_0	COMMAND SELECT ADDRESS
$\overline{CS}$	CHIP SELECT
CAS2 CAS0	CASCADE LINES
$\overline{SP}/\overline{EN}$	SLAVE PROGRAM ENABLE BUFFER
INT	INTERRUPT OUTPUT
$\overline{INTA}$	INTERRUPT ACKNOWLEDGE INPUT
IR0-IR7	INTERRUPT REQUEST INPUTS

Figure 6.11: 8259 Programmable Interrupt Controller—pinouts and internal structure.

The 8259 PIC acts like a receptionist, and each device is like someone who wants to talk to the boss who is, of course, the CPU. Like a receptionist, the 8259 has the job of only letting one device through at a time with some devices having a higher priority than others.

Each device has an interrupt line which runs to one of the eight interrupt input lines of the PIC. The 8259 PIC can be programmed to ignore or to monitor any combination of these lines. This selection is determined via what is called the *interrupt mask,* a byte which is sent to the PIC by the CPU through a port located in the I/O space. This is called a *control* port. The 8 bits in this mask correspond to the eight devices. To turn off interrupts from a device, you merely set the corresponding bit in the mask equal to 1. Thus, the PIC will ignore all eight devices if you send it a mask of 11111111B, and it will respond to all of them if you send the mask 00000000H.

If two or more devices (which are not *masked out)* signal the PIC for service at the same time, then the PIC determines which goes first according to several user-selectable schemes. These include a fixed priority and a rotating priority scheme. The devices not yet serviced wait their turn in a *reception area* which the PIC keeps track of. When a device begins to be serviced, the PIC moves it out of this waiting area into the working area.

There is one interrupt line which runs from the PIC to the interrupt input line, called interrupt request (INTR), on the 8086/8088 CPU. When the CPU gets a request on this line, it sends an acknowledge signal on the interrupt acknowledge (INTA) line. According to the type of CPU, the 8259 PIC continues servicing an interrupt request in one of two ways. When used with the 8080/8085, the PIC actually causes a CALL instruction to be sent to the processor, even providing the address of the subroutine. The processor is fooled into thinking that this instruction was fetched from memory. In the 8086/8088 mode, the 8259 interfaces cleanly with the rather nice interrupt handling system of the 8086/8088 described previously. It sends a byte which tells the CPU what *type* (location in the interrupt table) of interrupt should be executed. Of course, knowing Intel, the exact address of the subroutine (for 8080/8085) or the value of the interrupt type (for 8086/8088) is completely user-programmable. Well, actually, there is a whole block of addresses or types. In the case of the 8086/8088, the eight devices are assigned eight consecutively numbered interrupt types starting at any multiple of 8.

There are roughly 45 bits which can be used to program the 8259 PIC! These include the mask bits, the interrupt type bits, the CPU mode (8085 or 8086), the priority scheme, and a whole host of other possible options. These bits are set by sending the PIC sequences of bytes through its control port. The choices are rather overwhelming.

The 8251 Programmable Serial Interface Controller

The 8251 (see the figure below) is a programmable serial interface controller (PSIC). It assists in connecting devices to the computer which send 1 bit at a time. This is called *serial transmission*. Serial transmission is preferred over parallel transmission when information has to be transmitted over long distances. This is so for several reasons: sending 1 bit at a time uses less wire (two or three lines instead of eight or nine); serial lines are run at slower speeds, and thus there are fewer errors due to noise; and serial transmission is easily encoded and decoded for transmission over telephone lines. You use a modem for this.

PIN NAMES

D_7D_0	DATA BUS (8 BITS)	$\overline{DSR}$	DATA SET READY
C/D	CONTROL OR DATA IS TO BE WRITTEN OR READ	$\overline{DTA}$	DATA TERMINAL READY
$\overline{RD}$	READ DATA COMMAND	SYNDET-BD	SYNC DETECT / BREAK DETECT
$\overline{WR}$	WRITE DATA OR CONTROL COMMAND		
$\overline{CS}$	CHIP ENABLE	$\overline{RTS}$	REQUEST TO SEND DATA
CLK	CLOCK PULSE (TTL)	$\overline{CTS}$	CLEAR TO SEND DATA
RESET	RESET	$T_X E$	TRANSMITTER EMPTY
$\overline{T_X C}$	TRANSMITTER CLOCK	V_{CC}	+ 5 VOLT SUPPLY
$T_X D$	TRANSMITTER DATA	GND	GROUND
$\overline{R_X C}$	RECEIVER CLOCK		
$R_X D$	RECEIVER DATA		
$R_X RDY$	RECEIVER READY (HAS CHARACTER FOR 8080)		
$T_X RDY$	TRANSMITTER READY (READY FOR CHAR FROM 8080)		

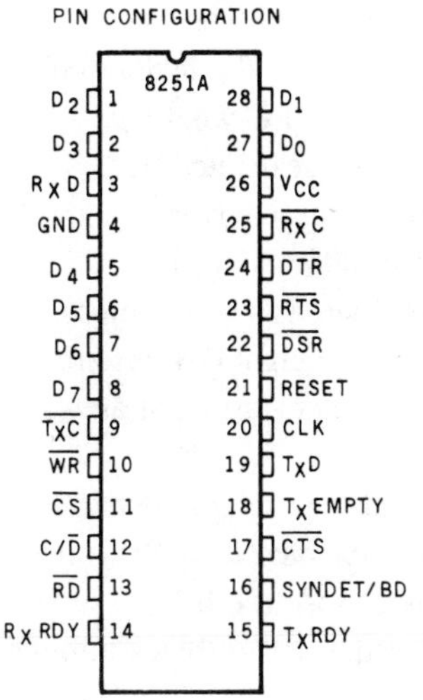

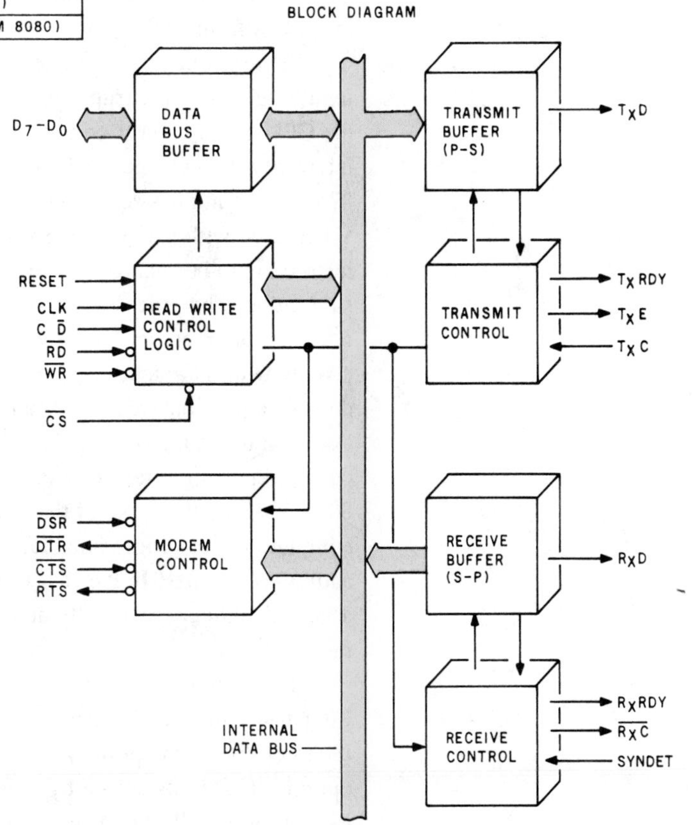

BLOCK DIAGRAM

PIN CONFIGURATION

Figure 6.12: 8251 Programmable Serial Interface Controller—pinouts and internal structure.

Since the computer internally deals with the data in parallel, a serial interface controller has to convert between parallel and serial. A device which does this is usually called a universal asynchronous receiver/transmitter (UART). The 8251 is actually a universal synchronous/asynchronous receiver/transmitter (USART). The difference is that the 8251 can operate both in an asynchronous mode and a synchronous mode. In the asynchronous mode each byte is handled separately. When a byte is ready for transmission, 1 or 2 bits are sent indicating that the next few bits belong to a byte of information. These are called the *start bits*. When all the bits of the byte have been sent, *stop bits* are sometimes transmitted. It usually takes about 10 bits to transmit one character this way. In the synchronous mode, a whole block of bytes is sent as a unit. There is a special starting pattern, but there are no extra bits sent with the individual bytes. The synchronous method is faster, but requires more software overhead and is only suitable for larger batches of information. In either mode the individual bits are sent at a rate called the baud rate. Some standard baud rates are 110, 300, 1200, 2400, 4800, 9600, and 19,200 bits per second.

The 8251 PSIC comes in a 28-pin package. It has to be initialized with a sequence of bytes usually sent through the system bus to the I/O space. The user can select synchronous or asynchronous transmission. For asynchronous transmissions, the user can also select the format for sending characters. This includes the number of start bits, stop bits, and the type of parity checking (including no parity). There is even a control for the speed of transmission. When used in conjunction with the 8253 Programmable Interval Timer, the 8251 Programmable Serial Interface Controller can adjust its speed to whatever speed the sender is using (just how this is done won't be discussed here). Figure 6.13 shows how to program the 8251 PSIC.

The 8255 Programmable Parallel Interface Controller

The 8255 Programmable Parallel Interface Controller (PPIC) (see figure 6.14) assists in connecting devices to the computer which send whole bytes (or even 12-, 16-, or 24-bit words) at a time. Parallel transmission is useful for high speed applications using devices which are not too far away from the computer. There is no special timing involved in parallel transmission. The bytes are sent as fast or as slow as the software allows. If the transmission needs to be slow, timing delays are put into the software. The upper limit on the speed is determined by how fast the system can shove them out. The fastest speed can be obtained by using DMA (see the section in this chapter on the 8237 Programmable DMA Controller).

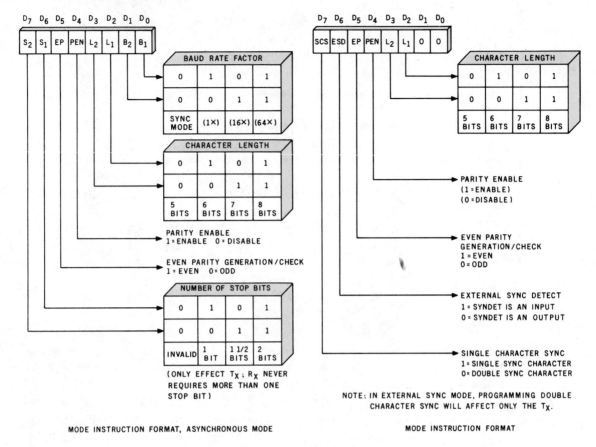

Figure 6.13: Programming in 8251 PSIC.

The 8255 comes in a 40-pin package (the same number as Intel's processors). It provides 24 bits of input or output lines which can be set by the user in a myriad of configurations. There are three basic transmission modes: mode 0 — basic input/output, mode 1 — strobed input/output, and mode 2 — bidirectional bus. The 24 lines are grouped in two 8-bit and two 4-bit groups. In mode 0, there are 16 ways that the directions (input vs. output) can be set for the four groups of bits. Data is simply sent or received over these lines. In mode 1, the two 4-bit groups are used for control and status and the 8-bit groups are used for data. Each 8-bit group can be set to run in either direction. In this mode, the user checks a certain bit in a status byte to see if the external device is ready. When the device is ready, the data byte can be transferred.

PIN CONFIGURATION

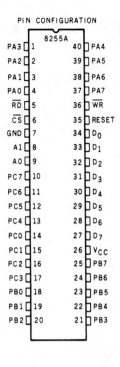

PIN NAMES

D_7-D_0	DATA BUS (BI-DIRECTIONAL)
RESET	RESET INPUT
$\overline{CS}$	CHIP SELECT
$\overline{RD}$	READ INPUT
$\overline{WR}$	WRITE INPUT
A0, A1	PORT ADDRESS
PA7-PA0	PORT A (BIT)
PB7-PB0	PORT B (BIT)
PC7-PC0	PORT C (BIT)
VCC	+5 VOLTS
GND	0 VOLTS

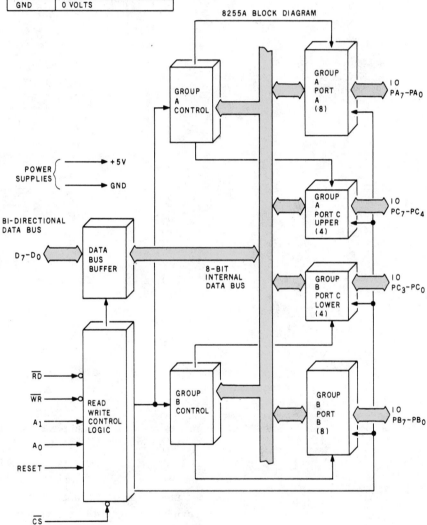

Figure 6.14: 8255 Programmable Parallel Interface Controller—pinouts and internal structure.

Commands are transmitted to the 8255 via a special I/O port. These commands affect such things as the grouping, the direction of the ports, and the assignment of control and status. The figure below shows how this works:

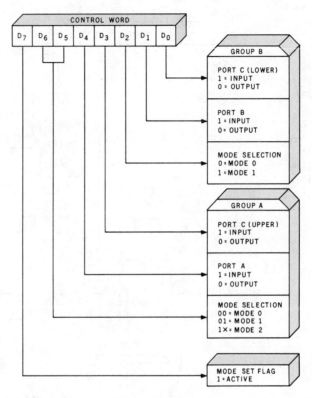

Figure 6.15: Programming the 8255 PPIC.

Figure 6.16 shows an example of a program which uses both the 8255 PPIC and the 8251 PSIC. The main program is a loop which makes the computer a terminal for another computer which could be some distance away. The communications line to this computer uses serial transmission, so we use an 8251 PSIC to interface with it. The local equipment is a keyboard and a video screen. Both of these are connected to our local computer via a single 8255 PPIC. The keyboard and video are considered to be the console for the total system.

The terminal routine first calls initialization routines for the 8255 PPIC and 8251 PSIC. These routines are included. Then the loop starts. First the PPIC is checked for keyboard input. If there is keyboard input, then the character is sent to the external computer via the PSIC, and the loop is started again. If no key was ready, then it checks the PSIC for a character from the external computer. If the external computer has a character, then it is sent to the video via the PPIC.

Three of the routines (CINP, XINP, and XOUT) use a status bit in a status byte to determine when the transfer is to be made. In contrast, the output routine for the console video uses a timing loop to insure that the device doesn't get information faster than it can safely handle.

```
                        ; TERMINAL LOOP
                        ; *************
0000'   E8 001E'        TERM:   CALL    CINIT       ;INITIALIZE PPI FOR PLOTTER
0003'   E8 0024'                CALL    XINIT       ;INITIALIZE USART FOR EXTRNL I/O
0006'   E8 0032'        TERM0:  CALL    CINP        ;LOOK FOR INPUT FROM CONSOLE
0009'   74 07                   JZ      TERM1       ;  IF FOUND GOTO TERM1
000B'   E8 004D'                CALL    XINP        ;LOOK FOR EXTERNAL INPUT
000E'   74 09                   JZ      TERM2       ;  IF FOUND GOTO TERM2
0010'   EB F4                   JMPS    TERM0       ;CONTINUE LOOKING FOR INPUT
0012'   8A E0           TERM1:  MOVB    AH,AL
0014'   E8 0053'                CALL    XOUT        ;TRANSMIT CONSOLE INPUT
0017'   EB ED                   JMPS    TERM0
0019'   8A E0           TERM2:  MOVB    AH,AL
001B'   E8 002C'                CALL    COUT        ;IF NO <ESC>, OUTPUT TO CONSOLE
001E'   E9 FFE5'                JMP     TERM0       ;CONTINUE LOOKING FOR INPUT
                        ;
                        ; CONSOLE (PPIC) INITIALIZATION
                        ; *****************************
0021'   B0 B8           CINIT:  MOVI    AL,0B8H     ;B8 HEX IS MODE CONTROL WORD
0023'   E6 E7                   OUTB    0E7H        ;SEND TO CONSOLE PPI
0025'   B0 03                   MOVBI   AL,03       ;03 IS BIT SET/RESET CONTRL WORD
0027'   E6 E7                   OUTB    0E7H        ;SET VIDEO STROBE BIT HIGH
0029'   C3                      RET
                        ;
                        ; EXTERNAL I/O (USART) INITIALIZATION
                        ; ***********************************
002A'   B0 AA           XINIT:  MOVBI   AL,0AAH     ;DUMMY COMMAND
002C'   E6 ED                   OUTB    0EDH        ;  SENT TO USART
002E'   B0 40                   MOVBI   AL,40H      ;RESET COMMAND
0030'   E6 ED                   OUTB    0EDH        ;  SENT TO USART
0032'   B0 CE                   MOVBI   AL,0CEH     ;USART MODE INSTRUCTION
0034'   E6 ED                   OUTB    0EDH        ;SEND MODE INSTRUCTION TO USART
0036'   B0 27                   MOVBI   AL,27H      ;COMMAND TO TRANSMIT & RECEIVE
0038'   E6 ED                   OUTB    0EDH        ;  SENT TO USART
003A'   C3                      RET
                        ;
                        ; CONSOLE INPUT ROUTINE
                        ; *********************
003B'   E4 E6           CINP:   INB     0E6H        ;LOOK AT CONSOLE PORT STATUS
003D'   24 40                   ANDBI   AL,40H
003F'   75 08                   JNZ     CIEND       ;RET IF NO INPUT WAITING
0041'   E4 E4                   INB     0E4H        ;GET INPUT FROM CONSOLE
0043'   F6 D0                   NOTB    AL
0045'   24 7F                   ANDBI   AL,7FH      ;STRIP OFF PARITY BIT
0047'   3A C0                   CMPB    AL,AL       ;SET Z BIT
0049'   C3              CIEND:  RET
                        ;
```

```
                       ; CONSOLE OUTPUT ROUTINE
                       ; ***********************
004A'   8A C4          COUT:    MOVB     AL,AH
004C'   E6 E5                   OUTB     0E5H           ;OUTPUT TO VIDEO
004E'   B0 02                   MOVBI    AL,02
0050'   E6 E7                   OUTB     0E7H           ;RESET PPI DEVICE
0052'   FE C0                   INCB     AL             ;SET PPI DEVICE TO PREPARE
0054'   E6 E7                   OUTB     0E7H           ;  FOR NEXT OUTPUT
0056'   B1 00                   MOVBI    CL,0           ;BEGIN TIMING DELAY
0058'   E2 FE          COUT1:   LOOP     COUT1
005A'   C3                      RET                     ;RETURN AFTER DELAY
                       ;
                       ; EXTERNAL INPUT ROUTINE
                       ; ***********************
005B'   E4 ED          XINP:    INB      0EDH           ;CHECK EXTERNAL INPUT STATUS WORD
005D'   F6 D0                   NOTB     AL             ;  FOR RAISED INPUT FLAG
005F'   24 02                   ANDBI    AL,02
0061'   75 06                   JNZ      XIEND          ;IF NONE THEN RETURN
0063'   E4 EC                   INB      0ECH           ;READ EXTERNAL INPUT
0065'   24 7F                   ANDBI    AL,7FH         ;STRIP OFF PARITY BIT
0067'   3A C0                   CMPB     AL,AL          ;SET Z BIT
0069'   C3             XIEND:   RET
                       ;
                       ; EXTERNAL OUTPUT ROUTINE
                       ; ***********************
006A'   E4 ED          XOUT:    INB      0EDH           ;CHECK USART OUTPUT STATUS.
006C'   24 01                   ANDBI    AL,01          ;  IF NOT READY FOR OUTPUT
006E'   74 FA                   JZ       XOUT           ;  CONTINUE CHECKING.
0070'   8A C4                   MOVB     AL,AH
0072'   E6 EC                   OUTB     0ECH           ;TRANSMIT CHARACTER
0074'   C3                      RET
                       ;
                                END
```

Figure 6.16: Terminal program using the 8255 PPIC and 8251 PSIC.

Intel now has a chip, the 8256 Multifunction Universal Asynchronous Receiver-Transmitter (MUART) which combines most of the functions of the 8251 PSIC, 8255 PPIC, and 8259 PIC. It has one serial port (with 13 different built-in baud rates), two parallel ports (one for data and one for status), and other features such as timers and an interrupt controller.

The 8275 Programmable CRT Controller

The 8275 Programmable CRT Controller (PCRTC) (see figure 6.17) is a 40-pin chip which provides the timing and control for displaying text on a video screen. The text is stored in a designated section of memory called the video text display RAM. The CPU puts the *digital* ASCII code for text characters into this display RAM, and the PCRTC produces the *video* signals necessary to display the corresponding symbols on the video screen.

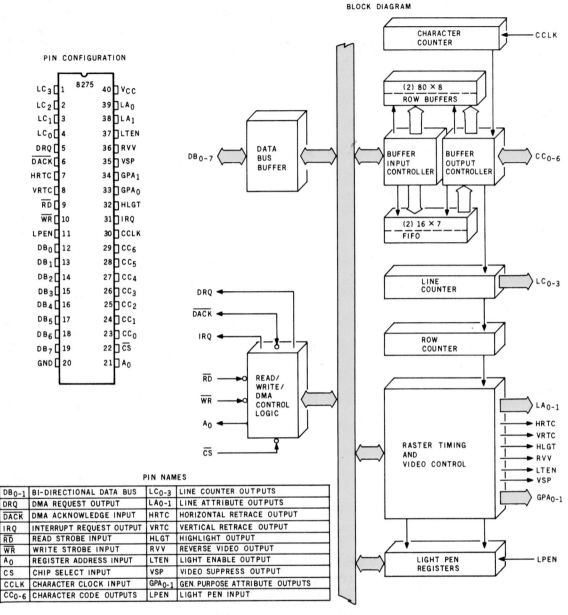

BLOCK DIAGRAM

PIN CONFIGURATION

PIN NAMES

DB$_{0-1}$	BI-DIRECTIONAL DATA BUS	LC$_{0-3}$	LINE COUNTER OUTPUTS
DRQ	DMA REQUEST OUTPUT	LA$_{0-1}$	LINE ATTRIBUTE OUTPUTS
DACK	DMA ACKNOWLEDGE INPUT	HRTC	HORIZONTAL RETRACE OUTPUT
IRQ	INTERRUPT REQUEST OUTPUT	VRTC	VERTICAL RETRACE OUTPUT
RD	READ STROBE INPUT	HLGT	HIGHLIGHT OUTPUT
WR	WRITE STROBE INPUT	RVV	REVERSE VIDEO OUTPUT
A$_0$	REGISTER ADDRESS INPUT	LTEN	LIGHT ENABLE OUTPUT
CS	CHIP SELECT INPUT	VSP	VIDEO SUPPRESS OUTPUT
CCLK	CHARACTER CLOCK INPUT	GPA$_{0-1}$	GEN. PURPOSE ATTRIBUTE OUTPUTS
CC$_{0-6}$	CHARACTER CODE OUTPUTS	LPEN	LIGHT PEN INPUT

Figure 6.17: 8275 Programmable CRT Controller—pinouts and internal structure.

The 8275 PCRTC repeatedly scans (at about a rate of 60 times a second) the computer's video memory starting at a specified location for a specified number of bytes mapping these memory locations over to positions on the screen, taking the numerical binary ASCII code in a memory cell to a symbol on the screen which has the corresponding ASCII code. For example, if the first byte of this memory contains 41H, which is the ASCII code for capital *A*, then the 8275 will cause a capital *A* to appear in the upper left corner of the screen (see the figure below). The rest of this stretch of memory gets mapped to the screen in rows from left to right, top to bottom.

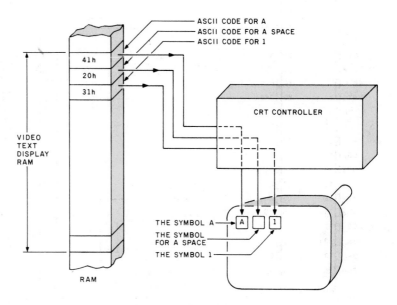

Figure 6.18: Mapping from video text display RAM to video screen.

The number of characters per row and rows per screen is programmed into the 8275 PCRTC by the user upon initialization of the device. The maximum values for these parameters are 80 characters per row and 64 rows per screen.

The 8275 has special features such as highlighting of characters, cursor control, support of a lightpen, and some graphics. These are programmed by the user via its special control port in the I/O space.

Many personal computers and terminals have a whole board filled with video text display control logic. Using a CRT display controller chip can significantly cut down on the cost, space, and power requirements of such circuitry at the price of reduced flexibility.

The 8272 Single/Double Density Floppy Disk Controller

The 8272 Single/Double Density Floppy Disk Controller (FDC) (see figure 6.19) is a 40-pin chip which provides the control circuitry for interfacing up to four floppy disks to a computer based on the 8080, 8085, 8086, 8088, or most any other microprocessor. It is designed to be compatible with both the IBM single density (IBM 3740) and the IBM double density (IBM System 34) disk formats.

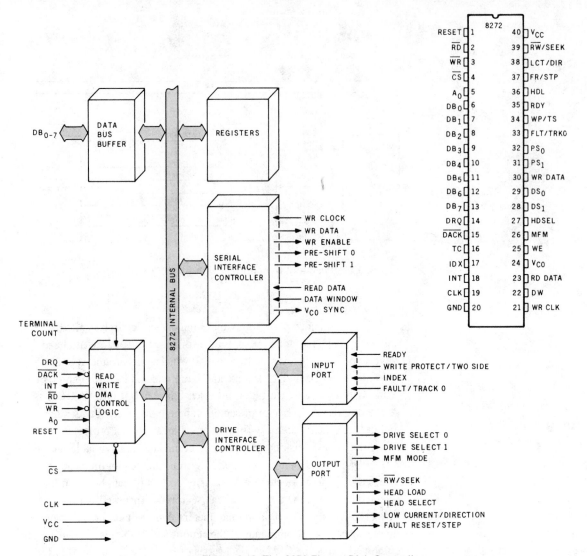

Figure 6.19: The 8272 Floppy Disk Controller.

The 8272 FDC is designed to work alone or in conjunction with a DMA controller (see figure 6.20).

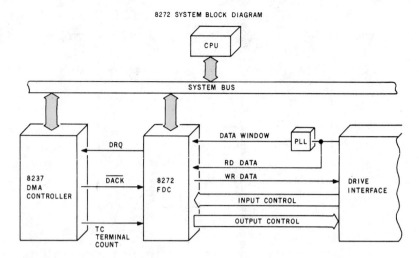

Figure 6.20: Using a DMA controller with the 8272 FDC.

Data is organized on floppy disks in concentric circles called *tracks,* and each track is divided into a number of sectors. A read/write head travels above (or below) the floppy disk which spins around at about 5 revolutions per second. Different tracks are selected by "stepping" the read/write head along a radial line (see figure 6.21). Once a track is selected, a particular sector or sectors can be transferred between the disk and the computer's memory (in a reserved area called a buffer).

Fifteen basic disk control function commands are available on the 8272 FDC. These include commands to move the read/write head of a selected drive to a selected track, transfer sectors of data between the selected drive and the computer, scan sectors for specified patterns, format disks, and set up timing parameters. For each command, there are three stages: 1) the command, 2) the action, and 3) the result. During the command stage, the CPU sends a series of bytes (the command) to the FDC. During the action stage, the FDC performs an action on the appropriate disk, possibly passing data back or forth between the FDC and the CPU (or system memory in the case of DMA transfers). During the result stage, the CPU grabs a series of bytes (the result) from the FDC.

More explicitly, the commands are as follows:

Read Data. This command causes one or more sectors of data to be transferred from the floppy disk to the computer. If you use a DMA controller, then you can place the bytes in these sectors directly into system memory, and if you don't, then you can route all bytes through the processor. This is a situation where the 8089 IOP could be used quite effectively. There is actually a series of 9 command bytes to invoke this command. These command bytes include such information as the drive

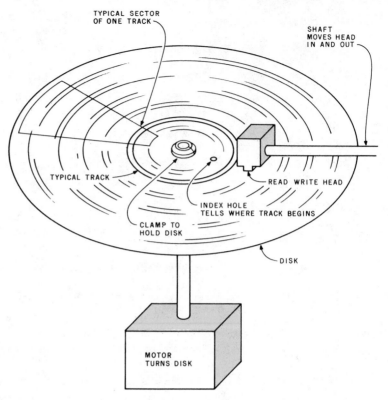

Figure 6.21: Floppy disk layout.

number, side number, sector number, number of bytes per sector, and length of this sector. The track number is not included because selecting the correct track is the responsibility of the Seek command.

Read ID. This command causes the FDC to read the identification information from the next sector to spin by under the read/write head of the currently selected disk. This information is sent back to the CPU as part of the result.

Read Deleted Data. This command is almost the same as the Read Data command, except that it causes a sector to be read even if a special electronic mark at the beginning of the sector, called the data address mark, indicates that the sector has been deleted (taken out of service).

Read a Track. This command reads a whole track from the disk drive and sends it to the CPU (or system memory in the case of DMA transfer).

Scan Equal, Scan High or Equal, and Scan Low or Equal. These scan commands are used to look for specified patterns on the disk. This can be useful for many different purposes associated with large data bases. For example, you might use these commands to look for a certain key indicating a certain customer.

Specify. This command is used to set timing parameters. These are: the Head Unload Time (HUT), Head Load Time (HLT), and the Step Rate Time (SRT). Since these are programmable, different kinds of disk drives can be used with this one chip.

Write Data. This command is used to transfer one or more sectors of data from the computer to the selected drive.

Format a Track. Before a disk can be used, it must be formatted. This command automatically performs this function for any given sector. To format a whole disk, you must set up a loop which calls this command over and over again.

Write Deleted Data. This command works the same as the Write Data command except that it puts a code indicating "deleted" into the data address mark for that selector. Thus the information is there, but the sector is officially out of service.

Seek. This command causes the read/write head to move (step) in and out among the different tracks as specified by the user.

Restore to Track 0. This command recalibrates a drive by sending the read/write head to track 0.

Sense Interrupt Status. The FDC can interrupt the CPU for a number of reasons. This command causes the FDC to return a couple of bytes, one of which indicates the cause of the most recent interrupt. This command is needed after the Seek or Restore commands to obtain resulting status.

Sense Drive Status. This command is used to get a byte from the 8272 Controller which contains information such as: the currently selected drive, whether or not there is an error, whether or not the disk was write protected, and whether or not the selected drive is busy.

Like many interface controllers, the 8272 FDC contains two accessible registers, a status register and a data register. The status register can be accessed at any time. Its 8 bits indicate when the controller and the individual drives are busy or ready, as well as such things as the direction of data flow (from processor to FDC or from FDC to processor). The data register is really a bidirectional port to a stack of registers in which commands, parameters, status, and data are stored. To get information into this stack during the command stage and out of this stack during the result stage, a polling method is used. That is, before each byte of data is transferred, the status must be checked (in a software loop) until the FDC is ready to make the transfer.

Like the situation with video text display circuitry, many computers have a whole board filled with a number of small general-purpose chips to handle what this particular Intel chip does by itself. The 8272 thus cuts down on space, cost, power, and design costs, and increases portability of the computer.

CONCLUSION

In the last few chapters we have been studying the Intel 16-bit processor chips: the 8086 and 8088 CPU chips, the 8089 IOP chip, and the 8087 NDP chip. In this chapter we have studied the additional chips necessary to build a complete computer. You can now look back at the two model computers in Chapter 2 which show how to connect all these chips together to form complete systems.

The chips in this chapter fall into five classes 1) system-timing, 2) bus-interface, 3) system controllers, 4) general-purpose device controllers, and 5) special-purpose device controllers.

Each chip we have studied is designed to remove a certain task from the direct control of the processor, whether the CPU or a peripheral processor such as the 8089 IOP. Each such *logical* task is assigned a different *physical* chip, making the whole system easy to understand. This is an example of the modern modular approach to design that makes the computer easy to design initially and easy to maintain when trouble occurs.

Chapter 7

Eleven Sample Programs For The 8086/8088

In this chapter we present a sequence of example programs, starting from the very elementary and building toward an interesting, moderately complex one. You can, with a minimum of fuss, actually try these programs on your system. Your computer does, however, need some hardware: the Godbout Dual 8085/8088 Processor Board and a floppy disk system with the CP/M-80 operating system. If, in addition, you have a memory-mapped video text display, then you will be able to clearly see the results of the first couple of programs. On the other hand, if your system is not so blessed, then we have provided a way for you to "peep" at a fictitious video screen. It is, in fact, not absolutely necessary to have CP/M-80. Preliminary versions were actually developed on an operating system other than CP/M. These examples are not intended to be virtuoso performances, but rather simple to moderately complex, natural, and useful examples of the type you might want to eventually write to improve your system's performance.

In this chapter, we have divided the 8086/8088 instruction set in an entirely different manner than in Chapter 3. This time we have organized the instructions in groups according to a way you might want to learn them, starting with data transfer, moving to simple loop control, and then on to arithmetic and more advanced concepts.

We will give you step-by-step instructions of how to assemble, link, load, and run these example programs. The general theory of developing assembly-language programs is discussed in Chapter 2. We will assume that you are acquainted with the terminology introduced there.

THE SET UP

We ran each example on an 8088 CPU with the Godbout dual 85/88 CPU board. We set up an S-100 bus system in an experimental mode. Perhaps you might want to set up your system similarly and try out each example on your own system as you read along. You will need the following hardware: a system including an S-100 bus mainframe, a floppy-disk system, a memory-mapped video text display system (optional), and the Godbout 85/88 dual processor board. For software, you will need the CP/M-80 operating system configured to your system and the Microsoft 8086/8088 cross-assembler (XMACRO-86). Figure 7.1 shows the requirements for hardware and how to set up the Godbout board for our purposes. In particular, please make sure that you set the switches so that the 8088 does a *cold start* each time.

1) S-100 bus mainframe.

2) Floppy disk system with CP/M operating system.

3) A memory mapped video text display board. If possible, place this in your system so that the RAM starts at E800H.

4) Keyboard or terminal input through an I/O port.

5) The Godbout 85/88 dual processor board. Set the switches as follows:

   a) SW1 position 4 should be *off* so that the 8085 does not restart when control is switched from the 8088 to the 8085.

   b) SW1 position 5 should be *on* so that the 8088 does restart when control is switched from the 8085 to the 8088.

   c) the other positions on SW1 should be set as required by your system. See the User's Manual provided with the board for details.

   d) SW2 (power on jump address) should be set as required by your system.

   e) SW3 should be set for the "standard" port address which is FDH.

Figure 7.1: Hardware requirements for running the software examples.

Once you have the hardware in place, you will need to type in a **loader program written in 8085 code (see figure 7.2).** Use the file name L88.ASM for the source code. It should be assembled using the ASM assembler (which comes with CP/M) and converted to COM file using CP/M's LOAD program. It will thus become a command from the CP/M operating system called L88. The L88 program is more of a *launcher* than a *loader,* because when it is invoked, it will sign on and give you the options of either returning to CP/M, jumping to an 8088 program, or displaying your video screen (possibly fictitious) on the console output device.

Before assembling L88.ASM, you will probably need to modify the *equate* for your particular system:

```
VIDEO    EQU       0E800H
```

This is the actual memory address of your memory-mapped video text board *(video screen).* If you do not have such a board, then find an area of free RAM, preferably at or above 2000H (because we will be loading our software in the region from 100H to 2000H). You will need less than 2 K bytes of RAM for this screen. You will see a similar equate in several of the example programs. Because the equates in the examples are for 8088 *segment paragraph addresses,* you should set these to one-sixteenth of the value used in this loader program (L88). For example, if we use E800H in the loader program, then we will use E80H in the 8088 example programs, and if we use 2000H in the loader program, then we should use 200H in the example programs.

The "go to 8088" option of the loader allows you to optionally specify a hexadecimal 8088 address of the form:

segment:offset

The default is 100:0. This means that the actual memory default location will be:

$$1000H = 100H * 10H + 0H$$

When the "go to 8088" command is executed, the loader program will load a few bytes of 8088 code and turn on the 8088. The 8088 begins executing this 8088 code which in turn causes it to jump to the specified address. This 8088 code is placed at FFFF0H because that's where the 8088 does its cold start. If you have the old 16-bit address, standard S-100 boards, then this location appears as the 16-bit address FFF0H. That is, the 16-bit addressing scheme on the 16-bit memory board will simply ignore the upper 4 bits of the 20-bit address. In any case, you must have a few bytes (13) of free RAM starting at the top of memory.

It is interesting to note that the method for switching from the 8085 CPU to the 8088 CPU is to execute an IN instruction on a preset port address (set to 0FDH here). Similarly, we use an IN Byte (INB) to switch back from the 8088 CPU to the 8085 CPU.

```
                ; LOADER FOR THE 8088
                ;
                ; This program starts the 8088 from CP/M
                ;
0005 =          BDOS    EQU     0005H           ; CP/M service
0000 =          WARM    EQU     0000H           ; warmstart
000D =          CR      EQU     0DH             ; <CR>
000A =          LF      EQU     0AH             ; <LF>
0020 =          SPACE   EQU     20H             ; space
FFF9 =          OFFSET  EQU     0FFF9H          ; offset address
FFFB =          SEG     EQU     0FFFBH          ; segment address
0100 =          CODE    EQU     0100H           ; 8088 default code segment
0040 =          STACK   EQU     0040H           ; 8088 stack segment
0000 =          ENTER   EQU     0000H           ; 8088 default entry point
E800 =          VIDEO   EQU     0E800H          ; video RAM address
003C =          LINELEN EQU     60              ; video line length
0005 =          LINENUM EQU     5               ; number of video lines
                ;
0100                    ORG     100H
```

```
                          ;
      0100 210402   OPT:   LXI     H,MESS1     ; option table header
      0103 CD3E01          CALL    MESOUT      ; is displayed
                   LOOP:
      0106 211A02          LXI     H,MESS2     ; option explanation
      0109 CD3E01          CALL    MESOUT      ; is displayed
      010C CDEB01          CALL    CONIN       ; input a character
      010F FE45            CPI     'E'         ; if it is an E, then
      0111 CA0000          JZ      WARM        ; jump to CP/M warmstart
      0114 FE47            CPI     'G'         ; if it is a G, then
      0116 CA2A01          JZ      J8088       ; jump to 8088
      0119 FE44            CPI     'D'         ; if it is a D, then
      011B CAA401          JZ      DISP        ; display screen
      011E C32101          JMP     ERROR       ; if not then error
                          ;
      0121 21B802  ERROR:  LXI     H,MESS4     ; error message
      0124 CD3E01          CALL    MESOUT      ; is displayed
      0127 C30601          JMP     LOOP        ; now try again

      012A CD4801  J8088:  CALL    LOAD88      ; load 8088 default jump
      012D CD5901          CALL    GETADD      ; get opt jump address
      0130 DA2101          JC      ERROR
      0133 DBFD            IN      0FDH        ; here the 8088 takes over
                          ;
      0135 21A102          LXI     H,MESS3     ; return from 8088
      0138 CD3E01          CALL    MESOUT      ; is displayed
      013B C30001          JMP     OPT         ; try again?
                          ;
                   MESOUT:                     ; message display routine
      013E 7E              MOV     A,M         ; get character
      013F 23              INX     H           ; next character
      0140 B7              ORA     A           ; was it the end?
      0141 C8              RZ                  ; if so return
      0142 CDDE01          CALL    CONOUT      ; output the character
      0145 C33E01          JMP     MESOUT      ; loop again
                          ;
                   LOAD88:                     ; load 8088 jump code routine
      0148 11F701          LXI     D,JMP88     ; point to the copy
      014B 21F0FF          LXI     H,0FFF0H    ; point to the destination
      014E 0E0D            MVI     C,LENGTH    ; this many bytes
      0150 1A       L88LP: LDAX    D           ; get a byte
      0151 13              INX     D           ; next source byte
      0152 77              MOV     M,A         ; put the byte
      0153 23              INX     H           ; next destination byte
      0154 0D              DCR     C           ; decrement the count
      0155 C25001          JNZ     L88LP       ; and loop
      0158 C9              RET                 ; return
                          ;
      0159 CDEB01  GETADD: CALL    CONIN       ; segment first
      015C FE0D            CPI     CR          ; carriage return?
      015E C8              RZ                  ; use default on both
      015F FE3A            CPI     ':'         ; colon?
      0161 CA6F01          JZ      GETAD1      ; use default on seg
      0164 CD7F01          CALL    HEX16       ; get 16 bits of hex
      0167 78              MOV     A,B
      0168 FE3A            CPI     ':'         ; check for colon
      016A 37              STC                 ; set carry for error
      016B C0              RNZ                 ; if not then error
      016C 22FBFF          SHLD    SEG         ; store segment address
```

```
016F CDEB01    GETAD1: CALL    CONIN        ; next number start?
0172 CD7F01            CALL    HEX16        ; get 16 bits of hex
0175 78                MOV     A,B
0176 FE0D              CPI     CR           ; check for carriage return
0178 37                STC                  ; set carry for error
0179 C0                RNZ                  ; return if error
017A 22F9FF            SHLD    OFFSET       ; store offset
017D B7                ORA     A            ; clear carry
017E C9                RET
                       ;
017F 210000    HEX16:  LXI     H,0          ; start clean
0182 CD9301    HEXLP:  CALL    CONDIG       ; next digit
0185 D8                RC                   ; return if error
0186 29                DAD     H            ; times 2
0187 29                DAD     H            ; times 4
0188 29                DAD     H            ; times 8
0189 29                DAD     H            ; times 16
018A 85                ADD     L            ; add the digit
018B 6F                MOV     L,A
018C CDEB01            CALL    CONIN        ; next character
018F 47                MOV     B,A          ; save it
0190 C38201            JMP     HEXLP        ; and loop
                       ;
0193 D630     CONDIG:  SUI     '0'          ; below zero?
0195 D8                RC                   ; return if so
0196 FE0A              CPI     10           ; above nine?
0198 3F                CMC
0199 D0                RNC                  ; return if not
019A D611              SUI     'A'-'0'      ; below A?
019C D8                RC                   ; return if so
019D FE06              CPI     'F'-'A'+1    ; above F?
019F 3F                CMC
01A0 D8                RC                   ; error if so
01A1 C60A              ADI     10           ; add 10 if ok
01A3 C9                RET
                       ;
01A4 CDD301    DISP:   CALL    CCRLF
01A7 21C902            LXI     H,MESS5      ; border
01AA CD3E01            CALL    MESOUT
01AD CDD301            CALL    CCRLF
01B0 2100E8            LXI     H,VIDEO      ; video RAM
01B3 1605              MVI     D,LINENUM    ; number of lines down
01B5 1E3C     DISP1:   MVI     E,LINELEN    ; line length
01B7 7E       DISP2:   MOV     A,M          ; get byte
01B8 23                INX     H            ; point to next
01B9 CDDE01            CALL    CONOUT       ; output it
01BC 1D                DCR     E            ; end of line?
01BD C2B701            JNZ     DISP2
01C0 CDD301            CALL    CCRLF        ; finish it
01C3 15                DCR     D            ; end of screen?
01C4 C2B501            JNZ     DISP1
01C7 21C902            LXI     H,MESS5      ; show a border
01CA CD3E01            CALL    MESOUT
01CD CDD301            CALL    CCRLF
01D0 C30601            JMP     LOOP
                       ;
```

```
01D3 3E0D      CCRLF:  MVI     A,CR            ; carriage return
01D5 CDDE01            CALL    CONOUT
01D8 3E0A              MVI     A,LF            ; line feed
01DA CDDE01            CALL    CONOUT
01DD C9               RET
                ;
               CONOUT:                         ; console output routine
01DE E5                PUSH    H               ; save the registers
01DF D5                PUSH    D
01E0 C5                PUSH    B
01E1 5F                MOV     E,A             ; E has the character
01E2 0E02              MVI     C,2             ; C has the function
01E4 CD0500            CALL    BDOS            ; call CP/M
01E7 C1                POP     B               ; restore the registers
01E8 D1                POP     D
01E9 E1                POP     H
01EA C9               RET                      ; and return
                ;
01EB E5        CONIN:  PUSH    H               ; save the registers
01EC D5                PUSH    D
01ED C5                PUSH    B
01EE 0E01              MVI     C,1             ; C has the function
01F0 CD0500            CALL    BDOS            ; call CP/M
01F3 C1                POP     B               ; restore registers
01F4 D1                POP     D
01F5 E1                POP     H
01F6 C9               RET                      ; and return
                ;
               JMP88:                          ; 8088 jump code
01F7 B8                DB      0B8H            ; MOVI   AX,STACK
01F8 4000              DW      STACK
01FA 8ED0              DB      08EH,0D0H       ; MOV    SS,AX
01FC BC0001            DB      0BCH,000H,001H  ; MOVI   SP,100H
01FF EA                DB      0EAH            ; JMP    ENTER,CODE
0200 0000              DW      ENTER
0200 0001              DW      CODE
000D =         LENGTH  EQU     $-JMP88
                ;
                ; message table
0204 3830383820MESS1:  DB  '8088 Loader Program',CR,LF,0
021A 5479706520MESS2:  DB  'Type your command:',CR,LF
022E 2020204520        DB  '    E              Exit to CP/M',CR,LF
0253 202020475B        DB  '    G[seg:offset]<CR>  Go to 8088',CR,LF
0276 2020204420        DB  '    D              Display screen',CR,LF
029D 0D0A2A00          DB  CR,LF,'*',0
02A1 0D0A526574MESS3:  DB  CR,LF,'Returned from 8088',CR,LF,0
02B8 0D0A53796EMESS4:  DB  CR,LF,'Syntax error',CR,LF,0
02C9 2A2A2A2A2AMESS5:  DB  '******** memory ********',0
                ;
02E2                   END
```

Figure 7.2: Loader program.

The rest of the programs are written in 8086/8088 code. They will all require this loader program.

THE PROGRAMS

For each instruction group we have a separate example program which uses instructions only in that or a previous group. We have set up these examples in a way which illustrates the power of Intel's segmentation method to package modules of code. We place each major set of subroutines in a separate segment. These segments are then treated as logical units and can be moved around in memory and then executed correctly by changing the contents of segment registers.

In each case, we list the new group of instructions and then explain what the program does and how it works. We shall never use all the instructions in the new group in the corresponding example, because it would be difficult and unnatural to do in our one-example-per-group format. Often, however, we will use more and more instructions from the group in later examples.

The Data-Transfer Group

The first group is *data transfer*. These instructions just move data around from one place in the system to another. The various places are: main memory, data registers, I/O ports, and segment registers.

The *data-transfer* instructions are:

MOV	Move
XCHG	eXCHanGe
IN	IN
OUT	OUT
XLAT	transLATe
LEA	Load Effective Address
LDS	Load Data Segment
LES	Load Extra Segment
LAHF	Load AH from Flags
SAHF	Store AH into Flags

The figure below shows our example for this group.

```
                              ; Example 1: (Data Transfer)
                              ;
                              ; Putting "HI" on the screen
                              ;
        0000'                          ASEG
        0E80                  VIDEO    EQU    0E80H
        0000                  SCREEN   EQU    0000H
                              ;
        0000   B8 0E80        ENTER:   MOV    AX,VIDEO      ; data segment is
        0003   8E D8                   MOV    DS,AX         ; screen RAM
                              ;
```

```
0005    C6 06 0000 48              MOVBI    SCREEN+0,'H'    ; 'H' in upper left
000A    C6 06 0001 49              MOVBI    SCREEN+1,'I'    ; 'I' next to it
                              ;
000F    E4 FD                      INB      0FDH            ; return to 8085
                              ;
                                    END                      ; End of code segment
```

Figure 7.3: Example 1: Putting "HI" on the video screen.

Comments: This is a warm-up example. It shows how just a few of the data-transfer instructions in conjunction with some of the addressing modes can create a visible effect, namely placing the message "HI" on the video screen. Perhaps, after you see how this works, you might want to try a longer message such as "HI THERE." This program is also a good test for your system with its new 8088 CPU.

The program is contained in a segment which can be located in any free area of RAM. We will load it into 1000H which is the "center stage" memory location for our example programs. This location is the default jump location for the loader program.

To run this example, use an editor to type in the source code exactly (except for the "video equate") as given in the above figure. Save it in a disk file called E1.MAC (the MAC file extension is needed to make the next step work correctly). Now assemble (translate from source code to partial machine code) using the Microsoft 8086 cross-assembler with the following command:

XM86 = E1/L

This causes the source code to be read from the file E1.MAC and the object code to be stored in the file E1.REL. The /L forces a listing to be stored in the file E1.PRN. The above command is in an abbreviated form. The official syntax for the command to assemble is:

XM86 objectfile,listfile = sourcefile

Here "objectfile" is the name of your object code file, "listfile" is the name of your list file, and "sourcefile" is the name of your assembly-language source code file. It is better not to include the file extensions because the assembler does it for you, and if you put the file extensions in the wrong place you just might destroy your original source code! Without file extensions the assembler will look for a source code file with the name you specify and a file extension MAC, produce an object file with the name you specify and a file extension REL, and produce a listing file with the name you specify and a file extension PRN. Usually, the same main name is used for all three files so the abbreviated form saves on keystrokes.

You cannot run the object code in E1.REL directly on the machine, but need to link it (see Chapter 2) using the command:

L80 E1,E1/N/E

This causes the object code to be read from the file E1.REL and the machine to be placed in the file E1.COM. Before finishing, the linker program will tell you that loading the code into the indicated spot in memory might be dangerous, but it gives you the option to do this anyway. You should select N for "no."

You can't abbreviate this time. The syntax is:

L80   objectfile1,objectfile2, . . . ,objectfilen,loadfile/N,options

Here the object code files:

objectfile1, objectfile2, . . . , objectfilen

are the source files for the linking operation. They are all to be combined into one machine-language program during this process. In our case, there is just one object file, namely E1.REL. Next comes loadfile/N. The "/N" is really an *option switch* which causes the file named just before it to be designated as the load file. In our case we want the load file to be named E1 also, so we typed "E1/N." Last come more options. In our case, we chose "/E" which causes the linker to save the load file (under the name specified by the /N option) and exit. File extensions *should not* be used in linker commands for the same reason that they should not be used with assembler commands. You *can* use them, but only at your own risk! If you do not use them, then the linker looks for object files with file extension REL and produces a load file with file extension COM.

Once the program has been linked and saved, you may load it into memory using the following command:

DDT E1.COM

DDT stands for *dynamic debugging tool* and is a CP/M system command. (For more information on DDT and other CP/M commands, see Murtha, Stephen; Waite Mitchell. CP/M Primer. Indianapolis, Indiana: Howard W. Sams & Co., Inc.)

Now use the following DDT command to move it into its true position:

M100,2FF,1000

If you wish to place it somewhere else, you can change the last number accordingly. Next a control C will bring you back to CP/M itself, and you may now type:

L88

This brings in and begins to execute the loader program discussed previously in this chapter. You should soon see the word "HI" on your screen. If you don't have a video screen, then press the *D* option from the loader to display your fictitious screen. You might return to CP/M, place spaces (20H) into your screen (with the DDT *fill command),* reload example one, and restart the L88 program. Now first display the screen with the "D" command, go to example one with the *G* command, and finally redisplay the screen with another *D*.

Now that we have seen how to run this example program, let's see how it works.

The program first initializes the data segment register so that it points to the RAM for our video screen. This means that now the programmer can think of the video screen RAM as a block of data with a starting address of zero. Notice that the segment register is loaded with **E80H, which is one-sixteenth of the actual RAM address. Recall that the** contents of the segment registers are multiplied by 16 when used to compute the actual address. Notice also that it takes two instructions to set the data segment register. It is not possible to move a constant directly into a segment register. If the paragraph address is stored in memory, then it is possible to move it directly into a segment register. We didn't do this here because such a memory access would use the data segment which is the register we are trying to initialize. We could, however, use a segment-override prefix and bring the information from the code segment (the segment which contains the program).

The first instruction in this two-step initialization process is a MOV instruction with immediate addressing mode for the source and register mode for the destination. With *double-operand* instructions on this processor, the destination always comes first, then a comma, and then the source.[1]

In the Microsoft cross-assembler, the immediate addressing mode is explicitly indicated with an *I* in the symbolic operation code, as in this first instruction. Only use the immediate mode with a source operand. If you think about it for a while, this should make sense. Consider that when an instruction has an operand in the immediate mode, the actual value of the operand is stored as part of the machine code. This data is

---

[1]This particular ordering of the operands is not universal with all processors. For example, in the PDP-11 minicomputer's assembly language, the source always comes first.

always the last part of the machine code. Thus, the operand is located within the instruction stream for the processor. In view of the way the 8086/8088 gets its instructions through a pipeline, this is a poor place to put a destination operand, and a very good place to put a source operand. Even on processors which don't use pipelining, the same rule applies. Having the destination in the instruction stream is poor programming practice because the program then actually begins to modify itself. In general, *self-modifying* code is bad because it is difficult to debug and maintain.

Notice that the destination of the first instruction, MOV, is a register. In fact it is a very special register, namely AX, the accumulator. The 8088 treats this as a special case and uses a shorter machine code.

Also, notice that the second instruction is a transfer from one register to another. Notice that the machine code for the second instruction is quite different from the machine code for the first, even though both are MOVe instructions. It takes only two bytes to specify a register-to-register MOVe.

In the next couple of instructions the ASCII code for *H* is moved to the first location of this video RAM, and the ASCII code for *I* is moved to the second location of the video RAM. The video board will cause the corresponding symbols to appear in the top row of the video screen starting from the left edge. In these instructions, the sources are in immediate mode and the destination is a direct memory reference. In the instructions that move the *H* and the *I,* there are plus signs in the expression for the destination. The assembler, not the CPU, has to evaluate this expression to find the address of the destination (which is the next location in the screen RAM). Both of these instructions are in byte mode. This is indicated explicitly by including a *B* in the symbolic operation code. Byte mode is useful for handling characters. Notice that the *B* appears before the *I*.

Finally the last instruction causes the 8088 to return control to the 8085 by executing the IN instruction from our standard port FDH. This is a data transfer instruction which is used for a quite different purpose, namely transfer of control between processors.

Simple Loop Control Instructions

The *simple loop control* instructions provide the most basic type of control over our programs. This group includes the following instructions:

INC	INCrement
DEC	DECrement
LOOP	LOOP
LOOPZ LOOPE	LOOP if Zero (Equal)
LOOPNZ LOOPNE	LOOP if Not Zero (Equal)
JCXZ	Jump if CX is Zero

Almost every useful program has at least one loop. A loop is a block of code with control to execute it several times. There are four popular types of loops: 1) *endless loops,* 2) *counting loops,* 3) *until loops,* and 4) *while loops.*

In the first type, endless loops, the block is repeated over and over again with no control to end it. This type is very popular with beginners. In BASIC such loops can be stopped with a control *C* (the panic button). In FORTRAN or machine language, you might have to resort to more drastic measures such as turning the computer off or pressing the reset button. In BASIC, FORTRAN, and Pascal, such loops are controlled by the GOTO statement, although the GOTO statement (and hence this type of loop) is frowned upon in Pascal. In 8086/8088 assembly language, the JuMP instruction is used (at the bottom of the loop). In keeping with the modern spirit of Pascal we shall also frown upon this type of loop, and therefore not include the JuMP instruction in the simple loop control instruction group. Here is an example:

```
START:                      ; top of the loop
       ....                  ; instructions
                             ; inside loop

       ....
       JMP       START       ; always go back to
                             ; START
```

In the second type, counting loops, the block is repeated a specified number of times (the *loop count).* Such loops are controlled in BASIC by the FOR/NEXT statements, in FORTRAN by the DO statement, and in Pascal by the FOR statement. In 8086/8088 assembly language, use the LOOP instruction. To use the LOOP instruction, you must load the count (CX) register with the loop count beforehand. Place the LOOP instruction at the end of the loop. Each time the LOOP instruction is encountered, the CX register is automatically decremented. If the result is not zero, then the LOOP instruction causes a jump to the beginning of the loop (as specified by the operand of the LOOP instruction) for another go around. Here is an example:

```
       MOVI      CX,8        ; for a count of 8
START:                       ; top of loop
       ....                  ; instructions
                             ; inside loop

       ....
       LOOP      START       ; decrement CX and
                             ; loop back
                             ; if CX is not zero
```

In the third type, until loops, a condition is checked at the bottom of the loop. If the condition is satisfied, then the loop terminates (after reaching the bottom). There is an *until statement* in modern, structured languages such as Pascal and the newest standards for BASIC and FORTRAN. In 8086/8088 assembly language, the LOOPZ, LOOPE, LOOPNZ, and LOOPNE control this type of loop. Actually, LOOPZ and LOOPE are different assembly-language names for the same machine-language instruction. LOOPNZ and LOOPNE also translate to a common machine code. These instructions actually combine the virtues of the counting loop with those of the until loop. As in the case of counting loops, the loop count must be loaded into the CX register beforehand, and the LOOP . . . instruction must be at the bottom of the loop. If the zero flag is set (for LOOPZ and LOOPE) or clear (for LOOPNZ and LOOPNE) at the bottom of the loop (when the LOOP . . . instruction is reached), then the loop will continue; otherwise it will terminate. Here is an example:

```
           MOVI      CX,100    ; count of 100
START:                         ; top of loop
           . . . .             ; instructions
                               ; inside loop

           . . . .
           CALL      TESTIT    ; this subroutine
                               ; sets ZF if done
           LOOPNZ              ; loop until done
```

In the fourth type, while loops, a condition is checked at the top of the loop. If the condition is *not* true, then terminate the loop. Like the until statement, the while loop is popular with modern structured programming languages. In 8086/8088 assembly language, the closest thing to while loop control is the Jump if CX is Zero (JCXZ) instruction. If this instruction is placed at the beginning of a loop and if the loop count is zero, then that loop will not be executed. Thus, this instruction gives better control on counting loops. In higher-level languages some FOR loops work in this way; that is, they will not execute even once if the loop count is zero. Here is an assembly-language example.

```
           MOVI      CX,50     ; count of 50
START:     JCXZ      END       ; top of loop
                               ; contains a test
           . . . .             ; instructions
                               ; inside loop

           . . . .
           LOOP      START     ; decrement and loop
END:                           ; continue to rest
                               ; of program
```

We have included the increment (INC) and decrement (DEC) instructions in this group, because they count either for loop control (when used in conjunction with a conditional jump) or some other quantity in a loop. We will cover the conditional jump instructions with the unconditional jump in another group later.

The figure below shows our example for the simple loop control group. This example can be put into a file named E2.MAC. Again, don't forget to set the equate for the video. The program can be assembled, linked, and run just as was done for the first example. That is, the command:

XM86 = E2/L

will assemble the source file, producing a relocatable machine code file (.REL) and a listing file (.PRN), and the command:

L80 E2,E2/N/E

will produce an absolute machine code file (.COM) called E2.COM. You need to use DDT to load and move this program into place just as with the previous example. When you use the "launcher" to run it, you will see the results on your screen (fictitious, if that's the case).

```
; Example 2: (Simple loop control)
;
; Putting the ASCII code on the screen
;
0000'                   ASEG
0E80            VIDEO    EQU    0E80H
                ;
0000    B8 0E80 ENTER:   MOVI   AX,VIDEO      ; point data segment
0003    8E D8            MOV    DS,AX         ; to video RAM
                ;
0005    B0 20            MOVBI  AL,20H        ; AL contains 1st printable
                                              ; ASCII code
0007    BB 0000          MOVI   BX,0          ; BX contains 1st location
000A    B9 0060          MOVI   CX,96         ; CX contains the count
                ;
000D    88 07   ASCII:   MOVB   [BX],AL       ; move character into place
000F    43               INC    BX            ; next position
0010    40               INC    AX            ; next character
0011    E2 FA            LOOP   ASCII         ; loop for the count
                ;
0013    E4 FD            INB    0FDH          ; return to 8088
                         END
```

Figure 7.4: Example 2: Putting the ASCII code on the screen.

Comments: This example shows how data transfer instructions can be combined with loop control instructions to efficiently display quite a few more characters on the screen. In this case the entire ASCII code is displayed on the screen.

This segment can be placed in memory at location 1000H to match the default jump address in the loader program.

As in the previous example, the data segment register is initialized in the first couple of instructions so that it points to the video RAM. The next few instructions initialize three data registers before the loop (AL, BX, and CX registers). The lower half of the A register contains the ASCII code starting with 20H (because we don't want *control characters*). The base register (BX) points to the location in memory where we want to place the characters. This is indicated by the addressing mode symbol [BX]. If we start BX at 0, then the characters will be placed in the video RAM starting at the first location of this RAM. The count register (CX) is used to hold the count 96 (for our subset of the ASCII code).

The loop begins with a label. This, in effect, names the loop. We have chosen the name ASCII.

After you move the character into place, increment both the ASCII code and the position and decrement the count. Notice that we have incremented all of AX while only AL actually contains the character. This is because we wished to take advantage of the special optimized 1-byte form of the INC for incrementing 16-bit registers. The contents of AH are not important and will not actually change as a result of running this example.

The last instruction in the loop (LOOP) takes care of the loop control. It automatically decrements the count, checks if the count is now zero, and loops if the count is not zero. Since the loop control instruction is at the end of the loop, the loop will always be executed at least once. If we were to set the count equal to zero before the loop, the loop would be executed 64K–1 times. If you want to safeguard against this, then put the JCXZ instruction at the beginning of the loop and jump to wherever you want if the count is zero to begin with.

The program finishes with the IN instruction which returns control to the 8085.

The TEST, CoMPare, And Jump Instructions

This group is really part two of the loop control group. The instructions in this group are:

TEST		TEST
CMP		CoMPare
JMP		JuMP
JE	JZ	Jump if Equal (Zero)
JNE	JNZ	Jump if Not Equal (Zero)
JS		Jump if Sign (negative)

JNS		Jump if Not Sign (nonnegative)
JP	JPE	Jump if Parity (Even)
JNP	JPO	Jump if Not Parity (Odd)
JO		Jump if Overflow
JNO		Jump if Not Overflow
JB	JNAE	Jump if Below (Not Above or Equal)
JNB	JAE	Jump if Not Below (Above or Equal)
JBE	JNA	Jump if Below or Equal (Not Above)
JNBE	JA	Jump if Not Below or Equal (Above)
JL	JNGE	Jump if Less than (Not Greater or Equal)
JNL	JGE	Jump if Not Less than (Greater or Equal)
JLE	JNG	Jump if Less than or Equal (Not Greater)
JNLE	JG	Jump if Not Less than or Equal (Greater)

Here we have conditional and unconditional jumps as well as the *virtual logical* and arithmetic instructions: TEST and CoMPare. By virtual, we mean that we perform the operation (logical AND for TEST and a subtract for CoMPare) and set the flags accordingly. However, we don't retain the result.

The figure below shows our example for the TEST, CMP, and JuMP group. This example doesn't use the video screen. Instead, it establishes communication through a port (serial or parallel).

```
                    ; Example 3: (TeST, CoMPare, and Jump)
                    ;
                    ; An I/O echo program
                    ;
0000'                       ASEG
0086                IFSTAT  EQU     86H             ; Input status port
0083                IPDATA  EQU     83H             ; Input data port
0080                OPSTAT  EQU     80H             ; output status port
0082                OPDATA  EQU     82H             ; output data port
0008                IMASK   EQU     08H             ; input status mask
0004                OMASK   EQU     04H             ; output status mask
0086                INITP   EQU     86H             ; initialization port
0014                INITM   EQU     14H             ; initialization mask
                    ;
0000    B0 14       CDINIT: MOVBI   AL,INITM        ; initialization
0002    E6 86               OUTB    INITP           ; procedure
                    ;
0004                LOOP:                           ; Main loop
0004                CDIN:                           ; input routine
0004    E4 86               INB     IPSTAT          ; status for input
0006    A8 08               TESTBI  AL,IMASK        ; test the status bit
0008    75 FA               JNZ     CDIN            ; loop until ready
000A    E4 83               INB     IPDATA          ; get the data
000C    8A E0               MOVB    AH,AL           ; return it in AH
                    ;
000E    3C 03               CMPBI   AL,03           ; control C
0010    74 0C               JZ      RETURN
                    ;
```

```
0012                              CDOUT:                              ; output routine
0012    E4 80                            INB      OPSTAT              ; status for output
0014    A8 04                            TESTBI   AL,OMASK            ; test the status bit
0016    75 FA                            JNZ      CDOUT               ; loop until ready
0018    8A C4                            MOVB     AL,AH               ; get data ready
001A    E6 82                            OUTB     OPDATA              ; put it out
                                  ;
001C    EB E6                            JMPS     LOOP                ; Always loops back
                                  ;
001E    E4 FD                     RETURN: INB     0FDH                ; return to 8085
                                         END
```

Figure 7.5: Example 3: An I/O echo program.

Comments: This example shows one way to program the 8088 to receive input from a keyboard or terminal and send output to a terminal or printer. First it waits for and then gets a character from the input device; next it waits for the output device to be ready and then sends this character out.

This program uses more advanced loop control. That is, the programmer would normally be more conscious (and conscientious) while using these instructions than those in the simple loop control group.

At the beginning of the program, the constants such as IPSTAT, IPDATA, OPSTAT, OPDATA, IMASK, OMASK, INITP, and INITM will have to be set differently for each computer. The conditional jumps such as JNZ may have to be reversed for this example to run on your computer. We will discuss the details just a little bit later. This code segment can be located at the standard stage center address 1000H.

The first instruction loads the (8-bit) accumulator (AL) with a bit pattern which we will use to initialize the I/O controller. Your computer may require a different pattern or even a sequence of patterns (see the discussion of the 8251 PSIC in Chapter 6). The second instruction puts this pattern into the control port of the I/O controller. You will have a different port, or perhaps you will have several ports to set up. You may find that you don't need initialization, or you may need a longer routine. You will have to consult the manual for your I/O system to see what you do need for your machine.

The next section of code takes in a character from the terminal or keyboard. First, the contents of status port for input are moved into AL. In most machines, 1 bit out of the 8 in a status byte indicates when input is ready. In this case it is bit number 3, and so we use the TEST instruction whose source (in immediate addressing mode) is equal to the bit pattern with a 1 in position 3 and 0 in every other position. This pattern is called a mask, because it helps *mask off* all but the desired bit. In this case the mask corresponds to the number 8. The figure below shows how this works.

```
7  6  5  4  3  2  1  0
0  0  0  0  1  0  0  0    =      08H
```

Figure 7.6: Computing the value of the mask.

Your computer will probably use a different bit and, hence, a different mask.

In our computer, a 0 in position 3 indicates that input is ready and a **1 in this position indicates that input it not ready, thus we use the JNZ** instruction to loop back if the keyboard (or terminal) is not ready. If your computer has this reversed, then you will need to use the JZ instruction.

The TEST and the conditional jump instruction work together in the following way: The TEST instruction does a logical, bit-by-bit AND of the source IMASK and the destination AL, storing the result in a temporary location inside the CPU, never to be seen by the programmer. All arithmetic and logic instructions (including this one) set the flags according to the result of the operation. That is, if the result is zero then the zero flag (ZF) is set; if the result is negative, then the sign flag (SF) is set; and so on. In this case, we watch the zero flag. If the status bit is 0 (ready), then the logical AND of the status byte with the mask is 0, and thus the zero flag is set (equal to 1). Conversely, if the status bit is 1 (not ready), then the logical AND of the status byte with the mask is equal to the mask, and thus the zero flag will be cleared (equal to 0). Thus ZF = 1 means ready, and ZF = 0 means not ready.[2]

The conditional jumps are designed to mesh with such a TEST instruction. That is, we should look at the TEST/Jump sequence as a unit. If the specified bit was 0, then JZ will cause a jump and JNZ will *fall through* to the next instruction. On the other hand, if the specified bit was not 0, then JZ will fall through and JNZ will jump. That is: the JZ instruction will branch on a zero result, and the JNZ will branch on a nonzero result. In either case, the combination of the TEST instruction and the conditional jump causes a branch according to what is contained in bit position 3 of the byte which was fetched from the input status port.

---

[2]Note that the Z flag is made exactly opposite to the result. Although this does cause confusion, it is logically correct. Just remember: ZF = 0 means *no*, the result is not 0, and ZF = 1 means that *yes*, the result is zero.

That is, JZ will branch only if this bit is 0 (ready), and JNZ will branch only if this bit is 1 (not ready). Thus, JNZ is used to branch back to test until ready.

The next instruction gets the character which is now waiting at the input port. The character is then saved into AH because AL is needed for further work.

Next we use the CoMPare instruction to see if the character is a control C. If it is, then we jump to an instruction which returns us to the 8085.

The output works similarly to the input. This time the same status port is checked, but a different bit is tested. Bit position 2 contains the status for output. Thus the output status mask is 00000100 in binary, which is 04H. Notice that we have used equates in the beginning of our program to set these values. This is good programming practice because if we wish to modify them, they are all together and need only one change to properly set each occurrence of any given constant throughout the rest of the code.

Again for output, 1 means not ready and 0 means ready; hence we have chosen JNZ as the conditional jump to loop until the output device is ready. When the output device is ready, then move the ASCII code for the character into the output port. Again, you will have to supply your own value for the address of this port.

The above method for I/O uses what is called polling (discussed in conjunction with the 8089 IOP in Chapter 5). The computer keeps checking until a device is ready and does no useful work while it is waiting.

Subroutine Calls and Returns

For efficient and readable programs both in assembly language and higher-level languages, subroutines are essential. The instructions in the subroutine call and return instruction group are:

CALL   CALL
RET   RETurn

The figure below shows how you can implement some really basic I/O subroutines for a computer system. We show both the subroutines and how they are called. This example does not use a video screen.

```
; Example 4:  (CALL and RETURN)
;
; I/O Routines
;
0000'            ASEG
0080     IO      EQU     0080H           ; paragraph address of I/O
0020     CDIN    EQU     0020H           ; offset of input routine
0026     CDOUT   EQU     0026H           ; offset of output routine
         ;.
```

```
0000                              ENTER:                          ; main loop
0000    9A 0020                           CALL    CDIN,IO         ; get a character
0003    0080
0005    3C 03                             CMPBI   AL,03           ; check for control c
0007    74 07                             JZ      RETURN          ; if so return
0009    9A 0026                           CALL    CDOUT,IO        ; print the character
000C    0080
000E    EB F0                             JMPS    ENTER           ; short jump to loop back
                                  ;
0010    E4 FD                     RETURN: INB     0FDH            ; return to 8085
                                          END                     ; end of code segment
```

Figure 7.7a: Example 4: Using I/O routines.

```
                                  ; I/O  Section
                                  ;
                                  ; This segment contains four console I/O routines
                                  ; which are designed to be called by routines in
                                  ; other segments.
                                  ;
                                  ; The routines are:
                                  ;
                                  ;     CDINIT: This routine initializes the console
                                  ;             device. It requires no input parameters
                                  ;             and returns none. It preserves all
                                  ;             register except AL.
                                  ;
                                  ;     CDBRK:  This routine checks for input from the
                                  ;             console. It requires no input parameters.
                                  ;             If no key was hit, it returns with the Z
                                  ;             flag clear. If a key was hit, then it
                                  ;             checks for control C or control S. If
                                  ;             neither, then it returns with ASCII code
                                  ;             of the key in both AL and AH. If control
                                  ;             C, then it returns to 8085. If control S,
                                  ;             then it waits for character which is
                                  ;             returned in both AL and AH. It preserves
                                  ;             all other registers.
                                  ;
                                  ;     CDIN:   This routine waits for a character from the
                                  ;             console input device. It requires no input
                                  ;             parameters. It returns with the ASCII code
                                  ;             for the key in both AL and AH. It preserves
                                  ;             all other registers.
                                  ;
                                  ;     CDOUT:  This routine sends a character to the
                                  ;             console output device. It requires the
                                  ;             ASCII code of the character to be in the
                                  ;             AH register. It preserves all other
                                  ;             registers.
                                  ;
0000'                                     ASEG
0086                              IPSTAT  EQU     86H             ; input status port
0083                              IPDATA  EQU     83H             ; input data port
0080                              OPSTAT  EQU     80H             ; output status port
0082                              OPDATA  EQU     82H             ; output data port
```

```
0008                     IMASK    EQU    08H         ; input status mask
0004                     OMASK    EQU    04H         ; output status mask
0086                     INITP    EQU    86H         ; initialization port
0014                     INITM    EQU    14H         ; initilization mask
                         ;
0000                     CDINIT:                     ; initialize the console
0000    B0 14                     MOVBI  AL,INITM    ; initialization mask
0002    E6 86                     OUTB   INITP       ; initialization port
0004    CB                        RETS               ; intersegment return
                         ;
0005                     KEY:                        ; local routine for input
0005    E4 86                     INB    IPSTAT      ; get status
0007    A8 08                     TESTBI AL,IMASK    ; test it
0009    75 04                     JNZ    KEYRET      ; return if nothing
000B    E4 83                     INB    IPDATA      ; otherwise get the data
000D    8A E0                     MOVB   AH,AL       ; return it in AH
000F    C3               KEYRET:  RET                ; intrasegment return
                         ;
0010                     CDBRK:                      ; console break routine
0010    E8 FFF2                   CALL   KEY         ; check for key
0013    75 0A                     JNZ    CDBRET      ; return if no key
0015    3C 03                     CMPBI  AL,03H      ; control C?
0017    74 18                     JZ     RETURN      ; if so return to 8085
0019    3C 13                     CMPBI  AL,13H      ; control S?
001B    74 03                     JZ     CDIN        ; if so wait for key
001D    3A C0                     CMPB   AL,AL       ; set Z to indicate key
001F    CB               CDBRET:  RETS               ; intersegment return
                         ;
0020                     CDIN:                       ; console input routine
0020    E8 FFE2                   CALL   KEY         ; check for key
0023    75 FB                     JNZ    CDIN        ; loop until key is hit
0025    CB                        RETS               ; intersegment return
                         ;
0026                     CDOUT:                      ; console input routine
0026    E4 80                     INB    OPSTAT      ; status for output
0028    A8 04                     TESTBI AL,OMASK    ; test it
002A    75 FA                     JNZ    CDOUT       ; loop until ready
002C    8A C4                     MOVB   AL,AH       ; get data ready
002E    E6 82                     OUTB   OPDATA      ; put it out
0030    CB                        RETS               ; intersegment return
                         ;
0031    E4 FD            RETURN:  INB    0FDH        ; return to 8085
                         ;
                                  END                ; END OF IO SEGMENT
```

Figure 7.7b: The I/O segment.

Comments: This example shows how you can implement two different kinds of subroutine calls and returns (intersegment and intrasegment).

There are two separate segments in this example, a segment containing the main program (located at the usual place, 1000H) and a segment filled with the primitive-level I/O routines. We have called the source code for the I/O segment EIO.MAC and the source code for the main program E4.MAC. The I/O segment should be loaded at address

800H. Its paragraph number (80H) is equated to the symbol IO in the main program, so any reference to it can be made by *name* rather than number.

You must have both segments in memory for this program to work.

You might want to create a file which contains both L88 (at 100H) and the I/O segment (at 800H). You can do this by using DDT to load in EIO.COM (machine code for the I/O segment) and move it into place. Then use the commands:

IL88.COM
R

to load in L88 while still in DDT. Now type control C, thus returning to the usual CP/M prompt. Now use the command:

SAVE 15 GO.COM

to save the region from 100H to 0FFFH as the command GO. Later you can add two system segments to this same area.

If you have created the above GO command, then you can run this and subsequent examples by using DDT to load the example and then (from the main CP/M prompt) typing GO.

The symbols CDINIT, CDBRK, CDIN, and CDOUT appear in the I/O segment as labels for the various IO routines. These also appear as equates for the main program. In practice, the manufacturer might supply the I/O segment and a file containing the equates. By linking or editing in this file, the user could make all necessary references to these routines by name rather than by address while writing applications programs.

Now let's look at the main program. It first calls CDIN, the console input routine, which waits for a character from the console input device. Notice that the CALL instruction is an intrasegment call; that is, it's a call from one segment to another. It has two operands: the *offset address* of the subroutine and the *paragraph number* of the segment in which it is to be found. Both operands are referenced by name as described above. In the Microsoft cross-assembler, the offset address always comes before the *segment paragraph number,* and these two quantities are separated by a comma.

CDIN returns the character in both AL and AH. A check is made to see if the character was a control C (the panic button). If so, a jump is made to the standard return of control to the 8085 CPU. If the character is not a control C, CDOUT is called. This is also an intersegment call (to the I/O segment). It accepts the character in AH and sends it to the output device. After the character is sent out, the program loops around for more.

The I/O segment begins with a long section of documentation. Each routine is described in detail. In this kind of documentation, the following points should be covered:

a) function or purpose of the routine
b) input parameters
c) output parameters
d) registers preserved or altered

It is important to have such documentation because routines such as these are going to be used and abused by others.

In addition to the four I/O routines for external use, the I/O segment contains a routine called KEY which is for internal use only. It cannot be successfully called from any other segment. This is because the return statement is an intrasegment RETurn instead of RETS for interSegment RETurn. An interSegment RETurn restores both the code segment and the instruction pointer registers while an intrasegment RETurn only restores the instruction pointer. Thus, a call of our routine KEY from another segment would probably not return back to the calling segment. The very last program will give us a way to actually see how differently these two calls work. We will be able to single step through the program watching the stack to see how the RET instruction *pops* one quantity (returning IP register) from the stack and the RETS pops two quantities (returning IP and CS registers).

The actual workings of the I/O subroutines are very similar to the I/O procedures described in the previous section of this chapter.

Again, you will have to *configure* them to your own computer system. If your system does not need an initialization routine, then you might want to replace the one we have by a sequence of four NOPs. Since we have not officially reached either the NOT or the NOP instruction, you will have to consider the last suggestion off-the-record.

The choice of JZ or JNZ depends upon how the bits are set on your status bytes. This can cause trouble all the way down the line into your application programs. If your bits are reversed, one way to nip this problem in the bud is to insert the logical instruction:

```
NOT      AL
```

right before the TEST instruction. Normally a couple of NOPs are inserted here to leave enough room in the machine code for a possible replacement by the NOT instruction. Again, this is off-the-record.

One peculiar point in the CDBRK routine is that the instruction:

```
CMPB      AL,AL
```

occurs just before the return. This just insures that the Z flag is set upon return, indicating that a character is ready. If your bits are still turned around on the input status, and you wish to change the conditional jumps rather than use the NOT instruction, then you might want to modify this instruction to

```
CMPBI    AL,03
```

Arithmetic Instructions

There are a whole bunch of instructions in the arithmetic group:

ADD GROUP

	ADD	ADD
	ADC	ADd with Carry
	AAA	ASCII Adjust for Addition
	DAA	Decimal Adjust for Addition

SUBTRACT GROUP

	SUB	SUBtract
	SBB	SuBtract with Borrow
	AAS	ASCII Adjust for Subtraction
	DAS	Decimal Adjust for Subtraction

MULTIPLY GROUP

	MUL	MULtiply
	IMUL	Integer MULtiply
	AAM	ASCII Adjust for Multiplication

DIVIDE GROUP

	DIV	DIVide
	IDIV	Integer DIVide
	AAD	ASCII Adjust for Division

CONVERSIONS

	CBW	Convert Byte to Word
	CWD	Convert Word to Double word
NEG		NEGate

We will demonstrate only a couple of these in our example program (see the figure below). You could spend the rest of your life working on examples for the ones we didn't get to.

```
; Example 5A: (Arithmetic Instructions)
;
; Multidigit counting on the screen
;
0000'             ASEG
0E80      VIDEO   EQU    0E80H
000A      SIZE    EQU    10
0080      IO      EQU    80H        ; paragraph address of IO
0010      CKBRK   EQU    10H        ; console break routine
```

```
                     ;
0000  B8 0E80        ENTER:  MOVI    AX,VIDEO        ; point data segment to
0003  8E D8                  MOV     DS,AX           ; video RAM
                     ;
                                                     ; initialize the number
0005  BF 004F                MOVI    DI,79           ; point to first position
0008  B9 000A                MOVI    CX,SIZE         ; CX contains the count
000B  B0 30                  MOVBI   AL,'0'          ; AL contains a '0'
000D  88 05          ENTER1: MOVB    [DI],AL         ; put digit in place
000F  4F                     DEC     DI              ; next position
0010  E2 FB                  LOOP    ENTER1          ; loop until done
                     ;
0012  BF 004F        LOOP:   MOVI    DI,79           ; main loop
0015  B9 000A                MOVI    CX,SIZE         ; set loop counter
0018  8A 25                  MOVB    AH,[DI]         ; use AH for carry
001A  FE C4                  INCB    AH
001C  8A C4          DLOOP:  MOVB    AL,AH           ; get the digit
001E  8A 65 FF               MOVB    AH,-1[DI]       ; get the next digit
0021  37                     AAA                     ; set the new carry
0022  04 30                  ADDBI   AL,'0'          ; convert back to ASCII
0024  88 05                  MOVB    [DI],AL         ; put it back
0026  4F                     DEC     DI              ; next position
0027  E2 F3                  LOOP    DLOOP           ; next digit
                     ;
0029  9A 0010                CALL    CKBRK,IO        ; check for interrupt
002C  0080
                     ;
002E  E2 E2                  LOOP    LOOP            ; always loops back
                     ;
                             END                     ; end of code segment
```

Figure 7.8a: Example 5A: Multidigit counting on the screen.

```
                     ; Example 5B: (Arithmetic Instructions)
                     ;
                     ; Multidigit counting to the terminal
                     ;
0000'                        ASEG
0E80'                VIDEO   EQU     0E80H
0080                 IO      EQU     80H             ; IO segment paragraph address
0026                 COUT    EQU     26H             ; console output
0010                 CKBRK   EQU     10H             ; console break
000A                 SIZE    EQU     10
                     ;
0000  B8 0E80                MOVI    AX,VIDEO        ; point data segment to
0003  8E D8                  MOV     DS,AX           ; video RAM
                     ;
                                                     ; initialize the number
0005  BF 004F                MOVI    DI,79           ; point to first position
0008  B9 000A                MOVI    CX,SIZE         ; CX contains the count
000B  B0 30                  MOVBI   AL,'0'          ; AL contains a '0'
000D  88 05          ENTER1: MOVB    [DI],AL         ; put digit in place
000F  4F                     DEC     DI              ; next position
0010  E2 FB                  LOOP    ENTER1          ; loop until done
                     ;
```

```
0012    BF 004F        LOOP:   MOVI    DI,79           ; main loop
0015    B9 000A                MOVI    CX,SIZE         ; set loop counter
0018    8A 25                  MOVB    AH,[DI]         ; use AH for carry
001A    FE C4                  INCB    AH
001C    8A C4          LOOP1:  MOVB    AL,AH           ; get the digit
001E    8A 65    FF            MOVB    AH,-1[DI]       ; get next digit
0021    37                     AAA                     ; adjust
0022    04 30                  ADDBI   AL,'0'          ; convert back to ASCII
0024    88 05                  MOVB    [DI],AL         ; put it back
0026    4F                     DEC     DI              ; next position
0027    E2 F3                  LOOP    LOOP1           ; next digit
                       ;
0029    9A 0010                CALL    CKBRK,IO        ; check for interrupt
002C    0080
                       ;
                                                       ; output the number
002E    BF 0045                MOVI    DI,79-SIZE      ; point to highest position
0031    B9 000B                MOVI    CX,SIZE+1       ; CX contains the count
0034    8A 25          OUT:    MOVB    AH,[DI]         ; get digit in place
0036    47                     INC     DI              ; next position
0037    9A 0026                CALL    COUT,IO         ; send it out
003A    0080
003C    E2 F6                  LOOP    OUT             ; loop until done
                       ;
003E    E2 D2                  LOOP    LOOP            ; always loops back
                       ;
                                END                     ; end of code segment
```

Figure 7.8b: Example 5B: Multidigit counting to the terminal.

Comments: There are two examples here, one for a video screen and one for a system with just a terminal. In either case, the example shows one way in which to do multidigit arithmetic with the 8088. In this example, there is a multidigit counter which is stored in the same place that it is displayed on the screen (or in the case of 5b, stored for offloading to the terminal). The digits are stored in their ASCII code with 1 digit per byte.

This code is contained in a segment which can be located in the standard memory location 1000H. The I/O segment must also be present for the call to CKBRK to work. (Do you have the flags right for the I/O?)

The program first initializes the number by loading each digit with a 0. This requires a short loop. Next comes the main loop of the program which is executed each time the counter is incremented. This loop initializes and then executes a smaller loop which takes care of each digit. Let's call this smaller loop the digit loop.

The digit loop uses a kind of pipeline to process the digits. It loads the next digit into the AH register after the current digit is put into AL. The AAA (ASCII adjust for addition) adjusts the current digit in AL by adding 6 to the lower nibble if it is greater than 9. Any carry-out of this nibble is automatically added to AH, which contains the next digit (by our design of the program). The AAA instruction also clears the upper nibble of AL, so the next instruction is required to add back the top nibble of the ASCII code for the digit. The digit is now put into place and the index register DI is pointed toward the next digit before looping back.

It is interesting to look at the timing for the digit loop. The units of time are the clock cycles, which are 200 nanoseconds for a 5-megahertz CPU. The figure below shows this.

			instruction	addressing	total
LOOP1:	MOVB	AL,AH	2	0	2
	MOVB	AH,-1[DI]	8	9	17
	AAA		4	0	4
	ADDBI	AL,'0'	4	0	4
	MOVB	[DI],AL	9	5	14
	DEC	DI	2	0	2
	LOOP	LOOP1	9	0	9

Figure 7.9: Timing for the digit loop.

The total time is 52 clock cycles or 10.4 microseconds. If there are 10 digits, then it will take very roughly 100 microseconds for each count. This is about 10,000 counts per second. We actually measured about 3,700 counts per second. There are at least three reasons for this loss of performance. One is that the instruction queue may not always be able to fetch instructions as fast as they are executed, another is that the video RAM may slow down the CPU by putting it into wait states, and another is the overhead from the larger loop.

By using string operations, which are discussed next, you should be able to increase the speed by about 20 percent.

String Manipulation

The string instructions allow us to rapidly move, compare, or scan through blocks of data. The instructions in this group are:

MOVC	MOVe string Character
MOVW	MOVe string Word
CMPC	CoMPare string Character
CMPW	CoMPare string Word
SCAC	SCAn string Character
SCAW	SCAn string Word
LODC	LOaD string Character
LODW	LOaD string Word
STOC	STOre string Character
STOW	STOre string Word
REP	REPeat
CLD	CLear Direction flag
STD	SeT Direction flag

We discuss these instructions reasonably extensively in Chapter 3, so we will avoid a general discussion here. Go back to Chapter 3 if you need to. The figure below shows our example program for this group.

```
                              ; Example 6:   (String operators)
                              ;
                              ; Outputting messages
                              ;
0000'                              ASEG
0E80                  VIDEO   EQU    0E80H          ; video RAM segment
0080                  IO      EQU    80H            ; I/O segment
0020                  CDIN    EQU    20H            ; console input routine
0026                  CDOUT   EQU    26H
007F                  DEL     EQU    7FH            ; ASCII code for DELETE key
0020                  SPACE   EQU    20H            ; ASCII code for SPACE key
000A                  LF      EQU    0AH            ; ASCII code for LINEFEED
000D                  CR      EQU    0DH            ; ASCII code for RETURN key
                              ;
0000                  ENTER:                        ; enter here
0000   8C C8                  MOV    AX,CS          ; make the data segment
0002   8E D8                  MOV    DS,AX          ; equal to the code segment
                              ;
0004   BE 0058        LOOP:   MOVI   DI,MESS0       ; main loop
0007   E8 003C                CALL   MESOUT         ; show the option table
                              ;
000A   9A 0020        LOOP1:  CALL   CDIN,IO        ; get the option
000D   0080
000F   9A 0026                CALL   CDOUT,IO       ; and show it too
0012   0080
0014   8A C4                  MOVB   AL,AH
                              ;
0016   3C 03                  CMPBI  AL,3           ; control C?
0018   74 3C                  JZ     RETURN         ; if so, return
                              ;
001A   3C 31                  CMPBI  AL,'1'         ; number 1?
001C   74 10                  JZ     DO1            ; send that message
                              ;
001E   3C 32                  CMPBI  AL,'2'         ; number 2?
0020   74 14                  JZ     DO2            ; send that message
                              ;
0022   3C 33                  CMPBI  AL,'3'         ; number 3?
0024   74 18                  JZ     DO3            ; send that message
                              ;
0026   BE 0160        ERROR:  MOVI   SI,MESS4       ; none of the above
0029   E8 001A                CALL   MESOUT
002C   EB D6                  JMPS   LOOP           ; loop back for more
                              ;
002E   BE 00A9        DO1:    MOVI   SI,MESS1       ; handle #1
0031   E8 0012                CALL   MESOUT
0034   EB D4                  JMPS   LOOP1
                              ;
0036   BE 0101        DO2:    MOVI   SI,MESS2       ; handle #2
0039   E8 000A                CALL   MESOUT
003C   EB CC                  JMPS   LOOP1
                              ;
003E   BE 0122        DO3:    MOVI   SI,MESS3       ; handle #3
0041   E8 0002                CALL   MESOUT
0044   EB C4                  JMPS   LOOP1
```

```
                                ;
0046               MESOUT:                            ; message output routine
0046   FC                CLD                          ; forward direction
0047   AC          MESLP: LODC                        ; get the character
0048   A8 FF              TESTBI  AL,0FFH             ; zero byte means
004A   74 09              JZ      MESEND             ; end of message
004C   8A E0              MOVB    AH,AL              ; send the character
004E   9A 0026            CALL    CDOUT,IO
0051   0080
0053   EB F2              JMPS    MESLP              ; loop around for more
                                ;
0055   C3          MESEND: RET                        ; return at the end
                                ;
0056   E4 FD        RETURN: INB     0FDH
                                ;
0058   0D 0A 54 79  MESS0: DB      CR,LF,'Type one of the following numbers:'
005C   70 65 20 6F
0060   6E 65 20 6F
0064   66 20 74 68
0068   65 20 66 6F
006C   6C 6C 6F 77
0070   69 6E 67 20
0074   6E 75 6D 62
0078   65 72 73 3A
007C   0D 0A 20 20         DB      CR,LF,'  1, 2, or 3'
0080   31 2C 20 32
0084   2C 20 6F 72
0088   20 33
008A   0D 0A 6F 72         DB      CR,LF,' or type control C to exit.'
008E   20 74 79 70
0092   65 20 63 6F
0096   6E 74 72 6F
009A   6C 20 43 20
009E   74 6F 20 65
00A2   78 69 74 2E
00A6   0D 0A 00            DB      CR,LF,0
                                ;
00A9   0D 0A 23 20  MESS1: DB      CR,LF,'# 1. Congratulations,'
00AD   31 2E 20 43
00B1   6F 6E 67 72
00B5   61 74 75 61
00B9   74 69 6F 6E
00BD   73 2C
00BF   20 79 6F 75         DB      ' you have made an excellent choice.',CR,LF
00C3   20 68 61 76
00C7   65 20 6D 61
00CB   64 65 20 61
00CF   6E 20 65 78
00D3   63 65 6C 6C
00D7   65 6E 74 20
00DB   63 68 6F 69
00DF   63 65 2E 0D
00E3   0A
00E4   4E 6F 77 20         DB      'Now try the other choices.',CR,LF,0
00E8   74 72 79 20
00EC   74 68 65 20
00F0   6F 74 68 65
```

```
00F4    72 20 63 68
00F8    6F 69 63 65
00FC    73 2E 0D 0A
0100    00
                                ;
0101    0D 0A 23 20             MESS2:   DB      CR,LF,'# 2. Poor choice, try again.',CR,LF,0
0105    32 2E 20 50
0109    6F 6F 72 20
010D    63 68 6F 69
0111    63 65 2C 20
0115    74 72 79 20
0119    61 67 61 69
011D    6E 2E 0D 0A
0121    00
                                ;
0122    0D 0A 23 20             MESS3:   DB      CR,LF,'# 3. Number 1 would be better.',CR,LF
0126    33 2E 20 4E
012A    75 6D 62 65
012E    72 20 31 20
0132    77 6F 75 6C
0136    64 20 62 65
013A    20 62 65 74
013E    74 65 72 2E
0142    0D 0A
0144    57 68 79 20                      DB      'Why don''t you try it now?',CR,LF,0
0148    64 6F 6E 27
014C    74 20 79 6F
0150    75 20 74 72
0154    79 20 69 74
0158    20 6E 6F 77
015C    3F 0D 0A 00
                                ;
0160    0D 0A 59 6F             MESS4:   DB      CR,LF,'You didn''t hit the right key!!!'
0164    75 20 64 69
0168    64 6E 27 74
016C    20 68 69 74
0170    20 74 68 65
0174    20 72 69 67
0178    68 74 20 6B
017C    65 79 21 21
0180    21
0181    0D 0A 00                         DB      CR,LF,0
                                ;
                                         END
```

Figure 7.10: Example 6: Outputting messages.

Comments: This program is designed to give you the runaround. It displays a message which asks you for a number from 1 to 3. Each number will cause a different message to be returned to you. You also have the option of hitting a control C to return to the loader program. The messages just lead you around in circles, but you can easily modify this program to make it output useful messages. This could be the beginning of a game or a program which performs various useful functions. The program uses the LODC string instruction.

This program can be located at the standard stage center address 1000H, and it requires the I/O segment to be located at its standard address 800H. If you have created the GO command, then this will happen automatically.

A main loop manages the program. It calls a subroutine called MESOUT to output messages and the subroutine CDOUT to input keystrokes from the user. MESOUT is within the same segment and CDOUT is in another segment (the I/O segment). The CoMPare instruction and conditional jumps are used to dispatch to the various options.

Within the MESOUT subroutine, the SI register is used to point to the character which is to be output. The LODC instruction moves the character from memory to the accumulator and increments SI so that it points to the next character. Before the character is output, it is checked to see if it is a zero. In our program zero signifies the end of the message. Notice that each message has a zero tacked onto it. Some assemblers actually have a special command which automatically places a zero after a message. There are couple of other standard ways to terminate messages, but we prefer this one. Notice that the carriage returns and linefeeds are included as part of the messages.

All messages are stored at the end of this program. This forms a nice structure. We could, of course, dedicate a whole segment to our messages. In any case the data segment register (DS) must point to the segment which contains the messages. In this program, this is done by moving the contents of code segment register (CS) to the data segment register.

Logical Instructions

The logical instructions are bit-by-bit operations which work on whole bytes or words. The instructions in this group are:

NOT	NOT
AND	AND
OR	OR
XOR	eXclusive OR

The figure below shows an example program in which logical operations are used to control a cursor while you type characters onto your video screen. If you do not have a video screen, then you cannot effectively try this example. If this is the case, then study it and go on to the next one, which also uses logical instructions.

```
                          ; Example 7:   (Logical operators)
                          ;
                          ; Typing a line on the screen
                          ;
0000'                             ASEG
0E80              VIDEO   EQU     0E80H        ; video RAM segment
00B0              PARM    EQU     0B0H         ; data parameters segment
0000              LINELOC EQU     0            ; address of beginning address
                                               ; of line
0080              IO      EQU     80H          ; I/O segment
0020              CDIN    EQU     20H          ; console input routine
007F              DEL     EQU     7FH          ; ASCII code for DELETE key
0020              SPACE   EQU     20H          ; ASCII code for SPACE key
000D              CR      EQU     0DH          ; ASCII code for RETURN key
                          ;
0000              ENTER:                       ; main loop
0000  B8 0E80             MOVI    AX,VIDEO     ; extra segment is video RAM
0003  8E C0               MOV     ES,AX
0005  B8 00B0             MOVI    AX,PARM      ; data segment points to data
0008  8E D8               MOV     DS,AX
000A  C7 06 0000          MOVI    LINELOC,0    ; initialize LINELOC
000E  0000
                                               ;
0010  8B 3E 0000  LINEBG: MOV     DI,LINELOC   ; DI has beginning address
0014  FC                  CLD                  ; forward direction
                                               ;
0015  26          LOOP:   $ES                  ; ES points to video RAM
0016  80 0D 80             ORBI    [DI],80H    ; put cursor
0019  9A 0020              CALL    CDIN,IO     ; get a character
001C  0080
001E  26                  $ES                  ; ES points to video RAM
001F  80 25 7F            ANDBI   [DI],7FH     ; remove cursor
0022  3C 03               CMPBI   AL,3         ; check for control C
0024  74 1F               JZ      RETURN       ; if so return to 8085
0026  3C 7F               CMPBI   AL,DEL       ; check for DELETE
0028  74 07               JZ      DELETE
002A  3C 0D               CMPBI   AL,CR        ; check for <CR>
002C  74 10               JZ      NXTLN        ; if so make a new line
                                               ; if none of the above
002E  AA                  STOC                 ; put the character in place
                                               ;
002F  EB E4               JMPS    LOOP         ; always loops back
                          ;
0031              DELETE:                       ; procedure to handle DELETE
0031  3B 3E 0000          CMP     DI,LINELOC   ; check for beginning of line
0035  74 DE               JZ      LOOP
0037  4F                  DEC     DI           ; back up
0038  26                  $ES
0039  C6 05 20            MOVBI   [DI],SPACE   ; blank it
003C  EB D7               JMPS    LOOP         ; and return to loop
                          ;
```

```
003E                          NXTLN:                        ; Procedure to make new line
003E   83 06 0000 50                  ADDI    LINELOC,80    ; new beginning of line
0043   EB CB                          JMPS    LINEBG        ; and return to loop
                                      ;
0045   E4 FD                 RETURN:  INB     OFDH          ; return to 8085
                                      END                   ; END OF CODE SEGMENT
```

Figure 7.11: Example 7: Typing a line on the screen.

Comments: This example shows how to turn the video screen into a terminal. String instructions and the logical operations OR and AND play important roles in controlling the display of the letters and the cursor.

This segment is located at the standard address 1000H. The IO segment must also be in its usual place, 800H.

There is one main loop with a couple of service procedures. The extra segment points to the video screen, and the data segment points to a storage area for variables.

The first line of text begins at location 0 of the VIDEO segment. The index register DI contains the current cursor position. The loop places a reverse video type of cursor on the screen by performing a logical OR whose source is the bit pattern 10000000 and whose destination is the current cursor position. This sets the leftmost bit of the displayed character. Then it waits for a character from the keyboard. As soon as the character is received, the cursor is turned off using a logical AND with the bit pattern 01111111. There is then a check to see if the character is a DELETE, ⟨CR⟩, or control C. If it is none of these, then the character is placed on the screen at the current cursor position using the string function STOre string Character (STOC). This automatically increments DI. The AND and OR require segment override instructions so that the extra segment is used rather than the data segment to access their destinations.

The service procedure to handle DELETE checks to see if you are at the beginning of the line. If so, you are prevented from backing up any further. If you are not, then you may delete. This is done by decrementing DI, thus backing up the cursor position, and moving a space into this backed-up position. Again, the segment override prefix is used to point to the extra segment.

The service procedure to handle ⟨CR⟩ adds 80 to the variable containing the memory location of the beginning of the line, thus making a new line. It then loops back to just before the normal loop where the index register DI is initialized to point to the beginning of the (new) line. If you have a different number of characters per line, you will want to add that number instead of 80.

The service procedure to handle control C is just the normal return to the 8085 CPU.

Starting with this basic skeleton, we encourage you to increase the number of special functions. For example, you could add scrolling by using the string instruction MOVC to move the screen up one line.

Shift, Rotate, And Carry Instructions

You can use the shift, rotate, and carry instructions for a number of different, assembly-language purposes. They basically allow you to multiply and divide by powers of 2. The instructions in this group are:

SHL SAL	SHift Left (Arithmetic)
SHR	SHift Right
SAR	Shift Arithmetic Right
ROL	ROtate Left
ROR	ROtate Right
RCL	Rotate through Carry Left
RCR	Rotate through Carry Right
CLC	CLear Carry
STC	SeT Carry

The figure below shows an example of how these operations are useful in preparing numbers for output.

```
; Example 8:   (Shift and rotate instructions)
;
; Hexadecimal arithmetic
;
0000'                      ASEG
0020             SPACE    EQU      20H          ; ASCII for SPACE
000D             CR       EQU      0DH          ; ASCII for RETURN
000A             LF       EQU      0AH          ; ASCII for LINEFEED
0080             IO       EQU      80H          ; IO segment
0010             CKBRK    EQU      10H          ; CKBRK offset address
0026             CDOUT    EQU      26H          ; CDOUT offset address
0090             SYS1     EQU      90H          ; SYS1 segment
0000             HEXOUT   EQU      00H          ; HEXOUT offset address
001B             HEXIN    EQU      1BH          ; HEXIN  offset address
004B             SPCOUT   EQU      4BH          ; SPCOUT offset address
0053             CRLF     EQU      53H          ; CRLF   offset address
0062             MESOUT   EQU      62H          ; MESOUT offset address
                          ;
0000   8C C8     ENTER:   MOV      AX,CS        ; make data segment
0002   8E D8              MOV      DS,AX        ; equal to code segment
                          ;
0004   BE 0090            MOVI     SI,MESS0     ; welcome message
0007   9A 0062            CALL     MESOUT,SYS1
000A   0090
                          ;
000C   9A 0053   LOOP:    CALL     CRLF,SYS1
000F   0090
0011   BE 00FA            MOVI     SI,MESS1     ; first number?
0014   9A 0062            CALL     MESOUT,SYS1
0017   0090
```

```
0019        9A 001B             CALL    HEXIN,SYS1        ; input the numbers
001C        0090
001E        89 16 008C          MOV     NUM1,DX
                            ;
0022        9A 0053             CALL    CRLF,SYS1
0025        0090
0027        BE 010A             MOVI    SI,MESS2          ; second number?
002A        9A 0062             CALL    MESOUT,SYS1
002D        0090
002F        9A 001B             CALL    HEXIN,SYS1        ; input the numbers
0032        0090
0034        89 16 008E          MOV     NUM2,DX
                            ;
0038        9A 0053             CALL    CRLF,SYS1
003B        0090
003D        BE 011A             MOVI    SI,MESS3          ; the sum
0040        9A 0062             CALL    MESOUT,SYS1
0043        0090
0045        8B 16 008C          MOV     CX,NUM1
0049        03 16 008E          ADD     DX,NUM2
004D        9A 0000             CALL    HEXOUT,SYS1
0050        0090
                            ;
0052        BE 0124             MOVI    SI,MESS4          ; the difference
0055        9A 0062             CALL    MESOUT,SYS1
0058        0090
005A        8B 16 008C          MOV     DX,NUM1
005E        2B 16 008E          SUB     DX,NUM2
0062        9A 0000             CALL    HEXOUT,SYS1
0065        0090
                            ;
0067        BE 0137             MOVI    SI,MESS5          ; the product
006A        9A 0062             CALL    MESOUT,SYS1
006D        0090
006F        A1 008C             MOV     AX,NUM1
0072        F7 26 008E          MUL     NUM2
0076        8B D0               MOV     DX,AX
0078        9A 0000             CALL    HEXOUT,SYS1
007B        0090
                            ;
007D        9A 0053             CALL    CRLF,SYS1
0080        0090
0082        BE 0147             MOVI    SI,MESS6          ; some stars
0085        9A 0062             CALL    MESOUT,SYS1
0088        0090
                            ;
008A        EB 80               JMPS    LOOP              ; loop back
                            ;
008C        0000        NUM1:   DW      0                 ; storage for number
008E        0000        NUM2:   DW      0                 ; storage for number
0090        54 68 69 73  MESS0:  DB      'This program does hexadecimal arithmetic.'
0094        20 70 72 6F
0098        67 72 61 6D
009C        20 64 6F 65
00A0        73 20 68 65
00A4        78 61 64 65
00A8        63 69 6D 61
00AC        6C 20 61 72
00B0        69 74 68 6D
```

```
00B4        65 74 69 63
00B8        2E
00B9        0D 0A 49 74              DB       CR,LF,'It computes the sum, difference,
00BD        20 63 6F 6D
00C1        70 75 74 65
00C5        73 20 74 68
00C9        65 20 73 75
00CD        6D 2C 20 64
00D1        69 66 66 65
00D5        72 65 6E 63
00D9        65 2C 20
00DC        61 6E 64 20              DB       'and product of two numbers.',CR,LF,0
00E0        70 72 6F 64
00E4        75 63 74 20
00E8        6F 66 20 74
00EC        77 6F 20 6E
00F0        75 6D 62 65
00F4        72 73 2E 0D
00F8        0A 00
00FA        46 69 72 73   MESS1:     DB       'First number:   ',0
00FE        74 20 6E 75
0102        6D 62 65 72
0106        3A 20 20 00
010A        53 65 63 6F   MESS2:     DB       'Second number: ',0
010E        6E 64 20 6E
0112        75 6D 62 65
0116        72 3A 20 00
011A        54 68 65 20   MESS3:     DB       'The sum: ',0
011E        73 75 6D 3A
0122        20 00
0124        20 20 54 68   MESS4:     DB       '   The difference: ',0
0128        65 20 64 69
012C        66 66 65 72
0130        65 6E 63 65
0134        3A 20 00
0137        20 20 54 68   MESS5:     DB       '   The product: ',0
013B        65 20 70 72
013F        6F 64 75 63
0143        74 3A 20 00
0147        2A 2A 2A 2A   MESS6:     DB       '**********************************',0
014B        2A 2A 2A 2A
014F        2A 2A 2A 2A
0153        2A 2A 2A 2A
0157        2A 2A 2A 2A
015B        2A 2A 2A 2A
015F        2A 2A 2A 2A
0163        2A 2A 2A 2A
0167        2A 2A 2A 00
                         ;
                                     END                      ; End of code segment
```

Figure 7.12a: Example 8: Hexadecimal arithmetic.

```
                    ; System segment #1
                    ;
                    ; This segment contains routines for outputting
                    ; various things such a hexadecimal numbers, spaces,
                    ; and carriage return - line feeds.  This segment
                    ; requires the IO segment.
                    ;
                    ; The routines are:
                    ;
                    ;    HEXOUT: This routine outputs the contents of the
                    ;            the DX register as a 16-bit hexadecimal
                    ;            number to the console output device. It
                    ;            requires one input parameter in the DX
                    ;            register. It returns none.   It destroys
                    ;            registers AX, BX, CX, and DX.
                    ;
                    ;    HEXIN:  This routine inputs a 16-bit hexadecimal
                    ;            number from the console input device.  It
                    ;            also echoes the digits as they are typed.
                    ;            It returns the number in register DX.  It
                    ;            destroys registers AX, BX, CX, and DX.  If
                    ;            a control C is hit, then it returns to the
                    ;            loader program.
                    ;
                    ;    SPCOUT: This routine outputs a space to the
                    ;            console output device. It requires no
                    ;            input parameters, and it returns none.
                    ;            It destroys the AX register.
                    ;
                    ;    CRLF:   This routine outputs a <CR> < LF> to the
                    ;            console output device.  It requires no
                    ;            input parameters, and it returns none.
                    ;            It destroys the AX register.
                    ;
                    ;    MESOUT: This routine outputs a message to the
                    ;            console output device.  The SI register
                    ;            must point to the beginning of the message,
                    ;            the end of the message is signified by
                    ;            a zero byte.
                    ;
0000'                       ASEG
0080                IO      EQU     0080H           ; IO segment
0010                CKBRK   EQU     0010H           ; CKBRK offset address
0020                CDIN    EQU     0020H           ; CDIN  offset address
0026                CDOUT   EQU     0026H           ; CDOUT offset address
0020                SPACE   EQU     20H             ; ASCII for space
000D                CR      EQU     0DH             ; ASCII for <CR>
000A                LF      EQU     0AH             ; ASCII for <LF>
                    ;
0000                HEXOUT:                         ; routine to output hex
0000    BB 0004             MOVI    BX,4            ; # of hex digits
0003    B1 04       HLOOP:  MOVBI   CL,4            ; a count of 4 for each
0005    D3 C2               ROL     DX,CL           ; to shift left
0007    8B C2               MOV     AX,DX           ; bring it into AX
0009    24 0F               ANDBI   AL,0FH          ; mask it
000B    27                  DAA                     ; add 6 if A-F
000C    04 F0               ADDBI   AL,0F0H         ; bump out a carry if A-F
000E    14 40               ADCBI   AL,040H         ; here is the ASCII
0010    8A  E0      HLOOP1: MOVB    AH,AL
```

```
0012    9A 0026                 CALL    CDOUT,IO        ; print digit
0015    0080
0017    4B                      DEC     BX
0018    75 E9                   JNZ     HLOOP           ; next digit
001A    CB                      RETS                    ; end of HEXOUT
                        ;
001B                    HEXIN:                          ; routine to input hex
001B    BA 0000                 MOVI    DX,0            ; initialize the number
001E    9A 0020         HEXIN1: CALL    CDIN,IO         ; input a digit
0021    0080
0023    3C 03                   CMPBI   AL,3            ; control C?
0025    74 4B                   JZ      RETURN
0027    9A 0026                 CALL    CDOUT,IO        ; otherwise echo it
002A    0080
                        ;
002C    8A C4                   MOVB    AL,AH           ; and
002E    2C 30                   SUBBI   AL,'0'          ; convert from ASCII
0030    72 18                   JB      HEXRET          ; too low?
0032    3C 0A                   CMPBI   AL,'9'-'0'+1    ; from 0 to 9?
0034    72 0A                   JB      HEXADD          ; if so, take it
0036    2C 11                   SUBBI   AL,'A'-'0'      ; from A to F?
0038    72 10                   JB      HEXRET          ; if not, return
003A    3C 06                   CMPBI   AL,'F'-'A'+1
003C    73 0C                   JNB     HEXRET
003E    04 0A                   ADDBI   AL,10           ; if so, adjust

0040    B1 04           HEXADD: MOVBI   CL,4            ; now
0042    D3 E2                   SAL     DX,CL           ; multiply old part by 16
0044    B4 00                   MOVBI   AH,0            ; and add new part
0046    03 D0                   ADD     DX,AX
0048    EB D4                   JMPS    HEXIN1
                        ;
004A    CB              HEXRET: RETS                    ; return when finished
                        ;
004B                    SPCOUT:                         ; space output routine
004B    B4 20                   MOVBI   AH,SPACE        ; space
004D    9A 0026                 CALL    CDOUT,IO        ; output it
0050    0080
0052    CB                      RETS                    ; end of SPOUT
                        ;
0053                    CRLF:
0053    B4 0D                   MOVBI   AH,CR           ; carriage return
0055    9A 0026                 CALL    CDOUT,IO        ; output it
0058    0080
005A    B4 0A                   MOVBI   AH,LF           ; line feed
005C    9A 0026                 CALL    CDOUT,IO        ; output it
005F    0080
0061    CB                      RETS                    ; end of CRLF
                        ;
0062                    MESOUT:                         ; message output routine
0062    FC                      CLD                     ; forward direction
0063    AC              MESLP:  LODC                    ; get the charcater
0064    A8 FF                   TESTBI  AL,0FFH         ; zero byte
0066    74 09                   JZ      MESEND          ; end of message
0068    8A E0                   MOVB    AH,AL           ; send the character
006A    9A 0026                 CALL    CDOUT,IO
006D    0080
006F    EB F2                   JMPS    MESLP           ; loop around for more
                        ;
```

```
0071   CB            MESEND: RETS               ; return at the end
                     ;
0072   E4 FD         RETURN: INB     0FDH       ; return to 8085

                             END               ; end of SYS1 segment
```

Figure 7.12b: System segment #1.

Comments: This example shows how to use shift operations to convert a
number between a binary and a hexadecimal representation. The
HEXOUT routine has a 16-bit binary number in the DX register as input.
The output is its hexadecimal representation on the console output
device, and the HEXIN inputs a hexadecimal number from the keyboard
and returns its binary representation in the DX register.

There are two segments introduced in this example. The main
program is located at the standard address 01000H. The SYS1 segment is
located at 900H. It contains the system routines HEXOUT, HEXIN,
SPCOUT, CRLF, and MESOUT. These are really I/O routines at a
slightly higher level than those in the segment called IO. They call the
routines in the IO segment so the IO segment must also be present at its
standard address 800H. Notice that MESOUT is almost the same as in
the last example. However, it is now designed to be called from another
segment in that it returns with the RETS instruction. You might want to
add this segment to your GO command.

The main program inputs two numbers (hexadecimal notation) and
then outputs the sum, difference, and product.

The routine HEXOUT grabs the 16-bit number 4 bits at a time and
uses some *clever code*[3] to convert each of these 4-bit numbers into the
ASCII code for its corresponding hexadecimal representation. In more
detail, the 16-bit number is rotated to the left by 4 places each time by
the two instruction sequence:

```
HLOOP:  MOVBI    CL,4              ; count of 4
                                   ; for each
        ROL      DX,CL             ; to shift
                                   ; left
```

---

[3]Clever code is code which uses ideas which are more difficult to understand to make the
machine run more economically.

Then it is moved into the accumulator where the lower 4 bits are masked off by ANDing the accumulator with 000FH. Next the following sequence of clever code is used to convert to ASCII:

```
DAA                      ; add 6 if
                         ; A-F
ADDBI   AL,0F0H          ; make a
                         ; carry if
                         ; A-F
ADCBI   AL,040H          ; here is
                         ; the ASCII
```

Since we have decided to use clever code, we should explain how it works. Although such code may work faster and take up less room in the computer, it may cost more in the long run, because of the time required to develop it and the time required for a new programmer to learn it every time it has to be maintained. Let's now see how our particular example of cleverness works in two cases:

1. If the number is from 0 to 9, then the DAA does not change anything, so the addition of F0H does not do much except change the upper nibble to a value of 15. In this case, there is no carry, and the next instruction just adds a 4 to the upper nibble, making it a 3. (Note that $15 + 4 = 19 = 16 + 3 = carry + 3$).
2. If the number is from 10 to 15, then the DAA adds a 6, causing the upper nibble to become 1. This makes the number "look like" its decimal representation. The addition of F0H then causes the upper nibble to be 0 and sets the carry. Thus, the accumulator holds the original value minus 10. The last instruction then adds the carry and puts a 4 in the upper nibble. This is the same as adding 41H which is the ASCII code for A, thus mapping these values into the symbols A through F. Here is a chart of what happens:

original number (hex)	0A	0B	0C	0D	0E	0F
after 1st instruction	10	11	12	13	14	15
after 2nd instruction	00	01	02	03	04	05
after 3rd instruction	41	42	43	44	45	46
corresponding symbol	A	B	C	D	E	F

Table 7.1: Tracing some clever code.

After this clever code the digit is sent out and the program loops back for the next digit.

Because the next three routines SPCOUT, CRLF, and MESOUT are used quite often, we have included them in this segment. You are welcome to add more routines to this segment.

Stack Instructions

One of the purposes of the system stack is to save data (the other is saving return addresses for subroutine calls). The stack instructions for saving data are:

PUSH	PUSH
POP	POP
PUSHF	PUSH Flags
POPF	POP Flags

The figure below shows an example of a program which uses the PUSH and POP instructions to save and restore the contents of the 8088 registers.

```
                    ; Example 9: (Stack Instructions)
                    ;
                    ; dumping all 8088 registers
                    ;
0000'                       ASEG
00A0                SYS2    EQU     0A0H            ; system #2 segment
0000                DISR    EQU     0000H           ; Display registers
                    ;
0000                ENTER:
0000    BB 0001             MOVI    AX,1            ; load AX, BX, CX, and DX
0003    BB 0002             MOVI    BX,2
0006    B9 0003             MOVI    CX,3
0009    BA 0004             MOVI    CX,4
000C    9A 0000             CALL    DISR,SYS2       ; display all registers
000F    00A0
0011    E4 FD               INB     0FDH            ; return to 8088
                    ;
                            END                     ; End of code segment
```

Figure 7.13a: Example 9: Dumping all 8088 registers.

```
                    ; System segment #2
                    ;
                    ; This segment contains a routine for displaying
                    ; the contents of all the 8088 registers.
                    ; There is also a local supporting routine.
                    ;
```

```
                              ; The main routine is:
                              ;
                              ;    DISR:     This routine displays the contents of
                              ;              the AX, BX, CX, and DX registers as
                              ;              16-bit hexadecimal numbers. It
                              ;              preserves all registers.
                              ;
0000'                         ASEG
0080            IO      EQU   80H               ; IO segment
0026            CDOUT   EQU   26H               ; CDOUT offset address
0020            CDIN    EQU   20H               ; CDIN  offset address
0090            SYS1    EQU   90H               ; SYS1 segment
0000            HEXOUT  EQU   00H               ; HEXOUT offset address
004B            SPCOUT  EQU   4BH               ; SPCOUT offset address
0053            CRLF    EQU   53H               ; CRLF  offset address
0062            MESOUT  EQU   62H               ; MESOUT offset address
                        ;
0000            DISR:                           ; display registers routine
                        ;
0000   9C               PUSHF
0001   50               PUSH  AX                ; save the EU registers
0002   53               PUSH  BX
0003   51               PUSH  CX
0004   52               PUSH  DX
0005   56               PUSH  SI                ; and selected BIU registers
0006   55               PUSH  BP
0007   1E               PUSH  DS
                        ;
0008   06               PUSH  ES                ; save them again
0009   1E               PUSH  DS                ; for display
000A   16               PUSH  SS
000B   0E               PUSH  CS
000C   50               PUSH  AX                ; (a ringer for the IP)
000D   54               PUSH  SP
000E   55               PUSH  BP
000F   56               PUSH  SI
0010   57               PUSH  DI
0011   9C               PUSHF
0012   52               PUSH  DX
0013   51               PUSH  CX
0014   53               PUSH  BX
0015   50               PUSH  AX
                        ;
0016   8B EC            MOV   BP,SP             ; fix some of these up
                        ;
0018   8B 46 2E         MOV   AX,[BP+46]        ; the CS
001B   89 46 14         MOV   [BP+20],AX
                        ;
001E   8B 46 2C         MOV   AX,[BP+44]        ; the IP
0021   89 46 12         MOV   [BP+18],AX
                        ;
0024   8B C5            MOV   AX,BP             ; the SP
0026   05 0030          ADDI  AX,48
0029   89 46 10         MOV   [BP+16],AX
                        ;
002C   8C C8            MOV   AX,CS             ; let data segment be equal
002E   8E D8            MOV   DS,AX             ; to the code segment
                        ;
```

```
0030    9A 0053              CALL    CRLF,SYS1        ; <CR><LF>
0033    0090
0035    BE 00BD              MOVI    SI,MESSAX        ; register AX
0038    E8 0066              CALL    REGOUT
003B    BE 00C2              MOVI    SI,MESSBX        ; register BX
003E    E8 0060              CALL    REGOUT
0041    BE 00C7              MOVI    SI,MESSCX        ; register CX
0044    E8 005A              CALL    REGOUT
0047    BE 00CC              MOVI    SI,MESSDX        ; register DX
004A    E8 0054              CALL    REGOUT
004D    BE 00D1              MOVI    SI,MESSFG        ; flags register
0050    E8 004E              CALL    REGOUT
                         ;
0053    9A 0053              CALL    CRLF,SYS1        ; <CR><LF>
0056    0090
0058    BE 00D9              MOVI    SI,MESSDI        ; register DI
005B    E8 0043              CALL    REGOUT
005E    BE 00DE              MOVI    SI,MESSSI        ; register SI
0061    E8 003D              CALL    REGOUT
0064    BE 00E3              MOVI    SI,MESSBP        ; register BP
0067    E8 0037              CALL    REGOUT
006A    BE 00E8              MOVI    SI,MESSSP        ; register SP
006D    E8 0031              CALL    REGOUT
0070    BE 00ED              MOVI    SI,MESSIP        ; register IP
0073    E8 002B              CALL    REGOUT
                         ;
0076    9A 0053              CALL    CRLF,SYS1        ; <CR> <LF>
0079    0090
007B    BE 00F2              MOVI    SI,MESSCS        ; register CS
007E    E8 0020              CALL    REGOUT
0081    BE 00F7              MOVI    SI,MESSSS        ; register SS
0084    E8 001A              CALL    REGOUT
0087    BE 00FC              MOVI    SI,MESSDS        ; register DS
008A    E8 0014              CALL    REGOUT
008D    BE 0101              MOVI    SI,MESSES        ; register ES
0090    E8 000E              CALL    REGOUT
                         ;
0093    9A 0053              CALL    CRLF,SYS1        ; <CR><LF>
0096    0090
                         ;
0098    1F                   POP     DS               ; restore the registers
0099    5D                   POP     BP
009A    5E                   POP     SI
009B    5A                   POP     DX
009C    59                   POP     CX
009D    5B                   POP     BX
009E    58                   POP     AX
009F    9D                   POPF
00A0    CB                   RETS                     ; End of DISR
                         ;
00A1         REGOUT:                                  ; routine display a register
00A1    9A 0062              CALL    MESOUT,SYS1      ; name the register
00A4    0090
00A6    8B EC                MOV     BP,SP            ; point to stack
00A8    8B 56 02             MOV     DX,2[BP]         ; get data off the stack
00AB    9A 0000              CALL    HEXOUT,SYS1      ; hex output
00AE    0090
00B0    9A 004B              CALL    SPCOUT,SYS1      ; couple of spaces
00B3    0090
```

```
00B5    9A 004B                         CALL    SPCOUT,SYS1
00B8    0090
00BA    C2 0002                         RET     2                       ; return and adjust stack
                                  ;
00BD    41 58 3D 20     MESSAX: DB      'AX= ',0
00C1    00
00C2    42 58 3D 20     MESSBX: DB      'BX= ',0
00C6    00
00C7    43 58 3D 20     MESSCX: DB      'CX= ',0
00CB    00
00CC    44 58 3D 20     MESSDX: DB      'DX= ',0
00D0    00
00D1    46 4C 41 47     MESSFG: DB      'FLAGS= ',0
00D5    53 3D 20 00
00D9    44 49 3D 20     MESSDI: DB      'DI= ',0
00DD    00
00DE    53 49 3D 20     MESSSI: DB      'SI= ',0
00E2    00
00E3    42 50 3D 20     MESSBP: DB      'BP= ',0
00E7    00
00E8    53 50 3D 20     MESSSP: DB      'SP= ',0
00EC    00
00ED    49 50 3D 20     MESSIP: DB      'IP= ',0
00F1    00
00F2    43 53 3D 20     MESSCS: DB      'CS= ',0
00F6    00
00F7    53 53 3D 20     MESSSS: DB      'SS= ',0
00FB    00
00FC    44 53 3D 20     MESSDS: DB      'DS= ',0
0100    00
0101    45 53 3D 20     MESSES: DB      'ES= ',0
0105    00
                                  ;
                                        END                     ; End of system #2
```

Figure 7.13b: System segment #2.

Comments: This example shows how to use the stack to preserve the contents of registers during subroutine calls. It also illustrates how to use the stack to pass values to subroutines.

Two segments are introduced in this example, the main program which can be located at the standard address 1000H, and SYS2, a second system segment which is located at A00H. The segments IO and SYS1 should be loaded in their usual places. At this point you had better make sure that all of these segments have been inserted into your GO command area (from 100H to 1000H).

The main program loads the registers AX, BX, CX, and DX with some numbers and then calls the register display routine DISR in segment SYS2.

The DISR routine first saves various registers by pushing them on the stack, and then saves all registers in reverse order. This last save puts a copy of these registers on the stack for use by the routine REGOUT. The routine REGOUT is called many times, once for each register. This routine requires that the SI register points to a message which *labels* the register to be displayed. The routine gobbles one 16-bit quantity from the stack, which is the contents of this register as it was in the main program.

The routine REGOUT works in the following way: First the register's label is sent out. Next, the contents of the stack pointer are placed in the base pointer (BP), and the contents of the register are pulled from the stack from the other side of the return address and placed in the DX register. The HEXOUT routine is then called to display the number, and then two spaces are skipped.

The return from REGOUT is with the instruction RET 2. This returns and then adjusts the stack pointer by 2 bytes to skip the data which has been passed to the routine.

After the call of REGOUT in DISR, it sends out a ⟨CR⟩ ⟨LF⟩ and restores the registers by popping them off the stack in the reverse order to that in which they were saved.

Notice that the stack is used for data (long-term data) as well as many subroutine calls. This requires special planning and a bit of careful maneuvering.

Processor Control

There are various instructions for controlling the CPU both in and of itself as well as in conjunction with other processors. The instructions in the processor control group are:

NOP	NO oPeration
HLT	HaLT
WAIT	WAIT
LOCK	LOCK
ESC	ESCape

The figure below shows an example of a program which uses just two of these instructions, namely the HaLT instruction.

```
; Example 10: (Processor control)
;
; No operation and Stop
;
0000'                   ASEG
00A0          SYS2   EQU   0A0H          ; System #2 segment
0000          DISR   EQU   0000H         ; DISR offset address
              ;
0000          ENTER:
0000   9A 0000          CALL   DISR,SYS2  ; display the registers
0003   00A0
0005   90               NOP               ; no operation
0006   9A 0000          CALL   DISR,SYS2  ; display the registers
0009   00A0
```

```
000B    F4                              HLT                      ; halt
000C    9A 0000                         CALL      DISR,SYS2      ; it shouldn't get this far
000F    00A0
0011    E4 FD                           INB       0FDH           ; return to 8088
                          ;
                                        END                      ; End of code segment
```

Figure 7.14: Example 10: No operation and stop.

Comments: This example shows what happens when you use the NOP instruction and you stop the CPU with the HLT instruction. The DISR routine monitors the progress through the code.

This routine can be loaded at the standard location 1000H. It also requires the segments IO, SYS1, and SYS2 to be in their usual locations. (Have you set up the GO command?)

Interrupt Instructions

There are several instructions to assist with the interrupt structure of the 8086/8088. The instructions in the interrupt group are:

STI	SeT Interrupt flag
CLI	CLear Interrupt flag
INT	INTerrupt
INTO	INTerrupt on Overflow
IRET	Interrupt RETurn

```
; Example 11: (Interrupts)
;
; DEBUG PACKAGE
;
            ASEG
SPACE   EQU     20H                     ; ASCII for SPACE
CR      EQU     0DH                     ; ASCII for RETURN
LF      EQU     0AH                     ; ASCII for LINEFEED
IO      EQU     80H                     ; IO Segment
CDOUT   EQU     26H                     ; Console output
CDIN    EQU     20H                     ; Console input
SYS1    EQU     90H                     ; System Segment #1
HEXOUT  EQU     00H                     ; Hexadecimal output
HEXIN   EQU     1BH                     ; Hexadecimal input
SPCOUT  EQU     4BH                     ; Output a space
CRLF    EQU     53H                     ; Output <CR><LF>
MESOUT  EQU     62H                     ; Output a message
;
;***********************************************************
; The following code initializes the interrupt vectors.
;
ENTER:                                  ; Initial entry point
        $CS
        POP     RETADD                  ; save return address
        $CS
        POP     RETADD+2
;
```

```
            PUSHF                       ; and restore stack
            $CS
            PUSH    RETADD+2
            $CS
            PUSH    RETADD
            PUSH    AX              ; save working registers
            PUSH    BX
            PUSH    CX
            PUSH    DX
            PUSH    SI
            PUSH    BP
            PUSH    DS
;
            MOVI    AX,0            ; point to
            MOV     DS,AX           ; beginning of memory
            MOV     AX,CS           ; and get this code segment
;
                                    ; set up interrupts
            MOVI    04H,IBRK        ; offset address
            MOV     06H,AX          ; segment address
            MOVI    0CH,JBRK        ; offset address
            MOV     0EH,AX          ; this code segment address
;
            MOV     DS,AX
;
            MOVI    SI,MESS0        ; welcome message
            CALL    MESOUT,SYS1
;
            JMP     JBRK            ; jump to restore and
                                    ; display registers
;
;***********************************************************
; The following code services the breakpoint interrupt.
;
JBRK:
            PUSH    AX              ; save standard registers
            PUSH    BX
            PUSH    CX
            PUSH    DX
            PUSH    SI
            PUSH    BP
            PUSH    DS
;
            MOV     BP,SP           ; BP points to stack
            $CS
            MOVB    AL,XBREAK       ; missing code byte
            DEC     [BP+0EH]        ; back up IP by one
            LDS     BX,[BP+0EH]     ; point to code
            MOVB    [BX],AL         ; put missing code byte in
;
JRET:       POP     DS              ; restore standard registers
            POP     BP
            POP     SI
            POP     DX
            POP     CX
            POP     BX
            POP     AX
            JMP     IBRK            ; jump to display registers
;
```

```
;*********************************************************
; The following code services a single step interrupt.
; It displays all of the 8088 registers, the stack, and
; the instruction queue.  It also allows you to modify
; registers, set breakpoints, and "GO" anywhere.
;
IBRK:                                   ; breakpoint procedure
;
        PUSH    AX                      ; save standard registers
        PUSH    BX
        PUSH    CX
        PUSH    DX
        PUSH    SI
        PUSH    BP
        PUSH    DS
;
                                        ; save again for display
        PUSH    AX                      ; (ringers for the stack)
        PUSH    AX
        PUSH    AX
        PUSH    AX
        PUSH    ES
        PUSH    DS
        PUSH    SS
        PUSH    CS
        PUSH    AX                      ; (a ringer for the IP)
        PUSH    SP
        PUSH    BP
        PUSH    SI
        PUSH    DI
        PUSH    AX                      ; (a ringer for the flags)
        PUSH    DX
        PUSH    CX
        PUSH    BX
        PUSH    AX
;
        MOV     BP,SP                   ; fix some of these up
;
        MOV     AX,[BP+54]              ; the flags
        MOV     [BP+8],AX


        MOV     AX,[BP+52]              ; the CS
        MOV     [BP+20],AX
;
        MOV     AX,[BP+50]              ; the IP
        MOV     [BP+18],AX
;
        MOV     AX,BP                   ; the SP
        ADDI    AX,56
        MOV     [BP+16],AX
;
        MOV     AX,[BP+56]              ; the stack
        MOV     [BP+28],AX
        MOV     AX,[BP+58]
        MOV     [BP+30],AX
        MOV     AX,[BP+60]
        MOV     [BP+32],AX
        MOV     AX,[BP+62]
        MOV     [BP+34],AX
```

```
        ;
IBRK0:  MOV     AX,CS           ; let data segment be equal
        MOV     DS,AX           ; to the code segment
        ;
BODY:                           ; now display them
        CALL    CRLF,SYS1       ; <CR><LF>
        MOVI    SI,MESSAX       ; register AX
        CALL    REGOUT
        MOVI    SI,MESSBX       ; register BX
        CALL    REGOUT
        MOVI    SI,MESSCX       ; register CX
        CALL    REGOUT
        MOVI    SI,MESSDX       ; register DX
        CALL    REGOUT
        MOVI    SI,MESSFG       ; flags register
        CALL    REGOUT
        ;
        CALL    CRLF,SYS1       ; <CR><LF>
        MOVI    SI,MESSDI       ; register DI
        CALL    REGOUT
        MOVI    SI,MESSSI       ; register SI
        CALL    REGOUT
        MOVI    SI,MESSBP       ; register BP
        CALL    REGOUT
        MOVI    SI,MESSSP       ; register SP
        CALL    REGOUT
        MOVI    SI,MESSIP       ; register IP
        CALL    REGOUT
        ;
        CALL    CRLF,SYS1       ; <CR><LF>
        MOVI    SI,MESSCS       ; register CS
        CALL    REGOUT
        MOVI    SI,MESSSS       ; register SS
        CALL    REGOUT
        MOVI    SI,MESSDS       ; register DS
        CALL    REGOUT
        MOVI    SI,MESSES       ; register ES
        CALL    REGOUT
        ;
        CALL    CRLF,SYS1       ; <CR><LF>
        MOVI    SI,MESSS0       ; stack + 0
        CALL    REGOUT
        MOVI    SI,MESSS1       ; stack + 1
        CALL    REGOUT
        MOVI    SI,MESSS2       ; stack + 2
        CALL    REGOUT
        MOVI    SI,MESSS3       ; stack + 3
        CALL    REGOUT
        ;
        CALL    CRLF,SYS1       ; <CR><LF>
        ;
        ;                               display queue
        MOVI    SI,MESSQU
        CALL    MESOUT,SYS1
        MOVI    SI,0
        CALL    DQUEUE
        MOVI    SI,1
        CALL    DQUEUE
        MOVI    SI,2
```

```
                CALL    DQUEUE
                MOVI    SI,3
                CALL    DQUEUE
                MOVI    SI,4
                CALL    DQUEUE
                MOVI    SI,5
                CALL    DQUEUE
        ;
                CALL    CRLF,SYS1       ; <CR><LF>
        ;
IBRK1:  MOV     AX,CS           ; set DS and BP
        MOV     DS,AX           ; equal to their
        MOV     BP,SP           ; standard values
        ;
                CALL    CDIN,IO         ; wait for key
        ;
        CMPBI   AL,'R'          ; check for commands:
        JZ      GORET           ; Return from subroutine
        CMPBI   AL,'E'
        JZ      EXIT            ; Exit debugger
        CMPBI   AL,'B'
        JZ      SETBRK          ; Set breakpoint
        CMPBI   AL,'G'
        JZ      GO              ; Go to specified address
        CMPBI   AL,'C'
        JZ      CONT            ; Continue (no single step)
        CMPBI   AL,'S'
        JZ      SETREG          ; Set register contents
        CMPBI   AL,SPACE
        JZ      GOSS            ; continue single stepping
        JMP     IBRK1           ; loop if none of above
        ;
GORET:                          ; Return from subroutine
        LDS     BX,[BP+0EH]     ; point to return address
        MOV     BX,[BP+14H]
        MOVBI   AL,0CCH         ; put breakpoint there
        XCHGB   [BX],AL         ; replacing code byte
        $CS
        MOVB    XBREAK,AL       ; save code byte for later
        JMP     CONT            ; and head on out
        ;
EXIT:   JMPL    RETADD          ; long indirect jump to return
        ;
SETBRK:                         ; Set breakpoint procedure
        CALL    CRLF,SYS1
        MOVI    SI,MESS2        ; offset message
        CALL    MESOUT,SYS1
        CALL    HEXIN,SYS1      ; get the offset
        LDS     BX,[BP+0EH]     ; point to breakpoint location
        MOV     BX,DX
        MOVBI   AL,0CCH         ; put breakpoint there
        XCHGB   [BX],AL         ; replacing code byte
        $CS
        MOVB    XBREAK,AL       ; save code byte for later
        JMP     IBRK1           ; more instructions?
        ;
GO:                             ; Go to specified address
        CALL    CRLF,SYS1
        MOVI    SI,MESS1        ; get segment
```

```
                CALL    MESOUT,SYS1
                CALL    HEXIN,SYS1
                MOV     [BP+10H],DX
                CALL    CRLF,SYS1
                MOVI    SI,MESS2        ; get offset
                CALL    MESOUT,SYS1
                CALL    HEXIN,SYS1
                MOV     [BP+0EH],DX
CONT:           ANDI    [BP+12H],0FEFFH ; clear single step
                JMP     IBRK3           ; leave debugger
;
GOSS:                                   ; single step
                ORI     [BP+12H],100H   ; set single step
                JMP     IBRK3           ; leave debugger
;
SETREG:                                 ; Set registers procedure
                CALL    CRLF,SYS1
                MOVI    SI,MESS3        ; Get register
                CALL    MESOUT,SYS1
                CALL    CDIN,IO         ; first letter into CH
                MOVB    AH,AL
                CALL    CDOUT,IO
                MOVB    CH,AH
                CALL    CDIN,IO         ; second letter into CL
                MOVB    AH,AL
                CALL    CDOUT,IO
                MOVB    CL,AH
;
                PUSH    CX              ; Save register name
                CALL    CRLF,SYS1
                MOVI    SI,MESS4        ; Get new contents
                CALL    MESOUT,SYS1
                CALL    HEXIN,SYS1
                POP     AX              ; now AX has register name
;
TSTAX:          CMPI    AX,'A'*100H+'X' ; AX?
                JNZ     TSTBX
                MOVI    SI,0CH          ; offset for AX
                JMPS    LDREG
TSTBX:          CMPI    AX,'B'*100H+'X' ; BX?
                JNZ     TSTCX
                MOVI    SI,0AH          ; offset for BX
                JMPS    LDREG
TSTCX:          CMPI    AX,'C'*100H+'X' ; CX?
                JNZ     TSTDX
                MOVI    SI,08H          ; offset for CX
                JMPS    LDREG
TSTDX:          CMPI    AX,'D'*100H+'X' ; DX?
                JNZ     TSTSI
                MOVI    SI,06H          ; offset for DX
                JMPS    LDREG
TSTSI:          CMPI    AX,'S'*100H+'I' ; SI?
                JNZ     TSTDI
                MOVI    SI,04H          ; offset for SI
                JMPS    LDREG
TSTDI:          CMPI    AX,'D'*100H+'I' ; DI?
                JNZ     TSTBP
                MOV     DI,DX           ; do this directly
                JMP     JRET
```

```
TSTBP:   CMPI    AX,'B'*100H+'P' ; BP?
         JNZ     TSTSP
         MOVI    SI,02H              ; offset for BP
         JMPS    LDREG
TSTSP:   CMPI    AX,'S'*100H+'P' ; SP?
         JNZ     TSTFL
         JMP     IBRK1               ; do not change SP
TSTFL:   CMPI    AX,'F'*100H+'L' ; FL?
         JNZ     TSTIP
         MOVI    SI,12H              ; offset for Flags
         JMPS    LDREG
TSTIP:   CMPI    AX,'I'*100H+'P' ; IP?
         JNZ     TSTCS
         MOVI    SI,0EH              ; offset for IP
         JMPS    LDREG
TSTCS:   CMPI    AX,'C'*100H+'S' ; CS?
         JNZ     TSTDS
         MOVI    SI,10H              ; offset for CS
         JMPS    LDREG
TSTDS:   CMPI    AX,'D'*100H+'S' ; DS?
         JNZ     TSTES
         MOVI    SI,00H              ; offset for DS
         JMPS    LDREG
TSTES:   CMPI    AX,'E'*100H+'S' ; ES?
         JNZ     TSTSS
         MOV     ES,DX               ; do this directly
         JMPS    LDREG
TSTSS:   CMPI    AX,'S'*100H+'S' ; SS?
         JNZ     TSTEND              ; do not change SS
TSTEND:  JMP     IBRK1               ; none of above
;
LDREG:   MOV     [BP][SI],DX
         JMP     JRET
;
IBRK3:   POP     DS                  ; restore the registers
         POP     BP
         POP     SI
         POP     DX
         POP     CX
         POP     BX
         POP     AX
         IRET                        ; End of IBRK
;
;****************************************************
; The following are subroutines used by IBRK
;
REGOUT:                              ; routine display a register
         CALL    MESOUT,SYS1         ; name the register
         MOV     BP,SP               ; point to stack
         MOV     DX,2[BP]            ; get data off the stack
         CALL    HEXOUT,SYS1         ; hex output
         CALL    SPCOUT,SYS1         ; couple of spaces
         CALL    SPCOUT,SYS1
         RET     2                   ; return and adjust stack
;
DQUEUE:                              ; display queue
         MOV     BX,[BP+18]
         MOV     AX,[BP+20]          ; old code segment
         MOV     DS,AX               ; to data segment
```

```
            MOVBI   DH,0                 ; set instruction byte
            MOVB    DL,[BX][SI]
            MOV     AX,CS                ; our code segment
            MOV     DS,AX                ; back again
            CALL    HEXOUT,SYS1          ; show value
            CALL    SPCOUT,SYS1          ; skip space
            RET
;
;**********************************************************
; The following are storage locations for variables
;
XBREAK: DB      0
RETADD: DW      0                        ; save the offset
        DW      0                        ; save the code segment
;
;**********************************************************
; The following are messages
;
MESS0:  DB      'Debug Program'
        DB      CR,LF,'R   = return from suroutine'
        DB      CR,LF,'B   = set to break point'
        DB      CR,LF,'E   = exit debug program'
        DB      CR,LF,'S   = set register'
        DB      CR,LF,'<SP> = single step'
        DB      CR,LF,'G   = go to address'
        DB      CR,LF,0
MESS1:  DB      'Code Segment: ',0
MESS2:  DB      'Offset:   ',0
MESS3:  DB      'Register: ',0
MESS4:  DB      'Contents: ',0
MESSAX: DB      'AX= ',0
MESSBX: DB      'BX= ',0
MESSCX: DB      'CX= ',0
MESSDX: DB      'DX= ',0
MESSFG: DB      'FLAGS= ',0
MESSDI: DB      'DI= ',0
MESSSI: DB      'SI= ',0
MESSBP: DB      'BP= ',0
MESSSP: DB      'SP= ',0
MESSIP: DB      'IP= ',0
MESSCS: DB      'CS= ',0
MESSSS: DB      'SS= ',0
MESSDS: DB      'DS= ',0
MESSES: DB      'ES= ',0
MESSS0: DB      'STACK+0= ',0
MESSS1: DB      'STACK+2= ',0
MESSS2: DB      'STACK+4= ',0
MESSS3: DB      'STACK+6= ',0
MESSQU: DB      'QUEUE = ',0
;
;**********************************************************
            END
;**********************************************************
```

Figure 7.15: Example 11: Debug package (source code only).

Comments: This is our grand finale. It is somewhat longer than the other examples and so, in the interest of space, we have only included the source code. The program allows you to debug any 8088 machine code including any of these examples. It shows the contents of all the 8088 registers and the stack at each step of the program, and the instruction queue. It also allows you several options including single stepping through 8088 code and setting breakpoints.

This program is not quite a full DEBUG package, because you cannot use it to dump or load memory locations or display assembly code. It would be a good exercise to add some of these features.

This segment can be located at the address 1000H and requires the segments IO and SYS1 to be in their standard locations. Why don't you add this segment to your GO command, expanding it upward to include this segment? You can call the whole thing DEBUG.COM.

The program first initializes several locations at the bottom of memory. These are used as interrupt vectors for the *single step* and *breakpoint* features. In Chapter 3, there is a discussion of the interrupt structure of the 8086/8088 CPU. In our example, the absolute locations 04h, 06h, 0Ch, and 0Eh are where the interrupt vectors are located for our program. The first two are for the *single step* interrupt, which is type 1, and the second two locations are for the *single byte* interrupt, which is of type 3. Recall that the "type" of an interrupt refers to the location of its *interrupt vector* (at four times the type) which contains a pointer (offset address and segment paragraph number) to the corresponding service routine. Warning: watch out for returns to the 8085 via the INB 0FDH instruction. This is because CP/M uses some of these interrupt locations for its operations. You will have to reboot if you wish to return to CP/M.

Next the program restores some registers and goes to the main body which displays the registers, stack, and queue and gives you a number of options. These include:

B	set Breakpoint
R	Return from subroutine
E	Exit from DEBUG
S	Set register
space	Single step
G	Go to specified location

Let's go through these commands starting with the single step command. To activate it just hit the space key. The result will be a new display of the registers, stack, and instruction queue. You should see the IP advance to the next instruction and the instruction queue move up accordingly. You should look at the assembly language to see how this command is implemented. You would see that a logical OR instruction is used to set the trap bit on the *copy* of the flags on the system stack. A subsequent IRET instruction causes this copy of the flags to be put into the real flags. With the single-step mode, there is an interrupt after each instruction. This causes the CPU to call the IBRK routine which shows the display. The CPU knows where IBRK is located because we loaded its segment and offset into interrupt vector number 1 at the bottom of memory.

The B command allows you to place the single byte interrupt instruction anywhere in the current code segment (as indicated by the value of CS in the display). To use this command, simply type B. The program will request an offset from you. Just type in the offset address of where you want the breakpoint (followed by a carriage return). The program will set the breakpoint and then wait for further commands. The program actually replaces the byte of code at the offset address by the single byte type 3 interrupt instruction and saves the code byte in a special location so that it can handle the breakpoint when it occurs. When the processor reaches such a breakpoint it vectors to JBRK, which causes the original byte of code to be replaced, and jumps to IBRK for a display and further commands.

The R command should be used only if you see the return address for a subroutine on the top of the stack (on the display). This normally happens as you single step through code and wish to skip past a subroutine. You would single step until the subroutine call has actually been executed, placing the return address on the system stack. This instruction automatically sets a breakpoint in a manner quite similar to the way the B command does.

The E command is designed to be used with a monitor or disk operating system (DOS) which calls the DEBUG from a different segment (CALL with two operands). The initialization sets the return address in a special location which is used by the E command to jump (indirect) back. If you have not called the DEBUG program in this manner, this command will *not* work!

The S command allows you to set any register except SP and SS. To set these would severely mess up the DEBUG program. To use this command, type S. It will ask you for a register. After you respond, it will ask you for its contents. Just type in the hexadecimal value, followed by carriage return. You will then see the display with the new value in the register you selected.

The G command allows you to jump to any address. It asks you for the value of the code segment and the value of the offset within this segment.

You should try this program out, using it to look at the other example programs; perhaps you might even use it to look at itself!

CONCLUSION

In this chapter we have given you a chance to get to know the 8086/8088 from an assembly-language programmer's point of view. We hope that this example software has given you a better understanding of how to effectively use the 8086/8088 instruction set to accomplish useful work for you.

We developed and tested these examples on the Godbout 8085/8088 Dual Processor Board. They actually work, producing results for you to see! We hope you enjoy the results.

Chapter 8

The Current Scene: 8086/8088 Products and Programs

In this chapter we will explore the current hardware and software scene for the Intel 8086, 8088, 8087, and 8089 processors. In 1978 when the 8086 CPU was first introduced, there was essentially no software and no hardware which used the 8086 CPU chip for anything other than a developmental purpose. Thus, you could learn about the chip and play with it but could make it do useful work only with difficulty. Soon Intel and other companies began to incorporate the 8086 (and then the 8088) in their systems and began to write the standard kinds of software for the common instruction set for these two processors. In 1981 IBM introduced its Personal Computer, based on the 8088 CPU. This brings the 8086/8088 CPU into the forefront as a leading contender for use as a workhorse microprocessor in the home, office, and school. In these familiar places it can take on educational applications as well as word processing, general processing, and business processing.

STARTING OUT — TWO APPROACHES

It is well known that without software a computer is totally useless, except perhaps as a room heater and conversation piece. There are two approaches to equipping a new type of CPU with the necessary software to make it useful: 1) start from scratch, developing software for a system entirely on that system, or 2) use a different well-developed system (the host) to write software for the new system (the target).

The *target-target* approach has been quite successful with the 8080/8085. This approach, however, can be painful because so many capabilities, especially file-handling and editing facilities, are lacking at first. This approach has been necessary because many developers of software for 8080/8085-based machines had no access to other machines. Only very well-funded individuals used minicomputers and maxicomputers for the host. For the most part, however, the well-funded were not interested in developing the full potential of the earlier microprocessors. Instead they concentrated at first on the larger machines. Now there is a great interest in these miniature machines throughout the computing community from the ''garage-type'' companies to the large giants such as XEROX, ITT, EXXON, and IBM.

The *host-target* approach requires the following three steps: a) source code is written and stored on the host, b) the source code is translated into the target's machine language using the host, and c) the machine code is transferred from the host to the target.

Step a) requires a host with good file-handling and editing facilities.

An *operating system* is used to help store and keep track of the files and an *editor* is used to enter and modify text.

Step b) requires programs which are called cross-assemblers and cross-compilers. A *cross-assembler* is a program which runs on the host but translates assembly language source code into machine language for the target. A *cross-compiler* is a program which runs on the host but translates *higher-level* language source code into machine code for the target. As machines become more sophisticated the difference between assemblers and compilers is becoming smaller. For example, the new Intel iAPX 432 is designed to be programmed at a very high level in the high-level language called Ada.

Step c) requires a method of communication from the host to the target. A common method is a serial data line, perhaps using the Intel 8251 Programmable Serial Interface Controller chip on either end of the line. Short programs on both the host and target machines are needed to control the transfer.

With the current widespread availability of sophisticated, 8080/8085-based computer systems, the second approach (host-target) is now being used to develop software for the 8086/8088. In the past when this second approach has been used, the host has often been a larger, more powerful computer, perhaps a minicomputer or maxicomputer. This is still done, but now there is a practical way of coming from the other end. Today's 8080/8085/Z80-based systems have very capable operating systems (such as CP/M by Digital Research) which can handle a large number of large files stored on floppy disks. In addition there are powerful, easy-to-use editors which run under these operating systems. It is now easier and much more efficient to use these editors than it is to use pencil and paper, and in many cases, easier to use than the editors available on the larger computers.

Another factor which makes this second approach (host-target) much more viable today is the large body of software in the form of source code already developed and working for the 8-bit machines. Much of this can be translated either manually or almost automatically (using a conversion program) so that it runs on the newer 16-bit machines. There are important reasons, however, why this translation process is not always the best route to take. One is that code translated line by line is actually less efficient than the original, both in its size and its speed. Another is that the new 16-bit machines are so much more capable than the older 8-bit machines that new approaches should be taken. The first place to start is with the operating systems. Most operating systems for 8-bit machines do one task at a time. The operator must wait at each step. On the other hand, the new 16-bit machines will support many tasks at once and the new operating systems will use this to great advantage. For example, XENIX which is now being developed by Microsoft as a refinement of the UNIX operating system, originally developed at Bell Labs, will allow a job to generate other jobs. All of these jobs run concurrently in your system and could then generate more jobs, getting lots of work done concurrently!

THE FIRST FOUR YEARS

The first manufacturer to develop hardware and software for the 8086, 8088, 8087, and 8089 processors was Intel itself. In recognition of the need to fully support these chips, Intel has invested in a large, modern building in Santa Clara, California, which is devoted to the design, manufacture, and sales of their *development systems*. A development system is a stand-alone computer system which has the necessary software and hardware to develop microprocessor software.

Development systems are key factors in securing sales for a chip-manufacturing company. The vast majority of sales are to other companies who will use these chips in electronic devices which they themselves design, manufacture, and sell. The chips thus provide the raw materials for work on a board or systems level. Companies which use the products of other manufacturers to develop their own products are called original equipment manufacturers, or OEMs for short. Cutting software and hardware development time to a minimum is essential for OEMs, because the market for such equipment is highly competitive. These companies will shop around to find the chip manufacturer who will give them the best support. They need support because the six months that it might require for them to develop the appropriate development tools could mean the loss of millions of dollars in sales. They want to be the first manufacturer in a market so that they can grab the most sales in two important areas: 1) in the short term, because the demand is much higher than the supply at first, and 2) in the long term, because the first product often sets the standard.

Intel basically uses the host-target approach. It has developed and marketed a whole suite of software which runs on its 8085-based *Intellec Microcomputer Development System*. The programs include: two assemblers, ASM86 (for the 8086/8088 and 8087) and ASM89 (for the 8089); three higher-level languages, PL/M-86, FORTRAN and Pascal; and various utilities, LINK86, LOC86, OH86, and LIB86. There is also a translation program CONV86 which will translate 8080/8085 assembly-language source code into 8086/8088 assembly-language source code. The host is their *Intellec Microcomputer Development System* and the target is their *iSBC 86/12 Single Board Computer*. Intel has been gradually making the transition to the 16-bit 8086 CPU in the development system itself. The *Series III Intellec Development Systems* now have two sides: one containing the older 8085 CPU and the other housing the newer 16-bit 8086 CPU, which can be coupled with an 8087 NDP. There are now two versions of the Intel development software, one for each side, and there are commands for switching back and forth. Gradually, certain software such as assemblers, linkers, and higher-level languages have made their way over to the 8086 side.

A number of other companies are offering either 8086/8088-based systems, software for these systems, or both. The following tables show many of the products available as of the date of this writing.

Manufacturer	Product
Action Computer Enterprises	8086 CPU Board
Apparat, Inc.	Add-on products for the IBM
A.S.T. Research	Memory cards and communications card for IBM
Cal-Tech Computer Services	8088 board for the Apple
Chrislin Industries, Inc.	Memory for IBM
Godbout	8085/8088 Dual Processor Board
Godbout	8086/8087 Coprocessor Board
IBM	IBM Personal Computer (8088 based)
Intel	Series III Intellec Development System
Intel	iSBC/12 Single Board Computer (8086 CPU)
Intel	SDK-86 System Design Kit
Lomas Data Products	LDP88 CPU Board and Complete System
Lomas Data Products	8086/8087/8089 CPU board
Metamorphic Systems, Inc.	8088 board for the Apple
Seattle Computer Products	8086 CPU Board and Complete System
TecMar	8086 CPU Board and Complete System
TecMar	Expansion Box for the IBM
TecMar	Add-in and Add-on Products for the IBM

Table 8.1: Some 8086/8088-based equipment.

Manufacturer	Product	Type
Digital Research	CP/M-86	Operating System and Utilities
Digital Research	MP/M-86	Operating System
Intel	IRMX88	Operating System
Intel	IRMX86	Operating System
Industrial Programming	MTOS-86	Operating System
Hemenway	SP/8086	Operating System and Utilities
Hemenway	MSP/8086	Operating System and Utilities
Phase One Systems	OASIS-8086	Operating System
Systems & Software	REX-80	Operating System
Microsoft	XENIX-8086	Operating System
Seattle Computer Products	86-DOS	Operating System and Utilities
IBM	DOS	Operating System
Intel	ASM86	8086/8088/8087 Assembler
Intel	LINK86,LOC86	8086 Utilities
Intel	ASM89	8089 Assembler
Microsoft	XMACRO-86	8086/8088 Cross-assembler
Microsoft	MACRO-86	8086/8088 Assembler
Intel	CONV86	Conversion Program
Sorcim	TRANS 86	Conversion Program
Intel	PL/M 86	PL/M Compiler
Digital Research	CBASIC-86	BASIC Interpreter
Microsoft	BASIC 86	BASIC Interpreter
Microsoft	BASIC 86	BASIC Compiler
Intel	FORTRAN 86	FORTRAN Compiler
Microsoft	FORTRAN-86	FORTRAN Compiler
Microsoft	COBOL-86	COBOL Compiler
Cybernetics, Inc.	RM/COBOL	COBOL Compiler
Microsoft	Pascal-86	Pascal Compiler
Sorcim	Pascal/M86	Pascal Compiler
Intel	Pascal 86	Pascal Compiler
MT Micro Systems	Pascal/MT+	Pascal Compiler
SofTech Microsystems, Inc.	UCSD Pascal	Pascal & Operating System
Intermetrics	PasPort 8086	PDP-11 Host Pascal Cross-compiler
Computer Innovations, Inc.	C86	C Compiler
Supersoft	C (8086 vers)	C Compiler
Information Unlimited Software	Easy-Writer	Text Editor
CompuView	VEDIT	Text Editor

Table 8.2: Some 8086/8088-based software.

Action Computer Enterprises, Inc.
55 West Del Mar Boulevard
Pasadena, CA 91105

Apparat, Inc.
4401 So. Tamarac Parkway
Denver, CO 80237

A.S.T. Research Inc.
17925 B Skypark Circle
Irvine, CA 92714

Cal-Tech Computer Services Inc.
4112 Napier St.
San Diego, CA 92110

Computer Innovations, Inc.
75 Pine St.
Lincroft, NJ 07738

CompuView
1955 Pauline Blvd.
Suite 200
Ann Arbor, MI 48103

Crislin Industries, Inc.
31352 Via Colinas
Westlake Village, CA 91362

Cybernetics, Inc.
8041 Newman Ave.
Suite 206
Huntington Beach, CA 92647

Digital Research
801 Lighthouse Rd.
Pacific Grove, CA 93950

Godbout Electronics
Box 2355
Oakland Airport
Oakland, CA 94614

IBM Corporation
Information System Division
Entry Systems Business
Boca Raton, FL 33432

Industrial Programming, Inc.
100 Jerico Quadrangle
Jericho, NY 11753

Information Unlimited Software, Inc.
281 Arlington Ave.
Kensington, CA 94707

Intel Corporation
3065 Bowers Ave.
Santa Clara, CA 95051

Intermetrics
733 Concord Ave.
Cambridge, MA 02138

Hemenway Associates
101 Tremont St.
Boston, MA 02108

Lomas Data Products
11 Cross Street
Westborough, MA 01581

Metamorphic Systems, Inc.
P.O. Box 1541
Boulder, CO 80306

Microsoft
10800 NE 8th St.
Bellevue, WA 98004

MT Micro Systems
1562 Kings Cross Drive
Cardiff, CA 92007

Phase One Systems, Inc.
770 Edgewater Dr.
Suite 710
Oakland, CA 94621

Seattle Computer Products, Inc.
1114 Industry Drive
Seattle, WA 98188

SofTech Microsystems, Inc.
9494 Black Mountain Road
San Diego, CA 92126

Sorcim Corporation
405 Aldo Ave.
Santa Clara, CA 95050

Supersoft Associates
P.O. Box 1628
Champaign, IL 61820

Systems & Software, Inc.
2801 Finley Rd.
Donnors Grove, IL 60515

TecMar Inc.
23600 Mercantile Rd.
Cleveland, OH 44122

Table 8.3: Some manufacturers of hardware and software.

Two of the first companies to come out with products for the personal and professional market which use the 8086/8088 CPU were Godbout and Microsoft. The Godbout 8085/8088 Dual-Processor board provides an inexpensive way for you to have both the host and the target in the same system, and Microsoft's 8086 cross-assembler provides the software to use this board. If you have an S-100 bus mainframe, then you can replace your 8080, 8085, or Z-80 CPU with the Godbout dual-processor board. This board contains both an 8085 CPU and an 8088 CPU. You can switch back and forth between the two processors under software control. You bring your system up using the 8085 CPU, develop your 8088 software, storing it on your floppy disks. Then you load it into memory and turn the system over to the 8088! The Microsoft XMACRO-86 cross-assembler can greatly assist you in this process, but you can do the assembly by hand if you are as masochistic as we were at first. The cross-assembler runs under the CP/M operating system and produces code for the 8086/8088. We have used this cross-assembler in conjunction with the Godbout Dual Processor board to complete the development and testing of the examples in the last chapter.

Digital Research now has a version of CP/M (control program for microcomputers) for the 8086/8088 called CP/M-86. See (Murtha, Stephen M.; Waite, Mitchell *CP/M Primer*. Indianapolis, Indiana. Howard W. Sams & Co., Inc.). CP/M-86 is very similar to the 8080/8085/Z-80-based CP/M (now called CP/M-80). Like the earlier CP/M-80, the new CP/M-86 has an assembler (ASM), editor (ED), file transfer program (PIP, short for peripheral interchange program), and a debugging tool (DDT, short for dynamic debugging tool). There is even a special version of the assembler which acts as a cross-assembler from your old 8080/8085/Z-80 system to your new 8086/8088 system. This is very useful if you use an older 8-bit machine to help set up your new 16-bit system. Disks produced on a CP/M-80 system should be readable by a CP/M-86 system (with the same disk drives.) It is interesting to note that the CP/M assembler is very similar to the Intel Assembler, depending more on the type of the operands than upon special mnemonics (such as the addition of the letter *I*) to determine the difference between immediate data and offset addresses for variables.

There is still a problem getting this operating system to work on your system: lack of compatibility among different disk drives. CP/M-86 was first available only on a pair of 8-inch, single-density diskettes. Thus, if you had had a 5 ¼-inch disk system (which is the other current standard size for diskettes), you would not even be able to fit the CP/M disk into your drive! As a rule, almost any 8-inch, single-density diskette can be read by any 8-inch disk drive microcomputer system. The situation is quite different in the 5 ¼-inch world. There are 16-sectored, 10-sectored, and one- (soft-) sectored diskettes. Many 5 ¼-inch-based drives will refuse to read anything but the correct type. Actually, this is only the beginning of the real problem, for you can always have someone copy the contents of an 8-inch distribution disk to whatever type of diskette used by your system. There are service companies which will do this for a fee, or you might know a friend who knows a friend who has a system with both types of drives and the software to run both at once. The real problem is making sure that your CP/M knows how to operate your disk. There is a special section of CP/M called the BIOS (Basic I/O System) which must be configured for each different computer system. The BIOS has two semi-distinct parts: the console/printer interface routines and the disk-drive interface routines. Writing your own console and printer routines is fairly straightforward. If you have read all the way through this book this far, you probably are quite capable (with the aid of the CP/M manuals) of writing your own version. On the other hand, the disk routines are often complicated and should be attempted only if you are very knowledgeable. The difficulty of doing this varies widely, depending upon how intelligent your disk-drive controller is (see the chapter on support chips). Most people will wait until Lifeboat Associates or some other company comes out with a version of CP/M-86 which will work on their system. This is now beginning to happen.

Once CP/M-86 and other disk operating systems become readily available in the various formats and have been properly interfaced for the various types of disk drives, there should be no lack of other types of software. Already, there are several companies offering versions of Pascal (see The Pascal Primer. Fox, David; Waite, Mitchell; Indianapolis, Indiana: Howard W. Sams and Co., Inc.) and other languages such as C and BASIC. Many of these companies already have assembly-language source code for the corresponding 8080/8085/Z-80 program. It will not be that hard to convert these into programs for the 8086/8088. It just takes a certain amount of time, so hold on.

It should also be noted that the higher levels of software are practically independent of the machine or, at least, of the particular CPU they are run on. Of course, such peripheral equipment as video graphics displays will tend to cause even the highest level of software to become somewhat machine dependent, but even here there are certain standards. As a result, if you have a BASIC, FORTRAN, C, Pascal, or even a FORTH program which works on your S-100 bus system now, then it should work unchanged if you change your processor to a new 8086 or 8088 CPU and get the corresponding new operating system and compiler or interpreter.

Figure 8.1a: The IBM Personal Computer.

Figure 8.1b: Inside view of the IBM Personal Computer.

THE IBM ACORN

One of the most notable developments for the Intel 8086 family of processor chips is IBM's choice of the 8088 CPU in their 1981 entry into the personal computer arena. This computer was developed under the project dubbed with the code name "ACORN," but it is being sold under the less imaginative but perhaps more accurate name of "The IBM Personal Computer." The computer, with a price range from $1260 to about $3830 (with a 48 K, one floppy-disk drive system going for $2235 at Computerland), is in direct competition with the Apple and Radio Shack computer offerings. The basic starter unit uses an audio cassette for mass storage and an ordinary television as the video display. The more expensive versions include up to two floppy-disk drives (about 160 Kbytes per disk) and such things as color monitors. Of course, remember that software is an additional but necessary cost. In fact, you could easily spend almost $3000 if you get the advanced BASIC from Microsoft ($40), the Pascal Compiler from Microsoft ($300), EasyWriter by Information Unlimited ($175), General Ledger by Peachtree Software ($595), Accounts Receivable by Peachtree Software ($595), Accounts Payable by Peachtree Software ($595), asynchronous communications support ($40), Adventure by Microsoft ($30), and Advanced Diagnostics Package ($155).

The IBM has a cassette interface which you can use for mass storage if you don't get the floppy disk system. However, you will supply the cassette tape recorder yourself.

The IBM machine has a main bus with an 8-bit data subbus (to match the 8-bit data bus of the 8088 CPU). There are five expansion slots for extra memory, I/O, or whatever else you can dream of. This is not the S-100 bus. In fact, there are only 62 signals on the IBM bus. Many of the 8088 signals such as the 20 address lines, the eight data lines, address latch enable (ALE), address enable [from the 8089 Bus Arbiter (AEN)], MEMory Read (MEMR), MEMory Write (MEMW), I/O Read (IOR), I/O Write (IOW), and CLOCK appear on this bus in demultiplexed or "separated" form, and in addition there is a set of new signals. These mainly have to do with the hardware interrupt facilities of the IBM. IBM is publishing the precise standards for its bus and is encouraging other smaller board-oriented manufacturers to develop their own boards to fit into these slots. Already there are advertisements for add-on products for the IBM.

The 8088 CPU in the IBM computer runs on a 4.77 MHz clock. However, the memory runs with a 2.44 MHz clock. This is along the lines of Motorola's suggestion that their MC68000 be run at a faster speed than the rest of the system. Since the cost of memory increases with its guaranteed speed, and since there are a number of instructions (in particular multiply and divide) on the 8088 CPU which take a sizeable number of clock cycles for internal processing, this should keep the cost of memory down while keeping performance up. Indeed, IBM will be offering memory expansion boards at quite reasonable costs (16 Kbytes for $90, 32 Kbytes for $395, and 64 Kbytes for $540). The access time for memory is supposed to be about 250 ns, which corresponds to a "virtual" clock speed of 4 MHz, the standard speed for a Z-80. The memory is organized in 9-bit words with an extra bit for error detection (see the discussion of error detection and correction in Chapter 4). Up to 256 Kbytes of user RAM can be added to the system, considerably more than the 64 Kbytes normally available for the older 8-bit processors with their 16-bit addressing. This is short of the 1 megabyte addressing capability of the 8088 CPU, but the IBM system uses some of this "missing" address range for system functions such as a 40 Kbyte ROM for an enhanced Microsoft BASIC and a 16 Kbyte video display ROM.

The computer is designed for ease of use. In particular, the keyboard can be put on your lap or on a table at various tilt angles. Both upper and lower case are supported, making word processing viable. Ten special function keys also assist in word-processing applications. The keyboard actually produces two special codes for each key. It sends one code when a key is pressed and another code when the key is released. Internally, the computer uses ASCII, which is quite something coming from IBM! (IBM had invented its own code for characters, called EBCDIC.)

Perhaps the most interesting feature of the IBM machine next to its use of the 8088 CPU is its color graphics capability (available at extra cost with a special adapter). It has a special 16 Kbyte RAM dedicated to the video display. There are two display formats for graphics: a medium-resolution 320 horizontal by 200 vertical pixels (dots), and a high-resolution 640 horizontal by 200 vertical pixels. The high-resolution format will only allow 1 bit per pixel and the medium-resolution format will allow 2 bits per pixel. There is also a test mode in which each character can have any one of eight foreground colors, any one of eight background colors, two levels of intensity, as well as a blinking or nonblinking display. This seemingly impossible feat is accomplished by providing 2 bytes of storage for each character on the screen. One byte contains an ASCII code for the character and the other contains all the display information.

Although the basic model displays its video through an ordinary television set, color monitors are available for the color graphics option. Because it uses a standard television signal, there is a problem in increasing the vertical resolution much higher than it is. For example, if the vertical resolution were doubled to 400 pixels, then the picture would start to flicker. This is because an ordinary television signal "paints" every other line of the screen during each frame. Thus, two frames are required to display the whole picture with the second frame interlacing in between the lines of the first. This happens at a rate of 60 frames per second (to match the 60-cycle house current). Thus, each pixel (dot) is "repainted" every $\frac{1}{30}$ second with dots which are adjacent vertically flashing on and off opposite to each other. On an ordinary television picture this is not a problem, but when there is a high contrast between adjacent pixels, such as in a computer-generated picture, the flicker becomes quite objectionable. The solution is to repeat the picture each time for the second interlacing frame, and that way the second interlacing frame reinforces rather than works against the first.

With the addition of an optional green-phosphor video monitor and a different adapter, the system makes an excellent word processor. The monitor will display 25 lines of 80 characters. Features such as underlining, high-intensity characters, blinking characters, and reverse video are available under software control. The special monitor is really needed because of the flicker problem and the poor ability of ordinary television sets to resolve 80 characters horizontally. To eliminate flicker, the monitor is specially equipped to hold the light longer each time it is activated. A *long persistence* phosphor is used. Such phosphors usually produce a green image.

IBM is tapping directly into the existing personal computer software market for this new computer. It has commissioned Microsoft to produce three versions of BASIC: Cassette BASIC, Disk BASIC, and Advanced BASIC. All have some very interesting features. Perhaps the most intriguing is the ability to pass graphics commands in the form of strings. For example, the string:

A$ = "r10;d30;l20;u10"

will define a box (right 10 units, down 30 units, left 10 units, and up 30 units). This string can be combined with other strings to form more elaborate patterns. The BASIC command DRAW will cause any such string to actually be drawn. Thus for example:

DRAW A$

will cause the box to be drawn on the screen.

IBM is offering a specially developed CP/M-like operating system called IBM Personal Computer DOS. This was developed for IBM by Microsoft as a result of difficulty in getting CP/M-86 through IBM's quality control. IBM's DOS has the same system calls (ways for application programs to call the operating system) as CP/M-86. However there are substantial improvements over CP/M. For example, there is a built-in editing system for entering commands. Each command creates a template for the next command, so if you make an error which involves just a few keystrokes, you don't have to retype the whole command. Even if you don't make errors (ha!), this feature will be very valuable in entering sequences of commands which are very similar.

In its initial marketing (October, 1981) the Microsoft DOS supported a full set of application-oriented software, including a Microsoft Pascal Compiler, Visicalc from Personal Software, Easywriter (a word-processing program by Information Unlimited), and an asynchronous communications program written in BASIC which IBM has promised to extend to allow the computer to imitate an IBM 3270 terminal. In addition, there is a business package which includes general ledger, accounts payable, and accounts receivable, all by Peachtree Software. IBM is also offering two other operating systems: CP/M-86 by Digital Research and UCSD p-System, which includes the famous UCSD Pascal.

IBM has formed a division just to handle this personal computer and the related software. It is encouraging an open-market approach to development of new software in the spirit of the existing microcomputer market.

CONCLUSION

We have explored the current uses for the 8086 family of processor chips. Many companies in addition to Intel have given strong commitment and support for the 8086 and 8088 CPUs by providing the basic systems and software for these processors. These companies include: Godbout (Dual 8085/8088 Processor Board), Seattle Computer (8086 Processor Board), Digital Research (CP/M-86), Microsoft (XMACRO-86, BASIC-86, and eventually XENIX), and IBM (The Personal Computer). In particular, IBM's choice of the 8088 CPU for its entry into the personal computer race promises to open a new era in personal and professional computing. IBM's approach should breed a tremendous amount of applications software and interesting peripheral hardware.

Appendix A

The iAPX 186 And The iAPX 286

Intel is currently developing certain improvements and extensions to the iAPX 86 and iAPX 88. The first is the iAPX 186, which is really a "faster" version of the iAPX 86; and the second is the iAPX 286, which extends the on-chip hardware and instruction set of the iAPX 86 into the areas of memory management and virtual memory.

THE iAPX 186

We start with the iAPX 186. The iAPX 86 was the first of the new generation of 16-bit machines, coming out before the Motorola and Zilog entries into this field. In comparison with these other, newer processors, the iAPX 86 is somewhat less efficient with certain kinds of instructions such as the string instructions, multiplication, division, shifts, and rotates. With the announcement of the iAPX 186 as a future product, Intel seems to have recognized these weaknesses and has promised a newer version of the 8086 which will execute these instructions at speeds which are more competitive with the other two processors. For example, multiplication and division on the 186 are now three to four times faster than on the 8086, and repeated string moves now execute almost as fast as the buses can handle them, thus making the string moves very much like DMA transfers.

As always, the new offering has some nice new surprises as well as the return of some older favorite features. For the iAPX 186, the new features include multilevel interrupt control, two high-speed DMA channels, and three 16-bit programmable timers. In other words, the 186 integrates into the processor many of the features found on the iAPX 86 family support chips, thus replacing whole circuit boards by a small fraction of a square inch of silicon. For the 186, the old features include the same core of 8086 instructions (with a few additions) plus an on-the-chip clock generator just as the 8085 has.

The iAPX 186 is intended for a wide range of applications which includes intelligent terminals, small business computers, data-acquisition systems, process-control systems, and I/O subsystems for larger computers such as an iAPX 432 computer system. This matches up with the kind of applications that the 8086 is already being used for. The 186 should make these applications much easier and more inexpensive, because it will reduce the number of chips needed in such systems, which will also reduce the physical size and complexity of such systems.

The additional iAPX 186 instructions include two instructions (ENTER and LEAVE) for use with procedure calls in structured, higher-level languages such as Pascal; two instructions to push immediate data (both 16-bit and 8-bit that is automatically extended to 16-bit) onto the system stack; two instructions for multiplying by immediate data; an array bounds checking instruction (just like the Motorola 68000); and shift and rotate instructions whose shift counts are specified by immediate data. Also included are PUSH ALL and POP ALL instructions, which are very handy when you want to write a procedure which does its own thing without bothering anything else. Of course, the PUSH ALL and POP ALL instructions are also useful when handling interrupts in a multitasking system. In addition to the above instructions, there are block move instructions whose source or destination can be the I/O space.

The iAPX 186 has a few more features in addition to the ones we have described, but what we have presented should give you a good idea of what the iAPX 186 can do, namely everything that an 8086 can do and more (and faster by about 30 percent) with a lot fewer support chips!

THE iAPX 286

The iAPX 286 has added a new level of sophistication to the basic 8086 architecture in that it now includes memory management as a natural extension of the processor's addressing capabilities. The 286 has elaborate, built-in data protection facilities which put its security provisions about halfway between those for the 8086 (none) and the 432 (covered in the next appendix). Further features of the 286 include all features of the new 186 instruction set and extension of the memory addressing space to 16 megabytes (using 24 bits for addressing). Virtual memory is now supported with an addressing space of about a gigabyte!

Like the 432, the 286 checks every access for instructions or data to see if there might be a violation of *access rights*. Unlike the 432, the 286 is designed to use a conventional operating system in which there are several levels of privilege. In such an operating system, there is a *kernel* which, as the name implies, is the innermost part of the operating system. The kernel has the most privilege and the applications programs have the least. It is interesting that the 286 operating system structures are called ''subjects'' by Intel. This is in direct contrast to the name ''objects'' which is used to describe the fundamental operating structures of the iAPX 432.

The 286 allows for four levels of privilege. Protection of data in such a system is achieved by having privileged instructions and privileged data and code segments as well as sets of access rights to each segment in the system.

To an ordinary user, the segment registers (code segment, data segment, extra segment, and stack segment) appear to have the usual 16 bits. However, these 16 bits do not actually point directly to memory as they do on the 8086. Instead, they point into special tables in memory called descriptor tables, some of which belong to the users and some of which belong only to the operating system. In addition to these 16 bits, each 286 segment register holds 57 other bits which are hidden from the user! Some of these (8 bits) are used by the hardware to hold access rights (read only, execute only, and so forth), some hold the actual address (now 24 bits) of the beginning of the segment, and some hold the permissible length of the segment (up to 64 Kbytes as specified by 16 bits to access 16 megabytes). Thus, the user is never told where he/she is in memory and is always kept within certain bounds. As an added feature, the user is never allowed to write into a code segment. This prevents a user from modifying a program to do illegal and potentially dangerous acts. There are even provisions to prevent a user from introducing a "Trojan horse" into the system which might sneak the user into a state of higher privilege.

The 286 has three new registers. These point to the currently active descriptor tables. These descriptor tables contain all information about the protected objects in the system. Any change of segment and any change of privilege must go through these tables. There are in addition several new flags (1-bit quantities) in the 286 hardware.

The 286 has several new instructions over those of the 186. All these instructions manipulate the memory management/protection system by doing such things as loading and storing contents of special flags and pointers, including the descriptor tables and their pointers.

CONCLUSION

It is encouraging to see Intel's announcements of these future products. Because of their compatibility with the current 8086/8088 chips, announcements of these new products mean that it is worthwhile to invest time and effort in the 8086/8088 now. That is, approaches and programs (computer code) developed now on the 8086/8088 will, with very little modification, be appropriate for the more powerful hardware of the future.

Appendix B

The Intel iAPX 432
32-Bit Microprocessor

This appendix gives an overview of one of the most exciting new developments in computer architecture, namely the Intel iAPX 432 microprocessor family. The 432 is not merely Intel's answer to the "pseudo 32-bit" microprocessors from other manufacturers. It is, instead, a bold departure from current practices in microprocessor architecture, because its hardware operates at a much higher level than ever before and because within this family many copies of the same microprocessor (theoretically up to 256!) can work together cooperatively and yet independently to form the heart of a large computer.

The iAPX 432 is, in fact, the first microprocessor to implement some recent theoretical research (some of which has been quite secret) about how to take advantage of the advances in the design of computer hardware to solve some very real and pressing problems. Briefly, these problems center around providing efficient service for a large number of users while at the same time preserving a high degree of security for sensitive data.

In this appendix, we shall begin with a general discussion of advances in computer hardware, new and expanding applications for computer systems, and the new design requirements brought on by these applications. We will then discuss how the iAPX 432 works and how it provides some very interesting ways to satisfy these fundamental requirements.

NEW ADVANCES AND OLD REQUIREMENTS
The Advances

Although advances in hardware design and manufacture are not problems in themselves, they have opened up opportunities full of challenge. That is, there is much to learn and master, and there are concepts and methods now practical which were only dreams a short time ago.

The advances in design and production of computer chips has permitted the packing of tremendous processing capabilities into smaller and less expensive packages. It is now possible to put more than 100,000 primitive electronic devices on a single chip the size of a small fingernail. This means that substantially more sophisticated computer systems can now be built for considerably less cost. Because these circuits use less power and dissipate less heat than before, the lower costs are for both the electronic circuits themselves and the support systems that house, power, and cool these circuits. Since these support systems are often made of metal and have a number of moving parts, any reduction in their size and capacity will lead to savings in cost of the total system.

These same advances have also enabled the production of extremely large memories at very reasonable prices. Gone are the days when every bit of memory had to be individually wrapped with its own coil of wire. Now memory is constructed of the same technology as the new processors and thus can be produced with the same high densities, low power consumption, and low costs.

In the past, computer systems were designed around the more limited processing power and smaller-capacity memories available at the time. Entirely different strategies are appropriate now. In particular, we now need new approaches to the design of operating systems, because the larger memories make it feasible for operating systems to be many times more sophisticated than ever before. We will see in this appendix how the iAPX 432 has incorporated some of these new approaches into its hardware.

The Requirements

At the same time these semiconductor hardware advances have been taking place, application areas such as banking, the military, big business, medicine, and aerospace have been demanding high-capacity, high-capability computer systems. The basic design requirements for a computer system for these users can be summed up by the following criteria: 1) speed, 2) security, 3) reliability, 4) expandability, and 5) ease of programming. In this section, we will give a point-by-point discussion of each of these.

Some of these computing requirements have been around for a long two at a time. This has limited systems, which do well in all five categories, to highly funded applications such as certain special categories to highly funded applications such as certain special government installations. Now, with ever-decreasing costs of memory and CPU hardware, it is becoming possible to develop systems at lower costs which satisfy these criteria much better. In fact, the price-versus-performance ratio is now dropping to the point where many commercial applications which were unthinkable before are becoming quite practical! The commercial arena is, of course, where most of the money will be spent, and as the unthinkable becomes possible, a lot of money will start to flow.

Now let's discuss each criterion in more detail.

Speed

Typically a moderate-to-large computer system has many persons using it at once in a time-sharing arrangement. The computer is designed so that each user gets a particular "slice" of processing time from the CPU, with the result that each user sees the computer as just working for him or her. Most users want to feel that they have the machine totally to themselves because they want to perform their own computations and not be held back by the programs of other users. With this type of use, the raw computing power (speed) of the machine is very important and determines to a large extent how fast the users get their jobs done. (Another very important factor in determining the speed in such applications is the data-transfer rate between the computer and its mass storage devices.) Speed of processing, therefore, is of paramount importance.

With future applications, many users will want to feel that they are connected to a system which has access to many resources, including large data banks, satisfactory computing power, and even other users. The computer system will essentially be an electronic marketplace. In any case, users will demand a very quick response in answer to each request for service. The users will not, however, expect that all requested service be completed instantly, only that each request be accepted by the system quickly and efficiently (within seconds) and that the requests be processed within a reasonable time (usually minutes). Thus, the accepting of requests and their processing are really two different matters. That is, the accepting and preliminary screening of requests is an interactive process and the processing of service is more a batch-oriented process.[1] The solution to providing this kind of multi-action system involves the use of multitasking (many jobs) with perhaps many different processors (many CPUs) within the one system. With this type of system, the raw computing power is not as important as how the system is organized. With so many jobs being performed at once and with some jobs dependent upon others, the computer becomes somewhat like a bureaucracy. If one part of the system gets hung up, it can block the progress of other parts, thus slowing down service for many. This happens when resources such as CPUs, memory, or peripheral devices are limited either through actual scarcity or through poor scheduling strategies. The iAPX 432 is designed to solve these problems by providing methods for dividing large jobs into smaller, more manageable ones, providing the groundwork for efficient scheduling schemes for these jobs and interactions between them as well as providing ways to easily attach many processors and other devices to the computer system. In fact, theoretically up to 256 copies of the 432 can work together within the same computer in a cooperative manner! As long as the processors don't interfere with each other, the more processors you have the faster your system will react to requests.

Security

Within a large computer system with many persons using it at once,

---

[1] *Batch* processing is an operating system strategy in which a user submits a whole job and then "disappears" until the job is done. *Interactive* processing is a strategy in which the user and the computer communicate with each other while a job is in progress.

each person should have a certain "profile" of *access rights* to the data within the system. An access right is a permission to read or modify a certain piece of data stored in a computer system. In general, each user has different access rights to the different pieces of data in the system. For example, for a bank computer system, a teller would have a completely different set of rights than a vice-president, and in fact, the various vice-presidents would normally have access rights different from each other's. In other words, for each user there is one set of data which can be created and modified by that user, another (possibly larger) set of data which can be read by that user, and another set to which there is no access. These various sets for the various users in the system overlap in complicated ways, forming a whole matrix of access rights for the entire system. Violations of these access rights could lead to losses of billions of dollars, directly in the case of banks, or indirectly in the case of private industry. Violations could also lead to loss of national security in the case of the government and certain key industries.

Security is not a problem just for banks and top-secret government institutions. Today's computer systems are not considered secure enough in many other areas. For example, many universities store grades and student financial records on the same computer systems they use for student programming assignments. Lack of security in such a case could lead to serious legal problems.

In today's systems, users give passwords to protect their accounts and individual data files within these accounts. In future systems, interactions among sets of data will be much more complex, frequent, and automatic, so passwords managed by humans alone will not be adequate. In such a system the computer will have to automatically assign and check "passwords" for *each* data access.

We shall see how the iAPX 432 uses an *object-based* operating system with a *capability-based* addressing scheme to greatly increase security. Within such a system, each job or task can be granted its own set of access rights, and any attempt to violate these rights would lead to an immediate error condition.

Reliability

In addition to possible violations of data by users, all data should be protected against being accidentally destroyed by hardware or software malfunctions. That is, a processor might fail or get hung up or a certain subroutine might start to perform operations on the wrong type of data, perhaps performing floating-point operations on its own processor instructions or starting to execute integer data as instructions. Since some of these systems are imbedded in medical equipment and in powerful weapons, such failures could mean loss of lives, perhaps all of us in the case of a major weapons malfunction!

For software reliability, we shall see how the object-based operating system of the iAPX 432 has built-in protection to prevent such tragedies.

The data in the 432 is *strongly typed* with automatic (hardware) type checking for each access. That is, each piece of information in the system is assigned a *data type*. Thus, 16-bit integers are one *type* of data, 80-bit floating-point numbers are another type of data, and processor instructions are yet another type. There is even provision for creation of user-defined data types. Every data access specifies a definite type for that data. Each type is stored in a separate segment of data. Before a 432 accesses the data in a segment, it must match data types between that of the segment and that of the requested data. If the data being accessed is not of the type requested, then the hardware automatically produces an error condition. For hardware reliability, there is also a special checker mode in which two copies of the 432 run the same instructions together and check on each other.

Expandability

For small applications you should use a small computer system; for larger applications you should use a larger system. That is, the capacity and hence the cost of a system should be commensurate with the demand on the system. The problem is that there has been incompatibility among systems with the various levels of performance. Each time a new level of performance was required, an elaborate *conversion process* was needed to move the data and programs from the old system to the new system. This is counterproductive, quite expensive, and time consuming. The iAPX 432 allows you to add new processors to an existing system without changing the operating system! This allows you to start with a one-processor system and gradually add more (recall, theoretically up to 256) processors as needed to handle the work. We will discuss this further when we look more closely at the 432's *object-based* operating system.

Ease of Programming

Still another problem which has been created by the proliferation of computers and applications for computers is the shortage of people to program these computers. This has led to rising costs of software development. The current methods are just too expensive and labor intensive. It is becoming more and more important to use standardized software and hardware building blocks to construct such systems, allowing systems designers at all levels to understand each other's work and thus be much more productive. That is, instead of programming all the pieces of a system, you can now work with *preprogrammed* pieces. The iAPX 432 actually incorporates this preprogramming into the hardware itself! That is, the 432 works on a new level of sophistication in that an extensive set of operating system ''primitives'' are actually part of its hardware instruction set. In other words, the 432 uses a silicon-based operating system. In addition, all its machine-code operations are completely symmetrical with respect to their operands. That is, there are no special cases and there are no special registers with their own "personalities."

PRELIMINARY CONCEPTS

Before getting into the details of how the iAPX 432 works, we will briefly describe two of the basic concepts behind its built-in operating system, namely the notions of *objects* and *messages*. The objects are the "pieces" of the operating system, and the messages are the way commands and information are transmitted among these pieces.

Objects

An *object* is an entity which resides in memory and both houses and protects a set of related information (data). An object might contain data for the operating system or processor instructions, or it might contain data for a particular application. In general, each object would contain only one type of data, although some types of data could be quite complex.

The objects in an operating system actually take on a life of their own, acting like workers in an office with their own job titles, job descriptions, and assigned tasks. They perform these assigned tasks and communicate with each other by sending "messages" back and forth. For example, several different objects containing floating-point vectors that represent different parts of some physical process could exchange information with each other about the process. Objects even have their own set of private telephone numbers where they can be reached!

There are actually many different types of objects in a system, each a specialist with its own role to play. For example, each (hardware) *processor* in the system has a unique object (in memory) called its *processor object*. This object acts as an "agent" for the processor in the system, storing vital data for the operation of that processor (see Figure B.1). To add a new processor to a system, it is merely necessary to add a corresponding processor object. On the other hand, each job in the system is divided up into subjobs called *processes*, each of which is also represented by an object (in memory) called a *process object*. Thus, the process object acts as an agent for a particular piece of work that needs to be accomplished, storing parameters for that job. Another type of object is called a *dispatching port object*. It acts as an employment bureau, assigning the various process objects (agents for the jobs) to particular processor objects (agents for the hardware "workers"). There are a number of other types of objects including *communication-port objects, carrier objects, instruction objects, storage-allocation objects, fault-handling objects,* and *user-data objects*.

The reason for having all these different objects is that each object contains only one type of information. This provides excellent control and protection of all the information in the system because one can use *type checking* as part of such a protection scheme. That is, every data access involves a check to see if that data is of the type requested. The protection scheme for data is quite interesting. Each object consists of

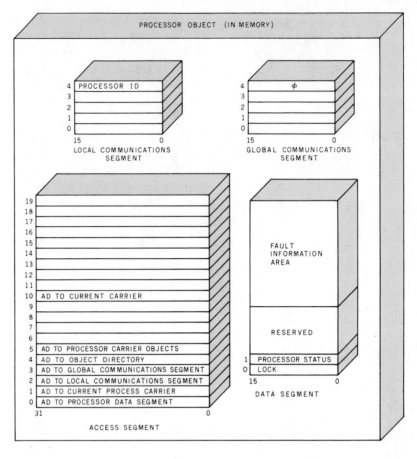

NOTE:
AD IS SHORT FOR ACCESS DESCRIPTERS

Figure B.1: Processor objects.

several *segments,* some of which are called *access segments* and the others *data segments*. The access segments provide access information and the data segments store all other types of data in the system.

An access segment is just a list or directory of what can be accessed by a given object. The individual items stored in an access segment are called *access descriptors*. You can think of an access segment as a private telephone directory which contains telephone numbers (the access descriptors) to various segments in the system. A given object is allowed access to only those segments for which it has a corresponding access descriptor, and, in fact, for only those *access rights* as specified by that access descriptor. These access rights include such things as creation, modification, and reading rights. In this way the access rights profile of a given user can be explicitly coded into the computer as a specific choice of access descriptors in some access segment.

If the user tries to request information that he/she is not entitled to, and if that request is not denied by higher levels of software, then primitive levels will catch it. When this happens, there will be either a case of a required access descriptor which will not be available or an attempted access through an access descriptor with not enough rights. In any case access will be denied to the user.

Messages

Now let's take a quick look at this business of *messages*. When data is needed, it is often not under the control of the particular process which needs it. That is, the data will always be under the protection of some object in the system which may or may not be currently accessible to the given process. In order to get the required data, the process sends a message requesting the data. Then another, perhaps more privileged (at least for that data) process can get the data, perhaps processing and specially packaging it before sending it back to the original process. In this way parts of the original data base which should not be seen can be left hidden.

Messages actually consist of access descriptors. Thus, a request for data is represented by an access descriptor pointing to a segment which describes what is needed, and the return message would be an access descriptor pointing to a segment containing the (perhaps processed) information.

Messages thus provide a way for the various processes in a system to work together without taking over more control than is needed. Messages, in fact, provide a good way of protecting data from illegal access while at the same time allowing detailed job specifications involving sensitive data to be communicated and carried out within the system. In practice, sending messages is similar to the idea of calling subroutines. An important difference is that in the case of messages, the original process need not wait until the message has been received before going on with its business, and, in addition, a perhaps different process might actually service a request sent as a message.

THE iAPX 432 FAMILY

Now let's get into the details of what the iAPX 432 is and how it works. The principal member of the iAPX 432 family is a 32-bit microprocessor called a General Data Processor, or GDP for short. The GDP consists of two chips, the 43201 Instruction Decoder/ Microinstruction Sequencer and the 43202 Execution Unit. At the time of this writing, there is one other member of the iAPX 432 family. This is the Interface Processor which is housed in a chip whose model number is 43203. See the figure below for a pinout diagram for each of these chips. Each of the 432 chips is mounted in a quad-in-line package (QUIP) with 64 pins. *Quad-in-line* simply means that the pins are arranged in *four* rows as opposed to one row for *single-in-line* packages (SIP) or two rows for *double-in-line* packages (DIP). Most of today's generation of chips are housed in DIPs, and there are packages of resistors which come in

SIPs. The QUIP package is a new approach used for this new generation of microchip, providing a large number of signal lines in a very compact package. The four rows of pins in the QUIP package are actually *two double* rows on two opposite edges of the chip package. Thus, a dip could quip that a QUIP is really a double DIP!

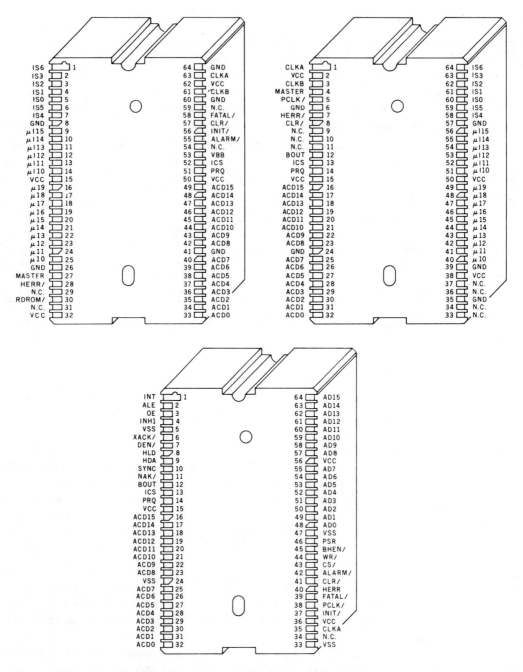

Figure B.2: Pinout diagrams of the iAPX family chips.

THE MICROMAINFRAME   Although the GDP is a complete microprocessor by itself, it is designed to work cooperatively with as many as 256 copies of itself to form the central computing unit of a large computer (see the figure below). Such a computer is called a micromainframe because it has the power and size of a maxicomputer and yet is constructed from microprocessors.

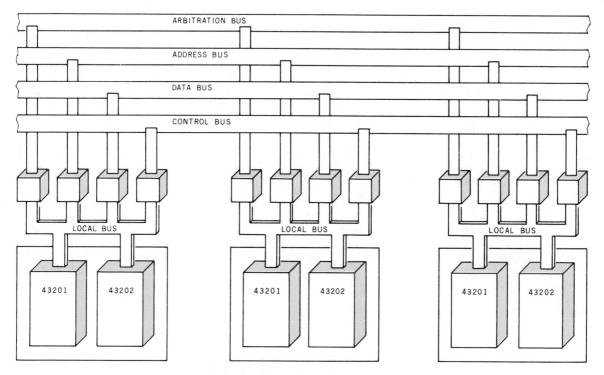

Figure B.3: Block diagram of a system with several GDPs.

A 432 micromainframe computer might consist of several modules. Each module would have one main internal bus which can consist of anywhere from 29 to 61 signal lines, depending upon how the signals are multiplexed. In any case, the internal data bus is 16-bits wide. Each GDP is mounted as a pair of chips, the 43201 Instruction Decoder/ Microsequencer (IDM) and 43202 Execution Unit (EU). These two chips lie right next to each other with about 23 signal lines running between them, but not out to the main bus. From the main bus, some of the lines run only to the IDM, others only to the EU, and some (for example, power) run to both. See figure B.4 for a pinout of the GDP as a unit.

In addition to the GDPs, a 432 micromainframe would contain one or more interface processors. An interface processor appears to be just

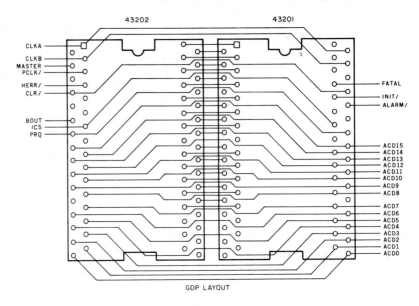

Figure B.4: Pinout diagram for the GDP unit.

like a GDP to the GDPs in the system. That is, it is connected to the main system bus and accepts the same kinds of interprocessor commands as a GDP, but it is also connected to a second bus (the I/O bus) to which the I/O processors and controllers are connected. Thus, the interface processors provide a 432 system with a way to communicate with the outside world. You could put various clusters of 8086s, 8088s, and 8089s on this exterior or I/O bus (see figure B.5). There are also "hooks" for integrating other types of processors onto the main bus as they become available. So far, plans for these other processors have not been made public (nor private, that we've heard of yet).

All the processors on the main internal bus share the same main memory, which can be quite enormous. In fact, the 432 has an addressing scheme for accessing as much as 2 to the 40th bytes of memory. This is over a trillion bytes or a million kilobytes! A segmentation scheme is used with special protection features and special look-up tables in memory for the segment addresses which are built into the hardware of the 432 processor.

SILICON OBJECT-BASED OPERATING SYSTEM

Besides a full set of instructions to perform arithmetic and logical operations on a rich assortment of data types, the iAPX 432 has an extensive set of instructions to perform operating system functions. Recall that an operating system is a "mother" program that oversees all actions of the application programs. The 432 operating system is based upon the notion of objects, a concept we have introduced earlier in this appendix.

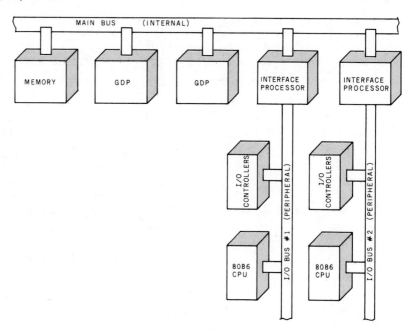

Figure B.5: Block diagram of a system with internal and I/O buses.

The 432 operating system instructions work by examining and modifying bits which belong to elaborate data structures in the computer's main memory. These data structures are called objects. As we mentioned before, these objects can consist of text, numbers, or even instruction code. Each object exists entirely in memory of a 432 computer system (although some of this memory is a special, fast kind of memory called *cache* memory). There are no user-accessible processor registers within the 432 itself! All processor registers are stored in memory within the *data segment* of special types of objects called *context objects,* which we will look at in a moment. Context objects have the interesting property that they are created and destroyed while a 432 goes about its business. Thus, quite frequently a 432 loses all its user registers!

It is important to note that although the objects act intelligently, they often do not contain a speck of processor instruction code! In fact, only an *instruction object* can hold active processor instructions. Instead most objects contain tables of information which tells the hardware what to do at a much higher level (almost like a high-level language).

To get a glimpse of what these objects look like on the inside, let's look more closely at the *context* objects.

Context Objects

Context objects play the key role in the actual running of 432 machine language. They are where most of the action is. *Context objects* are directly associated with each software procedure (subroutine), but only while that particular procedure is being executed. In other words, a context is created when a procedure is called and destroyed upon return from that procedure.

Internally, context objects consist of the following segments:

- a context *access* segment
- a context *data* segment
- a context *constants* segment
- a context *operand stack* segment

The access segment for a context contains a variable number of 32-bit access descriptors (like telephone numbers). The first 10 are special and must appear in the correct order, while the last ones depend upon the requirements of the particular procedure being executed by the context.

The data segment for a context contains 16-bit words which form the 432 working processor registers. These include: a status word, a stack pointer, an instruction segment identifier, and an instruction pointer. Having all user registers in memory is not a completely new concept. For example, the 16-bit Texas Instrument processor has a single user register on the processor which points to a work space in memory containing the other user registers. It is also true that large machines such as the CDC Cyber use environment tables in memory to keep track of what they are doing.

The constants segment contains the constants defined within the procedure. It is intended that whatever language the software is written in will have the ability to define named constants (as in Pascal). In fact, the intended language is Ada, a descendent of Pascal. Ada has an interesting history. It was developed in response to a request by the U.S. Department of Defense for a universal language for weapons system. It has taken on an even more universal usage now, although it is still at the stage where its standards are being firmed up. Ada was originally called the Green language and later was renamed after the first computer programmer, Lady Ada Augusta Byron, Countess Lovelace, daughter of the poet Lord Byron. Like the 432, Ada is "strongly typed." Similar to the 432, it deals with jobs in packages (objects for the 432). Ada has multitasking built into it, although the multitasking of the 432 and the multitasking in Ada so far have not been connected together.

The operand stack segment is optional. When it is present it allows the 432 to operate as a stack machine (within each procedure). The arithmetic and logical instructions allow references to either the stack or to operands stored as variables (or constants) in memory. In the chapter on the 8087 NDP we saw that the 8087 uses a stack to store its floating-point operands. It is easy and efficient to write compilers for a stack machine, making such machines very useful for higher-level languages.

The 432 processor instructions which operate on context objects are all some kind of CALL, RETURN, or BRANCH. For the CALL and RETURN instructions, the current context object is actually destroyed and a new context object is created, a rather drastic action! The BRANCH instruction works in a much more gentle manner, by modifying certain quantities stored within the context object.

You can think of the context objects as describing the current state of the processor running a particular job.

There are many more kinds of objects in the 432, including further program control objects as well as fault handling, data, and instruction objects. Other kinds of 432 operating system instructions cause data and access segments to be created or destroyed; create higher-level data types; and examine, move, and modify access descriptors. The best source for a detailed account is Intel's manual *iAPX 432 General Data Processor Architecture Reference Manual*. We hope that this short introduction has whetted your appetite for the heavier reading in this Intel manual.

BIT STREAM ENCODING

The iAPX 432 encodes its instructions in what is called a *bit-stream* as opposed to the *byte-stream* used by the iAPX 86,88. This means that the instructions for the iAPX 432 consist of strings or groups of bits which may be of any length. For example, there are instructions which are encoded in a string of 83 bits!

There are four *bit fields* (groups of bits) in the 432 machine code for each instruction. (See table B.1.) The first three fields are used to specify the operands and the last field is used to give the operation code for the instruction (what is actually to be done). This is similar to the way an HP calculator requires you to enter the data first and then key in the operation. The last field is not even present for some 432 instructions, because there is only one possible instruction whose operands match those described by the first three fields!

Each bit field has variable length and is encoded in a most ingenious manner, but, alas, that is another story.

The first field is called the class field. It is perhaps the most important. We will talk a bit about it and leave the other three fields (format, reference, and opcode) for your further reading if you are interested. Within the details of how these four fields work lies the secret of the 432's protection schemes for vital data.

The class field tells how many operands there are and how big each one is. There are 41 different *classes,* that is, 41 possible choices for number and size of operands. Five different operand lengths for data and one more length for branching reference are available. The possible lengths run from 8 bits to 80 bits. Table B.1 shows all 41 different classes which are actually used by the 432.

ORDER	OPERAND LENGTHS	CLASS ENCODING	OPERATORS IN CLASS
0	none	001110	1
	branch	101110	1
1	b,branch	0000	2
	b	011110	3
	db	111110	9
	w	000001	8
	dw	100001	2
	ew	010001	2
2	b, b	110001	6
	b,db	001001	1
	db, b	101001	5
	db,db	1000	17
	db, w	011001	5
	db,ew	111001	2
	w, b	000101	7
	w,db	100101	5
	w, w	0100	13
	w,ew	010101	3
	dw, b	110101	3
	dw,dw	001101	3
	dw,ew	101101	1
	ew, b	011101	3
	ew, w	111101	3
	ew,dw	000011	1
	ew,ew	100011	4
3	b, b, b	010011	10
	db,db, b	1100	9
	db,db,db	0010	25
	db,db, w	110011	4
	db, w, w	001011	4
	w, w, b	1010	9
	w, w, w	0110	15
	w, w,ew	101011	4
	w,ew,ew	011011	4
	dw,dw, b	111011	3
	dw,dw,ew	000111	4
	dw,ew,ew	100111	4
	ew, w,ew	010111	4
	ew,dw,ew	110111	4
	ew,ew, b	001111	3
	ew,ew,ew	101111	5
	reserved	011111	
	reserved	111111	

Note:

b	=	byte (8 bits)
db	=	double byte (16 bits)
w	=	word (32 bits)
dw	=	double word (64 bits)
ew	=	extended word (80 bits)
branch	=	branch information (10 bits or 16 bits)

Table B.1: The 41 different operand classes.

To see how these classes might be used, look at the following examples:

1) The 432 16-bit integer ADD instruction has three operands, each 16 bits in length. The first two are sources and the last one is a destination. That is, when this instruction is executed, the first two operands are added together and the result is placed in the location specified by the third operand.

2) The 32-bit integer ADD instruction also has three operands; however, this time they are each 32 bits in length.

3) The 32-bit integer NOT EQUAL instruction has mixed lengths for its operands. This instruction has three operands, of which the first two are words (32 bits) and the last is a byte (8 bits). The instruction compares the two words and returns the byte as the logical result of the comparison.

4) The temporary (80-bit) real MOVE instruction has just two operands, both extended words (80 bits). The first is the source and the second is the destination.

5) The instruction to make a 0 character has only one operand (the destination), which is 8 bits in length.

6) The RETURN instruction has no operands.

CONCLUSION

We have examined the iAPX 432 from several viewpoints: its role in society, its operating system structures, and its instruction encoding. There is much more to say about these topics, and there are many more topics concerning the Intel 432, but we hope this much discussion will give you an idea of what this grand experiment in microprocessor architecture is all about.

The 432 is probably the first in a long line of developments toward highly capable and complex computer systems. The 432 is now marketed in a rather expensive form (approximately $80,000 for a system), but the price will probably come down to about $1000 for a board. It still is not the ultimate answer because of several factors. For one, it is hard to start up. In fact, to start a 432 system, you fill the memory (perhaps from a disk) as though all the 432s in the system had been running for a long time, and then you actually start the 432s. Thus, the 432s are always in the middle of something, never at the start or finish. For another, a 432 is not very fast at ordinary computations. It was measured against a VAX and found to be about 10 times slower. It is really still too early to tell how a full-fledged 432 will do when it is used to its full potential because the necessary software is still being developed, a process which always takes unreasonably long. So keep a patient watch for further developments!

Appendix C

8086/8088 Instruction Set

8086
REGISTER MODEL

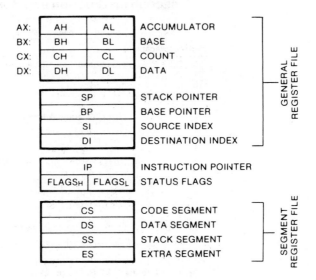

AX:	AH / AL — ACCUMULATOR
BX:	BH / BL — BASE
CX:	CH / CL — COUNT
DX:	DH / DL — DATA

GENERAL REGISTER FILE

SP — STACK POINTER
BP — BASE POINTER
SI — SOURCE INDEX
DI — DESTINATION INDEX

IP — INSTRUCTION POINTER
FLAGSH / FLAGSL — STATUS FLAGS

CS — CODE SEGMENT
DS — DATA SEGMENT
SS — STACK SEGMENT
ES — EXTRA SEGMENT

SEGMENT REGISTER FILE

Instructions which reference the flag register file as a 16-bit object use the symbol FLAGS to represent the file:

15							7							0
X	X	X	X	OF	DF	IF	TF	SF	ZF	X	AF	X	PF	X	CF

X = Don't Care

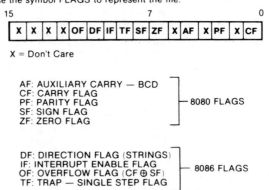

AF: AUXILIARY CARRY — BCD
CF: CARRY FLAG
PF: PARITY FLAG   8080 FLAGS
SF: SIGN FLAG
ZF: ZERO FLAG

DF: DIRECTION FLAG (STRINGS)
IF: INTERRUPT ENABLE FLAG
OF: OVERFLOW FLAG (CF $\oplus$ SF)   8086 FLAGS
TF: TRAP — SINGLE STEP FLAG

OPERAND SUMMARY

"reg" field Bit Assignments:

16-Bit (w = 1)	8-Bit (w = 0)	Segment
000 AX	000 AL	00 ES
001 CX	001 CL	01 CS
010 DX	010 DL	10 SS
011 BX	011 BL	11 DS
100 SP	100 AH	
101 BP	101 CH	
110 SI	110 DH	
111 DI	111 BH	

SECOND INSTRUCTION BYTE SUMMARY

mod	xxx	r/m

mod	Displacement
00	DISP = 0*, disp-low and disp-high are absent
01	DISP = disp-low sign-extended to 16-bits, disp-high is absent
10	DISP = disp-high: disp-low
11	r/m is treated as a "reg" field

r/m	Operand Address
000	(BX) + (SI) + DISP
001	(BX) + (DI) + DISP
010	(BP) + (SI) + DISP
011	(BP) + (DI) + DISP
100	(SI) + DISP
101	(DI) + DISP
110	(BP) + DISP*
111	(BX) + DISP

DISP follows 2nd byte of instruction (before data if required).

*except if mod = 00 and r/m = 110 then EA = disp-high: disp-low.

Operand Address (EA) Timing (clocks):
Add 4 clocks for word operands at ODD ADDRESSES.
Immed Offset = 6
Base (BX, BP, SI, DI) = 5
Base + DISP = 9
Base + Index (BP + DI, BX + SI) = 7
Base + Index (BP + SI, BX + DI) = 8
Base + Index (BP + DI, BX + SI) + DISP = 11
Base + Index (BP + SI, BX + DI) + DISP = 12

DATA TRANSFER

MOV = Move
Register/memory to/from register

1 0 0 0 1 0 d w	mod reg r/m

Timing (clocks): register to register   2
                  memory to register   8+EA
                  register to memory   9+EA

Immediate to register/memory

1 1 0 0 0 1 1 w	mod 0 0 0 r/m	data	data if w=1

Timing: 10+EA clocks

Immediate to register

1 0 1 1 w reg	data	data if w=1

Timing: 4 clocks

Memory to accumulator

1 0 1 0 0 0 0 w	addr-low	addr-high

Timing: 10 clocks

Accumulator to memory

1 0 1 0 0 0 1 w	addr-low	addr-high

Timing: 10 clocks

Register/memory to segment register

1 0 0 0 1 1 1 0	mod 0 reg r/m

Timing (clocks): register to register   2
                  memory to register   8+EA

Segment register to register/memory

1 0 0 0 1 1 0 0	mod 0 reg r/m

Timing (clocks): register to register   2
                  register to memory   9+EA

PUSH = Push
Register/memory

1 1 1 1 1 1 1 1	mod 1 1 0 r/m

Timing (clocks): register   10
                  memory   16+EA

Register

0 1 0 1 0 reg

Timing: 10 clocks

Segment register

0 0 0 reg 1 1 0

Timing: 10 clocks

POP = Pop
Register/memory

1 0 0 0 1 1 1 1	mod 0 0 0 r/m

Timing (clocks): register   8
                  memory   17+EA

Register

0 1 0 1 1 reg

Timing: 8 clocks

Segment register

0 0 0 reg 1 1 1

Timing: 8 clocks

XCHG = Exchange
Register/memory with register

1 0 0 0 0 1 1 w	mod reg r/m

Timing (clocks): register with register   4
                  memory with register   17+EA

Register with accumulator

1 0 0 1 0 reg

Timing: 3 clocks

IN = Input to AL/AX from
Fixed port

1 1 1 0 0 1 0 w	port

Timing: 10 clocks

Variable port (DX)

1 1 1 0 1 1 0 w

Timing: 8 clocks

OUT = Output from AL/AX to
Fixed port

1 1 1 0 0 1 1 w	port

Timing: 10 clocks

Variable port (DX)

1 1 1 0 1 1 1 w

Timing: 8 clocks

XLAT = Translate byte to AL

1 1 0 1 0 1 1 1

Timing: 11 clocks

LEA = Load EA to register

1 0 0 0 1 1 0 1	mod reg r/m

Timing: 2+EA clocks

LDS = Load pointer to DS

1 1 0 0 0 1 0 1	mod reg r/m

Timing: 16+EA clocks

LES = Load pointer to ES

1 1 0 0 0 1 0 0	mod reg r/m

Timing: 16+EA clocks

LAHF = Load AH with flags

1 0 0 1 1 1 1 1

Timing: 4 clocks

SAHF = Store AH into flags

1 0 0 1 1 1 1 0

Timing: 4 clocks

PUSHF = Push flags

1 0 0 1 1 1 0 0

Timing: 10 clocks

POPF = Pop flags

1 0 0 1 1 1 0 1

Timing: 8 clocks

ARITHMETIC

ADD = Add
Reg./memory with register to either

0 0 0 0 0 0 d w	mod reg r/m

Timing (clocks):   register to register   3
                   memory to register   9+EA
                   register to memory   16+EA

Immediate to register/memory

1 0 0 0 0 0 s w	mod 0 0 0 r/m	data	data if s:w=01

Timing (clocks):   immediate to register   4
                   immediate to memory   17+EA

Immediate from register/memory

1 0 0 0 0 0 s w	mod 1 0 1 r/m	data	data if s:w=01

Timing (clocks):   immediate from register   4
                   immediate from memory 17+EA

Immediate from accumulator

0 0 1 0 1 1 0 w	data	data if w=1

Timing: 4 clocks

SBB = Subtract with borrow
Reg./memory and register to either

0 0 0 1 1 0 d w	mod reg r/m

Timing (clocks):   register from register   3
                   memory from register   9+EA
                   register from memory   16+EA

Immediate from register/memory

1 0 0 0 0 0 s w	mod 0 1 1 r/m	data	data if s:w=01

Timing (clocks):   immediate from register   4
                   immediate from memory 17+EA

Immediate from accumulator

0 0 0 1 1 1 0 w	data	data if w=1

Timing: 4 clocks

DEC = Decrement
Register/memory

1 1 1 1 1 1 1 w	mod 0 0 1 r/m

Timing (clocks):   register   2
                   memory   15+EA

Register

0 1 0 0 1 reg

Timing: 2 clocks

NEG = Change sign

1 1 1 1 0 1 1 w	mod 0 1 1 r/m

Timing (clocks):   register   3
                   memory   16+EA

CMP = Compare
Register/memory and register

0 0 1 1 1 0 d w	mod reg r/m

Timing (clocks):   register with register   3
                   memory with register   9+EA
                   register with memory   9+EA

Immediate to accumulator

0 0 0 0 0 1 0 w	data	data if w=1

Timing: 4 clocks

(Continued on following page)

ADC = Add with carry
Reg./memory with register to either

| 0 0 0 1 0 0 d w | mod reg r/m |

Timing (clocks): register to register   3
                  memory to register   9+EA
                  register to memory   16+EA

Immediate to register/memory

| 1 0 0 0 0 0 s w | mod 0 1 0 r/m | data | data if s:w=01 |

Timing (clocks): immediate to register   4
                  immediate to memory 17+EA

Immediate to accumulator

| 0 0 0 1 0 1 0 w | data | data if w=1 |

Timing: 4 clocks

INC = Increment
Register/memory

| 1 1 1 1 1 1 1 w | mod 0 0 0 r/m |

Timing (clocks): register   2
                  memory   15+EA

Register

| 0 1 0 0 0 reg |

Timing: 2 clocks

AAA = ASCII adjust for add

| 0 0 1 1 0 1 1 1 |

Timing: 4 clocks

DAA = Decimal adjust for add

| 0 0 1 0 0 1 1 1 |

Timing: 4 clocks

SUB = Subtract
Reg./memory and register to either

| 0 0 1 0 1 0 d w | mod reg r/m |

Timing (clocks): register from register   3
                  memory from register 9+EA
                  register from memory 16+EA

Immediate with register/memory

| 1 0 0 0 0 0 s w | mod 1 1 1 r/m | data | data if s:w=01 |

Timing (clocks): immediate with register   4
                  immediate with memory 17+EA

Immediate with accumulator

| 0 0 1 1 1 1 0 w | data | data if w=1 |

Timing: 4 clocks

AAS = ASCII adjust for subtract

| 0 0 1 1 1 1 1 1 |

Timing: 4 clocks

DAS = Decimal adjust for subtract

| 0 0 1 0 1 1 1 1 |

Timing: 4 clocks

MUL = Multiply (unsigned)

| 1 1 1 1 0 1 1 w | mod 1 0 0 r/m |

Timing (clocks): 8-bit   71+EA
                  16-bit   124+EA

IMUL = Integer multiply (signed)

| 1 1 1 1 0 1 1 w | mod 1 0 1 r/m |

Timing (clocks): 8-bit   90+EA
                  16-bit   144+EA

AAM = ASCII adjust for multiply

| 1 1 0 1 0 1 0 0 | 0 0 0 0 1 0 1 0 |

Timing: 83 clocks

DIV = Divide (unsigned)

| 1 1 1 1 0 1 1 w | mod 1 1 0 r/m |

Timing (clocks): 8-bit   90+EA
                  16-bit   155+EA

IDIV = Integer divide (signed)

| 1 1 1 1 0 1 1 w | mod 1 1 1 r/m |

Timing (clocks): 8-bit   112+EA
                  16-bit   177+EA

AAD = ASCII adjust for divide

| 1 1 0 1 0 1 0 1 | 0 0 0 0 1 0 1 0 |

Timing: 60 clocks

CBW = Convert byte to word

| 1 0 0 1 1 0 0 0 |

Timing: 2 clocks

CWD = Convert word to double word

| 1 0 0 1 1 0 0 1 |

Timing: 5 clocks

LOGIC

NOT = Invert

| 1 1 1 1 0 1 1 w | mod 0 1 0 r/m |

Timing (clocks): register   3
                  memory 16+EA

SHL/SAL = Shift logical/arithmetic left

| 1 1 0 1 0 0 v w | mod 1 0 0 r/m |

Timing (clocks): single-bit register   2
                  single-bit memory 15+EA
                  variable-bit register 8+4/bit
                  variable-bit memory 20+EA+4/bit

SHR = Shift logical right

| 1 1 0 1 0 0 v w | mod 1 0 1 r/m |

Timing (clocks): single-bit register   2
                  single-bit memory 15+EA
                  variable-bit register 8+4/bit
                  variable-bit memory 20+EA+4/bit

SAR = Shift arithmetic right

| 1 1 0 1 0 0 v w | mod 1 1 1 r/m |

Timing (clocks): single-bit register   2
                  single-bit memory 15+EA
                  variable-bit register 8+4/bit
                  variable-bit memory 20+EA+4/bit

(Continued of following page)

ROL = Rotate left

1 1 0 1 0 0 v w	mod 0 0 0 r/m

Timing (clocks):	single-bit register	2
	single-bit memory	15+EA
	variable-bit register	8+4/bit
	variable-bit memory	20+EA+4/bit

ROR = Rotate right

1 1 0 1 0 0 v w	mod 0 0 1 r/m

Timing (clocks):	single-bit register	2
	single-bit memory	15+EA
	variable-bit register	8+4/bit
	variable-bit memory	20+EA+4/bit

RCL = Rotate through carry left

1 1 0 1 0 0 v w	mod 0 1 0 r/m

Timing (clocks):	single-bit register	2
	single-bit memory	15+EA
	variable-bit register	8+4/bit
	variable-bit memory	20+EA+4/bit

RCR = Rotate through carry right

1 1 0 1 0 0 v w	mod 0 1 1 r/m

Timing (clocks):	single-bit register	2
	single-bit memory	15+EA
	variable-bit register	8+4/bit
	variable-bit memory	20+EA+4/bit

AND = And
Reg./memory and register to either

0 0 1 0 0 0 d w	mod reg r/m

Timing (clocks):	register to register	3
	memory to register	9+EA
	register to memory	16+EA

Immediate to register/memory

1 0 0 0 0 0 0 w	mod 1 0 0 r/m	data	data if w=1

Timing (clocks):	immediate to register	4
	immediate to memory	17+EA

Immediate to accumulator

0 0 1 0 0 1 0 w	data	data if w=1

Timing: 4 clocks

TEST = And function to flags, no result
Register/memory and register

1 0 0 0 0 1 0 w	mod reg r/m

Timing (clocks):	register to register	3
	register with memory	9+EA

Immediate data and register/memory

1 1 1 1 0 1 1 w	mod 0 0 0 r/m	data	data if w=1

Timing (clocks):	immediate with register	4
	immediate with memory	10+EA

Immediate data and accumulator

1 0 1 0 1 0 0 w	data	data if w=1

Timing: 4 clocks

OR = Or
Reg./memory and register to either

0 0 0 0 1 0 d w	mod reg r/m

Timing (clocks):	register to register	3
	memory to register	9+EA
	register to memory	16+EA

Immediate to register/memory

1 0 0 0 0 0 0 w	mod 0 0 1 r/m	data	data if w=1

Timing (clocks):	immediate to register	4
	immediate to memory	17+EA

Immediate to accumulator

0 0 0 0 1 1 0 w	data	data if w=1

Timing: 4 clocks

XOR = Exclusive or
Reg./memory and register to either

0 0 1 1 0 0 d w	mod reg r/m

Timing (clocks):	register to register	3
	memory to register	9+EA
	register to memory	16+EA

Immediate to register/memory

1 0 0 0 0 0 0 w	mod 1 1 0 r/m	data	data if w=1

Timing (clocks):	immediate to register	4
	immediate to memory	17+EA

Immediate to accumulator

0 0 1 1 0 1 0 w	data	data if w=1

Timing: 4 clocks

STRING MANIPULATION

REP = Repeat

1 1 1 1 0 0 1 z

Timing: 6 clocks/loop

MOVS = Move String

1 0 1 0 0 1 0 w

Timing: 17 clocks

CMPS = Compare String

1 0 1 0 0 1 1 w

Timing: 22 clocks

SCAS = Scan String

1 0 1 0 1 1 1 w

Timing: 15 clocks

LODS = Load String

1 0 1 0 1 1 0 w

Timing: 12 clocks

STOS = Store String

1 0 1 0 1 0 1 w

Timing: 10 clocks

CONTROL TRANSFER

NOTE: Queue reinitialization is not included in the timing information for transfer operations. To account for instruction loading, add 8 clocks to timing numbers.

CALL = Call
Direct within segment

1 1 1 0 1 0 0 0	disp-low	disp-high

Timing: 11 clocks

Indirect within segment

1 1 1 1 1 1 1 1	mod 0 1 0 r/m

Timing: 13+EA clocks

Direct intersegment

1 0 0 1 1 0 1 0	offset-low	offset-high
Timing: 20 clocks	seg-low	seg-high

Indirect intersegment

1 1 1 1 1 1 1 1	mod 0 1 1 r/m

Timing: 29+EA clocks

JMP = Unconditional Jump
Direct within segment

1 1 1 0 1 0 0 1	disp-low	disp-high

Timing: 7 clocks

Direct within segment-short

1 1 1 0 1 0 1 1	disp

Timing: 7 clocks

Indirect within segment

1 1 1 1 1 1 1 1	mod 1 0 0 r/m

Timing: 7+EA clocks

Direct intersegment

1 1 1 0 1 0 1 0	offset-low	offset-high
Timing: 7 clocks	seg-low	seg-high

Indirect intersegment

1 1 1 1 1 1 1 1	mod 1 0 1 r/m

Timing: 16+EA clocks

RET = Return from CALL
Within segment

1 1 0 0 0 0 1 1

Timing: 8 clocks

Within seg. adding immed to SP

1 1 0 0 0 0 1 0	data-low	data-high

Timing: 12 clocks

Intersegment

1 1 0 0 1 0 1 1

Timing: 18 clocks

Intersegment, adding immediate to SP

1 1 0 0 1 0 1 0	data-low	data-high

Timing: 17 clocks

JE/JZ = Jump on equal/zero

0 1 1 1 0 1 0 0	disp

Timing (clocks):   Jump is taken   8
                   Jump is not taken   4

JL/JNGE = Jump on less/not greater or equal

0 1 1 1 1 1 0 0	disp

Timing (clocks):   Jump is taken   8
                   Jump is not taken   4

JLE/JNG = Jump on less or equal/not greater

0 1 1 1 1 1 1 0	disp

Timing (clocks):   Jump is taken   8
                   Jump is not taken   4

JB/JNAE = Jump on below/ not above or equal

0 1 1 1 0 0 1 0	disp

Timing (clocks):   Jump is taken   8
                   Jump is not taken   4

JBE/JNA = Jump on below or equal/not above

0 1 1 1 0 1 1 0	disp

Timing (clocks):   Jump is taken   8
                   Jump is not taken   4

JP/JPE = Jump on parity/parity even

0 1 1 1 1 0 1 0	disp

Timing (clocks):   Jump is taken   8
                   Jump is not taken   4

JO = Jump on overflow

0 1 1 1 0 0 0 0	disp

Timing (clocks):   Jump is taken   8
                   Jump is not taken   4

JS = Jump on sign

0 1 1 1 1 0 0 0	disp

Timing (clocks):   Jump is taken   8
                   Jump is not taken   4

(Continued on following page)

JNE/JNZ = Jump on not equal/not zero

0 1 1 1 0 1 0 1	disp

Timing (clocks):   Jump is taken   8
                            Jump is not taken   4

JNL/JGE = Jump on not less/greater or equal

0 1 1 1 1 1 0 1	disp

Timing (clocks):   Jump is taken   8
                            Jump is not taken   4

JNLE/JG = Jump on not less or equal/greater

0 1 1 1 1 1 1 1	disp

Timing (clocks):   Jump is taken   8
                            Jump is not taken   4

JNB/JAE = Jump on not below/above or equal

0 1 1 1 0 0 1 1	disp

Timing (clocks):   Jump is taken   8
                            Jump is not taken   4

JNBE/JA = Jump on not below or equal/above

0 1 1 1 0 1 1 1	disp

Timing (clocks):   Jump is taken   8
                            Jump is not taken   4

JNP/JPO = Jump on not parity/parity odd

0 1 1 1 1 0 1 1	disp

Timing (clocks):   Jump is taken   8
                            Jump is not taken   4

JNO = Jump on not overflow

0 1 1 1 0 0 0 1	disp

Timing (clocks):   Jump is taken   8
                            Jump is not taken   4

JNS = Jump on not sign

0 1 1 1 1 0 0 1	disp

Timing (clocks):   Jump is taken   8
                            Jump is not taken   4

LOOP = Loop CX times

1 1 1 0 0 0 1 0	disp

Timing (clocks):   Jump is taken   9
                            Jump is not taken   5

LOOPZ/LOOPE = Loop while zero/equal

1 1 1 0 0 0 0 1	disp

Timing (clocks):   Jump is taken   11
                            Jump is not taken   5

LOOPNZ/LOOPNE = Loop while not zero/ not equal

1 1 1 0 0 0 0 0	disp

Timing (clocks):   Jump is taken   11
                            Jump is not taken   5

JCXZ = Jump on CX zero

1 1 1 0 0 0 1 1	disp

Timing (clocks):   Jump is taken   9
                            Jump is not taken   5

8086 CONDITIONAL TRANSFER OPERATIONS

Instruction	Condition	Interpretation
JE or JZ	ZF = 1	"equal" or "zero"
JL or JNGE	(SF xor OF) = 1	"less" or "not greater or equal"
JLE or JNG	((SP xor OF) or ZF) = 1	"less or equal" or "not greater"
JB or JNAE	CF = 1	"below" or "not above or equal"
JBE or JNA	(CF or ZF) = 1	"below or equal" or "not above"
JP or JPE	PF = 1	"parity" or "parity even"
JO	OF = 1	"overflow"
JS	SF = 1	"sign"
JNE or JNZ	ZF = 0	"not equal" or "not zero"
JNL or JGE	(SF xor OF) = 0	"not less" or "greater or equal"
JNLE or JG	((SF xor OF) or ZF) = 0	"not less or equal" or "greater"
JNB or JAE	CF = 0	"not below" or "above or equal"
JNBE or JA	(CF or ZF) = 0	"not below or equal" or "above"
JNP or JPO	PF = 0	"not parity" or "parity odd"
JNO	OF = 0	"not overflow"
JNS	SF = 0	"not sign"

*"Above" and "below" refer to the relation between two unsigned values, while "greater" and "less" refer to the relation between two signed values.

INT = **Interrupt**
Type specified

1 1 0 0 1 1 0 1	type

Timing: 50 clocks
Type 3

1 1 0 0 1 1 0 0

Timing: 51 clocks

INTO = Interrupt on overflow

1 1 0 0 1 1 1 0

Timing: 52 clocks if pass   4 clocks if fail

IRET = Interrupt return

1 1 0 0 1 1 1 1

Timing: 24 clocks

PROCESSOR CONTROL

CLC = Clear carry

| 1 1 1 1 1 0 0 0 |

Timing: 2 clocks

CMC = Complement carry

| 1 1 1 1 0 1 0 1 |

Timing: 2 clocks

CLD = Clear direction

| 1 1 1 1 1 1 0 0 |

Timing: 2 clocks

CLI = Clear interrupt

| 1 1 1 1 1 0 1 0 |

Timing: 2 clocks

HLT = Halt

| 1 1 1 1 0 1 0 0 |

Timing: 2 clocks

LOCK = Bus lock prefix

| 1 1 1 1 0 0 0 0 |

Timing: 2 clocks

STC = Set carry

| 1 1 1 1 1 0 0 1 |

Timing: 2 clocks

NOP = No operation

| 1 0 0 1 0 0 0 0 |

Timing: 3 clocks

STD = Set direction

| 1 1 1 1 1 1 0 1 |

Timing: 2 clocks

STI = Set interrupt

| 1 1 1 1 1 0 1 1 |

Timing: 2 clocks

WAIT = Wait

| 1 0 0 1 1 0 1 1 |

Timing: 3 clocks

ESC = Escape (to external device)

| 1 1 0 1 1 x x x | mod x x x r/m |

Timing: 7+EA clocks

Footnotes:

if d = 1 then "to"; if d = 0 then "from"

if w = 1 then word instruction; if w = 0 then byte instruction

if s:w = 01 then 16 bits of immediate data form the operand

if s:w = 11 then an immediate data byte is sign extended to form the 16-bit operand

if v = 0 then "count" = 1; if v = 1 then "count" in (CL)

x = don't care

z is used for some string primitives to compare with ZF FLAG

AL = 8-bit accumulator

AX = 16-bit accumulator

CX = Count register

DS = Data segment

DX = Variable port register

ES = Extra segment

Above/below refers to unsigned value

Greater = more positive;

Less = less positive (more negative) signed values

See page 1 for Operand Summary.

See page 2 for Segment Override Summary.

Mnemonics © Intel, 1978.

Index

Absolute code, 65
Access rights, 326, 329
Access segment, 329
Account number, 68
ADA, 5, 63
ACD, 112
ADD, 110–112, 145–149
Address subbus, 18
Addressing:
  of 8086/8088, 79,
    82, 95–99
  of 8089, 208
  relative, 132
Airplane, 6
ALE signal, 26
AND, 117–118
Animation, 33–34
Arbitration scheme, 228
Arithmetic operations,
  190–191
Arithmetic shift, 272–275
ASCII code, 41
ASM assembler, 65
Assembler, 64
  ASM, 65
Assembler directive, 64
Assembly language, 60
  comments in, 98
  sixteen-bit, 63–73, 70–72
Autoinitialization, 231
AX register, 87

Base address, 95
BASIC, 4
Batch processing, 325
BCD (see Binary coded decimal)
Biased exponent, 160
Binary coded decimal (BCD),
  40–41
Binary coded decimal
  arithmetic, 123–125
  packed vs. unpacked, 124
Binary integer arithmetic,
  108–115
Bit, 36
Bit field, 336–338
Bit operation, 122–123
Bit-stream encoding, 336–338

Block, 36
  relocatable, 132
  task, 201
Block transfer, 128–129
Breakpoint interrupt, 94
Bus Arbiter (see 8289)
Bus Controller (see 8288)
Bus interface logic, 219–223
Bus interface unit, 60
Busy byte, 57
BX regiter, 87
Byte, 36

C, 5
Cache memory, 334
CALL, 131, 136–138, 267
Carry, sample program
  using, 282–289
Carry flag, 111
CBW, 115
CDC Cyber vs. 8087, 169
Central processing unit
  (CPU), 20
Character, 41
Checker byte, 194
Checksum, 66
Chip (see Microprocessor chip)
Circuit design, 25
Clever code, 287–289
Clock generator (see 8284)
Clock signals:
  of 8086/8088, 82
Cluster, 92
CMP, 134–135, 264–267
CMPC, 127–128
CMPW, 127,128
Comment, 98
Compiler, 67
Complement, 117, 123
Consumer products, 5
Context object, 334–336
Control byte, 192
Control subbus, 18
Control word, 179
Controller:
  board vs. chip, 24
  programmable, 25
Coprocessing, 55–56

Counting loop,   260
CP/M,   10
  binary machine language,   66
  file names in,   68–69
CP/M-86,   11–12, 311–312
Cross assembler,   69
Cursor control,   280
CWD,   114
CX register,   87
Cyber vs. 8087,   169
Cycle time,   141
Cyclic redundancy check,   194

Data subbus,   19
Data transfer:
  high-speed,   203
  instructions,   104–108
  sample program,   255–259
Data type,   34, 37–42, 111
  in iAPX 432,   326
  checking,   328
  and 8087,   166–169
  encoding,   37, 111
  storage requirements for,   35
DDT,   257
DEC,   115
Development approaches,
    305–306
Development system,   307
Device controller,   24–25,
    228–247
Digit loop,   274
Displacement,   96–97
DIP (double-in-line),   330
Dispatching port object,   328
DIV,   114–115
DMA Controller (see 8237)
Double-in-line (DIP),   330
Double look-up,   52
Double-operand
    instruction,   258
DX register,   87

8080 eight-bit processor,
    compared with 8085,   79
8082 Octal Address Latch,   29
8085 eight-bit processor:
  compared with 8088,   78
8086 General Purpose
    Processor:
  addressing,   79, 82, 95–99
  bit manipulation,   122–123
  clock signals,   82
  compared with 8088,   75
  compared with iAPX 186,
    319
  compared with MC68000,
    140–145

compared with Z8000,
    140–145
disadvantages of,   145
instruction set,   83, 103–140
I/O space,   80
logical operations,   115–118
machine language,   145–149
packaging,   82
program control,   130–138
register set,   81, 85–88
sample program,   149–153
segmentation in,   99–103
shift and rotate,   118–122
signals and pinouts,   88–91
string manipulation,
    125–130
system configuration,   28–34
system control,   138–145
8087 Numeric Data Processor:
  exception handling,   181
  instruction set,   173–179
  internal structure,   155
  pinouts,   155
  precision of,   161
  registers,   163
  stack,   170–173
8088 General Purpose Processor:
  addressing,   79, 82, 95–99
  advantages of,   77
  bit manipulation,   122–123
  clock signals,   82
  compared with 8085,   78
  compared with 8086,   75
  compared with MC68000,
    140145
  compared with Z8000,
    140–145
  disadvantages of,   145
  instruction set,   83, 103–140
  I/O space,   80
  logical operations,   115–118
  machine language,   145–149
  packaging,   82
  program control,   130–138
  register set,   81, 85–88
  sample program,   149–153
  segmentation in,   99–103
  shift and rotate,   118–122
  signals and pinouts,   88–92
  string manipulation,
    125–130
  system control,   138–145
8089 Input/Output Processor:
  addressing,   208
  functioning of,   197–204
  instruction set,   209–212
  local vs. remote mode,   199
  pinouts,   189
  register set,   204–205

sample program, 212–215
8237 Programmable DMA
    Controller, 30,228–231
8251 Programmable Serial
    Interface Controller,
    30, 234–235
8255 Programmable Parallel
    Interface Controller,
    30, 235–239
8256 Multifunction Universal
    Asynchronous Receiver-
    Transmitter, 240
8259 Programmable Interrupt
    Controller, 30, 231–233
8272 Programmable Floppy-disk
    Controller, 30, 242–247
8275 Programmable CRT
    Controller, 240
8284 Clock Generator,
    217–219
8286 Octal Data
    Transceiver, 30,
    219–223
8288 Bus Controller, 30,
    219–222
8289 Bus Arbiter, 223–227

Encoding, 27–28
Endless loop, 260
Error checking, 5
Error recovery (see Exception
    handling)
ESC, 139
ESCAPE, 162
Exception handling, 181
EXCHanGe, 106
Execution unit, 60
Expandability, 327
External reference, 65

File name, 68–69, 256
Flag, 139
Floating point notation, 40,
    156–162
Floating point operations in
    8087, 163
Floppy disk controller,
    242–247
FORTH, 5
Frame buffer, 229
Fujitsu, 75

Gate, 62–63
GDP (General Data Processor),
    332
Global call, 137
Global symbol table, 65

Godbout Dual Processor
    board, 311
Graphics (see Video graphics)

Hamming code, 193
HEX file, 66
HLT, 138, 139
HMOS, 3

iAPX 186, 319–320
    compared with 8086, 319
    instruction set, 319
iAPX 286, 320–321
iAPX 432, 323–338
    assembly language, 63
    bit-stream encoding,
        336–338
    context objects, 334–336
    disadvantages, 338
    family, 330
    operating system, 333–334
    system (micromainframe),
        332–333
IBM Personal Computer, 6,
    314–317
    operating system, 11
IN, 107
INC, 115
Index, 95
Input/Output (see I/O)
Input/Output Processor (see
    8089)
Instruction queue, 7, 59–60,
    84
Instruction set, 3
    of 8086/8088, 83
    of 8087, 162, 173–179
    of 8088 compared to
        8085, 78
    of 8089, 209–212
    comparisons between
        microprocessors, 140–145
    for coprocessing, 55–57
    data transfer, 104–108
    for floppy disk controller,
        244–247
    for iAPX 186, 319–320
    for multiprocessing, 56
INT, 138–139
Integrated circuit density, 20
Intel:
    floating point, 163
    HEX format, 65
    Intellec Development system,
        307
    Multibus, 27–28
    temporary real number, 160
Integer, 38, 156
Interactive processing, 325

Interlacing fields,   33
Interrupt,   8, 92
  for 8086/8088,   93–95
  breakpoint,   94
  flag,   94
  hardware,   94
  instructions,   294–304
  non–maskable,   90–94
  pinouts for,   90
  single step,   94
  vs. subroutine,   92
I/O
  address,   24
  data conversion,   192
  error detection,   192
  interrupt,   195–196
  polled,   195
  speed,   191
I/O control,   24–25, 191
  (see also Device control)

JMCE,   210
JMP,   132–133, 264–266
Jump,   130–135
  conditional,   133, 266–267

L80 Linker,   68, 70
L88,   250
Language (see Programming
  language)
LDS,   108
LEA,   107
Linker,   67–68, 257
Listing file,   65
Load file,   64, 68, 257
Loader,   64, 250–255
Local call,   137
Local mode,   199
Local reference,   65
LOCK,   56–59, 139
LODC,   130
Logical,   38
Logical operations,   115–118
  sample program,   279–282
Logical shift,   119–120
Long real format,   40
LOOP,   313, 135
Loop:
  counting,   260
  digit,   274
  endless,   260
  naming,   263
  sample program,   259–267
  until,   261
  while,   261

Machine language,   60
  for 8086/8088,   145–149
Macro,   123

Macrocode,   61
Mainframe vs. math chip,   169
Mask/Compare register,   210
Math chip,   4
  error checking in,   4–5
Matrix multiplicaton program,
  181–182
Maximum mode,   88
MC68000:
  addressing,   42
  compared with 8086/8088,
  140–144
Memory,   20–24
  access to,   3
  architecture of,   43–48
  board,   47
  cache,   334
  logical organization of,
  48–50
  management,   50–53
  moving programs in,   5
  types,   21
  units,   35–36
Memory management unit
  (MMU) chip,   49
Memory-read signal,   27
Memory-to-memory move,   143
Messages,   330
Microcode,   60–61
Microcomputer:
  architecture,   15–19
  components,   15
Micromainframe,   332–333
Microprocessor chip,   3, 20
  set,   166
  specialized,   4
Microsoft:
  L80 linker,   68, 70
  mnemonics,   103–104
  XMACRO-86 assembler,   69,
  311
Minimum mode,   88
MMU (Memory management
  unit) chip,   49, 51
Mnemonic,   60
  Microsoft,   103–104
Modular design,   75–77
Motorola:
  MC68000 (see MC68000)
  video display generator,   30
MOV,   104–106
MOVe string,   128
MS-DOS,   11–12
MUL,   112, 114
Multibus,   27–28
Multifunction Universal
  Asynchronous Receiver-
  Transmitter (see 8256)

Multiprocessing, 52–59
  using LOCK, 139

Nanocode, 61
NEC Electronics Video
    Processor, 30
NEG, 110
Nibble, 36
Non-maskable interrupt, 90,
    94
Normalization, 159
NOT, 118
Notation, 156–159
  floating point, 159–162
Numeric Data Processor (see
    8087)

Object, 328–330
Object code, 64, 65–67
Object file, 65
Octal Data Transceiver (see
    8286)
Octal latch (see 8282)
OEM (original equipment
    manufacturer), 28
Offset, 42, 48
Operating system, 10–12
  high-level, 5
  iAPX 432, 333–334
  IBM DOS, 316
Operation code, 64
Ordinal, 38
Orthogonal design, 16, 34
OUT, 107
Overflow flag, 111
Overlaying, 67

Packaging of 8086/8088, 82
Paging, 32
  logical, 50
  physical, 47
  vs. segmentation, 50
Parallel priority, 226
Parity bit, 193
PASCAL, 4, 5
Password, 326
PBX (private branch
    exchange), 6
PDP-11, 144
Pinout:
  for 8086/8088, 88–92
  for 8087, 155
  for 8089, 189
  for interrupt, 90
Pipelining (see Queue)
Plotter, smart vs. dumb, 192
Plotting program, 149–153
PLP (Presentation Level
    Protocol), 11

Pointer, 41
POP, 106
Pop, 171
Power subbus, 18
Power supply, 20
  for 8086/8088, 82
Precision, 157
  of 8087, 161
Prefix byte, 89
  REP, 127
Presentation Level Protocol
    (PLP), 11
Private branch exchange
    (PBX), 6
Process object, 328
Processor control, 293–294
Processor object, 328
Program control
  operations, 130–138
  sample program, 259–263
Program, moving in memory, 5
Programmable CRT Controller
    (see 8275)
Programmable DMA Controller
    (see 8237)
Programmable Interrupt
    Controller (see 8259)
Programmable Parallel Interface
    Controller (see 8255)
Programmable Serial Interface
    Controller (see 8251)
Programming, modular, 98
Programming language:
  assembly, 60
  higher level vs. lower
    level, 60
  machine, 60
Pseudo op, 64
PUSH, 106
Push, 171

Quad-in-line (QUIP), 330
Queue, 59
  instruction, 59–60, 83–84

RAM (random-access
    memory), 21
Range, 158
READY, 218
Real number, 156–157
Refresh rate, 32
  for high contrast
    graphics, 33
Register set, 8
  for 8086/8088, 81, 85–88
  for 8089, 204–208
Reliability, 326–327
Relocatable block, 132
Relocatable code, 65, 66, 102

Remote mode of 8089,
      199–200
REP,   127
RET,   132, 136–138, 267
ROM (read-only memory), 21
Rotate operation,   118,
      121–122
   sample program,   282–289
Rotating priority,   226
Rounding,   120
Run-time system,   52

S-100 bus,   16–17
   upgrading of,   77
SAR,   122
SBB,   112
SCAn,   127–129
Second source,   75
Security,   325
   with iAPX 286,   320–321
   with iAPX 326,   328–330
Segment identifier,   48
   software,   53
Segment register,   9, 49, 51
Segmentation,   7, 9, 48–50
   in 8086/8088,   99–103
   vs. paging,   50
Self-modifying code,   259
Serial priority,   226
Serial transmission,   234
Shift,   118–120
   arithmetic,   119, 122
   logical,   119
   sample program using,
      282–289
   static vs. dynamic,   121–122
Short real format,   40
Signals of 8086/8088,   88–92
Significand,   157
Single board computer,   27–28
Single/Double Denisty Floppy
      Disk Controller (see 8272)
Single-in-line (SIP),   330
Single step interrupt,   94
Software:
   development approaches,
      305–306
   for 8086/8088 system,
      9–12, 307–311
Source code,   63–64
Source file,   64
Speed,   324–325
   of 8086,   9
   of 8089 I/O chip,   191
   of floating point
      computation,   163
   and intelligence,   212

Stack:
   of 8087,   170–172
   instruction, sample
      program,   289–293
Stack pointer,   100
Status word,   180
STOC,   130
String,   41
   graphic commands,   316
   matching,   136
String manipulation,   125–130
   sample program,   275–279
Strobe,   91
SUB,   110–111
Subroutine,   136
   vs. interurpt,   92
   sample program,   267–272
   and stacks,   292
Swap,   173
System bus,   92
Symbol table,   65
   global,   65
System controller,   24

Task block,   201
Telephone answering
      machine,   6
Television monitor,   32–33
Temporary real format,   40,
      160
Termination circuitry,   17
TEST,   134, 265–266
Time multiplexing,   26–27
Time-sharing,   4
   I/O and,   195
Transistors,   63
   on chip,   3–4
Transistor-transistor logic
      (TTL),   25
Translation program,   10, 78
Triogonometric function
      program,   185
Two's complement numbering,
      38–39

UNIX,   5
Until loop,   261

Video controller,   240
Video equate instruction,   250
Video graphics:
   animation,   33–34
   controller,   30
   display,   32–33
   in IBM Personal Computer,
      315–316
   point-plotting program,
      149–153

system configuration,   30–34
using string command,   316
Voice communications,   6

WAIT,   56, 139
using 8087,   164
Weapons,   6
While loop,   261
Word,   36
sixteen bit,   22–23, 36
Workspace,   101
Write strobe,   91

XENIX,   11, 306
XFER,   211, 214
XLAT,   107
XMACRO-86,   69

Z8000:
addressing,   42, 49
compared with 8086/8088,
140–145
Zero,   159
to end message,   279

More BYTE Books Coauthored by Mitchell Waite

This is just one of four books coauthored by Mitchell Waite and published by BYTE/McGraw-Hill. You'll find the same friendly, easy-to-follow style and user-centered approach in each of the titles listed below. If you enjoyed and learned from this book, you'll certainly find the others in the Waite series equally helpful.

Computer Animation Primer, by Mitchell Waite and David Fox. Another in the ever-popular "Primer" computer book series, this engaging book introduces the exciting world of computer-animated graphics and presents the tools and techniques for creating original animated graphics on your personal computer. The book first describes the theory of animation and the potentials of various products, and then the authors go on to detail the actual programming techniques used in animation, focusing on character set, plotting, player-missile, and scrolling graphics. *Computer Animation Primer* features full-color illustrations and program listings in Atari BASIC and 6502 assembly language.

APPLE BACKPACK: Humanized Programming in BASIC, by Scot Kamins and Mitchell Waite. This book aids all computer users by establishing the "user-friendly" approach to programming in BASIC. The authors present concrete methods for developing programs that are not only easy to use, but also hard to misuse. Specific topics include clear screen formatting, crashproofing programs, developing built-in verifications and validations, presenting directions on the video display, and writing helpful, thorough documentation. Appendices feature an educational game program embodying the authors' user-centered approach and a humanized telephone-message-recording program with model documentation, both with complete Applesoft BASIC listings.

Word Processing Primer, by Mitchell Waite and Julie Arca. The first book of its kind, *Word Processing Primer* focuses on the newly available microcomputer-based text-editing programs. The authors begin with a review of the field, giving a working knowledge of the equipment and programs that make text editors work. A section on text formatting shows you how to control the final appearance of your printed copy, and a review of ancillary software, such as programs that check grammar or spelling and those that generate indexes or personalized form letters, shows the potential for customized applications. The book goes on to tell you what to look for when choosing a word processor, and a mini-catalog compares features, capabilities, limitations, and prices of many of the most popular pieces of software and equipment.